THIRTEEN YEARS AMONG
THE WILD BEASTS OF INDIA

THIRTEEN YEARS AMONG THE WILD BEASTS OF INDIA:

THEIR HAUNTS AND HABITS FROM PERSONAL OBSERVATION; WITH AN ACCOUNT OF THE MODES OF CAPTURING AND TAMING ELEPHANTS

G. P. SANDERSON

GYAN

Published by

Gyan Publishing House
5, Ansari Road
Daryaganj, New Delhi-110002
Phone: 011-47034999, 9811692060
E-mail: books@gyanbooks.com

Distribution Network
gyanbooks.com
India, USA, Canada, UK, Australia

ISBN: 978-93-7014-507-8 (HB)

First Published, 1879

2nd Impression 2025

Printed at: Gyan Press, Delhi.

THIRTEEN YEARS AMONG THE WILD BEASTS OF INDIA
Author: G. P. SANDERSON

THIRTEEN YEARS

AMONG THE

WILD BEASTS OF INDIA.

THIRTEEN YEARS

AMONG THE

WILD BEASTS OF INDIA:

THEIR HAUNTS AND HABITS FROM PERSONAL OBSERVATION; WITH AN ACCOUNT OF THE MODES OF CAPTURING AND TAMING ELEPHANTS.

BY

G. P. SANDERSON,

OFFICER IN CHARGE OF THE GOVERNMENT ELEPHANT-CATCHING ESTABLISHMENT IN MYSORE.

SECOND EDITION.

LONDON:
WM. H. ALLEN & CO., 13 WATERLOO PLACE, S.W.
Publishers to the India Office.
1879.

TO

COLONEL G. B. MALLESON, C.S.I.

LATE GUARDIAN TO HIS HIGHNESS THE MAHÁRÁJAH OF MYSORE.

My dear Colonel,

At the time that I commenced the operations of elephant-catching in Mysore, and when the experiment was regarded by many with at least distrust, you, unconnected with me by any official ties, came forward to give me the most practical proof of your confidence in my ultimate success by placing the resources in men and elephants of the Mysore Palace at my disposal. And you did this with such zeal and heartiness, your interest in my operations was so earnest, and your pleasure in my success so cordial, that I venture to ask you to accept the dedication of this account of my work, and of my life and adventures in the jungles of Mysore and Bengal—an account the compilation of which you suggested, and in the making up of which I have been encouraged to persevere by the example I have had before me in your own writings.

Believe me,

My dear Colonel,

Yours most sincerely,

GEORGE P. SANDERSON.

CONTENTS.

CHAPTER I.

SKETCH OF AUTHOR'S HUNTING EXPERIENCES.

CHAPTER II.

THE PROVINCE OF MYSORE.

CHAPTER III.

THE MYSORE JUNGLES.

CHAPTER IV.

A MYSORE VILLAGE.

CHAPTER V.

THE BILLIGA-RUNGUN HILLS.

CHAPTER VI.

THE ASIATIC WILD ELEPHANT (*ELEPHAS INDICUS*).

CHAPTER VII.

THE CAPTURING OF WILD ELEPHANTS.

CHAPTER VIII.

THE ELEPHANT IN CAPTIVITY.

CHAPTER IX.

THE MANAGEMENT AND FEEDING OF ELEPHANTS.

CHAPTER X.

ELEPHANT-CATCHING IN MYSORE.

CHAPTER XIV.

RIFLES AND CAMP-MANAGEMENT.

CHAPTER XV.

ELEPHANT-SHOOTING.

CHAPTER XVI.

INCIDENTS IN ELEPHANT-SHOOTING.

CHAPTER XVII.

INCIDENTS IN ELEPHANT-SHOOTING—(*continued*).

CHAPTER XVIII.

THE INDIAN BISON (*GAVÆUS GAURUS*).

CHAPTER XIX.

ADVENTURES IN BISON-SHOOTING.

CHAPTER XX.

THE TIGER (*FELIS TIGRIS*).

CHAPTER XXI.

TIGER-SHOOTING IN SOUTHERN INDIA.

CHAPTER XXII.

TIGER-SHOOTING IN SOUTHERN INDIA—(*continued*).

CHAPTER XXIII.

THE PANTHER, LEOPARD, AND CHEETA OR HUNTING-LEOPARD.

CHAPTER XXIV.

SPORT WITH PANTHERS AND LEOPARDS.

CHAPTER XXV.

SPORT WITH PANTHERS AND LEOPARDS—(*continued*).

CHAPTER XXVI.

THE INDIAN BLACK BEAR (*URSUS LABIĀTUS*).

CHAPTER XXVII.

DOGS FOR INDIAN HUNTING.

ILLUSTRATIONS.

THIRTEEN YEARS AMONG THE WILD BEASTS OF INDIA.

CHAPTER I.

SKETCH OF AUTHOR'S HUNTING EXPERIENCES.

I LAND IN MADRAS—APPOINTMENT IN MYSORE—MY FIRST TIGER—APPOINTED TO SUPERINTEND AN EXPERIMENT FOR THE CAPTURE OF WILD ELEPHANTS IN MYSORE—RESULTS—SIMILARLY APPOINTED IN EASTERN BENGAL—TRACTS VISITED—CAPTURE EIGHTY-FIVE ELEPHANTS—RETURN TO MYSORE—FURLOUGH TO ENGLAND—REMARKS.

I LANDED in Madras in 1864, and proceeded to a station in the Mysore country where I had friends. I was fresh from school and looked with delight upon the prospect of a coffee-planter's life, in which I had been promised a start by a friend, himself a planter. But coffee was in one of the vicissitudes with which that enterprise seems so frequently to be struggling —at least my friend's estate was—and before I had completed a voyage round the Cape he had been eaten out by the "borer" insect, or his prospects had shared the blight at that time affecting his trees' leaves—I forget which. My hopes of a jungle-life seemed to be doomed; my vision of wild elephants, tigers, and bison to be hopelessly dispelled! However, in a month or two a friend who was engaged in prosecuting some surveys for Government took me with him, and in the next six months I learnt a little of the country and surveying, and a good deal about duck and antelope shooting. I then applied myself to the study of Canarese, the vernacular of Mysore, for a year, which I look back upon as perhaps the most judiciously spent twelve months of my existence; and at the end of that time I obtained a Government appointment as Assistant Channel Superintendent.

Twenty-eight miles from Mysore, the former capital and still the seat of the native Court, is the Commissariat station of Hoonsoor, my appointed headquarters. My work consisted in looking after about 150 miles of river-drawn irrigation channels, all of them works of antiquity. Whilst traversing the Hanagode jungles through which the major portion of these flowed, I had sufficient leisure to gratify my taste for sport; in fact I had only to carry a rifle or gun with me on the channels to get frequent shots at spotted-deer, pig, and jungle-fowl, which small game quite contented me then. There was nothing large, except tigers; but though I used to be in some pleasurable apprehension of meeting them, as their footmarks were numerous, I never saw any. At last a friend, the Commissariat officer at Hoonsoor, got up a beat with elephants and took me with him, and I had the proud satisfaction of shooting my first tiger! Shall I ever forget how anxiously I watched Major M. as he rode an elephant up to the tiger, prostrate in a bush, to see if he was really defunct? How earnestly I adjured him from my tree, "not to shoot at him if he was dead;" and how he, naturally incensed at this advice from a griffin, stopped his elephant to inform me that he was "not such a —— fool as to shoot at a dead tiger!"

In two years, at the end of 1868, I attained a fair position owing to the advancement of officers above me, and reached the top of the tree of our small department. The whole of the irrigation channels in the Mysore province, aggregating 716 miles, then came under my charge, and the city of Mysore became my headquarters. I had a large extent of country, including several fine jungles in addition to my old haunts, to travel over in the prosecution of my work. I had a sufficient salary to afford a good battery, and the money necessary for getting good sport; and I spent most of my leave and all my cash upon it. In 1873 an opportunity was afforded me of changing what had hitherto been my favourite recreation only—sport—into the business of my life. I had before this time shot all the kinds of large game found in the Mysore country, and had become familiar with jungle matters. I had been especially interested in noting the habits of wild elephants; and upon my repeated representations, aided by the support of an official of high standing, a thorough sportsman, and able to form an accurate opinion on my proposals, the Mysore Government was induced to undertake the capture of some of the herds which roamed, useless and destructive, through various parts of the province, and I was appointed to carry out the experiment.

I succeeded, as I shall hereafter relate, in capturing a large number of elephants, and in consequence was appointed to the temporary charge of the Bengal Elephant-Catching Establishment, in September 1875. I worked in Bengal for nine months, during which time I visited the Garrow and Chittagong hill tracts, wild and little-known regions. I returned to Mysore in June 1876, after capturing eighty-five elephants in Chittagong.

But the famine which has recently devastated the south of India had then begun, and the scarcity of rain rendered elephant-catching impossible for a time, as fodder could not be procured for the support of any elephants that might have been captured; so myself and hunting establishment were employed in apportioning the border forests into grazing blocks for the starving cattle that flocked thither for pasture. Few of their owners had ever seen jungle before, and were terrified by exaggerated tales of tigers, wild elephants, and evil spirits. Unless provision had been made by Government for their being accompanied by men accustomed to jungle-life, they would merely have crowded the borders of the forests, and never have reached the best grazing grounds. After organising arrangements for their convenience, by placing trackers and jungle-men in charge of different sections of the forests, I found it necessary to return to England (in April 1877) on fifteen months' furlough on medical certificate, after a continued residence of thirteen years in India.

The peculiar opportunities which have been afforded me during that period from following my natural inclinations, and by the nature of my duties, of encountering the wild animals of Southern India and Eastern Bengal, have induced me to believe that my experiences may be of some interest to the general public, and perhaps of some service to the cause of natural history. In presuming to relate them I am but dealing with matters which have constituted my daily occupation. All that I narrate is from personal observation; and whilst no one can be more alive than myself to the fact that, if the wielding of my pen is to be taken as a test of my ability with the tools of sport, it will lead to but a poor opinion of my accomplishments, I claim one merit for my jottings which I hope will cover their numerous failings—at least in the eyes of brother sportsmen—and that is, that they are all strictly true. Any one who has devoted himself to Indian field-sports for some years as I have done must have been singularly unfortunate if he has not sufficient exciting facts noted in his journal to fill a book without the necessity of resorting to fiction or exaggeration.

I have dealt at some length upon the habits when wild, the mode of capture and training, and the management and conduct in captivity, of the elephant. The popular interest felt in that animal is perhaps more general than that attaching to any other, whilst regarding none are there more fallacies and erroneous impressions. Few writers have been in a position to deal with the subject in all its branches. Many sportsmen have shot large numbers of elephants, but have given us little information about their nature, disposition, and habits—matters with which it was at once my duty as a public servant, and my delight as a sportsman, to acquaint myself.

In the chapters on the other wild animals with which I have dealt I have separated my observations on their habits, and recitals of adventures with them, as I believe that arrangement will be a convenient one for all readers, whether lovers of natural history or of mere tales of adventure. I have endeavoured to select incidents in hunting the various animals illustrative of their dispositions and habits; and though in turning over the leaves of my journal the temptation to introduce more scenes of contest between rifle and wild beast has been considerable, I trust none will complain that my butcher's bill is too long!

I have given short accounts of the jungle-tribes with whom I have associated in pursuing their scarcely wilder fellow-inhabitants of the forests; and as my recitals will be more intelligible when my readers have been introduced to the country in which most of the incidents chronicled have occurred, I shall venture to devote a short chapter to a sketch of the province of Mysore. The accompanying map indicates its position in the peninsula of India.

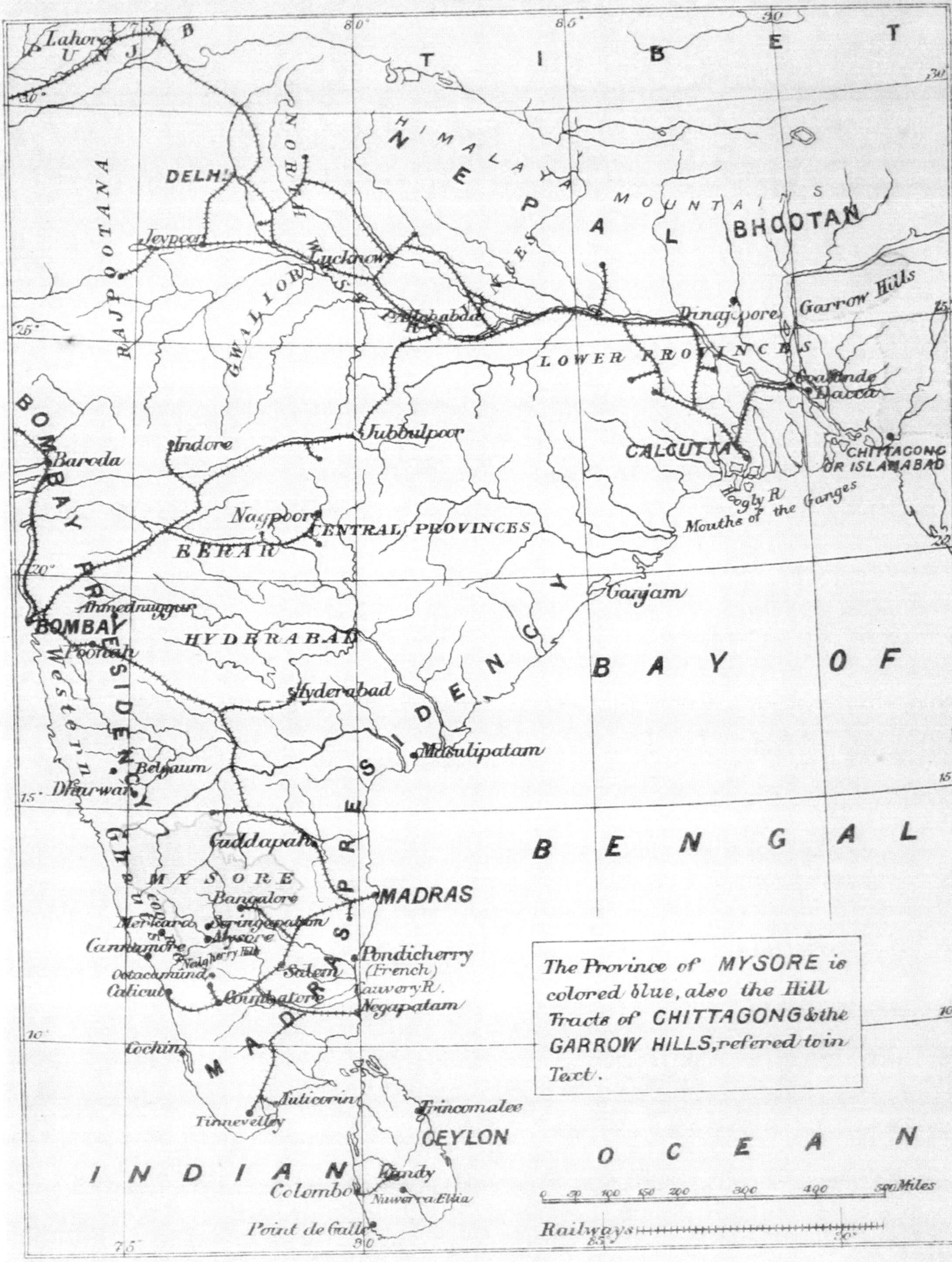

The Province of MYSORE is colored blue, also the Hill Tracts of CHITTAGONG & the GARROW HILLS, refered to in Text.
TIBET
NEPAL
HIMALAYA MOUNTAINS
BHOOTAN
Garrow Hills
Lahore
PUNJAB
DELHI
RAJPOOTANA
Jeypoor
Lucknow
GWALIOR
Dinagepore
LOWER PROVINCES
Dacca
CALCUTTA
CHITTAGONG OR ISLAMABAD
Hoogly R
Mouths of the Ganges
Jubbulpoor
Indore
Baroda
Nagpoor
CENTRAL PROVINCES
BERAR
Ganjam
Ahmednuggur
BOMBAY
BOMBAY PRESIDENCY
HYDERABAD
Poonah
Hyderabad
Masulipatam
Belgaum
Dharwar
Cuddapah
MYSORE
MADRAS
Bangalore
Mercara
Seringapatam
Mysore
Cannanore
Pondicherry
(French)
Ootacamund
Salem
Calicut
Coimbatore
Cauvery R.
Negapatam
Cochin
MADRAS PRESIDENCY
Tuticorin
Tinnevelly
Trincomalee
CEYLON
Kandy
Colombo
Nuwerra Elia
Point de Galle
BAY OF BENGAL
INDIAN OCEAN
Miles
Railways

CHAPTER II.

THE PROVINCE OF MYSORE.

DESCRIPTION—CLIMATE—POPULATION—REVENUE—THE LATE MAHÁRÁJAH—CHARACTER OF PEOPLE—CULTIVATION—RIVERS—CHIEF TOWNS—MYSORE BREED OF DRAUGHT-CATTLE—SEASONS.

THE Mysore country is an elevated, undulating plateau of 27,004 square miles, lying between 13° 6′ and 15° 0′ north latitude. Its length from north to south is 190 miles, and its width from east to west 230.

Mysore is bounded on the north by the Bombay Collectorate of Dhárwár and the Madras Collectorate of Bellàry; on the east and south by other districts of the Madras Presidency; and on the west by Coorg, a dependent province, and the Western Ghâts. Its chief town, Bangalore, is situated in the same latitude as, and 200 miles due west of, Madras. Mysore is a native State in subsidiary alliance with the British Government.

The general level of the country is from 2500 to 3000 feet above the sea, the lowest point being 1800 feet, and it descends steeply on all sides into the low country. High mountains, some 2500 feet above the ordinary level of the plateau, bound it on the west: these are called the Western Ghâts, and extend from the extreme south of India, through Travancore, Malabar, Mysore, and Bombay, to Kandeish, or about 950 miles, at a mean distance of some 50 miles from the coast. They break the force of the monsoon from the west; and the deluges of rain common in the country between them and the coast are modified in Mysore into showers and temperate rains.

Bounding Mysore on the south are the Neilgherry Hills, attaining an elevation of 8700 feet. Ootacamund, the chief sanitarium of Southern India, is easily accessible from Mysore. Its elevation is 7300 feet.

In the south-east are the Billiga-Rungun hills, the highest point of which is about 5000 feet above sea-level. Wild elephants are very abundant throughout this range and the forests at its foot.

The country in the interior of the province is undulating and in many parts hilly. A peculiar feature in many localities are the granite hills, often sheer rock, sometimes consisting of huge masses piled on each other, and forming caves where panthers and bears are occasionally found. Solitary fortified hills, called *droogs,* are numerous: many of these are still crowned with the remains of old fortresses which were used in former days as strongholds by robber chieftains.

The border mountains of Mysore are generally well wooded, but some of the highest summits are clear of forest, being grass downs with woods in the hollows, where moisture favours their growth.

The climate of Mysore is temperate, the mean deduced from observations (in the shade) at Bangalore being 72°6′. The mean diurnal range is 15°6′, the greatest recorded being 32° in one day in February. The greatest extremes recorded are 53° and 95°, in February and May respectively of 1866. The average rainfall is about 40 inches, though in the western forest tracts and hills it is frequently from 80 to 100 inches.

The last census, taken in 1871, gives the population at 5,055,412, of which 4,839,421 are Hindoos, 208,991 Mussulmáns, and about 7000 Europeans and half-castes.

The revenue in 1875 was £1,100,000; of this one-fourth is paid as subsidy to the British.

Mysore was acquired by the British in 1799, upon the death of Tippoo Sultán, at the siege of Seringapatam. The former dynasty was then restored by the British in the person of Krishna Ráj Wadeyar, then five years of age, who was installed as Rájah. The Government during his minority was ably conducted by the Bráhmin Dewán (or Prime Minister) Poornaya, under the control of the Political Resident, Colonel Sir Barry Close. The troops were commanded by Colonel Arthur Wellesley (subsequently Duke of Wellington).

His Highness's liberality and kindly disposition made him a universal favourite with both Europeans and natives. But he fell into the hands of injudicious advisers, and in 1830 the disturbed state of the country rendered necessary the intervention of the paramount Power. Since that period the territories of his Highness have been governed by a Commission, which is under the direct orders of the Government of India. Before his death in 1868 the Mahárájah, in the absence of male heirs, adopted a successor who is to resume the government of the country when he attains the period of majority—that is, the age of eighteen years—which will be about 1880.

Under European tutelage he is receiving a more liberal education than was within the reach of the late Mahárájah.

The Hindoo people of Mysore are peaceful, orderly, and good-natured, but lacking in enterprise. The Bráhmins are intelligent and ambitious; they have always filled most of the posts in Government offices. The Mussulmáns have sunk into deep poverty, chiefly through their own laziness, since the overthrow of the Mussulmán power in 1799. A few engage in mercantile and agricultural pursuits; many are enlisted in the Mysore Horse and the Sepoy corps; they also find employment as elephant and camel attendants, and horse-keepers. The domestic servants of Europeans in Mysore are all Madrassees, as the Canarese people have never taken to indoor service.

The country is well cultivated in many parts, the wisdom of former rulers having provided it with irrigation, both by channels drawn from the rivers passing through it, and from tanks or lakes formed by embankments thrown across the valleys. These ancient works are constructed upon such scientific principles that little can be done by European engineers to improve them. The lakes store the surplus rain-water for the use of the land further down the valley, and the cultivation thus artificially watered is called "wet" in India, in contradistinction to "dry," or that dependent on rainfall alone.

The chief rivers in Mysore are the Cauvery, Toongabhadra, Hemávutty, Cubbany, and Lutchmenteert; the latter three are tributaries of the Cauvery, joining it within the Mysore province. Where it leaves the plateau for the low country of Madras the Cauvery forms fine falls of about 200 feet in height. The falls of Gairsoppa in the north of Mysore are not so widely celebrated as they deserve to be. They are on the Sharávati river, and a portion of them have a sheer overfall of 960 feet.

The chief towns in the Mysore province are Bangalore (3031 feet above sea-level) and Mysore (2525 feet). Seringapatam, the celebrated fortress, is situated on an island in the Cauvery, nine miles from Mysore. From Bangalore to Mysore the distance is 88 miles. Bangalore is connected by rail with Madras, the distance being 216 miles; of this line 48½ miles only lie in Mysore, and there is no other railway in the province. There is no water carriage, as the rivers are rocky and swift. The roads, however, are excellent, and the Mysore breed of bullocks is celebrated for speed and endurance. Travelling is usually done by bullock-coach; for long distances from four to five miles an hour, with bullocks posted every five miles, is a fair pace. Bullock-carts do all the heavy trade. A pair of bullocks will draw a load of 15 cwt., exclusive of the cart, twenty miles a-night for many consecutive nights. Post-bullocks cost 3 annas (4½d.), and a baggage-cart and bullocks 1½ anna, per mile. Pack-bullocks penetrate the remoter tracts with merchandise. It was in a great measure owing to the superiority of the Mysore bullocks that Hyder Ali and Tippoo Sultán maintained a lengthened war with the British and Maharattas at the end of the last century. The best breed of bullocks is sedulously maintained at the Government Public Cattle Establishment at Hoonsoor, and extensive pastures are allotted for the grazing of the herds throughout the province. A certain number of first-class bulls are at times distributed to large villages for the free use of the agriculturists' herds.

The seasons in Mysore are three—the cold, hot, and rainy—and are distributed as below:—

COLD SEASON,	December. January. February.	Mornings and evenings cold and bracing; days bright and sunny.
HOT SEASON,	March. April. May.	Hot, and occasionally sultry, but the nights usually tempered by sea-breezes from the west. The hot weather in Mysore is by no means unbearable. Showers and heavy thunderstorms occur at intervals during April and May; these prelude the south-west monsoon.
RAINY SEASON,	June. July. August. September. October. November.	The south-west monsoon commences in June; heavy rains and showery and overcast weather prevail till September. In October the north-east monsoon commences, and thunderstorms and heavy downpours are common. In November the weather is often bright and cold, but rain falls now and again.

From May to December are the chief cultivation and harvest months, though some crops, as sugar-cane, &c., which are irrigated, are grown the whole year round.

CHAPTER III.

THE MYSORE JUNGLES.

BEST SEASONS FOR SPORT—MOVEMENTS OF GAME—JUNGLE-FIRES—FORESTRY—NATURAL CLASSES OF JUNGLE—DISTRIBUTION OF WILD ANIMALS—LIST OF ANIMALS FOUND IN MYSORE—REMAINS OF ANTIQUITY—RUINED VILLAGES IN THE FORESTS—ANCIENT IRRIGATION WORKS—A DESOLATED VALLEY.

IN the jungles the young grass commences to spring with the first showers in April, and by July has attained the height of a man. This is the case chiefly in hill tracts; in the low-country jungles it is more backward, as there is less rain and it is grazed down by cattle. By "grass" in Indian jungles is meant the broad-bladed and long-leaved lemon-grass and other coarse kinds, which grow in large tufts; also reeds in swampy ground, and small ground-creepers. This season is the time *par excellence* for stalking and shooting large game. The animals are intent on the new supply of fodder; occasional rain makes tracking easy; and after May the sky is usually obscured by clouds and driving mist in the hills, and considerable exertion may be undergone without discomfort.

From July to January the grass is so high and thick that game cannot be got at in it, and many places where good sport is obtainable earlier then become impenetrable. Driven out by the wet and discomfort, and tormented by myriads of flies, many animals leave the high and close cover at this time for the lighter shelter and choicer grazing to be had amongst the young and tender grass on the outskirts; but they retreat readily to the grass jungles if disturbed.

By January the grass has all seeded and become dry, and it is then fired by the jungle-people. The hitherto impenetrable jungles are now reduced to clear forests of trees, interspersed with separate evergreen thickets. Moving about in such forests is rendered easy, but warm, work, the heat rising from the blackened earth under a tropical sun being very trying where the forest is not dense. The jungle-people burn the grass to admit of their gathering certain fruits and jungle-products, especially the gall-nut, used in tanning. This burning insures a supply of sweet grass as soon as showers fall on the fertilising ash.

During the months when the jungles are clear, the wanderings of the game are necessarily curtailed, not only by want of cover, but also of food and water. The herds of elephants, bison, and deer collect in moist and deep valleys where the grass is green, and fires do not enter. The difficulty of finding these secluded places however, is great, as they are in such heavy and moist jungles that the very few wild people's dwellings that do exist are seldom near them, and unless the sportsman is well equipped for a march into difficult country, away from supplies of all kinds, they are inaccessible. To any one ignorant of the extent of the wild animals' hot-weather retreats it seems almost magical, after experiencing the difficulty of finding them during that season, to observe how they reappear on all sides with the first rains.

It is a magnificent sight to see the jungles of a hill-range burning. Sometimes immense tracts are on fire at once, and at night give forth a lurid blaze which lights up the country for miles round. If the fire is near, the roaring noise is truly appalling, and impresses one with a sense of the dread power of the element. Huge billows of thick smoke, in which lighted grass and leaves are whirled forward, roll heavily and slowly along, whilst a sound as of incessant discharges of small-arms is caused by the bamboos and grass stalks exploding. The noise lulls and swells with every alternation in the breeze and in proportion to the thickness of the undergrowth. Long after the main conflagration has passed, isolated bamboo-clumps and dried trees are seen burning fiercely like pillars of flame, till they fall over with a sullen crash, and are quenched. Many trees smoulder for months. I knew one of enormous size, the roots of which, some of the girth of a bullock, or greater, burnt for three and a half years, the fire smouldering slowly underground in the roots long after the parent stem had fallen.

During the day countless buzzards and fly-catchers hover over the smoke, preying on the bewildered insects which are escaping from it. The destruction of noxious vermin by the fires must be considerable; but many animals and reptiles, as the land-tortoise and snakes, whose powers of speed do not enable them to escape by those means, survive by burying themselves in holes or burrows amongst rocks.

I have never seen jungle-fires advance at any great rate, except in very dry and long grass, unshaded by trees, and under the influence of a strong wind. Here burning leaves and hot ashes are carried far ahead of the main fire, and a fresh blaze starts up at once where they fall. I do not think jungle-fires ever travel four miles in an hour. The devouring element licks up all before it in some places with wonderful rapidity, but it seldom proceeds far without a check. Wild animals retreat before conflagrations; but many, as for instance herds of elephants encumbered with young, could not always escape if the fires travelled at any great rate. I have never known any animals, except a few young sámbur, too young to walk far, to be caught in the fire; but jungle-people have been burnt on occasions. This has always occurred through their not heeding the danger, and staying to search for some near asylum, instead of at once starting for a known place of safety. Three men of a village near my camp in the Billiga-rungun hills, who were cutting bamboos, were burnt in this way, through not liking to leave their work further than the shelter of a ravine near, which proved insufficient to protect them from the wave of flame and smoke that passed over them.

Elephants, bison, &c., do not retreat straight before a fire, but to one side or the other. The fires seldom form a long front, so this outflanking movement readily succeeds. At the first distant crackle, or smell of smoke, wild animals at once retire. Fires are much less dangerous than is supposed if anything like prompt means are taken to effect a retreat. The jungle-people secure their houses by cutting some of the grass round, and firing it early in the season, before it is very dry. This stops the onward rush of the larger fires later on. Fires burn much more fiercely during the day than at night, as there is usually more wind, and everything is dry and brittle; whilst at night the heavy dews have a marked effect on the progress of the burning through making the grass damp ahead. The conflagrations are only fierce and general for one month, usually March; they begin in January.

A good deal is said in connection with forestry in India regarding the destructiveness of the annual fires to young trees, and attempts are constantly made, but rarely succeed, to exclude fires from reserved Government forests. It is, perhaps, doubtful whether they are so destructive as is believed, and whether the young plants of teak and other trees would flourish well if constantly choked and overshaded by undergrowth. At any rate there are splendid forests where, though fires have raged annually from time immemorial, the timber is as close as the ground can support it. The grass is not so high or thick under shade as in open ground, and as artificial teak nurseries are usually made in land from which the timber has been removed, and where, in consequence, grass grows apace, the fires are there more severe on the young plants than in their natural forests. There are always numerous young plants of timber-trees in every forest which can never live, as they grow more thickly than the ground can support when mature. The fittest survive; and though fires may scorch and shrivel up their leaves, I have not observed that the saplings which take root soon after the burning of one season are killed by the fires of the next, though many of those which are but a few months old when the fires commence are destroyed. I have been told by experienced jungle-men that timber-plants are burnt down for five or six consecutive years, the roots meanwhile thickening and strengthening underground, until they give birth to a plant sufficiently strong to withstand the effects of the momentary wave of flame.

The Mysore jungles may be divided into three classes. First, virgin forests of heavy timber, usually found in the hill-ranges along the borders of the province. They are naturally finest in such places as are inaccessible for the removal of timber; for from the more accessible parts the timber-supply of the country is drawn. The virgin forests are only inhabited by a few wild jungle-people. Secondly, the lighter belt of forest, usually about ten miles in width, intervening between the virgin forests and civilisation. From this tract the villagers procure the small timber and bamboos they require for household purposes. They also graze their cattle in it, seldom entering the heavier forest except during the hot weather, when pasturage elsewhere is very scarce. A few villages occur in this tract, but they are rather stations for cattle-grazing than for cultivation, nor are they often of a permanent nature. Thirdly, scrub-jungle of low and thorny bushes, which occurs at intervals throughout the open cultivated country in the sterile tracts, on the deserted sites of villages, &c. From this small firewood and bushes for fencing are obtained, and in it the cattle and flocks of the villagers in the interior are grazed.

In the heavy forests, elephants, bison, and sámbur are the chief game. These animals come at certain seasons into the lighter belt. But the legitimate occupants of the latter are the tiger, panther, bear, spotted-deer, and wild hog. The wild dog ranges through both heavy and light forests, and is terribly destructive to the deer tribe; he is never found in open country. In the scrub-jungle, particularly in those tracts near detached hills and low ranges, panthers, leopards, bears, ravine deer, wolves, and sometimes antelope, are found. Antelope and wolves, however, chiefly confine themselves to large tracts of open uncultivated country, on the borders of which the ryots' crops furnish the former with superior grazing, and his flocks are often pounced upon by the latter.

The following game-list comprises all the animals found in Mysore, except monkeys, squirrels, mungooses, ant-eaters, lemurs, flying-foxes, rats, and other small animals not objects of sport :—

LIST OF MYSORE GAME.

English.	Of Naturalists.*	In Canarese.	Remarks.
Elephant	Elephas indicus .	Ánay	Very numerous in border forests.
Bison or Gaur . .	Gavæus gaurus . .	Kárti, Kárd-yemmay, Kárd-korna, Doddoo.	Abundant throughout the ranges frequented by elephants.
Tiger	Felis tigris . . .	Hooli	Plentiful in suitable localities.
Panther	Felis párdus . . .	Dod-ibba	Less common than the leopard. A black variety is sparingly found in Mysore.
Leopard	Felis leopárdus . .	Kirba	Very common.
Cheetah or Hunting Leopard.	Felis jubáta . . .	Chircha, Sivungi .	Exceedingly rare in Mysore — almost unknown.
Bear	Ursus labiātus . .	Karadi.	Plentiful in certain localities.
Wolf	Canis pallipes . .	Torla	Not numerous.
Striped Hyæna . .	Hyæna straita . .	Kat-kirba . . .	Common.
Wild Dog. . . .	Cuon rutilans . .	Ken-naie, Kárdnaie	Do.
Sámbur	Rusa Aristotelis .	Kadavay	Common in the forest tracts.
Spotted-Deer . .	Axis maculātus . .	Sárga, Játi, Mikka	Very common.
Barking or Rib-faced Deer, Muntjac, Kákur, Jungle-Sheep.	Cervulus aureus .	Kárd or Kondkurri, Cháli.	Common.
Indian Antelope .	Antilope bezoartica	Hoolay-kara, Jinki	Not numerous.
Indian Gazelle or Ravine Deer.	Gazella Bennettii .	Sunk-hoolay . . .	Not common.
Wild Hog . . .	Sus indicus . . .	Kárd-hundi, Curry-játi.	Very numerous.
Crocodile	Crocodilus indicus .	Mosalay	Not numerous, and seldom over ten feet long.
Jackal	Canis aureus . . .	Nurrie	Very numerous.
Fox	Vulpes bengalensis	Kemp-nurrie . .	Not very numerous.
Common Jungle-Cat.	Felis chaus . . .	Kárd-bekkoo . .	Very common.
Leopard-Cat . . .	Felis bengalensis .	Bottina-bekkoo . .	Less common.
Otter	Lutra nair . . .	Neer-naie	Plentiful.
Porcupine . . .	Hystrix leucura .	Mool-hundi . . .	Do.
Mouse-Deer . . .	Memimna indica .	Koor-pundi . . .	Do.
Hare	Lepus nigricollis .	Molla	Do.

* Jerdon's *Mammals of India.*

The following animals of Indian sport are not found in Mysore:—

English.	Of Naturalists.*	In Canarese.	Remarks.
Rhinoceros . . .	Rhinoceros indicus	None.	Not found in Southern India.
Wild Buffalo . . .	Bubulus arni . .	Do.	
Neelgai	Portax pictus . .	Mayroo, Kárd-kudray.	Found in the Madras Presidency on the borders of Mysore.
Ibex, or the Neilgherry Wild Goat	Hemitragus hylocrius.	Kárd-árdoo . . .	

Birds.—Jungle-fowl, pea-fowl, and spur-fowl are common in the woods; bustard, floriken, red-legged partridge, quail, and rock-grouse in the open country; and wild duck, teal, snipe, wild geese, flamingoes, pelicans, and cranes in the lakes and rice-fields. Doves of several varieties are common both in the woods and open country.

Fish.—The rivers and artificial lakes in Mysore abound with excellent fish, but I have never succeeded in getting much sport with the fly. They may be taken by spinning or ground fishing—the latter chiefly at night. There is now in the museum at Bangalore the head and skin of a fish—a species of carp or *mahseer*, and called *billi*, or silver-fish, in Canarese—caught by me in 1871 in the Lutchmenteert, which measured 60 inches in length and 38 in girth. The circumference inside the mouth when caught was 24 inches. I was unfortunately unable to weigh this fish, but I estimated it by rough tests at not less than 100 lb. I have seen much larger fish, without doubt upwards of 150 lb., caught by natives, chiefly by netting during the months when the rivers are low. At such times two or three villages of professional fishermen will combine to net a single large fish known to be a prisoner in a pool during the hot weather. The pool may be a hundred yards long and broad, and the water fifteen feet deep, with cavernous rocks capable of sheltering fish; but by joining their nets, and diving and working for two or three days, they seldom fail to secure the prize.

The few crocodiles that are found in the Mysore rivers very rarely attack people; and fishermen—who pay no heed to them—have told me that if they come upon a crocodile whilst following their employment, it will skulk at the bottom and not move though handled, apparently believing it escapes observation. Crocodiles are, like all wild creatures, very timid where not encouraged, as is sometimes done by superstitious natives. In-

* Jerdon's *Mammals of India.*

credible though it may seem to readers with no knowledge of the saurians but that derived from stories of their boldness elsewhere, I may instance having seen several *bestas* (the professional boatmen, divers, and fishermen of Mysore) dive time after time into water twelve feet deep, and bring to the surface by the tail a crocodile seven feet long which I had wounded. The creature was not in any way crippled, but seemed overcome with fear. It offered no resistance till dragged near a rock where I stood with a rope, when it would turn and snap at the man pulling it, always sinking, however, the moment this demonstration made him let go its tail. Different divers went down successively, one at a time, and brought it to the surface; I at last killed it with a charge of shot.

Whilst in pursuit of game in the Mysore forests I have often been struck with wonder at the remains of the dwellings and works of a bygone population which are to be found, now engulfed in jungle. The whole country bears traces of having once been better populated than at present, and many of the remains are of a character that speak of the industry and culture of its inhabitants. Some of the temples, monuments, and sculptures are as grand in conception as they are admirable in execution. The old irrigation works of the country, consisting of stone dams across the rivers, often many hundred yards in length, and composed of blocks far beyond any of the native appliances of the present day to deal with; canals; and reservoirs, or lakes; mark the material prosperity of the country ages ago. Granite of excellent quality is found throughout the country, and the extensive use of this imperishable material in the old structures has preserved them intact to the present time. Wherever a village of importance existed remains of interest are to be seen. The sportsman wandering in the forest is often tempted to rest on his rifle, and muse sadly over the scenes of former life and industry, where the voices are now hushed, and wild Nature, deprived of her dominion for a few short years, again reigns supreme. The elephant rests at mid-day under the sacred peepul-tree, once in the centre of the village, where old and young met at evening,—the former to discuss village matters and rest after the fatigues of the day; the latter to amuse themselves, thoughtless of the future. Where are they now? Broken images and disused querns lie around; the wells are choked and dry; bears and panthers find shelter in the very temples where offerings were presented to the village gods, and where festivals were held. But the people have passed away without other record than the jungle-overgrown ruins, which have defied time. And may not similar changes follow again? Where the sportsman now tracks the elephant and tiger, cultivation may smile and happy voices be heard long after his own insignificant existence is more effectually forgotten than that of the people over whose traces he now muses.

Amongst scenes whither my duty or pleasure led me, I always felt particular interest in a portion of the Hoonsoor jungles which lies within the watershed of the Cubbany river. A chain of ancient channels here forms a wonderful system of irrigation, but they have caused the ruin of the land they once fertilised.

Often as I sat and overlooked the unbroken stretch of jungle which had swallowed up the country did I speculate on its former condition, and the causes that had led to the change. These seem evident. The whole tract must have been comparatively healthy at one time, as the remains of large towns testify to its former population; it must then have been open country, as cities do not spring up in jungle - encumbered tracts in India. The people, however, sighed for water to increase the fertility of their land, dependent upon rainfall alone, and a remarkable physical feature placed an unlimited supply of the fertilising element at their command. The valley which contains the channels runs nearly due west to east, and is about twenty miles long by five broad. From its upper or west end to its termination on the Cubbany river to the east, there is a fall of probably 500 feet. At the upper end, just over the watershed ridge and not more than 50 feet below it, flows the Lutchmenteert river, a considerable stream in the rainy season, and never quite dry; its course here is approximately from south to north, and it is within half a mile of the ridge. The former inhabitants of the valley to the east had cut a channel through the ridge, and introduced Lutchmenteert water into the Cubbany vale. With water thus available on the top of the watershed, irrigation was practically unlimited, and channels were led contouring along each side of the valley at a high level for many miles. The drainage water of these was caught up again and again by tanks or artificial lakes thrown across the valley.

These mighty works, though in ruins, still bear testimony to the former ability and industry of the inhabitants. But the fertilising element which now surrounded them became the means of their extinction. Land not cultivated must soon have been overgrown with rank jungle, nurtured by the moisture. The culturable area, too, must have been gradually reduced by about four-fifths, as irrigated land produces so much more valuable crops, and its cultivation is so much more arduous, that a small portion of what each man cultivated before as dry land would now suffice for his wants and engage all his labour.

Thus, each community in the valley found itself gradually shut in by jungle and rank herbage instead of the former open land. The whole valley became permeated with moisture, and the exhalations from the ground caused malarial fevers which eventually depopulated it, and which at this day prevent its reoccupation. The sites of the chief towns are now only marked by overgrown and weather-beaten earth-work fortifications, or by stone temples of a solidity that has defied the ravages of time; and all traces of many smaller villages have been lost.

The largest of the towns in the valley was Rutnapoori-korté (the City of Rubies), and it is probably at least 150 years since the last inhabitants left it. There are some granite slabs engraved in old Canarese characters near a fine old temple which covers a large area, and these probably contain some account of the founding or history of the temple. The temple is composed of massive pillars and beams of solid granite, many of which have fallen and lie strewn around. I learnt from the legends of the surrounding country that seven sisters formerly lived in Rutnapoori. These were the concubines of the rájah of the place, and each chose a site for the construction of a lake in the valley. These seven tanks, three of them now breached, are named after the sisters. The lowest of the seven was built by the youngest, and has the advantage of catching the surplus water from the others. It is still a splendid sheet of water, called Kurrigul, near the road from Mysore to Manantoddy in the Wynaad country. This road passes through the lower portion of the valley, running parallel with the Cubbany river; and, as the country is more open and accessible here, several large villages and patches of cultivation which had never quite died out have been resuscitated, and are extending.

For the upper portion of the valley, overgrown with dense unwholesome forest, nothing can be done at present. Population has long since moved elsewhere, and the tract is not yet required for producing food. A few hamlets spring up occasionally, as some small capitalist is tempted by the richness of the land, and the easy terms on which it is obtainable from Government, to cultivate a portion. But the wretched ryots who undertake the work live in a miserable condition. They are soon affected with enlarged spleens, the invariable accompaniment of fevers induced by a bad climate and bad water, and either give up, or decamp with the advances of money they have received. These spasmodic attempts at reclamation seldom last long. The capitalist finds the advantages of the soil are counterbalanced by the difficulty of the position. As long as it is sought to establish villages in the valley far below the level of the upper channels and their cultivation, so long must failure follow, as the unhealthiness of the locality is insurmountable. The only thing possible would be to restore the chain of tanks in the valley, and to abandon the cultivation on the heights. The tanks could be filled once or twice a-year from the Lutchmenteert, and, the upper cultivation being abandoned, the sides of the valley would not be pervaded with moisture. The breezes would be more healthy, and the villages cultivating the land below the tanks would be above the level of the dampness, and some portion of the former salubrity of the place would be restored. As long as water is kept running at a high level and drenching the soil, the bottom of the jungle-encumbered valley must be inimical to human life.

The land below the high-level channels has, however, been largely reclaimed during the past ten years. The cultivators live in Hoonsoor and adjacent villages, not in the tract itself, only visiting it for the purpose of cultivation. The low grounds in the valley are given up to the grazing of the Commissariat cattle at Hoonsoor, and this is the best use, perhaps, they can now be put to. These grazing grounds are essential in different places over the country, and there is usually enough cultivable land available without invading them.

CHAPTER IV.

A MYSORE VILLAGE.

THE VILLAGE OF MORLAY—ADVANTAGES OF NEIGHBOURHOOD FOR ELEPHANT-CATCHING—ATTRACTIONS TO THE SPORTSMAN—THE VILLAGERS—THEIR TENURE OF LANDS—EXPERIENCE IN HUNTING—NETTING GAME—CRUELTY OF THE MORLAYITES TO AN ELEPHANT—THEIR HOUSES—FOOD—CLOTHING—TEMPERANCE—WOMEN—INFIDELITY AMONGST—CASTE RULES ON THE SUBJECT—MATRIMONY IN MORLAY—THE VILLAGE HEADMAN—TRAINING THE MORLAYITES—MY TRACKERS—REMARKS ON NATIVE SHIKÁRIES.

WHEN I commenced the work of elephant-catching I left Mysore for the neighbourhood of a village called Morlay, in the Chámráj-Nuggar *talook,* in the south-eastern corner of Mysore, where I was forty-one miles from the city of Mysore, and within eight of the foot of the Billiga-rungun hills, where wild elephants abound. Morlay was an excellent place for my object, as the elephants had been in the immemorial habit of visiting the cultivation around it and adjacent villages at certain seasons, and of remaining at such times in the jungles close at hand for weeks together. Thus there was no necessity for following them into their hill fastnesses, where much hardship would have had to be undergone by all engaged in their pursuit. I lived in a civilised and accessible country, dotted about in which were plenty of villages from which labourers could be obtained when required. This relieved Government of the cost of keeping up a large permanent establishment.

Morlay is a charming place.* The views of the Billiga-rungun hills and the more distant Neilgherries, the splendid sheets of water close at hand and the stretches of green rice-fields which they nourish, the groves of date-trees and cocoanut-gardens fringing the borders of artificial lakes for

* My home and headquarters in India are still there. During my absence in England a reduced establishment is maintained for the up-keep of the kheddahs.

irrigation, are very beautiful. The jungle is so close at hand to the east that pea-fowl, jungle-fowl, and partridges can be heard sounding their cheery cries, the sportsman's pleasant reveille, before daybreak. Such a place as Morlay for sport surely never existed, at least for diversity of game. Within a radius of half a mile of my bungalow, elephants, tigers, panthers, bears, pig, and spotted-deer; and a little beyond, bison, sámbur, two kinds of antelope, and bustard, are to be found; whilst good duck, pea-fowl, jungle-fowl, and snipe shooting are at my very doors. Any one acquainted with Indian shooting-grounds will know that such a variety of game is rarely found in one place.

Morlay is not, however, a very healthy place, and my people and myself have all suffered severely from fever at various times. The least healthy months are from November to February, when the nights are cold, with occasional fogs, and the days hot; and if the rains (from June to November) are excessive and continuous the dampness caused gives rise to fever and dysentery.

I had with me until lately at Morlay an overseer named Jones. Born and bred in the country, he understood natives well, and talked Canarese, Hindoostáni, Tamil, and Teloogoo fluently. He was, moreover, skilful and patient in managing the large bodies of ignorant villagers we employed on occasions, and his services were invaluable. He had a wife and two children, but one child soon succumbed to fever, as did also an old European pensioner and his wife whom I employed to preserve my sporting trophies. During our second year at Morlay we lost at the rate of two hundred *per mille per annum* amongst servants, &c., which is, I believe, about five times the death-rate of the most unhealthy towns in England.

We did better afterwards, however, and Morlay is such an advantageous and delightful place for my work, that I have stuck to it through all vicissitudes; but Jones has lately had to leave it on account of his health, so I am now the last, as I was the first, European there.

I knew Morlay for three years prior to the time of taking up my residence near it in September 1873. I had shot one or two proscribed solitary elephants in the neighbourhood, and had then noticed the advantages it presented for elephant-catching—at least I remembered them afterwards, when I was casting about for a suitable locality for a commencement.

Morlay itself is a village, or rather two villages in one, those of Dod (large), and Chick (little), Morlay. The two are within a quarter of a mile of each other, and the families are all inter-allied. The people are *Oopligas*, or salt-makers, and the manufacture of earth-salt is the legitimate calling of their caste. The tribe is not numerous in Mysore, and is necessarily confined to those places where the earth from which salt is obtained is found. In former times they followed this pursuit almost exclusively; but more recently the impulse given to cultivation and other pursuits by the increased safety of property under good government, and the more equal distribution of products which has followed the opening up of the Mysore country by roads, have tended to break down the hard and fast line of hereditary employments of the different castes. Thus Oopligas, stone-cutters, and weavers, &c., have in many cases turned cultivators; whilst the Brinjárries or gipsies, whose occupation in former times was the carrying of grain and salt upon pack-bullocks into localities inaccessible by other means (combined with pillage and cattle-lifting), have taken to grazing the herds of the villagers during the hot weather in jungle localities, bringing firewood for sale into towns, and cultivation.

The lands the Morlay villagers till are generally held by Bráhmins, and the Oopligas are either their *jeetagárs* (agricultural serfs) or *wáragárs* (cultivators under agreement). The Bráhmin proprietors live in villages in the more open country, and only visit their lands occasionally. The arrangement between proprietors and jeetagárs, is one of the greatest antiquity, and is as follows :—

A labourer may be in want of a loan—say a pound or two, a large sum to many millions in India—for his wedding expenses or other exigency. A land-holder accommodates him on his giving a bond and entering his service. It is generally understood that the principal will not be repaid, but the creditor obtains a legal right over the services of the debtor until it is. The debtor's position is analogous to that of an articled servant, except that no limit, but the payment of his debt, is placed on the connection.

The debtor is required to do his master's bidding in all things, his services counting instead of interest on the debt; whilst the master is bound to feed him, and interest himself in all matters affecting his jeetagár. The established subsistence allowance to the jeetagár is forty seers (80 lb.) of *rági* (the staple grain of the country) *per mensem*, and four annas (sixpence) in cash. The grain is ample for his food, and the money for tobacco and betel. From time to time the jeetagár probably obtains small sums—or more commonly grain—from his master, which are added to his debt. If the jeetagár dies one of his sons must take his father's place until he can clear off his liabilities, even under the inheritor from the original creditor. This obligation is, I believe, strictly binding in the Mysore law courts.

Jeeta-service is universal throughout Mysore, and is well suited to the conditions of the agricultural classes, both proprietors and servants. A home and sufficiency of food is assured to thousands who have no desire beyond; whilst land-holders, who from their caste or position may be unable to work themselves, obtain a hold upon what would otherwise be a very unreliable class of servants. Jeetagárs who have been many years in families are frequently treated more as sons than servants. On the occasion of marriages or other rejoicings they are not forgotten. Good masters not infrequently free the jeetagárs, should the latter desire it, after some years of approved service, without payment of the original debt. It is not uncommon for jeetagárs to continue for generations in the same family. It is a remarkable fact that their remuneration is exactly what it used to be as far back as can be traced, though the ordinary rates of labour in the country have advanced considerably of late years. May not this be regarded as an indication of the favour with which this vassalage is regarded by the agricultural labourer?

The arrangement for *wára,* or half-share cultivating, is as follows:—

The owner of the land pays the Government assessment (the average rate in Mysore is about two shillings per acre for unirrigated fields and twelve shillings for irrigated land), gives half the manure required, furnishes the seed grain, and contributes half the expenses of reaping and threshing. The cultivator (wáragár) uses his own plough and bullocks, gives his labour and half the manure, pays for the weedings of the crop (necessary in India), the mid-day meals of the reapers, and half the threshing expenses. The produce is then equally divided between owner and wáragár. Should the owner not give half the manure, all the straw goes to the wáragár.

Living on the borders of the jungle amongst the game, the Morlayites have for generations applied themselves to hunting. They have no guns, only spears and nets. They have strict caste rules on the subject, and maintain excellent discipline in their hunts. Each house has to supply a man with a net and spear when big game is followed, and a net and cudgel in hare-hunting. Their nets are of two kinds,—the first for tigers, bears, deer, &c.; and the second for small game. They are both made of home-grown hemp (jute, *Crotolarea juncea*), and are manufactured by themselves. The large nets are made of rope as thick as a finger, and are forty feet long and twelve deep, with a mesh large enough to admit a man's head. The small-game nets are of twine, and are one hundred and eighty feet long and four deep, with a mesh to admit a small fist.

With fifty to a hundred of these nets, large or small, a considerable extent of country can be enclosed. Whether deer or pig with large nets, or hares, mouse-deer, or porcupines with the small nets, are hunted, the plan pursued is to support the nets on upright light props across the line of country which the game, when driven, is expected to take ; a man is posted in ambush here and there behind the line of nets, and the remainder drive the jungle. The animals generally gallop into the nets, their heads become entangled in the meshes, the net falls and envelopes them, and they are speared while struggling. Powerful animals, as sámbur deer, large boars, &c., often tear through the nets, and tigers and bears occasionally bite the rope. When much hunted, beasts grow cunning, and frequently break back; or when one knocks the net down the others make for the gap and escape at that point.

With tigers, panthers, and bears, a different plan is pursued to that adopted for deer and pig. The Oopligas of Morlay had seldom molested dangerous animals before I hunted with them, but I showed them how the Torrea caste in Heggadévan-korté surround and kill tigers, &c., and we soon disposed of a good many. An animal is tracked to his lair; a circle of nets is then formed round him at some distance, in perfect silence, during the heat of the day: and he is either shot when roused, or speared as he precipitates himself against the nets. I shall speak further of this sport in treating of the tiger.

From their constant experience with game, the Oopligas soon became excellent assistants in elephant-catching. They had been accustomed from childhood to guard their fields against elephants at night, so did not fear them much, and if well led always behaved boldly. When the elephants were especially troublesome before I came to Morlay the men used to drive them with horns and tomtoms to the hills. As an instance of the pertinacity of elephants on occasions, they once drove an unusually troublesome herd (which we subsequently caught in June 1874) into the hills, and as it rained heavily that night, and there seemed to be no immediate fear of elephants, the field-watchers were withdrawn. In the morning they found some of the *jowáree* (*Sorghum vulgare*, the Indian maize) fields had been destroyed by the same elephants, which were in their original position again in the jungle close at hand!

About thirty years ago there was one particular male elephant which caused the Morlayites much loss by constantly feeding in their rice-fields. One morning he was seen close to the village about daybreak, when such a hue and cry was raised that in his fright the elephant attempted to cross a strip of morass which bordered the rice-fields and lay in the most direct route to the jungle. The surface of the bog gave way when he was half-way over, and he sank through to his middle. His pursuers pelted him with stones and cudgels, till, it becoming evident he could not extricate himself, some of the boldest approached and threw bundles of straw upon him, and then fired them. The wretched beast was terribly burnt on the back and hind-quarters, but not disabled; and whilst the villagers were casting about for some means of doing him mortal injury, he worked himself through the bog to firmer ground further on, and finally, after having been several hours in his unpleasant position, made his escape, and lived for many years, branded like a felon, to follow his old courses. Though the Morlayites' conduct on this occasion was very cruel, it must be said for them that they were incessantly troubled by this and other elephants, and as they possessed no guns they could do nothing effectual towards killing this freebooter.

Natives' ideas of cruelty are peculiar. They differ widely from ours. They think nothing of letting a domestic animal, with broken limbs or sores swarming with maggots, linger to death rather than raise a finger to put it out of its misery. They would consider taking its life under any circumstances cruel. Humanity as understood by us is a feeling of which they have no conception. When orders are issued at certain seasons by Government for the destruction of starving and half-rabid pariah dogs, by which Indian towns are infested—a merciful course to the animals themselves, and one necessary for the protection of the public—even educated Hindoos are seldom wanting to raise an outcry against the step. The same men would pass, without notice or pity, a donkey or cow by the roadside suffering from raw wounds at which crows were pecking (no uncommon sight in India), whilst the maddened animal made vain attempts to defend itself. I have never heard any native when with me shooting suggest such a thing as putting a wounded animal out of its pain. They have frequently said, "Why waste another bullet on it? it will die." A Shōlaga (hill-man) in my employ recently found a bison in an elephant pitfall; he had a gun, but rather than expend a shot on an animal that was useless to him, he left it there to starve to death: it did not die till the thirteenth day. When my men caught pea-fowl in snares they would pull out a feather, poke the stem through both eyelids, and fasten up the birds' eyes, to prevent them fluttering and spoiling their plumage, which "master would want." None of my men ever thought of sparing the youngest animal we might find in the jungle. If permitted to do so, they would consign fawn or leveret, whose helplessness might have been expected to excite even their compassion, to the game-bag without a regret, except at its size.

The Oopligas' houses are mere huts with earthen walls and thatched roofs, devoid of any aperture but the door. Before *kheddah* operations were begun they lived from hand to mouth a good deal, and during times of scarcity they ate, as they still do, many jungle-products, as the heart of the frond of date-palms, succulent roots which grow in immense quantities in the beds of some lakes after the water has receded, and several kinds of leaves. Their staple food, and that of all the lower classes in Mysore, is rági (*Cynosurus corocanus*), a small grain about the size of No. 7 shot, and hardly distinguishable, except in being a little larger, from common turnip-seed. The price of this varies in good and bad seasons from 100 lb. down to 20 lb. per rupee. During the recent famine it has been 11. Two pounds are required by a man *per diem.*

The grain is prepared for food by grinding it in the common double-stone hand-mill. One woman will grind five or six pounds per hour. The flour is boiled into a stiff pudding in an earthen pot, being stirred the while with a stick, and is then made into balls. This is the chief food of all the labouring classes in Mysore and many parts of Southern India. The poor cannot afford to eat rice, which is ordinarily three times the price of rági; but even if procurable, rice is not regarded with favour by those who have hard work to do. Some condiment is commonly used with it, generally a mixture of chillies, coriander, tamarind, garlic, onions, and salt. Meat, pulse, or greens are boiled with the condiments if procurable.

Rági is stored in subterranean granaries. They are usually situated on somewhat high ground, and in gravelly soil or decomposed rock. Their construction is simple. A circular hole about two feet in diameter is dug to three feet in depth, when a domed chamber of an oval shape is excavated, capable of containing from ten to twenty cart-loads of grain. Neither masonry nor props are used. A little straw is laid on the floor, and against the walls of the chamber to a third of their height, when the grain is filled in. A slab is placed over the pit at the bottom of the short shaft that enters it, and the shaft is then filled in with earth. Rági thus stored will keep for an indefinite number of years. It is safe from insects and rats, and is not easily accessible to thieves, as the pits are generally situated near the village—sometimes in the streets—and it takes some little time to dig to the grain. Moreover it is highly dangerous to enter a rági-pit till twelve hours or more after it has been opened. The carbonic acid gas generated therein is instantaneously fatal, and though natives are well aware of this, accidents frequently happen through their descending the pits before they are well aired. Three brothers died in this way near Morlay in one pit in attempting to rescue each other when overcome by the fumes of the gas.

In former days, when villages were subject to pillage by Brinjárries and gang-robbers, grain-pits were often dug in the fields and ploughed over for concealment. It occasionally happened that through the death of the owner or other eventuality, the existence of certain pits was forgotten, and these are not unfrequently found at the present day, many probably two or three hundred years old. The grain in them is generally perfectly sound. It would be thought that moisture would penetrate the pits; but from the nature of the soil, and the site chosen, this seldom appears to occur. Money and jewels are often hidden at the bottom of rági-pits for safe keeping. A corps of men is said to have been attached to invading armies in Mysore in former days to search for rági on the sites of villages temporarily left by their inhabitants. The searchers were provided with steel testing-rods, and from constant practice knew pretty well where to look for the hidden stores. They are said to have been guided chiefly by the smell of the tip of the rod on withdrawing it as to whether they had "struck rági."

Few of the Oopligas when I began work at Morlay had more than a piece of cloth to wrap round their loins, and a coarse blanket, or *cumbly*, as a protection against wet or cold. When hunting or working they wear absolutely nothing but the *langoty*, which is a string round the loins and a piece of cloth about a hand's-breadth fastened to it in front; this is carried between the legs, and is tucked under the string again behind. It is an extremely practical attire, light and airy in appearance, as far as it can be seen, and one that does not hamper their activity. There are few large or well-conditioned men amongst the Oopligas. Their endurance, however, in hunting or work is remarkable. They take two meals a-day—one about ten o'clock in the morning, the other at eight in the evening. Meat is a great treat to them, and I frequently shoot deer or pigs for them. They do not eat cow's flesh, nor even that of the bison, which they consider to be of the same holy caste, though they eat jackals, wild cats, field-rats, iguana lizards, &c. They never drink any intoxicating liquor. Though they live in a date-grove, from the trees in which "toddy" is daily drawn in large quantities for sale elsewhere, and although from the pots tied to the trees they might drink on the sly at any time, not a single Oopliga ever, to my certain knowledge, does so. It is not an hereditary usage, and they no more long for liquor than an Englishman does for blubber or train-oil.

Their women are mostly very ugly. They only possess the charms attaching to budding youth for a few years, after which they sink at once into hideous frights. At about twenty-five their youth is gone, and they seem to betake themselves to fifty forthwith without any intermediate stage. They are of course married early, like all Hindoos, and often have children before they are fourteen years of age. They were at first so poor that they barely had enough rags to satisfy even their very moderate ideas of decency's requirements; and I have often felt amused whilst commiserating some of the girls who, with a short cloth wound lightly round their loins, and reaching but to their knees, endeavoured to pass muster as I rode through the village, or when they were collected at camp for grinding rági, by holding their hands up to their chins and covering their bosoms with their elbows! They were anxious for cloths, and I latterly insisted on the money they earned by grinding flour for our men being applied to their own gratification in this respect, and not to their husbands'.

There is never any violent crime amongst these simple people. They live in family harmony, and any little differences are settled by village regulations. Infidelity amongst their women is common enough, but their rules and ideas on this subject are very moderate, and a husband who feels himself aggrieved, instead of flying into a temper, addresses himself to the headman, a *punchayet* or council is convened, and the defendant is probably fined a few rupees. At the same time, a check is placed on husbands having recourse to too much litigation by fining them occasionally for having adulterous wives!

If a woman does not like her husband, and any other man, married or otherwise, fancies her, she may go with him if he pays the husband Rs. 45, which is the fixed capitalised value of the marriage expenses. These transactions always have to be carried out through the headman, who has his regular fees. This purchasing of wives cannot be indulged in, however, to any great extent, as the devoted lovers can seldom raise enough money except by selling themselves into bondage, which has probably already been done to their full value.

This looseness in the matrimonial rules may seem sufficiently shocking to English notions, but it must be considered that marriage in Morlay is purely an arrangement of convenience; and though it is literally so with ourselves, a halo of religious feeling has come to surround this civil contract, and moral turpitude is connected with any breach of its provisions, of which natives of the lower classes understand nothing. Their rules suit themselves very well. If a woman's husband cannot support her, she may find some one else who can; or if a man has a useless or termagant wife, he may get some one else who will manage better for him, though he is bound to continue the support of his first wife as long as she remains with him.

The hereditary headman of the Morlay Oopligas is a young fellow called Lingah. He was one of the first to take employment under me, and has always since been a most faithful adherent. It is a great pity and a disadvantage that the hereditary authority of headmen of villages and castes has been gradually undermined. The Mysore Government has, however, done much lately towards restoring their power, which is undoubtedly a wise measure and one in accordance with the feelings of the people.

Paternal despotism seems to be the best method of government for the Hindoo.

I shall never forget what an untutored lot my Morlayites were when I first knew them, and they often laugh and joke at it now themselves. They needed an immense amount of training before they became efficient for work in which considerable discipline was necessary. One of their chief duties was to direct large numbers of men when we were driving elephants, and it was therefore necessary that they themselves should be smart, and learn to carry out orders promptly and exactly. Of such matters, or of the importance of time, they had not naturally the remotest idea. They considered to-morrow as good as to-day in all matters, and hours of no consequence at all. The apathy and unreliableness of Hindoos are sufficiently trying to the naturally energetic Englishman. It can easily be imagined, then, that for some time my poor ignorant Morlayites truly exercised my soul. However, by degrees Jones, who drilled them, introduced quite military precision amongst them. When once their natural apathy was shaken we found them very teachable. They were made to stand in a line for muster, instead of the mob they naturally affected ; to make their salaams morning and evening on coming from and returning to the village; and to run on all occasions when sent on any short errand. The most difficult thing was to get them to carry a verbal message correctly, but by constantly calling them back and making them repeat what they were bid to say this was at last managed fairly. They soon began to pride themselves on belonging to the kheddah service, and it is now amusing to hear them abusing and ordering their fellow-villagers at work or in sport; they regard their untrained brethren as a very degenerate lot.

Five of the best men were appointed as elephant-trackers, their duty being to go to the jungles within a certain circuit of Morlay every morning to examine tracks of elephants or tigers, to find out their whereabouts, and generally to keep me informed of all jungle occurrences. In elephant or other hunting these scouts are my right-hand men. They have the most dangerous duties to perform, and I shall have occasion often to mention them further on. More plucky and reliable men I never had, and their knowledge of the habits of all animals is only equalled by their skill in following them, or anticipating what their line of conduct or of country will be. After our first capture of elephants I had a small silver elephant stamped for each to wear on a green cap, and they are very proud of this badge of office. Their names are: Dodda Sidda, Koon Sidda, Máda, Murga, Mástee.

And here let me say a few words upon trackers. The skill of certain tribes of American Indians in following a trail is proverbial, but I engage to say it cannot excel that of jungle-people in India. Human eyesight is pretty much the same all the world over. It would be incorrect to represent any class of people, as some writers have done, as able to follow a track over ground where there is no mark discernible to the untrained eye. It is not to be supposed that a print which is visible to an Indian would not be equally so to a European if pointed out to him. The skill of tracking lies in first observing, and reading, what an untrained eye would pass over, or be unable to interpret.

I know nothing more interesting than to see really good trackers at work. There is a dash about men accustomed to hunt together, and who thoroughly understand the game they are after, which makes sport of what is often the rather tedious part of a chase. Jungle-people in India are under constant necessity to avoid formidable animals, as they have neither the means nor the stomach to oppose them. They thus become preternaturally quick in noting sights and sounds which do not attract the attention of ordinary persons. The slight ruffling of the surface which alone marks, in hard ground, where the tiger's paw has pressed; the horns of a deer lying in the grass, matching so closely with twigs and undergrowth as to be undistinguishable from them by the inexperienced eye; the bee, scarcely larger than a house-fly, entering a hole high in a tree overhead—a point of interest to men who spend much of their time in searching for its stores,—alike attract the quiet glance of the Kurraba and Shōlaga.

In cases where actual footprints fail, trackers are guided in following an animal by broken twigs, displaced blades of grass, dew shaken from the leaves whilst others are covered by it, and other signs. They can also judge with wonderful correctness of the date of different trails. When an animal has been moving about in the same locality for hours, and many different impressions have been left, much skill is required to determine the latest. Some may have been exposed to the burning rays of the sun, others sheltered from it. In such case the latter, though possibly hours older than the former, looks fresher, and would mislead the inexpert. A tiger's track of late the night before and early next morning may easily be confounded. The necessity of knowing which is which is evident. To follow the one would be to go through the many wanderings of his night's prowl in search of food; the other leads to where he may be found concealed for the day. Other points than its actual appearance aid in forming a correct diagnosis of a track's date. I remember one morning several of my Morlay men and I started early to look up a particular tiger we were anxious to fall in with. We intended to cast about in the most likely places for his morning's tracks; could we find these we should be able to discover his lair. It was cold, and the two trackers, Dodda Sidda and Murga, strode along in front of my riding elephant, their mouths muffled in their cloths after the sensible habit of all natives during the raw early hours. The path was dusty, and footprints were clearly visible. Presently the large square "pug" of the tiger we were in search of appeared, traversing the path before us. Some of the beaters who were following ran up in great excitement, and one asked the trackers if they had no eyes. Dodda Sidda removed his muffler for a moment as he still held on, to say, "Yelah, Korna, návu pattay-gáraró? Koombáraró? eely yesht' hottinelli tiroogárdootavó?" "Buffalo"—native synonym for stupid—"are we trackers or potters? When do the rats run about?" The questioner fell back abashed. The Indian field-rat (the jerboa-rat, *Gerbillus indicus*) issues from its burrows in great numbers during the night, but is always home again before daylight. The trackers had observed these creatures' tiny footprints overlying those of the tiger, and knew the latter had passed in the early part of the night.

On another occasion a panther's footprint in soft soil was under discussion. Some of the men contended it was of the evening before, others that it had been made about dawn. The minute threads of mould thrown up by a small earth-worm in the print made by the larger pad of the foot decided the date. That kind of worm only worked near the surface during the night. The print had been made the evening before.

Native shikáries are often very plucky fellows, and even those who are not so, and who know anything about their work, will do many things from their acquaintance with wild animals that they know they may do without risk, but which to the uninitiated sportsman appear venturesome. Even timid jungle-men who would not approach a horse, it being an unfamiliar quadruped, will lead the way after a vicious elephant or a wounded bison. They understand the habits of the latter, but from never seeing the former they do not know what to expect of it.

Men who serve a judicious master and who know they will not be unnecessarily exposed gain great confidence, and behave with a courage which the sportsman cannot but feel complimentary to himself, as reflecting their reliance on his coolness and skill. It is only right that a sportsman should remember not to allow any of his men to do that at which he would himself hesitate. I laid down this golden rule for myself early in my sporting days, and it is a great pleasure to me to think that I have never had a man killed in encounters with wild animals. I have often restrained beaters when they would willingly have ventured on some too dangerous service, and if natives see such consideration exercised on their behalf they are never wanting when required to share danger with their master.

I have sometimes heard sportsmen (elect) speak of their attendants getting "pale with fright," "blue with funk," "bolting up trees like lamp-lighters," &c. One cannot but comment mentally in many cases on the probable grounds their followers had for changes of complexion and feats of agility. Natives who have never seen a sportsman before are often called upon to show game. It is natural that they should be doubtful of the qualifications of a stranger, and they show their good sense in taking steps for their safety until they see they can place confidence in their employer. Natives often have good reason to be cautious. Cases of beaters being killed by dangerous animals are unhappily not of infrequent occurrence. Some men in the excitement of sport will urge natives to do things which they would be sorry upon reflection to do themselves. A man safely posted in a tree is liable to forget, in his chagrin at want of determination on the part of the beaters, what his own feelings would be if, with only a rag round his loins and a stick in his hand, he were required to turn a tiger out of a thicket. If only for the sake of sport care is necessary, as the story of an accident will precede a sportsman with telegraphic rapidity, and he will find beaters very chary of risking their persons at his next camp.

CHAPTER V.

THE BILLIGA-RUNGUN HILLS.

EARTHEN WALLS—MORLAY HALL—HONHOLLAY RIVER-VIEW—IRRIGATION—INCURSIONS OF WILD ANIMALS INTO CULTIVATION—THE RÁMASAMOODRUM LAKE—METHOD OF TAKING FISH—SLUICES—A NATIVE DROWNED—MEANS USED TO RECOVER HIS BODY—THE BILLIGA-RUNGUN HILLS—FOREST AND VEGETATION—A DESERTED VILLAGE—PROBABLE REASONS OF ABANDONMENT OF JUNGLE-VILLAGES—A NOTED BULL BISON—SHOOT HIM—LAKE ON THE HILLS—HAMLETS OF YELSÁRIGA AND POONJOOR—BOMMAY GOUDA—THE KOOMBAPPAN GOODY TEMPLE—CHARACTER OF THE GOD—FATE OF THE LAST PRIEST—RITUAL OBSERVED—YOUNG MARRIED WOMEN'S PRAYERS—RELIGION OF NATIVES—PROPITIATING KOOMBAPPAH—THE HOLEY DOINGS OF A HOLY MAN.

I WAS so busy for the first few months at Morlay that I had no time to build a house, so I lived in tents; but during the hot weather of 1874 I ran up a comfortable bungalow and outhouses for servants and Government stores. My bungalow consists of two rooms, each twenty by fourteen, and a bathing-room. The walls are of clay, smoothened and white-washed. The red gravelly soil common in many parts of Mysore is good material for wall-making. Many remains of earth-work forts which have been exposed to the vicissitudes of the weather for probably two or three hundred years, are to be seen throughout the country, built of this material only, without even a facing of stone, and though the walls are deeply indented and guttered by rain they waste but slowly. Earth for wall-making is first dug up and water is poured on it in the pit, after which it is tempered by men trampling it for some time. It is then built in layers half a yard high, and the required length of the wall; one day must be allowed for each layer to dry. Ordinary house-walls are one and a half foot thick at bottom, decreasing upwards. Wall-building is generally contracted for by the coolies at work, who take about eightpence for each

Phototint

H. M. Wright & Co. London.

Morlay Hall

six feet in length, the standard height being six feet. When dry, earthen walls are usually smoothened with a plaster of red earth mixed with sand. House-walls thus built are cheap, strong, and quickly run up; the only disadvantage connected with them is that white-ants are apt to work up through them into the roof of the house. This can, however, be easily prevented by a single course of brick-in-mortar upon the top of the wall.

The roof of my bungalow consists of a single areca-nut tree, fifty feet long, as a ridge-pole, and bamboo rafters which rest upon the walls. Over these are bamboo mats to prevent the ends of the grass with which it is thatched hanging down inside, and a layer of one foot of rice-straw makes it quite water-tight. The floor is of concrete to keep out white-ants, and is covered with bamboo mats.

"Morlay Hall," as I named this edifice, is situated about a quarter of a mile to the east of Morlay, on the site of a deserted village called Byádamooll, which is now only marked by irregular mounds and lines where the houses were, and by an old stone temple and some fine banian and peepul (*Ficus religiosa*) trees. The village ceased to exist fifty years ago. There are many such, thus deserted, of various degrees of antiquity, further in the jungles. I shall have occasion to speak of them further on, and to consider the probable causes which led to their abandonment.

My bungalow faces eastwards, towards the Billiga-rungun hills, which are eight miles distant and extend for twenty miles in front of me. They attain an elevation of about 6000 feet, or 3500 feet above the general level of the country around Morlay. Between my house and the hills the jungle consists chiefly of bamboo clumps and moderate-sized trees, with thick covers (the favourite resort of tigers, wild hog, &c.) on the river-banks and in the damp hollows. A few low detached hills lie near the foot of the range, and afford cover to bears and panthers. Parallel with the hills runs the Honhollay, a river about thirty yards broad, which, though rarely dry, is only a considerable stream at intervals during the rainy season. It then sometimes rises twenty feet above its bed, but is seldom impassable for more than a day together. During the first freshes of the rainy season it brings down large quantities of wood and bamboos, and the water is discoloured by the charcoal and black ashes washed from the hills after the hot-weather conflagrations. The water is considered bad within the jungles at this time, and also in December and January; but at all other times it is good. The reason of its being unwholesome in January and February is, that the hill streams have then shrunk almost to their lowest limits, and the leaves of the forest-trees which fall at the end of the year rot in large quantities in the water, and thus contaminate it by decaying vegetable matter; and though perfectly clear, it is bitter to the taste, and if constantly drunk is injurious to health. Several large villages in the open country are dependent for drinking-water on the river after it leaves the jungle. The water here seems good at all seasons, probably from undergoing a filtering process over beds of sand, where it is not shaded by trees.

The Honhollay rises in the Billiga-runguns, the parent branch being joined soon after its exit from the hills by two tributaries; one from Poonjoor, near the southern end of the range—the other, a large stream called the Chickhollay, from the open country towards the Neilgherries. After emerging from the Billiga-runguns through a gap about the centre of their western face, the river turns sharp north, and flows parallel with the range, and about four miles distant from it, through the Chámráj-Nuggar and Yellandoor *talooks,** and joins the Cauvery fifteen miles above the celebrated falls of Seevasamudrum. During its course its waters are drawn off by several small channels for purposes of irrigation. The first of these, the Honglewaddy, is fed from an *anicut* or stone dam, about twelve feet in height, made of large, rough blocks of granite, faced with a brick wall to prevent leakage: it is built across the stream from bank to bank. This raises the level of the water to a height sufficient to admit of its being drawn off by the channel, which runs for nine miles and feeds the Rámasamoodrum lake close to Morlay. The anicut, channel, and lake or tank, are works of some antiquity. The anicut and channel are now overgrown with dense jungle. The channels further down the river are smaller, and the dams used for turning the water into them are mere temporary structures of stakes, bushes, &c., thrown up after the floods subside.

There was formerly a good deal of cultivation under the Honglewaddy channel at several points between its source and the lake, but almost the whole of this has been gradually abandoned, owing to the depredations of elephants and tigers. Up to the time of my settling at Morlay it was no uncommon occurrence for a tiger to rush out and kill one or both the bullocks in a plough, if the driver left them for a moment. With the destruction of the tigers and reduction in the number of elephants, land is being gradually taken up again, and the cultivators can now follow their avocations in peace. There is no necessity to watch the fields at night, except occasionally to drive away deer and wild hogs, which is lighter work than the keeping out of elephants used to be.

The Rámasamoodrum tank at the end of the Honglewaddy channel is a beautiful sheet of water, nearly two miles in length and five hundred yards broad. It has, however, been silted up to a considerable extent by the

* Divisions of the country corresponding roughly to counties in England.

deposit brought into it for many years, and is not now capable of storing as much water as formerly. The two villages of Morlay are built near the edge of the water-spread, and my bungalow a quarter of a mile from it, on high and dry ground. The embankment of the lake has been raised at various periods to keep pace with the silting, and the bed is now several feet higher than the land irrigated on the lower side of the embankment. Through the embankment at different points run four sluices for drawing off the water to the rice-land below, which aggregates 903 acres, and yields an annual revenue to Government of Rs. 4688. These sluices have of late years fallen into partial disrepair; and from this cause, and the silting up of the bed, the tank now usually runs dry during the hot weather. There are no fish of large size in it, but a great quantity of moderate-sized ones and small fry are caught every year. In January 1874, when the tank had not been dry for five years, and the fish had had time to grow, a large haul was made by the Morlayites. As the water contracted to a very narrow space I caused the tank to be guarded day and night to prevent any villagers, except those who assisted in elephant-catching, from taking fish in it; and when the water was but two feet deep, and only a few acres in extent, a day was appointed for fishing it. Hundreds of men, women, and children were engaged with all sorts of devices, among which the chief was a basket of the shape of a flower-pot, but without the bottom, about three feet in height, two in diameter at the lower end, and one at the top. These open cylinders were merely plumped down upon the bottom, the wider mouth downwards, on chance, and if a fish were covered it flopped about inside, and was taken out through the top. As the pool was crowded the sport was exciting, and in a few hours many hundredweights were caught. The women and children removed baskets upon baskets of small fry which, suffocated by the disturbed mud, came to the top floating on their backs, when they were scooped up with sieves.

Speaking of sluices for drawing off water from lakes, it is remarkable that no contrivance has been introduced in supersession of the somewhat rude plan of old days, which is still in use. This is as follows: A covered masonry culvert runs through the embankment; at its inner end (that is, the end within the lake) two upright granite slabs are erected, so as to stand above the highest level of the water; they are often twenty-five feet in height. At every six feet or so cross-slabs are placed between them. Through each of the cross-slabs a hole is drilled for guiding a vertical pole which passes through them, and attached to the lower end of which is a wooden plug. This plug fits into a vent in the horizontal covering-slab over the mouth of the culvert, and when raised or lowered opens or closes the culvert. To move the pole and attached plug a man stands on the cross-slabs. This method answers well enough for small tanks, but in many of large size there is an additional vent in the vertical slab which closes the mouth of the culvert vertically, and in this a horizontal vent is drilled, to close which a flat stone is usually employed. This stone has to be placed against the hole by hand; and to all large tanks there are attached one or more men, called Toobmullegies or sluice-divers, to whom free lands are granted as remuneration for attending to the distribution of the water. It would be very easy to have a vertical shutter, in the shape of a spade, with a long handle reaching to above the surface of the water, to close this dangerous horizontal vent. It is remarkable how seldom accidents happen to the divers, as they keep to the guiding granite pillars at either side, and place the stone in front of the vent without getting before it themselves; but mishaps sometimes occur, and six years ago a diver was drowned by being sucked into the vent of one of the sluices of the Rámasamoodrum tank. There was a depth of nineteen feet of water above the sluice at the time. The danger of approaching a vent of one foot in diameter, through which the water was issuing under this pressure, may be imagined. In some way the unfortunate man was caught; both his legs were drawn into the vent up to the thighs, and he sat, when drowned, with his body resting against the vertical slab. I was in charge of the tank at the time, but it was some days before I could attend to getting him out, as I thought the natives would manage it; as they could not, I went to the spot myself. Standing on the top of the sluice slabs, the corpse was twenty feet below; only three or four men could get footing to pull at it together, and it defied all attempts at withdrawal. We tried for two days without effect. I at last had two hide-ropes secured by a diver round the corpse, and ordered a raft of plantain-stems to be made capable of floating ten people: this was stationed above the corpse, and sufficient people stood on it to sink it a foot, whilst the hide-ropes were secured to it. On the people getting off, the raft's floating power pulled up the body, not at all decomposed, though it had been eleven days under water: the man's never having been exposed to the air after death was probably the cause of this. His dark skin was bleached quite white. One of the legs was torn off at the hip-joint and carried through the sluice.

The Billiga-rungun hills consist of three main parallel ranges running due north and south, with various offshoots. The Cauvery river flows round their northern end, whilst they are separated from the Neilgherry hills at their southern extremity by a gap of about twenty miles of level country. They are about thirty miles in length from north to south, and ten in width;

but only about ten miles of the central portion is densely covered with forest, as towards the end the hills become lower and the jungle lighter. The Mysore territory includes the most western parallel; the rest of the hills lie in the Coimbatore district of the Madras Presidency. A good road passes through a gorge towards their southern end, and descends by the Hássanoor Ghât into the Coimbatore district, which is about 1000 feet below the general level of the Mysore plateau. The hills are practically unknown to Europeans. A few Survey and Forest officers have been to some of the most prominent points, and in former days some officers of the Mysore Commission who were fond of sport occasionally visited them, but of late years hardly any one but myself has set foot in them. The only inhabitants are a few Shōlagas—a wild, uncivilised, but inoffensive race. They occupy isolated hamlets of five or six huts.

The Mysore range is lower than the ranges further east. It is covered with comparatively small timber and bamboos, as there is no great depth of soil, and crags and rocks frown here and there amongst the jungle. Towards the northern end, in the Yellandoor talook, is a precipitous mass of granite, facing westwards, named the "Billikul" or "Billigiri" (white rock); and from this the whole range is geographically designated, though, as is common in India, the natives of the vicinity have names for each portion of the hills, and do not know the whole by any collective appellation. The range is, however, usually known to people at a distance as the Billigiri-runguns; but this, I think, is not a correct term, and that Billiga-runga, the local name amongst the common people, is the right one. *Billi* means white in Canarese, and *kul*, a rock or stone; in Canarese Billi-kul-runga becomes Billiga-runga by euphony. *Giri* is Sanskrit for mountain, and the union of a Canarese and Sanskrit word is unnatural. The hills are generally termed "Shwétadri" by Bráhmins, which is admissible as pure Sanskrit, and means "white-mountain." Runga is the name of a god.

The interior ranges, as seen from Morlay, present a splendid panorama of woods and open grass downs. The hills are rounded and are all of about the same elevation. The woods are confined chiefly to the hollows where moisture favours their growth; the open downs between them are covered with dense lemon-grass, which attains a height of eighteen feet. Between the Mysore range and the next range to the east lies a deep valley, along which the Honhollay stream flows southwards before its exit westwards into open country. This deep, forest-encumbered valley is a tract of great interest; and there are many places which I have penetrated where, I believe, other European foot never trod. Wild swamps there are where the strangest forms of vegetation are seen, some found nowhere else in the hills. The whole neighbourhood has a weird character. Aged trees of huge dimensions, whose ponderous arms are clad with grey moss and ferns far out to their points; tough, gnarled, leafless creepers, as thick as a child's body, growing from one root, whither they mount the tall trees around, and thence spread like the arms of a cuttle-fish in every direction, curling round some trunks, clearing long spans in places, and often extending for three hundred yards without varying much in thickness,—make some of the chief features of the woods in these deep valleys. Few flowers are found; the whole is a damp, gloomy, hoary forest, sacred as it were to the first mysteries of nature. Game—even elephants and bison—are seldom seen here; the dense foliage overhead prevents grass growing beneath, so there is nothing for them to eat; but they form safe retreats for animals in their neighbourhood when the jungles are burning during the hot weather. When any animals escaped us in the first range, or the lower jungles of the open country, and reached this haven, which is known as "Mullay Kárdoo," or the Rain Forest, we generally had to abandon the chase, as it required a well-organised expedition to penetrate the tract.

Close to the mouth of the gorge by which the Honhollay river emerges into the lower jungles through the most westerly or Mysore range, is the site of an old and long-deserted village called Dodda Goudan Parliah, and from this I have named the gorge. The last inhabitants of this place apparently left about 1820, but it must have been practically deserted at least twenty years before that time. The divisions of the fields, broken rági-grinding stones, and stone terraces built round the foot of the trunks of old tamarind and peepul trees, are still to be seen. It was once a populous village, in which iron-smelting was carried on. The site of the village and the fields are still comparatively free of jungle; but by August the grass grows very high about them, and the place is then a favourite resort of game, especially bison, whilst in the low country.

In addition to Dodda Goudan Parliah, there are the remains of other villages, apparently contemporary with it, in different parts of the lower jungles, but I have tried in vain to obtain any very authentic explanation of the causes of their abandonment. From the tales which some of the oldest Shōlagas remember their fathers relating of the ransacking to which villages were frequently subjected in these parts during Hyder and Tippoo's days, and the early days of the British (between 1780 and 1800), at the hands of Brinjárries (gipsy grain-carriers), who, when conveying grain to the troops between Mysore and Coimbatore, passed through this country,

Phototint. H. M. Wright & Co London.

The Dodday Gowdan Parliah Gorge.

I believe the hardships and robberies to which the people were subjected to have been the chief cause of their leaving their homes. Their granaries were sacked, their herds driven off, and their women abducted by these freebooters. Consecutive years of scarcity or sickness may also, in some cases, have tended to this result; but as all Indian villages have small beginnings, if the site chosen proves unhealthy it is soon given up; and consequently, when the remains of any village formerly of importance are found, it is more reasonable to look to other causes for its abandonment than unhealthiness, which should rather decrease (except epidemics) with the growth of the village, and the greater area from which the surrounding jungle is removed, than increase. Some villages have evidently been ruined through the action of their inhabitants, as those mentioned in Chap. III.; but there are no such causes visible in the deserted villages at the foot of the Billiga-runguns, and doubtless the ancestors of the Brinjárries, who now quietly graze cattle over their ruins, had a main share in bringing about their downfall.

There used to be a famous old solitary bull bison, well known to the Shōlagas as having frequented the vicinity of Dodda Goudan Parliah for twenty years. I had learned that he was generally to be seen in the cool hours of the morning and evening grazing in the short grass on the outskirts of the jungle, preparatory to retiring into it for the day. One morning I was going from a place called Koombár-goondy to fish in the deep pools of the Honhollay, within the gorge, and was riding my small pad elephant Soondargowry, which did not bring my head to the level of the grass, then ten feet high, when, as I passed along, I saw through a gap in the grass the head of a bison lying under a bamboo clump some sixty yards to my right. I pulled up to make sure. Yes! there he was, a splendid old bull, chewing the cud peacefully, and not looking in our direction! I knew instantly he must be *the* bull I had heard so much of, and which I had been singularly unsuccessful in falling in with before. My heavy rifles were at hand, so I jumped off the elephant, and with a tracker crept through the grass towards the bull. As we came to the clear ground under the bamboo clumps, he suddenly upreared his gigantic black form to our right; he had caught a slant of our wind. He stood stern on; and as I feared he might dash away, I took the best shot I could, and broke his right hip-joint. I was using an 8-bore rifle and ten drams. At the shot the bull rushed amongst the bamboo clumps, his disabled leg swinging like a flail. Another tracker joined us, and we followed him without loss of time; but he got into a narrow belt of grass and young bamboo a hundred yards away, and here we heard him breathing heavily. We kept to the shelter of trees whilst making a near advance, when the bull, hearing us, showed himself, and I stepped out and faced him at thirty yards. He did not charge, however, though he snorted furiously, and I killed him with a shot in the neck as he turned. This was the work of two or three minutes from my first seeing him. He was an immense animal, eighteen hands at the shoulder, and very old. He had foot-and-mouth disease.

The villagers of this tract in past times evidently made much use of the grazing grounds on the top of the hills during the dry weather, and have constructed a fine tank, called the Hannaykerray, on the summit. This holds water at all seasons. The name signifies the tank on the brow, *hannay* meaning forehead in Canarese.

At the foot of the Hannaykerray hills is a Shōlaga hamlet called Yerlsáriga, or the "seven fields." Around it is a little cultivation, but it is chiefly a cattle-grazing station. It is eight miles from Morlay, and by keeping a Shōlaga there in kheddah employ I always have early news of any elephants coming down the hills; and when bison-shooting, or looking after elephants, I generally make it my headquarters. The Dodda Goudan Parliah gorge, being a broad and gradually ascending means of ingress to the hills, contains the main elephant and bison track between them and the low jungles.

There is a hamlet called Poonjoor, on a tributary of the Honhollay, four miles to the south of Yerlsáriga, along the foot of the hills. It is close to the Hássanoor Ghât road, just at the point where the road enters the pass through the hills towards Coimbatore. There is only one family at Poonjoor; the headman, old Bommay Gouda, has always been one of my greatest allies in sport, and I must honour him with some mention.

Bommay Gouda is a man of about fifty-five years of age. He is of good caste, being a Shivachár or Lingáyet, and lives by cultivation and breeding and selling cattle. Of all the cheery jungle-companions I know Bommay Gouda stands first. He has literally lived amongst wild animals all his life and possesses the most consummate knowledge of their habits, but the tiger and the elephant are his chief game. At a story by the camp-fire he is unrivalled, and he is still as tough as he is keen. I please him by telling him he is "my father" in sport, the filial position being founded on his having piloted me up to my first elephant, bison, and bears. One thing distresses him, which is that after he is gone there will be no one to keep up his name, as his eldest son is good for nothing at sport, no chip of the old block. I shall frequently have occasion to mention Bommay Gouda, as we have done many good days' sport together.

From living in this unhealthy place for so many years, amongst the wild beasts of the forest, Bommay Gouda has come to be regarded with superstitious awe by the inhabitants of the open country. Few would dare to offend him, as his powers of injuring them by supernatural means are never doubted. Neither he nor any of his family eat meat, but in his younger days he occasionally shot sámbur and bison with his old match-lock, to barter their flesh for grain. He also used to make a good deal by shooting elephants and tigers. The reward for a tiger was Rs. 30, and for an elephant Rs. 70; but whilst the reward for the tiger has been increased to Rs. 50, that for the elephant has been withdrawn, and protection substituted.

Of late years there has been a police-guard stationed at Poonjoor, as a check to the numerous robberies on the Hássanoor road, but owing to its unhealthiness the men have to be changed frequently. Bommay Gouda's family, from long usage to the place, enjoy fair health, but it is hurtful to new-comers. It is a favourite grazing station when drought in the open country obliges the ryots to send their cattle to the jungles. Shōlagas and Brinjár-ries are mostly engaged to take charge of these herds. In the jungles around Poonjoor when there is plenty of rain, game of all descriptions, from elephants downwards, is abundant. At all times tigers are, or were before I thinned them, numerous, attracted by the herds of cattle; but the same marauders visited Morlay (eleven miles distant through the jungles), and there they were laid low.

Three miles from Morlay, situated in a beautiful glade on the banks of the Honhollay river, surrounded by fine trees and jungle, is Koombappan Goody, or the temple of Koombappah, the shrine whither the Morlayites and other adjacent villagers repair at certain times to pay their devotions. The temple is sixteen feet long, eight broad, and nine high; it has a flat roof, and is composed throughout of large dressed slabs. It was built in old days, probably when an adjacent village, the site of which is now marked by ancient trees and stones, flourished. Worship has been kept up though the village has ceased to exist. Mondays and Fridays are the *poojah* or service days, when the priest attends. Only such people visit it as have some request to prefer, usually connected with their families, their crops, or their bodily ailments. They are not continually found about their church, as they do not consider it necessary either for their spiritual welfare or for the sake of respectability.

Koombappah is regarded as an *evil* god who must be propitiated. The priest often told me he was "a very bad god indeed," and if his *poojah* were not conducted properly, it would be a poor look-out for himself. I have often witnessed the doings at the shrine when, after a morning's work or sport in the jungles, I have been enjoying a cheroot after breakfasting under the trees near the temple. The proceedings are conducted as follows:—

The priest, an ordinary ryot, turns up about mid-day after having his breakfast comfortably, usually attended by a few villagers who have requests to make. Company is desired by all, as the last incumbent, the present one's father, was carried off by a man-eating tiger on his way to conduct service, and a tigress which was killing when I arrived at Morlay kept the present divine in a lively state of trepidation. With him the cry of the "Church in danger" means more than it often does elsewhere.

The first thing to be done by the Poojáree after opening the door of the temple with a crooked piece of iron in lieu of a key, and sweeping out the first of the two chambers into which it is internally divided, is to go down to the river with a brass vessel, and after performing his ablutions in the stream, to bring back water for sprinkling within the holy of holies, into which he alone may enter, and before which a cloth is kept suspended. He then places incense and a light in the inner chamber, and whilst giving Koombappah time to contemplate these, the Poojáree adjourns to a shed near, where he commences cooking rice and vegetables. Whilst the pot is boiling the service is begun by his taking the plantains and cocoanuts, or handfuls of grain, brought by those present, and placing them before the god, mentioning the worshippers' requests at the same time. One promises to feed a dozen poor people before the temple if he is relieved from fever or other ailment; another to give a small brass bull, the emblem of Shiva, if disease leaves his cattle; and so on. The Poojáree the while tinkles a cracked bell in his left hand; and as he is not very well up in the ritual and psalmody which are the fashion in more important Eeshwara temples, he confines himself pretty much to vociferating "Shivané Gooroo; avana pádavé gatie" (Shiva is our teacher; his feet are our salvation). The congregation respond in similar phrases.

The rice being cooked by this time, is placed before the god, after which it is distributed, and every one eats. The offerings of fruit are then returned to the offerers, together with a consecrated flower out of the temple; the latter is put into their turbans. Of the fruit, some is occasionally given back by the people to the Poojáree, or they eat it themselves. The fear in which Koombappah's power of good and evil is held in the neighbourhood is very great.

In these gatherings at the temple there is, as in most Hindoo religious ceremonies, none of the penitential dejection and show of remorse which we sometimes see as accompaniments to our religious observances. No one comes to the temple with a long face, but each is dressed in his or her best, and with a view to enjoying him or herself; and they go away with a confidence that their wishes will be granted pleasant to see. Should the result be unpropitious, they merely consider that something has been amiss in their offerings, and are no more discouraged than better educated people at the failure of their prayers. Whilst service is going on every one chatters away without restraint, and I was often amused by the scenes I witnessed. Sometimes young married women (they generally came in company for mutual countenance), would be rolling round and round the temple on the soft turf, to move Koombappah to give them children. As the trackers stood leaning on their long spears, they carried on a running fire of chaff against the unfortunate girls, expressing themselves freely (and sometimes in terms which would certainly have aggravated an English female into giving them a bit of her mind) as to their opinions of the revolvers' points, as, tightly enveloped in their cloths, all dripping from a purificatory plunge in the river, these rolled over and over.

There is no Government grant to this temple. The people support it amongst themselves, and all give the Poojáree a bundle of their crops at harvest, which, together with the established perquisites at the temple, is sufficient for his livelihood. I have heard people exclaim in India against the Government's policy of maintaining grants-in-aid of what they are pleased to call heathenism. The extension of views gained by mixing much with many different people must teach any one who is not an unthinking Christian, that there is good in everything, and as much that is suitable to the intellectual status of the people in their religious institutions as in their costume, food, and manner of life. Is the Government to do away with ancient endowments, and to interest itself with those who would force one or other of the numerous religious beliefs of a comparatively small portion of the human race upon two hundred and fifty millions? Personally I have learned to respect the feelings and earnestness of the simple village communities around me. I can say that there is not a hypocrite in the country-side, nor one who decries the religion of his neighbour—rather a contrast in the latter respect to the jealous wranglers of various denominations who do their own causes injury by their intolerance of each other in the same mission-field.

Good-natured and charitable, a pattern of amiability in his family relations, and ever ready to help his needy relatives, the rustic Hindoo is a creature whom one cannot but like greatly, despite his constitutional mendacity and other little peculiarities that clash with English notions.

When we were catching elephants or hunting tigers, Koombappah was always in request, and the promise of a sheep, or so many cocoanuts and plantains, would be made by the trackers to insure his co-operation. In the event of success, I had, of course, to stand expenses. The bargains were invariably made dependent on Koombappah's performing his part first; no one ever thought of trusting him beforehand! Once I expended thirty rupees in having his premises whitewashed and repaired, upon the occasion of our catching our first elephants. All the villagers asked after Koombappah the moment they were mustered to drive the elephants on the eve of the eventful day, and when they were told of the munificent inducement which had been held out to him to insure them against accidents, they entered on their work with a confidence that conduced not a little to success. Poor fellows! was I, merely because I did not myself believe in Koombappah, to leave them in fear because their god had not been propitiated?

On another occasion when elephants were near our enclosures at Koombappan Goody, I thought the ringing of the old cracked sheet-iron bell, and the noise and talking of the people, might disturb the herd, so I asked the Poojáree if he could not take Koombappah somewhere else for a time. He said that if I would lend some men to build a temporary shed further down the river, and give him seven rupees (fourteen shillings) for incense and other expenditure, he would move Koombappah. This I gladly acceded to, and with much ceremony by the ryots, Koombappah was escorted to his new quarters. There was no image to represent him; he was supposed to move in the spirit. I sometime afterwards got access to the holy of holies, and found Koombappah was only represented by a circle and other figures on the floor-slabs.

In talking of natives and their religion, I cannot refrain from narrating an amusing pious fraud which was practised on the credulous villagers near Morlay by three sharp fellows from the Hyderabad country. The very simple means they employed were as follows: They arrived at Hurdenhully, a village near Morlay, and took up their abode in a *tope*, or clump of trees. One was represented to be an ascetic on a pilgrimage from Kási (Benáres) to Ráméshwaram, the holy cities of Northern and Southern India; the other two were his attendants. The holy man soon attracted the attention of the people by the austerity of his religious observances. He had long, unkempt locks, a rag round his loins, and his body was plentifully besmeared with cow-dung and ashes, after the manner of Indian devotees. He spent his time in sitting apart in a reverential attitude, muttering incantations and invocations, and appeared to be wholly wrapped up in the contemplation of divine things. His companions attended to his few wants, and took care to extol his great piety, his advanced religious state, and unworldly spirit, in the villages near. Hundreds of people soon began to visit the Gooroo (spiritual guide) and to pay their reverence to him.

At last it began to be rumoured about that his long contemplation of sacred things had gained this holy man the Divine approval, that supernatural powers had been granted to him, and that he proposed a descent to Pátárla (the regions existing under the earth, according to Hindoo mythology), and a return after seven days. This produced tremendous religious interest for many miles round. An abundant harvest was just over; it was the dry weather and the people had nothing to do; so thousands flocked to bow before the saint who, unmoved as ever, appeared to be in a rapture of contemplation. Charitable contributions of grain poured in from all sides, and after being offered to the still oblivious Gooroo, were cooked for the consumption of the attendant crowds. After a few days, moved by the spirit, he transferred the scene of his devotions to some open ground a mile distant, and here, under the directions of his two companions, his newly-attached disciples commenced the excavation of a hole in the ground, about five feet deep and three in diameter, which was to be his starting-point for the lower regions. Over this was built a substantial earth-work shrine, with a small door at one side; surmounting the whole was the figure of a bull, the emblem of Shivite worship, in clay. At a distance of about twenty feet from this structure the two attendants erected a small hut of branches: this was carefully closed in with cloths, and during the few days when the shrine was being prepared, the man of ashes spent the whole of his time in it, fitting himself (it was supposed) by renewed diligence in prayer for his projected visit to the other world.

The public excitement was kept up at all hours by incessant tom-toming and horn-blowing, and the charitable and well-to-do ryots who were present distributed food gratuitously to the daily-increasing crowds. At last the eventful day for the mystical disappearance arrived. The chief men amongst the multitude pressed round the shrine as the Gooroo approached it chanting a song of adoration, and implored his blessing. The devotee then entered the hole below the shrine, and it was securely closed and thenceforth sedulously watched day and night pending his resurrection, and in accordance with his parting instructions.

During the intermediate time interest in his performance was kept alive by exciting news of his having been seen first at Bissalwadi, a hill five miles to the west; shortly afterwards, in the jungle ten miles in an opposite direction. In fact, his appearance and reappearance were as unsettling as that of Mr Toots at the church windows during the publishing of the banns of marriage between Walter and Miss Dombey. Whilst public speculation pointed to some particular direction as a probable one for his next manifestation, a messenger would suddenly arrive in camp with news regarding the ubiquitous one which set all calculation at defiance. The fact that he was wandering about the country instead of being in Pátárla, does not appear to have struck any of his believers as a departure from his original undertaking; it was possibly thought these flittings were the performances of his disembodied spirit.

At the expiration of the appointed seven days the expectant multitude was massed round the shrine, which at a given signal from the inside was opened, and the wonder-worker calmly stepped into the daylight, shaking the soil from his matted locks, and merely seeming a little dazed by the glare of day. He was received as a god, and seated on the figure of the bull. A blanket was spread at his sacred feet by his companions, who regarded this as a favourable opportunity for making the collection—an essential part of religious performances in the East as elsewhere. One eager worshipper after another now pressed forward to touch the holy feet with his forehead, and drop his coin on the rapidly-increasing pile on the blanket. Some gave as much as thirty or forty rupees; and a sum of upwards of £200 was thus contributed.

The holy man then made a progress from village to village, levying further contributions with a cupidity scarcely consistent with his unworldly character. He stated the object of his pilgrimage to be the collection of funds for constructing a well for travellers at one of the entrances to Ráméshwaram, and that the amount already subscribed was insufficient for the purpose. If any one declined to contribute, his holiness resorted to the effective practice known in India as "Dherna," which consists in the claimant's seating himself at the entrance of a house, and vowing neither to eat, drink, nor go away until his request is complied with. To avoid incurring the sin of allowing such a sacred character as our hero to suffer at his door, the persecuted tenant was generally impelled to purchase his departure.

The Gooroo and his two friends shortly proceeded on their pilgrimage. I should mention that the hole into which he had descended had been filled in immediately on his reappearance, in accordance with some superstitious representations made by his attendants, and some months elapsed before the sequel of the story transpired. It was during the following rainy season that some of the ryots of the neighbourhood noticed that the earth had sunk in an extraordinary manner about the scene of the wondrous achievement, and an examination of the place showed that the devotee and his companions had dug a small burrow or tunnel, merely sufficient to admit of a man's squeezing himself along it, between the shrine and the adjacent place of his retirement; this had been done before the Gooroo's entombment, and the work had now collapsed. Through it the Gooroo had made his way after his descent, and had effected his escape after nightfall. He had then shown himself here and there, with what result has been seen, and had managed his reappearance by the same means. His dupes, whilst regretting their cash, displayed none of the vindictiveness which an Englishman would certainly have done at being so taken in, and much amusement prevailed amongst them, particularly at the expense of those of their number who had contributed most liberally to the well at Rámésliwaram.

CHAPTER VI.

THE ASIATIC WILD ELEPHANT (*ELEPHAS INDICUS*).

DISTRIBUTION OF THE ASIATIC ELEPHANT—HABITS OF WILD ELEPHANTS—NUMERICAL EXTENT OF HERDS—A FEMALE ALWAYS THE LEADER OF A HERD—THE ELEPHANT-FLY—ELEPHANT CALVES—ELEPHANTS SWIMMING—ROGUE ELEPHANTS—THE MANDLA ELEPHANT—NIGHT SCENE AT THE HONGANOOR LAKE—DEPREDATIONS OF ELEPHANTS LESS SERIOUS THAN USUALLY SUPPOSED—HEIGHT OF ELEPHANTS—MEASUREMENT OF FOOT—AFRICAN ELEPHANTS—AGE ATTAINED BY ELEPHANTS—WHERE DO ELEPHANTS DIE?—NATIVE BELIEFS—MURRAIN AMONGST ELEPHANTS—PERIOD OF GESTATION—"MUST" ELEPHANTS—FEMALE "MUST" ELEPHANTS—MEANS OF TELLING AGE OF ELEPHANTS—AGE AT WHICH FEMALES BREED—TWO CALVES AT A BIRTH—HEIGHT AND WEIGHT OF CALVES AT BIRTH—THE FEMALE ELEPHANT'S AFFECTION FOR HER YOUNG—SIZE OF INDIAN ELEPHANTS' TUSKS—CONSIDERATION OF THE USES OF THEIR TUSKS TO ELEPHANTS—ABSENCE OF TUSKS IN CEYLON ELEPHANTS—MUCKNAS—GUNÉSHES—FEMALE ELEPHANTS' TUSHES—PACES AND SPEED OF ELEPHANTS—INABILITY TO LEAP.

MY observations of the habits of wild elephants have been made chiefly at Morlay, near the Billiga-rungun hills, where I commenced elephant-catching in Mysore, and also in the Goondulpet and Kákankoté forests, where I had shot elephants previously, as well as in the Garrow and Chittagong hills in Bengal.

The wild elephant abounds in most of the large forests of India, from the foot of the Himalayas to the extreme south, and throughout the peninsula to the east of the Bay of Bengal—viz., Chittagong, Burmah, and Siam; it is also numerous in Ceylon. There is only one species of elephant throughout these tracts.

In Mysore large numbers frequent the forests of the Western Ghâts which bound Mysore on the west and south, the Billiga-rungun hills in the south-east, and a few are found in portions of the Nugger Division in the extreme north. There being no heavy forests in the interior, elephants do not, as a rule, occur far within the borders of the province, but are commonly met with in the belt of lighter jungle which intervenes between the virgin forest and cultivation.

Herds of elephants usually consist of from thirty to fifty individuals, but much larger numbers, even one hundred, are by no means uncommon. When large herds are in localities where fodder is not very plentiful, they divide into parties of from ten to twenty; these remain separate, though within two or three miles of each other. But they all take part in any common movement, such as a march into another tract of forest. The different parties keep themselves informed at all times of each other's whereabouts, chiefly by their fine sense of smell. I have observed that tame elephants can wind wild ones at a distance of three miles when the wind is favourable. Each herd of elephants is a family in which the animals are nearly allied to each other. Though the different herds do not intermix, escaped tame female elephants, or young males, appear to find no difficulty in obtaining admittance to herds.

In a herd of elephants the females with their calves form the advanced-guard, whilst the tuskers follow leisurely behind; though, if terrified and put to flight, the order is speedily reversed, the mothers with calves falling behind, as the unencumbered tuskers have no one to see to but themselves. I have never known a case of a tusker's undertaking to cover the retreat of a herd. A herd is invariable led by a female, never a male, and the females with young ones are at all times dangerous if intruded upon. The necessity for the convenience of the mothers of the herd regulating its movements is evident, as they must accommodate the length and time of their marches, and the localities in which they rest or feed at different hours, to the requirements of their young ones; consequently the guidance of a tusker would not suit them.

Elephants make use of a great variety of sounds in communicating with each other, and in expressing their wants and feelings. Some are uttered by the trunk, some by the throat. The conjunctures in which either means of expression is employed cannot be strictly classified, as fear, pleasure, want, and other emotions, are sometimes indicated by the trunk, sometimes by the throat. An elephant rushing upon an assailant trumpets shrilly with fury, but if enraged by wounds or other causes, and brooding by itself, it expresses its anger by a continued hoarse grumbling from the throat. Fear is similarly expressed in a shrill brassy trumpet, or by a roar from the lungs. Pleasure by a continued low squeaking through the trunk, or an almost inaudible purring sound from the throat. Want—as a calf calling its mother—is chiefly expressed by the throat. A peculiar sound is made use of by elephants to express dislike or apprehension, and at the same time to intimidate, as when the cause of some alarm has not been clearly ascertained, and the animals wish to deter an intruder. It is produced by rapping the end of the trunk smartly on the ground, a current of air, hitherto retained, being sharply emitted through the trunk, as from a valve, at the moment of impact. The sound made resembles that of a large sheet of tin rapidly doubled. It has been erroneously ascribed by some writers to the animals beating their sides with their trunks.

The ranges of wild elephants are very extensive, and are traversed with considerable regularity. In the dry months—that is, from January to April, when no rain falls—the herds seek the neighbourhood of considerable streams and shady forests. About June, after the first showers, they emerge to roam and feed on the young grass. By July or August this grass in hill tracts becomes long and coarse, and probably bitter, as tame elephants do not relish it. The elephants then descend now and again to the lower jungles, where the grass is not so far advanced. They here visit salt-licks and eat the earth—strongly impregnated with natron or soda—in common with most wild animals: also a fruit which grows at certain seasons on a dwarfed tree in the low country. I have been unable to ascertain its botanical name with certainty. It is said by natives to produce intoxication in elephants, under the influence of which they break surrounding trees, &c. I have never seen any signs of this myself, but the notion is widely spread amongst jungle-people.

Another reason for their leaving the hills during continued rain is the annoyance caused by the flies and mosquitoes which then become very troublesome. The elephant-fly is always less numerous in the low-country jungles. This truly formidable pest appears in the rains; it lives mostly in long grass, and attacks bison and sámbur as well as elephants. When the grass becomes very wet, these flies collect on any passing animals, and so great is the irritation they cause, that elephants and bison are always found about the outskirts of the jungle at this time. The elephant-fly is dark grey in colour, about the size of a small bee, and has a most formidable proboscis; it is very soft, and the slightest blow kills it.

Whilst in the low-country jungles a few elephants, chiefly males, occasionally stray into cultivation; the mothers with calves keep aloof from the vicinity of man's dwellings. About December, when the jungles become dry, and fodder is scarce, all the herds leave the low country, and are seldom seen out of the hills or heavy forests until the next rains.

Whilst in open country the herds move about a good deal during the day in cloudy, showery weather. On very stormy and inclement days they keep to bamboo cover which is close and warm. During breaks, when the sun shines for a few hours, they come out eagerly to warm their huge bodies. They are then fond of standing on the sheet rock so common in the Mysore country about hill-ranges. The young calves and staid mothers, in small groups, half dozing as they bask, form tranquil family pictures at such times. Elephants are partial to rocky places at all seasons.

Whilst marching from one tract of forest to another, elephants usually travel in strict Indian file. They seldom stay more than one or two days at the same halting-place, as the fodder becomes exhausted. They rest during the middle hours of the night, as well as during the day. Some lie down, and they usually dispose themselves in small distinct squads of animals which seem to have an affection for each other. (Tame elephants frequently display a particular liking for one or other of their fellows.) About three o'clock they rise to feed or march, and by ten o'clock in the day they are again collected, and rest till afternoon; at eleven at night they again rest. In showery cool weather elephants are frequently on the move all day long.

Elephants generally drink after sunrise and before sunset. They seldom bathe after the sun is down, except in very warm weather. Whilst fording water on cold nights, tame elephants curl up their trunks and tails to keep them out of it; and if taken at a late hour to be washed after their day's work, frequently show their dislike to the unseasonable bath.

Though a few calves are born at other seasons, the largest number make their appearance about September, October, and November. In a herd of fifty-five captured in June 1874, in Mysore, there was only one calf under six months of age, whilst seven were from eight to nine months. Amongst the females captured, eight calved between September and November. In eighty-five elephants captured in Chittagong, in January 1876, the bulk of the calves were from one to three months of age. I observed in Mysore that the herds invariably left heavy jungle about October for more open and dry country, on account of the wet and discomfort to the calving females and their offspring.

When a calf is born the herd remains with the mother two days; the calf is then capable of marching. Even at this tender age calves are no encumbrance to the herd's movements; the youngest climb hills and cross rivers assisted by their dams. In swimming, very young calves are supported by their mothers' trunks, and held in front of them. When they are a few months old they scramble on to their mothers' shoulders, helping themselves by holding on with their legs, or they swim alone. Young calves sent across rivers in charge of our tame elephants often did this, though they could swim by themselves if necessary.

Full-grown elephants swim perhaps better than any other land animals.

A batch of seventy-nine that I despatched from Dacca to Barrackpur, near Calcutta, in November 1875, had the Ganges and several of its large tidal branches to cross. In the longest swim they were six hours without touching the bottom; after a rest on a sand-bank, they completed the swim in three more; not one was lost. I have heard of more remarkable swims than this.

Much misconception exists on the subject of rogue, or solitary elephants. The usually accepted belief that these elephants are turned out of the herds by their companions or rivals is not correct. Most of the so-called solitary elephants are the lords of some herds near. They leave their companions at times to roam by themselves, usually to visit cultivation or open country, whither less bold animals, and the females encumbered with calves, hesitate to follow. Sometimes, again, they make the expedition merely for the sake of solitude. They, however, keep more or less to the jungle where their herd is, and follow its movements. Single elephants are also very frequently young, not old, males—animals not yet able to assert a position for themselves in the herd, and debarred from much intimate association with it by stronger rivals. They wander by themselves on the outskirts of the herd, or two or three such are found together, so that solitary is rather a misleading appellation. A really solitary elephant is, in my experience, and according to native hunters, an animal rarely met with. I do not believe in any male elephant being *driven* from its herd. If unable to cope with some stronger rival, it has merely to keep on the outskirts and give way, and it avoids molestation. I have seen this constantly; and where elephants are really solitary I believe the life is quite of their own choosing. Young males are only biding their time until they are able to meet all comers in a herd.

I once met with a remarkable instance of a young male elephant, about two years old, which had lived a solitary life for three or four months. Its mother had probably fallen into one of the numerous old elephant-pits on the Billiga-rungun hills, and the calf must have remained near after the herd left the vicinity. It subsequently took up its quarters in the low country, and though one herd visited the locality, the young one was refused admission, and it remained in the same place after the herd left. I captured it soon afterwards.

Single male elephants spend their nights, and sometimes days, in predatory excursions into rice and other fields in the immediate vicinity of villages. They become disabused of many of the terrors which render ordinary elephants timid and needlessly cautious. These elephants are by no means always evilly disposed. A solitary elephant I knew intimately at Morley was a most inoffensive animal, and, although bold in his wanderings, never injured any one. Some male elephants, however, as much wandering herd tuskers as really solitary animals, are dangerous when suddenly come upon, but rarely wantonly malicious.

Of cases recorded of really vicious animals perhaps the most notable is that of the Mandla * elephant, an elephant supposed to have been mad, and which killed an immense number of persons about five years ago. It is said to have eaten portions of some of its victims, but it probably only held their limbs in its mouth whilst it tore them to pieces. The Mandla elephant was shot, after a short but bloody career, by two officers.

I have only known one instance of two full-grown male elephants, unconnected with herds, constantly associating together. These were a tusker and *muckna* (or tuskless male), in the Kákankoté forests. They were inseparable companions in their night wanderings, but always remained a mile or two apart during the day. I knew the pair well in 1870-72; in the latter year I shot the tusker, as he had become dangerous, and had been proscribed by Government for killing people.

Natives who live in localities frequented by elephants become very bold in driving them away from their fields at night. I once saw a stirring scene at the Honganoor tank or lake at the foot of the Billiga-rungun hills. It was in November 1870, and the rice-crop was nearly ripe, when I encamped at Bellatta, on the border of the wide expanse (some 600 acres) of level rice-fields. The stream from the Billiga-runguns which feeds the Honganoor lake emerges from a deep gorge; a mile farther on is the lake; between the gorge and the lake the water is diverted by many small runnels over the rice-land. This lake is artificial, of very great antiquity and beauty, and when full is dotted with floating islands of white and rose-coloured lotus, and a sort of water-convolvulus. Teal, duck, pelicans, flamingoes, wild geese, and cranes and storks of several kinds, are to be seen there at certain seasons in numbers; pheasant-tailed jacánas walk on the lotus-leaves, uttering their musical cry; and snipe are plentiful from November to February in the short grass round the water-spread. Many birds build their nests in the fringe of green rushes round the small bays; amongst these the beautiful blue coot with red wattles is numerous.

At evening as I rode into camp the scene across the waving sea of ripening paddy was very beautiful. To the west the lake shone like silver in the level rays of the sun, just dipping behind the old tamarind-trees on its embankment. To the east the glorious hills, their dark woods and frowning cliffs seeming close at hand, were bathed in purple. In the glistening

* Near Jubbulpore, Central Provinces.

rice-fields, unbroken by fences, trees stood here and there, in which nestled the watchers' platforms. The smoke of fires near each showed that the men were cooking their evening meal; and when darkness came on, the lights dotted over the plain both at the foot of, and on the platforms up in, the trees, with the voices of the watchers, made the scene a cheerful one.

I had just finished dinner, and was enjoying a smoke before the blazing camp-fire, which lit to their topmost branches a pair of magnificent tamarind-trees under which my tent was pitched, when I heard a distant shout of "ánay" (elephants). At once lights began to flit over the plain, moving towards one point; tom-toms were beaten, and rattles, made from split bamboos, sounded. An elephant trumpeted shrilly, the men yelled in defiance, till the intruders retreated to the jungle. The cover bordering the cultivation was so dense as to afford secure shelter to elephants close at hand even during the day. After some little time, when the tom-toming and noise had ceased, a similar commotion took place at another point; again the Will-o'-the-wisp lights moved forward with a repetition of the shouting and trumpeting. The villagers who were keeping up my camp-fire told me it was only on occasional nights that the elephants visited the cultivation. The watchers were evidently in for it now, and they became thoroughly alert at all points.

Once the elephants came within 200 yards of my camp, and long after I went to bed I heard the shouting and rattling of the watchers. These men were Shōlagas from the hills; they were hired annually for a month or two at a fixed payment in grain for watching their crops by the low-country cultivators, who are themselves less able to stand the exposure in a rice-flat, and less bold in interfering with the elephants. The watchers provide themselves with torches of light split bamboos in bundles about eight feet long and eight inches in diameter. These are lighted at one end when required, and make a famous blaze. Armed with them the men sally forth to the spot where the elephants are feeding. Some carry the torches, the others precede them, so as to have the light behind them. The elephants can be seen in open ground at 100 yards, should they wait to let the lights get so close. Sometimes troublesome rogues get beyond caring for this, though the men are very bold and approach to within 40 or 50 yards. Natives have frequently told me of particular elephants letting them get to within a few yards, and then putting their trunks into their mouths, and, withdrawing water, squirting it at the lights! I need hardly say the latter part of the statement is entirely imaginary; the idea, doubtless, arises from the attitude elephants often assume when in uncertainty or perplexity, putting the trunk into the mouth, and holding the tip gently between the lips.

The large area of rice-fields within the bed of the Honganoor lake was assessed long ago at one-third the usual rates on account of the depredations of elephants. The actual damage caused to crops by wild elephants is much less than is popularly supposed. The chief evil of their presence is the bar they oppose to any advance in certain localities. Agricultural progress in India is always on a very small scale. One cultivator secures an acre or two of land, and opens it up in rough style, but as he possesses little capital to withstand a bad season, he generally abandons his land if his first crop be eaten up by elephants or other animals. Reclamation in jungle-localities only succeeds where several ryots open land together. In Mysore every facility is given by Government in granting jungle-land free of rent for some years, and on a reduced rental for a further term; but the country bordering jungle-tracts is seldom sufficiently populous to necessitate any extensive incursions upon the surrounding jungles. When the necessity arises elephants can be easily driven back.

The usually received notions of the height which elephants attain are much in excess of fact. Out of some hundreds of tame and newly-caught elephants which I have seen in the South of India and in Bengal, also from Burmah and different parts of India, and of which I have carefully measured all the largest individuals, I have not seen one 10 feet in vertical height at the shoulder. The largest was an elephant in the Madras Commissariat stud at Hoonsoor, which measured 9 feet 10 inches. The next largest are two tuskers belonging to his Highness the Mahárájah of Mysore, each 9 feet 8 inches, captured in Mysore some forty years ago, and still alive.

Of females, the largest I have measured—two leggy animals in the stud at Dacca—were respectively 8 feet 5 inches and 8 feet 3 inches. As illustrating how exceptional this height is in females, I may say that, out of 140 elephants captured by me in kheddahs in Mysore and Bengal, in 1874 and 1876, the tallest females were just 8 feet. The above are vertical measurements at the shoulder.

In India elephants are often measured by throwing a tape over the shoulders, or even back, the ends being brought to the ground on each side, and half the length taken as the animal's height.* Even the same elephant varies with its condition when measured in this way. An 8-feet elephant, in fair condition, gives a height of 8 feet 9 inches by this method.

There is little doubt that there is not an elephant 10 feet at the shoulder in India. As bearing on this subject, I may quote the following from the *English Cyclopædia.* The Mr Corse referred to therein was a gentleman evidently thoroughly conversant with elephants, probably in charge of the

* This accounts for the 11 or 12 feet elephants we sometimes hear of.

Government animals in Bengal. His paper on the elephant was read before the Royal Society in 1799.

"During the war with Tippoo Sultan, of the 150 elephants under the management of Captain Sandys, not one was 10 feet high, and only a few males 9½ feet high. Mr Corse was very particular in ascertaining the height of the elephants used at Madras, and with the army under Marquis Cornwallis, where there were both Bengal and Ceylon elephants, and he was assured that those of Ceylon were neither higher nor superior to those of Bengal."

. . . .

"The Madras elephants have been said to be from 17 to 20 feet high. Now let us see how dimensions shrink before the severity of measurement. Mr Corse heard from several gentlemen who had been at Dacca that the Nabob there had an elephant about 14 feet high. Mr Corse was desirous to measure him, especially as he had seen the elephant often at a former period, and then supposed him to be 12 feet high. He accordingly went to Dacca. At first he sent for the *mahout* or driver, who without hesitation assured him that the elephant was from 10 to 12 cubits—that is, from 15 to 18 feet high. Mr Corse measured the elephant exactly, and was rather surprised to find that the animal did not exceed 10 feet in height."

Twice round an elephant's foot is his height, within one or two inches; more frequently it is exactly so. Persons unacquainted with elephants not unfrequently guess from ten to fifteen times round the foot as the height. As the diameter of a large male elephant's foot is 18 inches, ten circumferences would make his height 47 feet.

The height of African elephants is greater than that of Asiatic elephants, both in the males and females. Sir Samuel Baker, in his *Nile Tributaries of Abyssinia*, says both sexes average about one foot taller than the Asiatic elephant.

The age to which the elephant lives is, as must ever be the case with denizens of the jungle, uncertain. The general opinion of experienced natives is that it attains 120 years in exceptional cases, but more generally to about 80 years. This view, however, is based on observations of elephants in captivity; under the more favourable conditions of a natural life the elephant must attain a greater age than when confined. My own opinion is that the elephant attains at least to 150 years.

One of the best instances I have seen from which to form conclusions is the case of a female elephant, Bheemruttee, belonging to his Highness the Mahárájah of Mysore. This elephant was captured in Coorg in 1805, and was then a calf of three years of age. She is still, at 76, in good working condition, and does not present the appearance of a particularly aged elephant, which is always shown in the lean and rugged head, prominent bones, deeply-sunk temples, and general appearance of decay. Bheemruttee is, however, past her prime.

In captivity she has lived under much less favourable conditions than a wild elephant, in being exposed to heat, often underfed, and subjected to irregularities of all kinds. Amongst newly-caught elephants I have seen many females evidently older than Bheemruttee with young calves at heel. Mahouts believe that female elephants breed up to about 80 years of age.

One of the most remarkable facts in connection with elephants is the extreme rarity of any remains of dead ones being found in the jungles. This circumstance is so marked as to have given rise to the notion amongst the Shōlagas of the Billiga-rungun hills that elephants never die; whilst the Kurrabas of Kákankoté believe that there is a place, unseen by human eye, to which they retire to end their days. In my own wanderings for some years through elephant-jungles I have only seen the remains of one female (that we knew had died in calving), and one drowned elephant brought down by a mountain torrent. Not only have I never myself seen the remains of any elephant that had died a natural death, but I have never met any one amongst the jungle-tribes, or professional elephant-hunters, who had seen a carcass, except at a time when murrain visited the Chittagong and Kákankoté forests. Bones would not decay for some years, and teeth and tusks would survive for some time, yet not a single pair of ivories has ever, as far as I know, been found in the Mysore jungles during the time I have known them. In Chittagong, in January 1876, I found a portion of a large tusk in a morass, much eaten by exposure; it weighed 33 lb. Another was found in Tipperah, almost fossilised, weighing 36 lb.; there were no other remains in either case.

The fact of remains of bison, deer, and other wild animals seldom being found is equally singular. Their bones would be sooner disposed of than those of elephants; still it is strange that, except in cases of epidemics amongst these animals, they are hardly ever seen. Certain classes of wild animals may possibly retreat to quiet localities when they find their powers failing them, as places where alarms and necessity for flight are unlikely to overtake them. But this is not the case with such gregarious animals as elephants. It may be supposed that in thick forests vultures do not attract attention to their carcasses, and monsoon rains and jungle-fires soon dispose of them. Still one would think that some carcasses at least would be found, whereas they never are; and though it is certain the animals do die, I know of no reasonable explanation of what becomes of them.

The following interesting reference to the subject of dead elephants never being seen is made by Sir Emerson Tennent in his *Wild Elephant.* I venture to quote it as showing the similarity of opinion of the natives of Ceylon and the wild tribes of Mysore :—

"The natives generally assert that the body of a dead elephant is seldom or never to be discovered in the woods. And certain it is that frequenters of the forest with whom I have conversed, whether European or Singhalese, are consistent in their assurances that they have never found the remains of an elephant that had died a natural death. One chief, the Wanyyah of the Trincomalie district, told a friend of mine, that once after a severe murrain which had swept the province, he found the carcasses of elephants that had died of the disease. On the other hand, a European gentleman, who for thirty-six years, without intermission, had been living in the jungle, ascending to the summits of mountains in the prosecution of the trigonometrical survey, and penetrating valleys in tracing roads and opening means of communication—one, too, who has made the habits of the wild elephant a subject of constant observation and study—has often expressed to me his astonishment that, after seeing many thousands of living elephants in all possible situations, he had never yet found a single skeleton of a dead one, except of those which had fallen by the rifle.

"The Singhalese have a superstition in relation to the close of life in the elephant: they believe that, on feeling the approach of dissolution, he repairs to a solitary valley, and there resigns himself to death. A native who accompanied Mr Cripps when hunting in the forests of Anarájapoora, intimated to him that he was then in the immediate vicinity of the spot 'to which the elephants come to die,' but that it was so mysteriously concealed that, although every one believed in its existence, no one had ever succeeded in penetrating to it. At the corral, which I have described at Kornegalle, in 1847, Dekigame, one of the Kandyan chiefs, assured me it was the universal belief of his countrymen that the elephants, when about to die, resorted to a valley in Saffragám, among the mountains to the east of Adam's Peak, which was reached by a narrow pass with walls of rock on either side, and that here, by the side of a lake of clear water, they took their last repose."

This belief of a universal sepulchre is, however, quite untenable as regards Mysore, as there is no spot in its jungles that is not penetrated at times by the Shōlagas or Kurrabas. Nor is the idea defensible on other grounds.

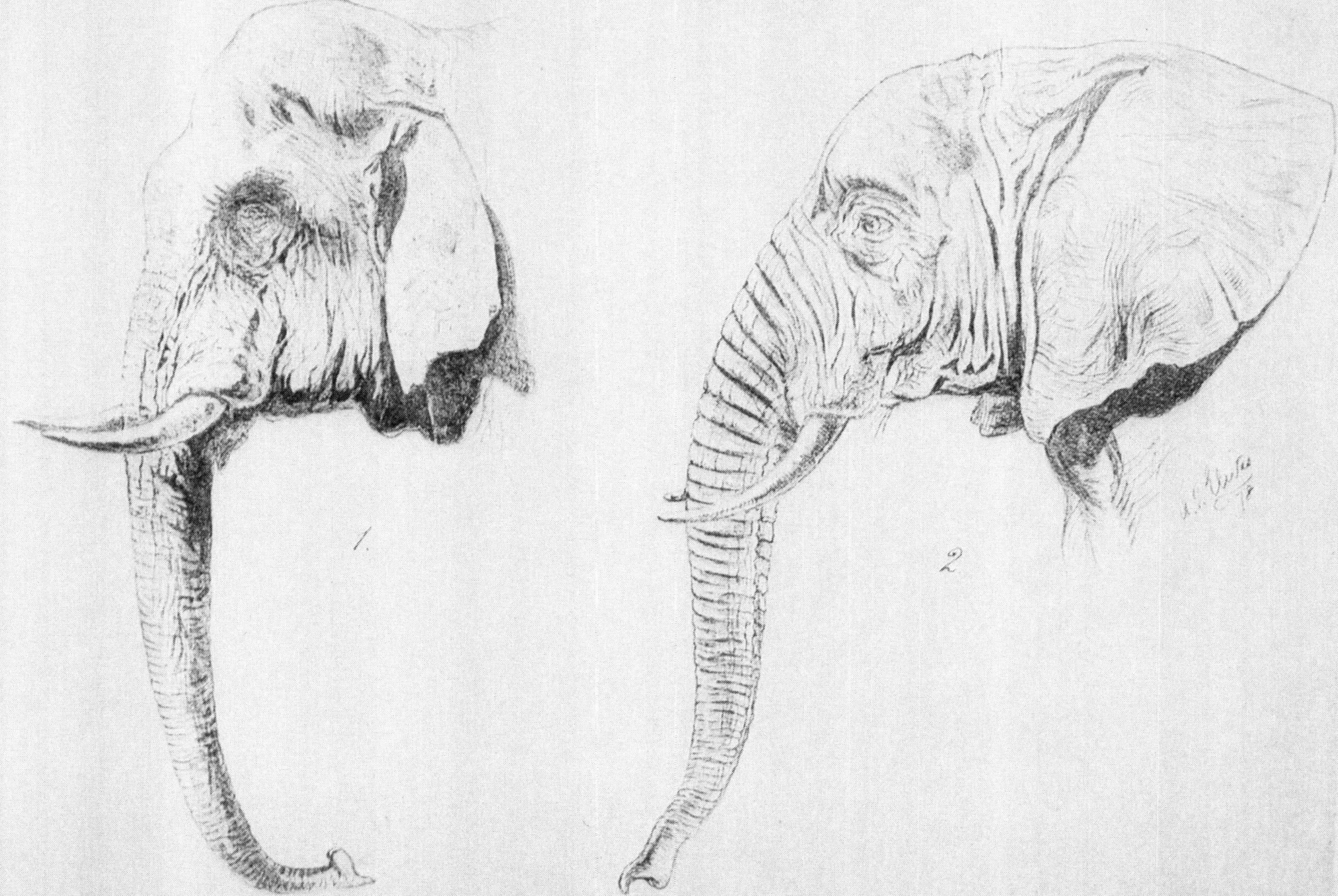

Phototint

H. M. Wright & Co London

Heads of
(1). Indian Elephant.

There is an epidemic disease, corresponding to murrain in cattle, from which wild and tame elephants suffer at long intervals. It attacked the elephants in the Government stud at Dacca, in Bengal, about thirty years ago, and carried off nearly fifty per cent of a total of upwards of three hundred. It lasted, with varying virulence, for more than ten years. The animals in best condition suffered most; only two, both in poor condition, are recorded as having recovered after seizure. The symptoms were, breakings-out and gatherings on the throat and legs, spots on the tongue, and running from the eyes. With the cessation of the flow from the eyes the animals died, usually on the second day after attack. In 1862 a similar epidemic carried off large numbers of elephants in the Chittagong forests. A few years later the herds in the Kákankoté jungles in Mysore were attacked; but the mortality was not great, and the disease soon left. On this occasion the fact of the elephants dying was well known to the Kurrabas.

The period of gestation in the elephant is said by experienced natives to vary as the calf is male or female, being twenty-two months in the case of the former, and eighteen in the latter. I cannot of my own observation afford conclusive proof that such is the case, though I believe there is some truth in the statement. I have known elephants to calve twenty months after capture, the young always being males when eighteen months were exceeded, and it was not known how long the mothers had been in calf before capture. The female elephant receives the male again about eight or ten months after calving.

Male elephants of mature age are subject to periodical paroxysms, supposed to be of a sexual nature. They are said to be *must*, or mad, when under their influence. Fits of *must* differ in duration in different animals; in some they last for a few weeks, in others for even four or five months. Elephants are not always violent or untractable under their influence, being frequently only drowsy and lethargic. The approach of the period of *must* is indicated by the commencement of a flow of oily matter from the small hole in the temple on each side of the head, which orifice is found in all elephants, male and female. The temples also swell. The elephant frequently acts somewhat strangely, and is dull and not so obedient as usual. In the advanced stages the oily exudation trickles freely down from the temples, which are then much swollen.

On the first indications the elephant is strongly secured. If he becomes dangerous his food is thrown to him, and water supplied in a trough pushed within his reach. Fatal accidents are of common occurrence in cases of *must* elephants getting loose. They usually attack man or any of their own species near, and the society of a female does not appear always to appease them. I once saw one of our tuskers, which was then only under suspicion of an approaching fit, break away from the control of his mahout as he was being ridden to water, and, despite severe punishment, attack and knock down a female at her picket near; and, had his tusks not been cut, he would without doubt have killed her on the spot. He was at last driven off by spears thrown at his trunk and head, when he stalked across the open plain with his mahout on his neck, fury in his eye, master of all he surveyed, and evidently courting battle with any created being. The men had a difficult and dangerous task to secure him. His hind-legs were at last tied from behind the trunk of a tree near which he stood, and the mahout having drawn up a chain by a cord, and secured it round his neck, he was moored fore and aft. I shall never forget the mahout's fervent ejaculation of "Allah! Allah!" as he slipped over the elephant's tail when he was made fast.

The flow of *must* occasionally, but very seldom, occurs in female elephants. I have seen it twice in newly-caught females in the prime of life, and in very full condition. It never occurs, I believe, in tame female elephants.

Mahouts can usually tell the age of elephants tolerably correctly. A young animal, though of full size, or a very old one, cannot be mistaken, but it requires much experience to estimate those of middle age. I have known even experienced men differ about the same animal to the extent of fifteen years. The general appearance of the animal suffices in some cases. A very old elephant is usually in poor condition, and the skin looks shiny and shrivelled. The head is lean and rugged, the skull appearing to have little but skin upon it; the temples and eyes are sunken; and the fore-legs, instead of bulging out above the knee with muscle, are almost of the same girth throughout. Instead of walking firmly and planting the feet flat, an aged elephant brings the feet to the ground somewhat in the manner of a plantigrade animal, touching with the heels first. But all the above symptoms may be present in a greater or less degree in debilitated, middle-aged animals, and are consequently not conclusive; but the appearance of the elephant's ear will probably settle the question. The ear is relied upon in ageing elephants as the teeth are in a horse. In very young elephants —up to six or seven years—the top of the ear is not turned over (as in man); but with advancing years it laps over, in old elephants very much so, and the ear is ragged and torn along the lower edge.

The elephant is full grown, but not fully mature, at about twenty-five years of age. At this period it may be compared to a human being at eighteen; and it is not in full vigour and strength till about thirty-five. Female elephants usually give birth to their first calf at sixteen years of age, sometimes at thirteen or fourteen, but are then palpably immature themselves. I have heard of what appears to be a well-authenticated case of a female elephant having two calves at a birth. Many wild female elephants are accompanied by two, sometimes three, calves of different ages.

Elephants breed about once in two and a half years. Two calves are usually sucking at the same time; and I have even seen the eldest of three, a young elephant five and a half feet high, and about five years old, that had to stoop to reach its mother, suck occasionally. I need hardly say that the young elephant sucks with its mouth, not its trunk.

Calves usually stand exactly three feet high at the shoulder when born; the trunk is then only ten inches long, and possesses little flexibility. The average weight of several calves I have weighed on the second day after birth has been 200 lb. They live entirely upon milk till six months old, when they eat a little tender grass; their chief support, however, is still milk for some months.

The elephant very rarely breeds in confinement, but this is owing to the segregation of the sexes, and also to the physical causes of insufficient food or hard work. It would not answer from an economic point of view to breed elephants in India, as, before they were of a useful age—fifteen years—they would have cost more than would suffice to capture a number of mature wild ones, ready for work. It is said that they are bred in a semi-wild state, and with little expense, in parts of Burmah and Siam. The females there are shackled and left at large in the forests during the non-working months, where wild males have access to them. But in Burmah fodder is plentiful, and the young stock cost nothing till taken up for sale.

The female elephant evinces no peculiar attachment to her offspring. The statement of Knox, quoted by Sir Emerson Tennent, that "the shees are alike tender of any one's young ones as of their own" is incorrect. Much exclusiveness is shown by elephants in the detailed arrangements amongst themselves in a herd, and if the mothers and young ones be closely watched, it will be seen that the latter are very rarely allowed familiarities by other females, nor, indeed, do they seek them. I have seen many cases in the kheddahs where young elephants, after losing their mothers by death or other causes, have been refused assistance by the other females, and have been buffeted about as outcasts. I have only known one instance of a very gentle, motherly elephant in captivity allowing a motherless calf to suck along with her own young one.

Sir Emerson Tennent mentions the belief that if a wild female elephant happen to be separated from her young for only two days, though giving suck, she never after recognises or acknowledges it. I apprehend that this idea arose from the fact that amongst newly-captured elephants, through the anxiety and exhaustion attending the mother's efforts to escape, her milk is invariably dried up for the time being. I have then seen elephants repel their calves, whose importunities annoyed them. But with the return of milk after a few days' rest and cooling food they have suckled them as before. In captivity the female is by no means jealous of her young being handled, and strangers may approach and fondle her calf immediately after its birth without incurring her resentment.

It is exceedingly entertaining to note the gravity of young calves, and the way in which they keep close to their bulky mothers. The extreme gentleness of elephants, the care they take never to push against, or step upon, their attendants, doubtless arises from an instinctive feeling designed for the protection of their young, which a rough, though unintentional, push or blow with the legs of such huge animals would at once kill. Amongst all created creatures the elephant stands unrivalled in gentleness. The most intelligent horse cannot be depended upon not to tread on his master's toes, and if terrified makes no hesitation in dashing away, even should he upset any one in so doing. But elephants, even huge tuskers whose heads are high in the air, and whose keepers are mere pigmies beside them, are so cautious that accidents very seldom occur through carelessness on their part. In the kheddahs, though elephants are excited by struggling, they never overlook the men on foot engaged in securing the captives; and though there would seem to be great danger in being amidst the forest of huge legs and bulky bodies of the tame elephants, they evince such wonderful instinct in avoiding injuring the men that I have never seen an accident occur through them.

When an alarm occurs in a herd the young ones immediately vanish under their mothers, and are then seldom seen again. A herd containing a large number of calves would be supposed under these circumstances by the uninitiated to consist entirely of full-grown elephants. I have only known two young elephants disabled in many rushes and crushes of large herds that I have witnessed. The mothers help their offspring up steep places with a push behind, and manage to get them through or over every difficulty with great ingenuity.

The tusks of the Asiatic elephant are much smaller than those of the African. The largest tusks of any elephant that I have myself shot measured respectively 4 feet 11 inches and 5 feet in length, outside curve; 16½ inches in circumference at the gum; and weighed 74½ lb. the pair. An elephant with one enormous tusk, and one diseased and broken, was shot in the

Billiga-rungun hills in 1863 by Sir Victor Brooke and Colonel Douglas Hamilton. An account from the pen of the former gentleman of their adventures with this elephant appears in Chap. XVII.; and the following dimensions and weight of both tusks, from the same source, may be relied upon :—

RIGHT TUSK.

	Feet.	Inches.
Total length, outside curve,	8	0
Length of part outside socket or nasal bones, outside curve,	5	9
Length of part inside socket, outside curve,	2	3
Greatest circumference,	1	4.9
Weight,	90 lb.	

LEFT TUSK.*

	Feet.	Inches.
Total length, outside curve,	3	3
Outside socket, do.,	1	2
Inside do. do.,	2	1
Greatest circumference,	1	8
Weight,	49 lb.	

Tusks are firmly embedded in sockets or cylinders of bone which run up to the forehead and end at a line drawn from eye to eye. Tusks, except those of very aged elephants, are only solid for a portion of their length; the hollow is filled with a firm, bloody pulp. In young animals the tusks are only solid for a portion of their length even outside the gum, and are hollow throughout the embedded portion. With age the pulp cavity decreases in depth, till, in very old animals, it becomes almost obliterated. In the large tusk referred to above, the pulp hollow extends from the base through half the embedded portion (about 13½ inches). In a pair of tusks belonging to Colonel Douglas Hamilton it is 10½ inches in an embedded length of 25. As a rule, tusks show barely one half of their total length outside the jaw of the living animal. The length within and without the nasal bones is generally exact, but the lip or gum hides a few inches of the projecting half. As the sockets or nasal bones of a large elephant are from 1 foot 6 inches to 1 foot 9 inches in length, this admits of an elephant's having a tusk 3½ feet long, of which only 1½ foot (the gum hides about 4 inches) is

* Sir Victor Brooke says: "The diseased (left) tusk is a very remarkable example from a pathological point of view. The pulp cavity is entirely obliterated, a mass of excessively dense nodular dentine being formed in its place. As far as I can judge, the tusk has been broken off short after attaining large dimensions, and in the rupture a deep longitudinal rent extended backwards into the pulp cavity, giving rise to diseased condition of the pulp. The stench from the tusk when extracted was horrible."

visible. This rule holds pretty closely for all elephants until they become aged, when, if the tusks grow abnormally long, which is not always the case, the exposed portion becomes longer than the embedded, as the latter is limited to the length which the nasal bones attain—viz., about 1¾ foot in the largest skulls.

The points are usually cut from the tusks of tame elephants, and the extremity is encircled with a brass or iron ring to prevent the tusk splitting, and for show. In cases where too much has been cut from the tusk and the hollow portion entered, dreadful mischief ensues. I have seen a tusker, one of whose tusks had rotted away from this cause, with the socket far into the head filled with maggots. Tusks if once lost are never renewed.

Sir Emerson Tennent considers at some length the use for which the tusks of male elephants can be designed. He says:—

"But here there arises a further and very curious inquiry as to the specific objects in the economy of the elephant to which its tusks are conducive. Placed as it is in Ceylon, in the midst of the most luxuriant profusion of its favourite food, and with no natural enemies against whom to protect itself, it is difficult to conjecture any probable utility which it can derive from such appendages. Their absence is unaccompanied by any inconvenience to the individuals in whom they are wanting; and as regards the few who possess them, the only operations in which I am aware of their tusks being employed is to assist in ripping open the stems of the joggery palms and young palmirahs to extract the farinaceous core; and in splitting up the juicy shaft of the plantain.

"If the tusks were designed to be employed offensively, some alertness would naturally be exhibited in using them. So peaceable and harmless is the life of the elephant, that nature appears to have left it unprovided with any special weapon of offence; and although in an emergency it may push or gore with its tusks, their almost vertical position, added to the difficulty of raising its head above the level of the shoulder, is inconsistent with the idea of their being designed for attack, since it is impossible for the animal to deliver an effectual blow, or to wield its tusks as the deer and the buffalo can wield their horns.

"Among elephants, jealousy and other causes of irritation frequently occasion contentions between individuals of the same herd; but on such occasions their general habit is to strike with their trunks, and to bear down their opponents with their heads. It is doubtless correct that an elephant, when prostrated by the force or fury of an antagonist of its own species, is often wounded by the downward pressure of the tusks, which in any other position it would be almost impossible to use offensively."

Before treating on this question I must refer to Sir Emerson Tennent's work, *The Wild Elephant*, published originally in 1859, and again in 1866. This is, I believe, the most recent work on the elephant, and has been serviceable in removing some of the grossest misapprehensions regarding it; but it is full of the errors which are unavoidable when a man writes on a subject with which he has no practical acquaintance, and musters information without having sufficient knowledge to enable him to choose the good and reject the evil. The book is written in such a fascinating and earnest style that it is difficult to believe that the author is mostly romancing, and before I knew anything of elephants I revelled in his descriptions. But when on even short personal acquaintance with the noble animal I found that, amongst his numerous accomplishments, the power to take all four feet off the ground at the same moment was not one, I was obliged to conclude that the elephant in the case quoted by Sir Emerson as having cleared a barricade 15 feet high, only carrying away the top bar, could not have accomplished the feat; and though Sir Emerson subsequently wrote to the person from whom *he* had the information, who wrote to the Cutchery Modliar of Kornegalle who had told *him*, who sent a *native* to measure the place again, who said he found the elephant had only made a clear jump of 9 feet, because he had climbed on to a white-ant's hill from which he sprang, I found myself unable to place further belief in the author. More extended acquaintance with elephants entirely dissipated my faith in the wild elephant of Sir Emerson Tennent's imagination and of my inexperienced days. Sir Emerson Tennent has, in many places in his work, substituted theory and fancy for fact.

In the above matter of tusks he has indulged in pure theory. In his account of the two or three captures of elephants he witnessed (the largest number caught at one time being apparently nine), he does not mention any tuskers having been taken, though the artist in the illustrations to his work (which are excellent and lifelike pictures) has thrown in a tusker amongst the captives. Sir Emerson Tennent being confessedly no sportsman probably never saw a wild tusker. In Ceylon tuskers are few and far between, and no one but a sportsman who constantly followed elephants would be likely to fall in with them.

Far from tusks being useless appendages to elephants, and of little service for offence, they are amongst the most formidable of any weapons with which Nature has furnished her creatures, and none are used with more address. They are not placed almost vertically, as stated by Sir Emerson Tennent,* and they can be used at almost any angle. In a herd of elephants the tuskers maintain the height of discipline. Every individual

* This will be seen in the illustrations of elephants.

gives way before them, and in serious fights amongst themselves one or other is frequently killed outright. So great is the dread entertained by all elephants of a tusker, that our stanchest tame females shrank if any of the tame tuskers turned suddenly in their direction. Superiority in a herd appears to attach to the different tuskers in proportion to the size of their tusks; no tusker thinks of serious rivalry with one of heavier calibre than himself. In the kheddahs in Mysore we found the services of tuskers invaluable; we had two, amongst others, that were taller and with longer tusks than any wild ones we captured, and their presence was always sufficient to awe the most obstreperous wild male whilst the men were securing it. Our tame elephants' tusks were cut and blunt, but we had steel glaives to slip on if necessary, with which they could have killed any elephant in a very short time.

Tusks are not used to assist the elephant in procuring food. Small trees are overturned by pushing with the curled trunk, or feet if necessary; and to get at the core of a palm-tree, or break up the plantain, the pressure of his feet alone is used.

On the continent of India *mucknas,* or male elephants *born* without tusks, are decidedly rare. The word *muckna* is derived from *mookh,* the mouth or face. Mucknas can hardly be distinguished from females at the first glance, but if they are full-grown animals their superior size shows their sex. Their tushes or prongs are generally a little longer and thicker than those of female elephants. It is a common belief that mucknas are larger as a rule than tuskers. This is not the case, but they are generally stouter and more vigorous animals. Their good development is sought to be accounted for by their being said to be allowed by their mothers to suck after young tuskers have been driven off, when their sharp little tusks hurt their mothers; but this, though an ingenious explanation, is not a correct one, as the young tusker can suck without its tusks touching its mother, and I have always seen them suckled as long as the female calves are.

A common belief that mucknas are usually vicious animals is also groundless. They are generally much ill-treated by the tuskers of the herd, upon whom they are powerless to retaliate, and I have seen one or two decidedly timid in consequence. A timid elephant is always less safe than one of better courage, but I have not found mucknas to be naturally ill-tempered. The absence of tusks appears to be a merely accidental circumstance, as the want of beard or whiskers in a man. Mucknas breed in the herds, and the peculiarity is not hereditary nor transmitted. This is a known fact, and is demonstrated by the occasional occurrence of tuskers, doubtless from tuskless sires, in Ceylon herds.

In Ceylon a male elephant with tusks is a *rara avis:* Sir Samuel Baker says that not more than one in 300 is provided with them. Out of 140 elephants, of which 51 were males, which I captured in Mysore and Bengal in 1874-76, only 5 were mucknas.

It is difficult to imagine what can cause the vital difference of tusks and no tusks between the male elephant of continental India and Ceylon. The climate may be said to be the same, as also their food; and I have not seen any theory advanced that seems at all well founded to account for their absence in the Ceylon elephant. There is a somewhat similar case in the common antelope (*Antilope bezoartica*) of Southern India's having inferior horns to those of Central India, an 18-inch black buck being a decided rarity in Mysore, and 14 inches being the average, whilst in other parts of India they attain to 26 or 27 inches. Sámbur (*Rusa Aristotelis*) in the Chittagong and other forests to the east of the Bay of Bengal have inferior horns to those of the Neilgherries and other parts of India.

Elephants occasionally lose one tusk, sometimes both, in accidents in the jungle, and some have only one tusk from birth. The latter are known as "Gunésh" (the name of the Hindoo god of wisdom) by Hindoos, and are reverenced by them if the tusk retained be the right-hand one.

The tusks of the male elephant-calf show almost from birth. I believe that they are never renewed, and that the first tusks are permanent. In many works on the elephant it is stated that the first tusks are shed before the second year, but I believe this to be an error—one that has gained ground through so many writers deriving their information from a common source. I have made this a point of particular inquiry amongst experienced elephant-attendants, and have found them unanimous in dissenting from the idea of any such process of renewal. It is impossible that such an important matter could have escaped their notice (natives are keen observers), and I apprehend that the error—as it undoubtedly is—has arisen through some *savant's* diagnosis of the elephant's dentition, based on analogy, or the confounding the teeth and the tusks, as the same word is used to denote either in several native languages. Jerdon has given his support to the statement as far as adopting it goes, but this is a case in which a deservedly trusted writer could hardly have had the information from his own observation. I have had many young elephants in my charge, and never noticed anything of the change alluded to.

The Indian female elephant is always born with *tushes* or short downward prongs in the upper jaw, rarely more than four inches in length out of the gum: these, whilst present, are used for stripping bark off trees, &c.; but they are seldom retained long, being generally broken off early in life, and they do not appear to be at all necessary to the elephant. Female elephants use them amongst themselves in striking each other, raising their trunks in doing so, and bearing downwards with their tushes. These tushes are never renewed. A young female which I had, in trying to overturn a tree, broke both her tushes one after the other.

The only pace of the elephant is the walk, capable of being increased to a fast shuffle of about fifteen miles an hour for a very short distance. It can neither trot, canter, nor gallop. It does not move with the legs on the same side together, but nearly so. A very good runner might keep out of an elephant's way on a smooth piece of turf; but in the ground in which they are generally met, any attempt to escape by flight, unless supplemented by concealment, would be unavailing.

As before stated, an elephant cannot jump, and, though very clever in surmounting obstacles, can never have all four feet off the ground together. Whether it is the peculiar formation of the hind-legs, with knees instead of hocks, or the weight and bulk of the animal that incapacitates him, I cannot say, but he is physically incapable of making the smallest spring, either in vertical height or horizontal distance. Thus a trench seven feet wide is impassable to an elephant, though the step of a large one in full stride is about six and a half feet.

The idea that wild elephants have decreased of late years is not uncommon in India. It appears to have arisen from the fact of orders having been issued of late years by the Supreme and Local Governments for their protection; also from their undoubted decrease in Ceylon. But the case of that island is hardly analogous to that of the continent. In Ceylon elephants have always been made a peculiar object of pursuit by large numbers of sportsmen and paid native hunters, whilst their range is not without its limits. In continental India the actual numbers shot by European sportsmen has always been very small, and it was only for a few years that natives were induced to turn their attention to killing them by a reward given for their destruction in the Madras Presidency. This was soon withdrawn, when the natives' interest in their pursuit ceased; and the representations of humane officials having further led to the curtailment of the wasteful methods of trapping them practised by native hunters, the wild elephant now enjoys perfect immunity throughout the Western Ghâts, and those boundless jungles extending for hundreds of miles along the foot of the Himalayas into Burmah and Siam. The number annually caught by the Government establishments is comparatively very small; and there is no doubt that all the forest ground that can be legitimately allowed to the wild elephant is as fully occupied at present as is desirable. I have examined the elephant-catching records of the past forty-five years in Bengal, and the present rate of capture attests the fact that there is no diminution in the numbers now obtainable; whilst in Southern India elephants have become so numerous of late years that the rifle will have to be again called into requisition to protect the ryots from their depredations, unless more systematic measures for their capture and utilisation than are at present in vogue be maintained. It cannot but be a matter of hearty congratulation to all interested in so fine and harmless an animal that there is no chance of the sad fate that is pursuing his African congener, and leading to his rapid extinction, affecting the Asiatic elephant.

CHAPTER VII.

THE CAPTURING OF WILD ELEPHANTS.

METHOD ADOPTED FOR TAKING HERDS—CONSTITUTION OF A KHEDDAH PARTY—SKETCH OF OPERATIONS—THE CATCHING OF SINGLE ELEPHANTS—FOLLOWING THEM DURING THE NIGHT—PITFALLS—BARBARITY OF THIS METHOD—NOOSING—JUDGMENT REGARDING RECAPTURED ELEPHANTS IN A CASE BEFORE THE HIGH COURT OF JUDICATURE, CALCUTTA.

THE following are the chief methods adopted for the capture of wild elephants :—

Driving into *kheddahs* or enclosures.

Hunting with trained females.

Pitfalls.

Noosing from trained elephants' backs.

The kheddah plan is the only one adapted for the capture of whole herds, the others being for single elephants. It is the method in vogue by the Government hunting establishments in Bengal, and is conducted as follows: A hunting party is collected which consists of 370 men, all accustomed and trained to the work. Their duties and scales of pay are shown in the following roll. They are under the immediate control of the jemadar, or native sergeant, who is responsible, under the European officer, for the collecting of the men and the whole operations of the party. In addition to their pay each man is allowed free rations at the rate of 2 lb. of rice *per diem*, and 2 lb. of salt fish, chillies, and salt, *per mensem*. These provisions ordinarily cost about Rs. 3 per head *per mensem*; and the total cost of a party is Rs. 3800 (£380) *per mensem*.

Attached to each elephant-hunting party there must be a number of tame elephants, or *koonkies*, to deal with the wild elephants when captured; the number of which latter must depend upon the strength of the koonkie establishment, as it is useless to catch more than the tame ones can deal with efficiently. Not only have the wild ones to be led out of the jungles, and loosed from picket and taken to drink and bathe daily, but each requires an elephant's load of fodder, which the tame ones have to bring. Consequently two wild ones to each tame one is the maximum that can be managed.

No.	Detail.	Rate of pay per mensem.	Remarks.
		Rs.	
1	Jemadar,	25	To collect establishment and conduct operations.
1	Interpreter,	10	To Hillmen.
1	Writer,	9	To furnish reports, accounts, &c.
1	Head-tracker,	9	To go in advance and ascertain the position and number of herds, and to lead the party in surrounding a herd.
2	Mate-trackers,	7½	
15	Trackers,	7	
20	Head-coolies,	9	To surround and guard the herd, construct enclosure, or kheddah, and drive the elephants in.
20	Mate-coolies,	7½	
280	Coolies,	7	
1	Havildar,	9	To keep a check on the circle of coolies by going round at short intervals; also to mount guard at the superintendent's camp. These men are furnished with guns.
1	Naik,	7½	
14	Sepoys,	7	
1	Head-nooser,	9	To bind the wild elephants when impounded in the enclosure.
4	Noosers,	7	
1	Head-pulwán,	9	These men are furnished with guns and take post at any point where the elephants show a determination to force the cordon of coolies.
4	Pulwáns,	7	

The hunting party proceeds to the forest at the commencement of the dry weather—usually in December—equipped for two or three months, and the scouts having found a herd (a large one is always sought, as there is no more trouble in catching it than a small one), the hunters are halted within a mile, when half of them file off to the right and half to the left. Along these diverging lines, which are to meet beyond the herd and enclose it, two men are left at every fifty yards or so as a guard. The surround when completed is often six or eight miles in circumference, as if the ground is favourable the men are posted more widely apart than two at fifty yards. It is a rule in elephant-catching that, this circle being once completed, the herd can only escape through great carelessness on the part of the guard. In a couple of hours the hunters run up a thin fence of split bamboos all round the ring, and make rough shelters of boughs for themselves. Their only duty then is to see that the elephants do not break out of the circle. The animals are seldom seen during the day: at night large fires are kept up, and if they approach, shouts and shots are used to drive them back. The bamboo fencing serves to show the jemadar and his assistants where the elephants have broken out should they escape, so that the particular men who are to blame can be detected. The surround is always made as extensive as possible, as with plenty of cover, fodder, and water inside, the elephants give less trouble than if confined in a small space. The investment may have to be maintained for a week or so, sometimes much longer. The elephants give some little trouble for the first two nights, but after that time they seldom try to force the guards unless fodder becomes scarce inside. The guards are supplied with provisions, and cook their meals at their posts.

The construction of the kheddah, inside the large circle, is commenced as soon as the elephants are surrounded. For this work one of the two coolies is taken from each post from 8 A.M. till 4 P.M., as the elephants give little trouble during the day, and a single sentry suffices. The Hindoostánee word kheddah means the enclosure or pound intended for imprisoning the herd. This is formed of stout uprights about twelve feet in height, arranged in a circle of from twenty to fifty yards in diameter, and strongly backed by sloping supports and binders behind. An entrance of four yards in width is left for the ingress of the herd. The enclosure is built on one of the elephants' chief runs, and in a spot where the thickness of the cover screens it from view. Elephants keep strictly to beaten tracks in traversing the jungles—a circumstance of great service in arranging plans for their capture. To guide the elephants to the gate, two lines of strong palisades are run out from it on each side of the path by which they will approach. These guiding wings diverge to perhaps fifty yards across at their commencement, which may be a hundred yards or so from the gate. When the herd is once within this funnel-shaped approach, it is easily driven forward by the beaters closing in from behind. The gate is made very strong, and is studded with iron spikes on the inside. It is slung by rope-hinges to a cross-beam, and is dropped by the rope being cut as soon as the elephants have entered. Inside, round the foot of the palisade, a ditch is generally dug about four feet wide and deep, to deter the elephants from trying the stockade, or should they do so, to prevent their standing in a position to use their strength to advantage. Elephants rarely attempt to force the palisades; they never do so in a body. Occasionally an enterprising animal will try his strength on them; and strong though the stockade is, I have known a determined tusker go through as if it had been made of corn-stalks. The men closed up at once on this occasion, and none of the others attempted to follow their leader—an instance of the elephants' lack of intelligence in certain matters.

As soon as the kheddah is completed, probably in four or five days from the time of the surround, arrangements are made for driving the herd. For this purpose one man is taken from each picket of the original circle on the morning of the day when the drive is to take place, and a smaller interior circle is formed by commencing at the ends of the guiding wings of the kheddah and posting the men until the elephants are again surrounded. They are then driven forward towards the kheddah, and when near it the men close in from all sides with shouts and shots, and the elephants generally enter the trap without hesitation. Should they suspect danger, however, and refuse to proceed, or break back through the beaters, fatal accidents are not uncommon.

After the elephants have been impounded in the kheddah, the tame elephants are admitted with their mahouts upon the neck of each, and a rope-tier seated behind. It is a remarkable circumstance that the wild ones very seldom attempt to dislodge the riders, though they might do so with ease. I never knew of a case (except one which happened to myself) of a rider being attacked by any of them. The duty of the tame elephants is to secure the wild ones by separating them one by one from their companions, when their hind-legs are tied together by the men, who slip to the ground for the purpose. A rope is then secured round each captive's neck and another to one hind-leg, and they are led out and picketed in the forest near, until they have been sufficiently subjugated to be removed. Further details will be found in the account of capturing elephants in Mysore.

HUNTING WITH TRAINED FEMALES.

The largest male elephants are seldom caught with the herd by the kheddah plan, from their habit of frequently absenting themselves from their companions, or making their escape out of the circle of men by their greater boldness. They are the most valuable animals, and are usually caught in the following manner, or some modification of it:—

Four or five steady females, ridden by their mahouts, who partly conceal themselves with a dark-coloured blanket as they lie on their elephants' necks,* are taken to the jungle where the single male is known to be, and are allowed to graze as though they were wild ones, and to gradually approach the male if he does not himself take the initiative. Some wild males make off at once, probably scenting the men on the elephants' necks, but many do not appear to notice them. When the male

* The term "decoy" is entirely misapplied to trained elephants used for catching wild ones, as they act at the command of their riders, and use no arts to divert the male's attention, as has been asserted.

can be got to abandon himself without reserve to the society of the females, they keep in close attendance upon him; and as it is sometimes two days and nights before he can be secured, a party of spare mahouts follows on foot to relieve the riders every twelve hours. For this purpose the tame females are withdrawn one at a time, and the mahout is changed out of view of the wild one. The relieving party also generally has a spare elephant carrying the ropes and chains required when the elephant is secured.

At night the wild male probably leaves the forest to visit the fields of the adjacent villages, whither he is closely escorted by his treacherous friends. If he enters a field to graze one female is posted at each corner, and by a signal gives notice to the others when he leaves it. This is to avoid the damage which the whole party's entering the corn would cause.

Towards morning the elephant retires to the forest, and when he shows signs of going to sleep the tame ones close round him. Should he not appear to be very somnolently inclined, devices are used to keep him awake, such as moving off all the tame elephants, when he generally follows, so as to keep him without rest, and tire him until he shall resign himself to slumber without reserve. (Some elephants can be got to eat opium in sugar-cane, when, the mahouts say, they are soon reduced to helplessness, but I have never had an opportunity of using it myself.) The tame Delilahs, under the direction of their riders, close round their victim when he is really asleep, and two mahouts slip off with coils of rope and tie the slumbering Samson's hind-legs together very securely. Half an hour is frequently spent in doing this. The tame elephants then withdraw, and the men on foot perhaps slap the wild one behind and tell him to be of good cheer.

His terror on perceiving men so close to him may be imagined, and his rage and dismay at finding his legs bound together pass description. If he has been secured to a tree he uses every effort of which he is capable to snap his bonds. If his hind-legs have merely been fastened together he makes off as best he can, dragging them after him. The other elephants follow at a distance, and when he is completely exhausted they again approach, keeping out of reach of his tusks, as he will now use them, and the men fasten him to a convenient tree, and camp close at hand. In a day or two a cable is fixed on his neck, and with one still on one hind-leg, he is led away to an appointed station to be trained. A large proportion of the fine elephants captured in this way die from the injuries they receive from the severe restraints necessary to control them during the first few days.

PITFALLS.

A most barbarous method of catching wild elephants is by pitfalls dug in their paths, and into which they fall with a readiness which is remarkable in animals which are usually so cautious in all sorts of ground. The pits are generally arranged in some confined pass, at seasons when elephants are not in the neighbourhood, or under particular trees which they are in the habit of visiting for their fruit or leaves. The standard native measurement for pits in Mysore is ten and a half feet long by seven and a half broad, and fifteen feet deep. This is a tight fit as to area for a large elephant, but is purposely made so to prevent male elephants using their tusks to dig down the sides. This they, however, generally manage to effect in a day or two if they are left to themselves. The depth of the pits being so great, it may be imagined that an immense majority of the elephants that make the descent have their limbs dislocated or broken, or receive permanent internal injury, even if they are not killed on the spot, as sometimes happens. To prevent such mishaps as far as possible, a strong bar is fixed across the mouth of the pit in the centre, upon which the elephant's neck usually falls; and though it bends or breaks with his weight, it tends to make him go down more level than he would otherwise do. It is seldom the hunters trouble themselves to put boughs in the bottom of the pit to break the force of the elephant's descent. In Mysore a perfect network of pitfalls used to be maintained by the Mahárájah, the Forest Department, and a few by lessees, as also in Madras; in these a large number of animals were taken annually. An immense proportion died from the effects of this violent mode of capture, and those that lived were only small ones, whose weight did not lead to such serious effects as in full-grown elephants.

The Shōlagas and Kurrabas used, when pits were in vogue in Mysore, to be intrusted with their supervision. If an elephant fell into one they were supposed to take the news to the station where the tame elephants were kept, near the jungles, and these would then be taken by their drivers to secure the animal. Between the delay made by the jungle-people and the laziness of the elephant-men, many elephants were starved to death in the pits, or so reduced as never to be got out of the jungle alive. Many other wild animals fell into the pits besides elephants. I have myself known of several bison, a pair of bears, and two pairs of tiger cubs falling into them. Deer constantly did so; and it was for the sake of their flesh, as much as for the trifle that they were paid, that the jungle-people used to attend to the pits. In the hot weather when cattle were taken to graze in the forests they frequently fell in, and were of course left to their fate, as their legs or ribs were more often broken than not. The Commissariat and Forest Departments soon gave up the pit plan; but the Mahárájah required a few elephants annually, and even though ten or twenty were killed for every one that lived, it was his only method of procuring them. As the forests were full of herds, it did not matter from an economic point how many were killed. I have heard of four elephants falling into one pit together, and, strange to say, three survived on this occasion, probably from having the fourth as a cushion at the bottom: this one was trampled to death, and almost out of all shape.

The pits were often arranged with great art by the hunters, an open one being perhaps left in view, in avoiding which an elephant would fall into a covered one alongside; or several were dug in close proximity, into which others might fall when fleeing in terror at the bellow of fright which the first gave on finding the earth sinking under him. On one occasion I was riding through a strange part of the Billiga-rungun hills, when, coming to a felled tree, I turned my pony aside to go round it. One of the Shōlagas with me fortunately stopped me, just in time, by screaming "Koppoo! koppoo!" (pit, pit)—and almost under my pony's nose I saw a hole through the covering caused by the falling of a deer into the pit. The tree had been felled with the object of making the elephants go round it, as I had done.

Since the Mahárájah's death the pit system in Mysore has happily been given up. The atrocious cruelties to which elephants were subjected by it are too horrible to think of.

NOOSING FROM TRAINED ELEPHANTS' BACKS.

This is the most spirited and exciting, though by no means advantageous, manner of hunting the wild elephant. It is practised in parts of Bengal and Nepaul, but is unknown in Southern India. It is far from an economic method, as the wear and tear of the tame elephants engaged is very great, nor can full-sized wild ones be captured by it. I have never myself seen a hunt by this method, but I have had men in my employ who were adepts at it. It is conducted as follows: Three or four fast tame elephants are equipped with a rope each; at one end is a noose, the other is girthed securely round their bodies; on some the noose is to the near side, on the others to the off. Each elephant has three riders—the mahout on its neck to guide it; the nooser kneeling on a small pad on its back, holding the open noose in his hands; and a driver seated near the root of its tail, whose duty it is to hammer it unmercifully in the region of the *os coccygis* with a spiked mallet. This impels an elephant to much greater exertions than any use of the driver's goad will, though that inducement is by no means omitted.

Thus equipped the elephants approach the wild ones. These at once make off, and the chase commences through or over everything, the men saving themselves from being swept off, if the jungle is thick, as best they can. Where the ground is favourable two tame elephants endeavour to range up on opposite sides of a fleeing wild one, encouraged thereto by the unlimited use of the *a posteriori* argument of the mallet man. When the elephants are well up with the wild one the nooses are cast, and generally encircle its neck. If this is effected the tame elephants are checked, and other nooses are soon secured, but the choking of the wild one, or fatal accidents to the tame ones or their riders, by being pulled over or dragged into ravines, are not unusual accompaniments of this rough work.

Hand-noosing is practised only in Ceylon, where a couple of hunters on foot manage with wonderful skill and activity to noose the hind-legs of an elephant when running away, and to secure the trailing ends of the rope to a tree as it passes.

It has not unfrequently happened in Bengal, where numbers of elephants are kept by native land-owners, that animals have escaped and joined wild herds, and have been recaptured along with them in the Government kheddahs. The question of ownership of such elephants has often been raised. The following is a case on appeal, decided in the High Court of Judicature, Calcutta, in favour of the Government establishment that recaptured an escaped elephant:—

Plaintiff, a zemindar, alleged that he had the female elephant in question in possession for six years, when she fled to the jungles. He made diligent search for her, and reported her loss at the nearest district police station. He heard a year later that she had been recaptured in the Sylhet District, in the Government kheddahs. His claim to the animal being rejected by the Superintendent of Kheddahs, he instituted a suit for her recovery in the Court of the Collector of Sylhet. The Collector gave judgment in favour of the Superintendent of Kheddahs on behalf of Government. Plaintiff thereupon appealed to the High Court of Judicature, Calcutta, but his appeal was dismissed on the grounds that such animals being originally *feræ naturæ*, are no longer the property of man than while they continue in his keeping. If at any time they regain their natural liberty his property ceases, unless they have *animus revertandi*, which is only to be known by their usual custom of returning—or unless instantly pursued by their owner, for during such pursuit his property remains. In this case pursuit had ceased, and the animal had returned to its natural and independent state.

CHAPTER VIII.

THE ELEPHANT IN CAPTIVITY.

CONSIDERATION OF THE ELEPHANT'S INTELLIGENCE—THE DOMESTIC ELEPHANT'S TEMPERAMENT — FALLACIES REGARDING THE POWER OF THE TRUNK—ORIENTALS' IDEAS OF PERFECTION IN ELEPHANTS—THEIR BREEDS OR CASTES—KOOMERIAHS—DWÁSALAS—MEERGAS—DISTINGUISHING POINTS—WHITE ELEPHANTS—SPECIAL VALUE OF TUSKERS—RULE AND REASON FOR CUTTING TUSKS—ECONOMIC USES IN DRAUGHT—AS BEASTS OF BURDEN — OF DISPLAY — RIDING-ELEPHANTS — SHIKÁR ELEPHANTS — ELEPHANT-MARTS—EXPORT FROM CEYLON—PRICES OF ELEPHANTS—PAST—PRESENT—PROBABLE FUTURE OF THE MARKET—REQUIREMENTS IN ELEPHANTS AND MEANS OF SUPPLY TO THE BENGAL GOVERNMENT—THE DACCA KHEDDAH ESTABLISHMENT—BENGAL LICENCE SYSTEM OF CAPTURING ELEPHANTS — MEANS OF SUPPLY OF ELEPHANTS TO THE MADRAS GOVERNMENT — KHEDDAHS IN THE MADRAS PRESIDENCY — THE BURMAH MARKET—APPENDIX ON BREEDING OF ELEPHANTS.

THE opinion is generally held by those who have had the best opportunities of observing the elephant, that the popular estimate of its intelligence is a greatly exaggerated one; that, instead of being the exceptionally wise animal it is believed to be, its sagacity is of a very mediocre description. Of the truth of this opinion no one who has lived amongst elephants can entertain any doubt. It is a significant fact that the natives of India never speak of the elephant as a peculiarly intelligent animal; and it does not figure in their ancient literature for its wisdom, as do the fox, the crow, and the monkey.

The elephant's size and staid appearance, its gentleness, and the ease with which it performs various services with its trunk, have probably given rise to the exalted idea of its intellect amongst those not intimately acquainted with it. And its being but little known in Europe, whilst what is known of it justly makes it a general favourite, leads to tales of its intelligence being not only accepted without investigation, but welcomed with pleasure. Many of the stories about it are intended for the edification of little folks, and as such are well enough; but in a sober inquiry into the mental capacity of the animal they must be duly examined.

One of the strongest features in the domesticated elephant's character is its obedience. It may also be readily taught, as it has a large share of the ordinary cultivable intelligence common in a greater or less degree to all animals. But its reasoning faculties are undoubtedly far below those of the dog, and possibly of other animals; and in matters beyond the range of its daily experience it evinces no special discernment. Whilst quick at comprehending anything sought to be taught to it, the elephant is decidedly wanting in originality.

What an improbable story is that of the elephant and the tailor, wherein the animal, on being pricked with a needle instead of being fed with sweetmeats as usual, is represented as having deliberately gone to a pond, filled its trunk with dirty water, and returned and squirted it over the tailor and his work! This story accredits the elephant with appreciating the fact that dirty water thrown over his work would be the peculiar manner in which to annoy a tailor. Is such a feat of reason possible in any beast? How has he acquired the knowledge of the incongruity of the two things—dirty water and clean linen? He delights in water himself, and would therefore be unlikely to imagine it objectionable to another.

An incident which I saw narrated in a book as having been observed by an officer in India is palpably disentitled to belief. It was to the effect that a gunner, whilst seated on one of the heavy guns in a column of artillery on the march, fell off, and would have been crushed under the wheel in another moment, when an elephant, in attendance on the guns, perceiving the man's danger, seized the wheel, lifted it over his prostrate body, and put it down on the other side of him! How did the elephant know that a wheel going over the man would not be agreeable to him? We comprehend it as it is a matter within the range of our experience; but could the elephant imagine himself in the man's place, and therefore understand what his sufferings would be if crushed under the wheel? Would a Newfoundland dog—certainly a more intelligent creature than an elephant—rescue a child from drowning if it had never been taught to bring objects to the bank? And if totally untrained, and not even accompanied by its master—in fact, quite uninfluenced, as the elephant in the story is represented to have been—is it possible to believe it capable of such an effort of intellect as to understand the danger of a person drowning, and the necessity for prompt assistance? If the elephant were possessed of the amount of discernment with which he is commonly credited, is it reasonable to suppose that he would continue to labour for man, instead of waving his keepers adieu and turning into the nearest jungle?

Let us consider whether the elephant displays more intelligence in its wild state than other animals. Though possessed of a proboscis which is capable of guarding it against such dangers, it readily falls into pits dug for catching it, and only covered with a few sticks and leaves. Its fellows make no effort to assist the fallen one, as they might easily do by kicking in the earth around the pit, but flee in terror. It commonly happens that a young elephant falls into a pit, near which the mother will remain until the hunters come, without doing anything to assist it, not even feeding it by throwing in a few branches. This, I have no doubt, is more difficult of belief to most people than if they were told that the mother supplied it with grass, brought water in her trunk, or filled up the pit with fagots, and effected her young one's release. Whole herds of elephants are driven into ill-concealed enclosures which no other wild animals could be got to enter, and single ones are caught by their legs being tied together by men under cover of a couple of tame elephants. Elephants which happen to effect their escape are caught again without trouble; even experience does not bring them wisdom. These facts are certainly against the conclusion that the elephant is an extraordinarily shrewd animal, much less one possessed of the power of abstract thought to the extent with which he is commonly credited. I do not think I traduce the elephant when I say it is, in many things, a stupid animal; and I can assert with confidence that all the stories I have heard of it, except those relating to feats of strength or docility performed under its keeper's direction, are beyond its intellectual power, and are mere pleasant fictions.

It often happens that persons who do not understand elephants give them credit for performing actions which are suggested to them, and in which they are directed, by the mahout on their necks. There is no secret so close as that between a horse and his rider, or between an elephant and his mahout. One of the chief characteristics in the domestic elephant's temperament is, as before stated, its obedience, and it does many things at the slightest hint from its mahout, whose directions are not perceived by an onlooker unacquainted with the craft of elephant-guidance. This has led to such mistakes as Sir Emerson Tennent makes * in describing the conduct of tame elephants while engaged in capturing wild ones in Ceylon, when he says: "The tame ones displayed the most perfect conception of every movement, both of the object to be attained and the means to accomplish it. They saw intuitively a difficulty or a danger, and addressed themselves *un-*

* *The Wild Elephant*, by Sir J. Emerson Tennent.

bidden to remove it." Another writer on a capture of elephants in Travancore says: "It may be interesting to mention a trait of one of the trained elephants, which shows such a degree of intelligence and forethought that it deserves to be placed on record. While the animals were being driven towards the enclosure, one of the trained elephants, a large tusker, was observed to pick up stones from the ground with his trunk, and hand them up to his keeper on his neck. He did it in such a deliberate and matter-of-fact manner, that it was plain he comprehended perfectly the reason for which stones were required."

Such are the notions with which those with superficial acquaintance with elephants fly away. I have seen the cream of trained elephants at work in the catching-establishments in Mysore and Bengal; I have managed them myself, under all circumstances; and I can say that I have never seen one show any aptitude in dealing, undirected, with an unforeseen emergency. I have a young riding-elephant at present, Soondargowry, often my only shooting companion, which kneels, trumpets, hands up anything from the ground, raises her trunk to break a branch, or passes under one in silence, stops, backs, and does other things at understood hints as I sit on her pad; but no uninitiated looker-on would perceive that any intimation of what is required passes between us. The driver's knees are placed behind an elephant's ears as he sits on it, and it is by means of a push, pressure, and other motions, that his wishes are communicated, as with the pressure of the leg with trained horses in a circus. As well might performing dogs which spell out replies to questions be credited with knowing what they are saying, as elephants with appreciating the objects to be gained by much which they do under the direction of the rider.

So much for the intelligence of the elephant. Let us now consider its temperament in captivity. I think all who have had to deal with elephants will agree in saying that their good qualities cannot be exaggerated, and that their vices are few, and only occur in exceptional animals. The not uncommon idea that elephants are treacherous and retentive of an injury is a groundless one. Male elephants are subject to periodical fits of *must*,* of the approach of which, however, due warning is given, and during the continuance of which care is necessary in dealing with them, as they are quite irresponsible for their actions. But at all other times the male elephant is generally perfectly safe, rarely suddenly changeable in temper. Female elephants are at all times the most perfect-tempered creatures in the world. Amongst some hundreds which I have known, only two have had any tricks. Of these, one would not allow herself to be ridden by a strange

* This is treated of in Chapter VI.

mahout; the other had a great aversion to any natives but her own two attendants approaching her. She was, however, perfectly friendly with Europeans, as I used to feed and pet her; and when engaged at the kheddahs in Mysore, she was frequently fed by the ladies present.

The elephant's chief good qualities are obedience, gentleness, and patience. In none of these is he excelled by any domestic animal, and under circumstances of the greatest discomfort, such as exposure to the sun, painful surgical operations, &c., he seldom evinces any irritation. He never refuses to do what he is required, if he understands the nature of the demand, unless it be something of which he is afraid. The elephant is excessively timid, both in its wild and domestic state, and its fears are easily excited by anything strange. But many have a good stock of courage, which only requires developing; the conduct of some elephants used in tiger-hunting demonstrates this.

Much misapprehension prevails regarding the uses and power of the elephant's trunk. This organ is chiefly used by the animal to procure its food, and to convey it, and water, to its mouth; also to warn it of danger by the senses of smell and touch. It is a delicate and sensitive organ, and never used for rough work. In any dangerous situation the elephant at once secures it by curling it up. The idea that he can use it for any purpose, from picking up a needle to dragging a piece of ordnance from a bog, is, like many others, founded entirely on imagination. An elephant might manage the former feat, though I doubt it; the latter he would not attempt. Elephants engaged in such work as dragging timber invariably take the rope between their teeth; they never attempt to pull a heavy weight with the trunk. In carrying a light log they hold it in the mouth as a dog does a stick, receiving some little assistance in balancing it from the trunk. Tuskers generally use their tusks for this and similar purposes, and are more valuable than females for work. An elephant is powerful enough to extricate a cannon from a difficult situation, but he does it by pushing with his head or feet, or in harness—never by lifting or drawing with his trunk. The story adverted to above, of the elephant lifting the wheel over the prostrate gunner, is a physically impossible one. Elephants do not push with their foreheads, or the region *above* the eyes, but with the base of the trunk, or snout, about one foot below the eyes.

An elephant rarely uses its trunk for striking other elephants or man. Newly-caught ones seldom attempt even to seize any one coming within their reach with their trunks; they curl them up and rush at the intruder. Should any accident happen to an elephant's trunk to prevent it conveying water to its mouth, it drinks by wading into deep water and immersing the mouth in the manner common to most quadrupeds. In drinking, only about, fifteen inches of the end of the trunk are filled with water at a time; the trunk is then curled backwards so as to reach the mouth, and the water is blown into it. Wild elephants' trunks are occasionally cut by the sharp edges of split bamboos whilst feeding. One which I saw had more than a foot of the outer cuticle stripped off the trunk; another, a healed gash penetrating to one of the nostrils of the trunk from the outside.

The elephant is essentially a native's animal. Natives alone have fully studied his peculiarities and classified him into castes; his capture, training, and keeping, are in native hands, as well as the trade; and the native standard of merit regulates the market.

Commercially elephants come under only two classes—the one of pageantry, the other of utility. Every native prince or nobleman of distinction in India keeps elephants to swell his retinue: Government and private persons, as timber contractors, &c., require them for work.

The native requirements in an elephant differ essentially from ours. They prize the animal chiefly as an adjunct to court display and temple processions. Consequently perfection of form and carriage are paramount from their point of view. As we require it for economic purposes, strength, docility, and courage are first considerations with us. The most perfect shooting elephant may be of small value to a native, whilst gaudy animals, with perhaps nothing but their looks to recommend them, are highly valued.

The native standard of a good elephant does, however, comprise all essentials to excellence for any purpose; and putting aside minor and whimsical requirements, consisting in certain lucky or unlucky marks, correctly distinguishes the most desirable animals. In fancy beasts, a too short or too long tail, a black mark on the tongue, or a less number of nails than eighteen (some elephants have but sixteen; the usual number is five on each fore foot, and four on each hind), are defects sufficient to disqualify the best animals.

Elephants are divided by natives into three castes or breeds, distinguished by their physical conformation; these are termed in Bengal *Koomeriah*, *Dwásala*, and *Meerga*, which terms may be considered to signify thorough-bred, half-bred, and third-rates. The term *Koomeriah* signifies royal or princely. *Meerga* is probably a corruption of the Sanscrit *mriga*, a deer; the light build and length of leg of this class of elephants suggest the comparison. *Dwásala* in Persian means two things or originals, and in reference to the elephant, signifies the blending of the first and third castes into the intermediate one.

Only animals possessing extreme divergence rank as Koomeriahs or

Meergas; and the points of these breeds (if they may be so called) do not amount to permanent, or even hereditary, variation. Whole herds frequently consist of Dwásalas, but never of Koomeriahs or Meergas alone; these I have found occur respectively in the proportion of from ten to fifteen per cent amongst ordinary elephants.

The Koomeriah, or thorough-bred, takes the first place; he alone can reach extreme excellence, but all the points required for perfection are very rarely found in one individual. He is amongst elephants what the thorough-bred is amongst horses, saving that his is natural, not cultivated, superiority. The points of the Koomeriah are: Barrel deep, and of great girth; legs short (especially the hind ones) and colossal, the front pair convex on the front side from the development of muscle; back straight and flat, but sloping from shoulder to tail, as an upstanding elephant must be high in front; head and chest massive; neck thick and short; trunk broad at the base and proportionately heavy throughout; bump between the eyes prominent; cheeks full; the eye full, bright, and kindly; hind-quarters square and plump; the skin rumpled, thick, inclining to folds at the root of the tail, and soft. If the face, base of trunk, and ears, be blotched with cream-coloured markings, the animal's value is enhanced thereby. The tail must be long, but not touch the ground, and be well feathered.

The illustration represents a first-class Koomeriah, and is from a photograph of an animal captured in the kheddahs in Chittagong whilst I was in charge. This elephant was probably sixty years of age when captured. His height was 9 feet 2 inches (vertical) at the shoulder. He exhibited the magnanimous and urbane temperament common to these first-class animals, and was easily managed a few days after capture. He was designed for the Viceregal State howdah, being the finest elephant captured in Bengal for many years; but he died after I left Dacca—from what cause I have not learnt.

The Dwásala class comprises all animals below this standard, but which do not present such marked imperfection as to cause them to rank as Meergas, or third-rates; all ordinary elephants (about seventy per cent) are Dwásalas.

A pronounced Meerga is the opposite to the Koomeriah. He is leggy, lank, and weedy, with an arched, sharp-ridged back, difficult to load, and liable to galling; his trunk is thin, flabby, and pendulous; his neck long and lean; he falls off behind; and his hide is thin. His head is small, which is a bad point in any elephant; his eye is piggish and restless. His whole appearance is unthrifty, and no feeding or care makes him look fat. The Meerga, however, has his uses; from his length of leg and lightness he

Photolint

E. M. Wright & Co. London

"Koomeriah" Elephant.

Phototint.

H. K. Wright & Co. London

"Meerga" Elephant

is generally speedy: the heavier Koomeriah is usually slow and stately in his paces.

The illustration of a Meerga is from a photograph of one captured in the same herd with the above-mentioned Koomeriah, and presents all the characteristic points of its class.

The temper of Koomeriahs, both male and female, is generally as superior to that of the Meerga as their physical conformation. Though gentleness and submissiveness are characteristics of all elephants, the Koomeriah possesses these qualities, and equanimity, urbanity, and courage in a high degree. The Meerga's ill-favoured look frequently bespeaks the nervousness and meanness of his temperament. His want of courage, and, consequently, apprehensive nature, often lead to his being dangerous through his fears. He may strike at a stranger, or injure his own attendants when overcome with fear, whilst the Koomeriah, through his superior courage, is unmoved. As a nervous horse or cowardly dog is ever the first to kick or bite, so poor-couraged elephants are the animals which are least trustworthy.

The elephant is said to be subject to albinism. I have never myself seen a really white one, nor have any of the experienced native hunters whom I have met. There is at present in his Highness the Mahárájah of Mysore's stables a young tusker, captured twelve years ago, which is of a somewhat light colour, both as to his skin and hair, and his eyes are light blue. Amongst those I captured in Mysore, in 1874, was a calf of a very light shade, somewhat of a dirty cream colour; ordinary calves are quite black. Regarding the white elephants of which we read as forming the most cherished possessions of the King of Ava, I am unable to give any information. I have never heard of any trustworthy European writer's having seen them.

Real vice in any elephant is a thing almost unknown. Natives attach less importance than we do to the temper of elephants; all can be managed by some means, and the possession of an unruly animal, if of good figure, is sometimes regarded as rather desirable than otherwise.

No male elephant can reach high merit without good tusks; the longer and heavier they are the more is their possessor valued; but they must be of good shape, curving upwards like the runners of a cradle, and diverging gracefully from each other. Tuskers are far more valuable for work than females, not only from their greater strength, but from the good use they make of their tusks in turning and carrying logs, &c. A tusker, if given the end of a rope to pull, puts it over one tusk, and holding the end between his teeth, can move a weight with this purchase which a female with only the hold with her teeth would be unable to manage. Tusks usually require cutting once a-year: the elephant is made to lie down in water, and the portion to be removed is then sawn off. This gives him no pain, and is necessary to prevent elephants injuring each other, not as a precaution for the safety of their attendants. The rule for cutting an elephant's tusk is as follows: Measure from the eye to the insertion of the tusk in the lip; this length measured from the latter point along the tusk will give the spot where it should be cut. In young animals a little more should be allowed, as the above measurement may approach too nearly the medullary pulp of the tusk.

Elephants are used by Government for the transport of troops, for provisioning outpost stations which are not connected by roads, &c. The progressing development of roads and railways in India may be expected to do away with the necessity for the services of some in the most accessible localities, but it will always be necessary to keep a certain number in case of movements in rough and uncivilised countries. Elephants were indispensable in the Abyssinian, Looshai, and other petty wars and expeditions in recent years, and similar services may be required at any moment.

The merely useful elephant, whose employment is to assist the movement of troops, to transport timber from the forests to river-banks, for shooting purposes, &c., is usually of the Dwásala or Meerga class. Amongst these the tuskers cost much more than the females. For work males are more powerful; their tusks enable them to perform a variety of services which the female renders less efficiently; and for shooting their superior courage is indisputable. A male elephant bears about the same relation in appearance and power to the female as a domestic bull does to a cow. From females being more generally employed in shooting, being more readily procurable, males seldom have the opportunity of showing their natural superiority in courage and strength; but where they are employed they are immeasurably superior.

For draught, elephants are very valuable, as logs can be brought by their aid from localities where they would otherwise be inaccessible. The elephant's power is most advantageously employed where a great exertion is required for a short distance, through a limited space of time. When elephants are harnessed, the dragging-rope is either attached to a collar round the neck or to a girth behind the shoulders. The latter plan is the better of the two, as it gives more bearing surface, and there is less liability to gall. To pull from the girth, the elephant's pad is first put on, to prevent the girth-rope from galling the back. The girth, a strong rope ninety feet in length, is then passed tightly several times round the elephant behind the shoulders, and a small breast-rope is attached to prevent it slipping backwards. The pulling rope or chain is then fastened to the girth, half-way up the elephant's side.

Native attendants are very careless, and pulling-ropes are constantly breaking, which makes elephants that have once been frightened in this way cautious about throwing themselves into the collar. But an elephant with confidence in his gear will make the most extraordinary exertions, leaning forward far beyond his centre of gravity, or kneeling and almost resting on his forehead, in his attempts to move the load. In dragging light timber a rope about three feet long is generally fastened round one end of a log. The elephant takes the rope in its teeth, and thus raising one end clear of the ground, half drags, half carries it away. An elephant can be harnessed to a cart in the same way as a horse. In Dacca two elephant-waggons were employed for carrying away the litter from the elephant-lines.

As a beast of burden the elephant can scarcely be considered satisfactory in all respects, chiefly from his liability to gall under such heavy weights as he is otherwise able to carry. This difficulty can be avoided with great care, but it requires constant attention from more heedful and humane masters than ordinary elephant-attendants. Some of these do not attempt to prevent a sore back—rather the reverse—when elephants are on long and arduous service. A sore back once established, the elephant cannot be used for weeks, often months, and its attendants escape work, even the bringing its fodder. The best preventive has been found to be putting every one connected with the elephant on half-pay till the animal has recovered. An elephant well packed will carry an immense bulk and weight; and in difficult country, especially hilly or swampy districts, their place cannot be taken by any other means of carriage. For transporting light guns in mountain warfare they are invaluable. An elephant's gear consists of a thick, soft-padded cloth, covering the whole of the back from the nape of the neck to the croup, and hanging half way down the animal's sides. Over this comes a saddle, which consists of two pads or flat bags of stout sacking, each six feet long, and two and a half broad. These are stuffed to one foot in thickness with dried grass or cocoanut fibre, and are attached by cross-pieces, so that one lies on each side of the elephant's backbone, which is thus protected from pressure. Upon the first pair of pads is another large single pad. On this the load is placed. Thus all the weight should rest on the upper part of the animal's ribs, without touching the spine, as in a horse with a well-fitted saddle.

Half a ton is a good load for an elephant for continuous marching. In hilly country seven hundredweights is as much as he should carry. I have known a large female carry a pile of thirty bags of rice, weighing 82 lb. each, or one ton and two hundredweights, from one storeroom to another, three hundred yards distant, several times in a morning. By the Bengal Commissariat code elephants are expected to carry 1640 lb., exclusive of attendants and chains, for which 300 lb. extra may be added; but this is too great a weight for continued marching. The weight of one of his Excellency the Viceroy's silver State howdahs and trappings is a little over half a ton, as below:—

	Cwts.	qrs.	lb.
Howdah, ...	6	1	22
Gold cloth, ...	1	0	14
Punkahs, &c., ...	0	2	25
Ropes and gear, ...	1	5	15
	10	2	20

Elephants are kept by natives of rank in India solely for the purposes of display, and in this sphere the animal is more at home than in any other. The pompous pace of a procession suits his naturally sedate disposition, and the attentions lavished upon him please his vanity. Only male elephants are valued for this purpose, and tuskers are preferred to mucknas. Every inch of height adds immensely to an elephant's value after nine feet at the shoulder has been passed. I have already said in the last chapter that ten feet at the shoulder is probably the extreme height of the Asiatic elephant. One or more elephants are attached to most temples of note in India, and take part in the religious processions connected with them.

Government elephants are often used for riding by the European officers who have charge of the departments in which they are employed, and they are of much use in country where horses cannot be taken. Though an elephant is but a poor means of progression on a highroad, in jungly or hilly country he is most useful, as guides and gun-bearers are always in attendance in such places, and the elephant can move as quickly as the party would be able to proceed without him. A light elephant, trained for *sowári*, or riding, if active and free, is a very pleasant mount. Half-grown ones are the best. As a rule, long-legged, lanky animals of the Meerga caste are the most active walkers. Calves are always quick movers. I have used them as small as thirteen hands at the shoulder, with a soft pad and stirrups, bestriding them as a pony. They are wonderful little creatures for getting up or down any difficult place; they give no trouble; and will keep up with a man running at any pace before them.

Elephants very rarely stumble; should they even do so they never fall from that cause, as they can go down on one or both knees—an easy position for an elephant. I have sometimes, but rarely, known them fall flat on their sides in slippery soil during wet weather.

Elephants can always be guided, except when frightened, by the slightest tap with a small stick on either side of the head, the pressure of the knee, or even by a word; but if alarmed, they have to be controlled or urged forward by the driving-goad. An elephant is as much afraid of this implement as a horse is of the curb, and can be restrained by it as well. When under the influence of fear, of course the elephant may run away, as a horse does, regardless of punishment. It is a terrible thing to be bolted with in jungle by an elephant; the rider is fortunate if he escapes with whole bones. I have felt on the one or two occasions on which it has happened to me as a man might if bestriding a runaway locomotive, and hooking the funnel with the crook of his walking-stick to hold it in!

It is very difficult to cure a confirmed bolter, as the habit has its origin in fear, and the animal is always liable to be startled by unexpected sounds or sights, chiefly the former. It is a rare trick, however, and I have only known two elephants subject to it. One was a fine baggage animal, but almost useless for jungle-work from this trick. I, however, cured her in the following way: I had a stout hoop of iron made, with sharp spikes on the inside to encircle one of her hind-legs. This was kept in its place round the leg by being suspended from the pad by a rope, and it fitted the leg loosely, so as not to inconvenience the elephant except when required to do so. To the ring was attached a chain fifteen feet long, at the other end of which was a pickaxe's head. This grappling apparatus was slung to the pad by a small cord in a slip-knot, handy to the mahout. If the elephant began to run, one pull freed it, and before the anchor had been dragged many yards it caught in roots or bushes, and brought the elephant up with such a twinge that she soon began to think twice before making off.

Howdahs are not pleasant things to ride in, nor are they necessary except for State purposes and tiger-shooting. For ordinary riding a soft pad is much more pleasant; upon it there is none of the swaying motion felt in a lofty howdah. A *chárjáma* is frequently used; this is merely a broad board with cushions upon it, and foot-boards attached on each side. It is made for four persons, two on each side, seated back to back, and has a rail at each end.

Four miles an hour is a good pace for an elephant, but long-legged ones will swing along at five or upwards for a moderate distance, say ten miles. I have known thirty-nine miles done at a stretch at a moderate pace. Single wild elephants that have been wounded or much frightened will often travel as far as this in a few hours without a halt.

The elephant's use in tiger-shooting is well known, and speaks volumes for the tractability of an animal naturally so timid and disinclined for such work. Female elephants are more commonly used than males for tiger-shooting, being more easily procurable. But a well-trained male elephant is infinitely superior to any female, from his greater courage and strength. Unless they are well disciplined, however, there is danger of some male elephants attacking the tiger when they see him, which is a dangerous habit, as the occupants of the howdah may be shaken out during the animal's endeavours to crush the tiger.

A case of this kind occurred at Dacca, in May 1876, whilst I was there. A lady and her husband, Mr and Mrs I——, were at a tiger-hunt in a howdah on a female elephant, when a tigress charged across the open ground where they were stationed, not so much at the elephant as to get into a piece of cover behind it. The elephant rushed to meet the tigress, in this case more from excitement and terror than real courage. I—— fired and rolled the tigress over in front of the elephant, which kicked at her. The tigress grasped one of the elephant's hind-legs with teeth and claws, and the elephant was pulled, or fell, down on to her. I—— was thrown out, his rifle going off in the shock of his fall, but fortunately without doing any harm. He helped Mrs I—— from the howdah, and they ran to the protection of another elephant at some distance. The tigress was killed on the spot by the fall of the elephant upon her. In this case, had the elephant stood her ground, I—— would probably have killed the tigress before she got to close quarters.

As elephants are not bred in captivity, the demand for them from the forest is unwavering. Kábul merchants are the chief agents for the supply of high-class animals. These energetic traders frequently attach themselves to Courts where liberal prices are given, and in their service penetrate the remote tracts of Burmah and Siam. Here they purchase tuskers for figures seldom exceeding £100 on the spot, and march them, perhaps occupying more than a year on the road, to India. Their outlay is considerable in feeding them highly and in marching them slowly. I have heard of a case where a tusker, which had cost the merchant much money and labour, died almost at the gate of the city of the rájah for whom he was designed; who, when the merchant appeared with the elephant's trappings and tusks, bewailing his misfortune, ordered, with true Eastern munificence, that he should be paid the full value of the animal!

The chief marts for the supply of elephants to India hitherto have been Ceylon, Burmah, Siam, and a few of the forests of continental India; but from several causes the number brought into the market is now smaller than formerly, and prices are rising accordingly. The following statistics have been obligingly furnished me by the Secretary to the Government of

Ceylon, of elephants exported from the island during the years 1863-76. The sudden decrease in 1870 is due to the imposition in that year of an export duty of £20 per head, and lately the export has been entirely closed as a temporary measure, as it was feared that under the then existing rules for their capture and destruction, the practical extinction of elephants in the island might be expected at no distant date.

ELEPHANTS EXPORTED FROM CEYLON FROM 1863 TO 1876.

Year.	Number.	Year.	Number.
1863, ...	173	1870, ...	30
1864, ...	188	1871, ...	63
1865, ...	270	1872, ...	51
1866, ...	202	1873, ...	83
1867, ...	148	1874, ...	77
1868, ...	163	1875, ...	7
1869, ...	199	1876, ...	3

The great annual fair held at Sōnepoor, on the Ganges, is the chief mart in India for the sale of elephants. It is held on the occasion of the gathering of some hundreds of thousands of pilgrims to worship at a noted shrine of Shiva, and bathe in the Ganges, at the full moon of the month of October—November. Thousands of horses and hundreds of elephants are collected there, and for this point all dealers in elephants make. Such elephants as they do not then dispose of are taken about amongst rájahs and native princes. Traders in elephants are, as to character, pretty much on a par with dealers in horses all the world over. I once met a humorous old Kábul merchant at Dacca. He and some fellow-dealers came to the *peelkhána* (elephant-stables) day after day, and importuned me to sell some of the newly-caught elephants from Chittagong. It is not uncommon to dispose of such as, from some cause, may be unfit for Government service; but on this occasion all were required for filling up vacancies in the Commissariat Department. There was one very old female, however, that I knew would never be fit for work, whilst being handsome, and in good condition, she might suit a native for show. I therefore offered her to the dealers for 400 rupees (£40), a very low figure. We proceeded to her picket, where the head dealer, a patriarchal-looking old fellow, examined her with attention for some time, and then turned away with a sigh. I asked him if the price was too high. "No," he said, "it is not that. The sight of the elephant makes me think of my poor old grandmother. She died when I was a lad. What an elephant that would have been for her!"

The price of elephants throughout India has increased enormously of late years. A considerable number were formerly purchased at Sōnepoor and elsewhere by the Bengal Government, but of late years prices have become almost prohibitory. In 1835 the price of elephants was £45 per head; in 1855 about £75; in 1874, twenty were purchased at Sōnepoor for the Bengal Government at £132, 15s. each; in 1875, seventy were required at Sōnepoor, for which £140 per head was sanctioned, but not one was procurable at that figure. £150 is now the lowest rate for which young animals, chiefly females, and not fully grown, can be obtained. The price of good females of the working class is at present from £200 to £300. The value of tuskers is very capricious; it depends mainly upon the nearness of approach of their points to those of the Koomeriah. The best are only found in the possession of those who can pay fancy prices, but all male elephants are in high demand for the retinues of rájahs and temple purposes. Scarcely any limit can be placed on the price of a really perfect Koomeriah; £2000 is not an unknown figure. Tuskers of any pretensions at all command from £800 to £1500. Two newly-caught tuskers of no particular merit were sold out of the Daçca stud, in 1875, for £1600 the pair.

The elephants required for the service of Government in Bengal are mostly captured by the Government Kheddah (or elephant-catching) Establishment, the headquarters of which are at Dacca, in Eastern Bengal. This establishment is under a European officer, and contains a large number of trained elephants and native hunters, and yearly in December penetrates some of the forests of Assam, Chittagong, or other tracts, and captures elephants, which are marched to Dacca before the rains commence in May. Here they are trained for service, and about November are despatched to Barrackpoor, near Calcutta, whence they are allotted to different Commissariat stations. The average annual number of elephants captured by the Dacca Establishment during the seven years prior to 1875-76 was fifty-nine.

The Superintendent of Kheddahs at Dacca is also empowered to grant licences to natives of capital to capture elephants upon certain terms, by which Government secures a further annual supply. These lessees work in forests where the Government kheddahs are not working, and the terms usually are that half of the elephants measuring over six feet, and below eight and a half feet, at the shoulder, are to be handed over as Government rent; whilst all below six feet, and over eight and a half feet in height, are the exclusive property of the lessee. Government is further at liberty to purchase any or all of the lessee's share of the elephants between six and eight and a half feet at £5 per foot of height at shoulder (for instance, £40 for an eight-feet elephant), which is very much below the usual price of newly-caught elephants.

This system is advantageous both to the Government and the lessee. Should the hunt be unsuccessful the former is not saddled with a money payment, whilst any really valuable tuskers, over eight and a half feet high, fall to his share. On the Government's part, the entire expenses of the kheddah are borne by the lessee, so no loss can be sustained. Should Government give any assistance in tame elephants for securing the captives when impounded, ten per cent of the latter are taken as remuneration.

The supply of elephants to Government must always be kept up by kheddahs and the licence system. The figure for which they are now captured need probably never be exceeded. The outer market is not likely to become easier, as, though the demand will decrease to some extent as the less wealthy native notables, and a few Europeans who keep elephants for sport, must curtail their studs to the ability of their pockets, the supply has decreased in a disproportionate degree owing to restrictions in hunting. An elephant which costs Government £40 to capture would cost at least £150 in the market.

The Madras Government is entirely dependent for its supply of elephants on Burmah, as there is no Government catching-establishment in the Presidency, as in Bengal, and the immense number of elephants roaming the Madras forests is turned to no account. The elephants are shipped from Moulmein to Coconada in vessels specially chartered for the purpose. A batch of about 60, imported eight years ago, cost £176 each when landed. Prices have risen since. The Collector of Coimbatore, a district of Madras, commenced elephant-catching in 1874, upon the plan adopted in Mysore, and between 1874 and 1877 captured 76 elephants, but the cost has been so great (about £13,000), and so many have died, that the scheme has been a financial failure. The idea, however, is a move in the right direction. The experiment has necessarily cost proportionately more than further operations need cost. It is evidently inexpedient that a distant market should be trusted to, in which prices are rising fast, and must continue to rise, whilst the jungles of the Madras Presidency abound with elephants. A catching-establishment cannot be got into order in a day, nor by the isolated efforts of one officer. The Dacca establishment has been working in one form or other since the beginning of the century. If the Madras Government is convinced of the necessity of keeping up its present stud of elephants—a matter admitting of much consideration, now that good roads, railways, and the settled state of the country have modified the former military requirements—it would seem to be a matter deserving of consideration whether the Commissariat requirements in elephants cannot be met from local sources. A fallacious idea that the Madras elephants are less hardy than those of Burmah has sprung out of the fact that many die before they are fit for service. But this is the case everywhere. Those imported from Burmah have been already seasoned, and consequently the mortality amongst them is lighter.

THE BREEDING OF ELEPHANTS.

The question has sometimes been raised whether it is the male or female elephant which comes into season. I have heard the opinion advanced that it is the former; but it is an erroneous one, probably founded on the fact of most male elephants in captivity having periodical paroxysms of *must*. Some male elephants never, or only at long intervals, have these fits; in others they are of tolerably regular occurrence. They occur also in wild individuals, chiefly in the cold weather from November to February. The temples swell, and an oily matter exudes from them, as in tame elephants, but the wild elephant, I believe, shows no violence whilst under their influence. The occurrence of *must* in tame elephants is connected with their condition, and rarely appears in animals much below par. It does not appear in animals under about thirty years of age, though tuskers breed from the age of twenty.

There is ample proof that it is not the male elephant that comes into season. In following single males with a view to capturing them with trained females, they may always be relied upon to make advances to the females, usually to some particular one, and the efforts of the mahouts are frequently necessary to keep her out of the male's reach.

The period of heat is not marked by any particular signs in the female, which has probably helped to strengthen the erroneous opinion spoken of. In approaching a male elephant, a female desirous of his attentions utters certain sounds, and courts his society; but only those conversant with elephants would notice this. It has frequently happened that the tame females of the kheddah parties have been found in calf after work in the jungles, where wild males have had access to them, though no indications of their being prepared to receive the male were observed even by their keepers.

It has been a disputed point as to the manner in which the connection between the two sexes takes place. Some have supposed that the female kneels or lies down to receive the male, but this is not the case. I have myself, on four different occasions, witnessed the act—once, by two animals belonging to a wild herd in the jungles; on the others, by animals which had just been caught, and which were at large within the kheddah enclosures. On each, the female elephant stood to receive the male in the manner common to all quadrupeds. The opposite opinion may have arisen from the fact that it is possible for a heavy male to bear down to her knees a female much smaller than himself. On none of these occasions did the male elephant exhibit signs of *must,* which shows that it is not only when under its influence that male elephants court the society of the females.

CHAPTER IX.

THE MANAGEMENT AND FEEDING OF ELEPHANTS.

ELEPHANTS' ATTENDANTS — MISMANAGEMENT OF THEIR CHARGES — CHIEF AILMENTS OF ELEPHANTS — KINDS OF FODDER — GRASS — BRANCHES — UNDER-FED ELEPHANTS — THE ELEPHANT FEEDS CONSTANTLY IN ITS WILD STATE — ALLOWANCE OF FODDER TO GOVERNMENT ELEPHANTS IN BENGAL AND MADRAS — REMARKS ON THE ABOVE SCALES — THE AMOUNT AN ELEPHANT WILL EAT.

THE proper management of the elephants attached to the military and other departments in India is a subject of much importance, both financially and from a humane point of view. It is, however, unfortunately a matter but little understood by the European officers of the various departments, who are almost entirely dependent upon their elephants' native attendants for information on the subject. These men are rascals more often than not, and all are invariably grossly superstitious and ignorant. Captain Forsyth, in his *Highlands of Central India*, notes their making their elephants swallow pieces of tigers' liver to give them courage in hunting; and the eyes of the owl, torn from the living bird, to enable them to see well in the dark!

It would be out of place in this book to offer any detailed suggestions for improving the management of elephants; but a few general remarks on the subject may be of use to some who have the charge of them, but have not had opportunities of familiarising themselves with the requirements of the animals. Such should bear in mind that almost all elephants' attendants are guided in their conduct by two great principles—namely, to spare themselves as much work as possible, and to make as much as they can out of their elephants' allowance of rice or other grain. They also invariably make their charges' comfort and convenience subservient to their own, and though they are rarely wantonly cruel, they subject their animals to much passive inhumanity, which a little supervision from those over them might prevent. Thus, on days when the elephant is not required for work, the mahout and grass-cutter will, if left to themselves, cook their morning meal, smoke, and pass the time until nearly mid-day, without even loosing their elephants, except to take them to water. They should be required to hobble them early, and turn the poor beasts out to graze and stretch their limbs till wanted; but as this would give them the trouble of going in search of them if they strayed, they will not do it unless seen after. When there are fields near, one attendant can accompany the elephant to prevent it doing damage.

Then, instead of cutting its fodder early, and taking the elephant out to bring in its load in the cool hours of morning or evening, the grass-cutter, who does not mind the hot sun himself, often takes it at mid-day, as that arrangement suits his hours of breakfasting, &c. Even the best mahouts, extraordinary though it may seem, seldom take the trouble of putting their elephants under a tree at mid-day; and if the unfortunate animal throws dust and litter upon its back, to shield itself in some measure from the sun, it is heartily abused for giving the attendants the trouble of cleaning it afterwards. Those in charge of the elephants and their attendants cannot do better than bear in mind what the natural requirements of the former are, and make the attendants' hours and habits conform to the elephants', instead of the reverse, as is too frequently the case.

The most common ailment amongst elephants is *yaarba'hd.* It is of two kinds: one called dropsical *yaarba'hd,* in which the neck, chest, abdomen, and sometimes the legs, swell with accumulations of water beneath the skin; the other is wasting *yaarba'hd,* in which the animal falls gradually away to mere skin and bone. Both kinds are exceedingly fatal if they become established. They are most common amongst newly-caught elephants—in fact, hardly any such escape the affection to some extent. I have never seen a wild elephant suffering from it. The disease is induced by the radical change of food and habits undergone by newly-caught elephants. Freedom from unnecessary restraint, liberty to graze at will, protection from all debilitating causes, such as exposure to the sun or inclement weather, are the best preventives and restoratives. Medicine is of little avail; and, if the disease is once allowed to become serious, there is every probability of a fatal termination.

Sore backs, from the chafing of gear, are exceedingly tedious to cure. The mistake usually made by mahouts is to allow the wounds to heal on the surface whilst mischief may be going on inside. A free use of the knife, great care in cleansing the wound, and the application of plenty of turpentine, strongly impregnated with camphor, are the best methods for insuring a speedy cure. The deep, burrowing holes usually present in sore backs should be well packed with tow steeped in the camphorated turpentine. This stuffing prevents the wounds closing up too quickly; the growth of new flesh should be encouraged from the bottom, not at the surface of the sore. A cloth steeped in *margosa** oil should be tied over the wound, to prevent flies approaching it and irritating the elephant.

Elephants occasionally become foot-sore from working in gravelly or stony soil. An elephant does not limp, but goes more slowly and tenderly when its feet become painful. Rest is the best cure.

When elephants require purgative medicine they eat a considerable quantity of earth, kicking it up with their toes, and conveying it to their mouths with their trunks. They usually eat from three to five pounds. This is resorted to when they are troubled by worms in the alimentary canal, and sometimes as much as 25 lb. weight of these parasites are passed by them. Certain soils, usually black and impregnated with a kind of natron, are preferred. Purging ensues in from twelve to twenty-four hours.

The chief fodder of tame elephants should consist of various kinds of grasses, which in India grow to a considerable length and thickness. But where these cannot be procured—or too often owing to the laziness of the grass-cutters, who find lopping branches easier work than cutting grass—elephants are almost entirely restricted to leaves and branches of trees. This is not a natural diet: wild elephants eat but sparingly of tree fodder. However, tame elephants become accustomed to it, and in many parts of the Madras Presidency hardly anything else is procurable.

There is, perhaps, no animal less liable to sickness than the elephant if well fed. This point is of paramount importance, and without it good management in other matters is of no avail. It is common enough to see elephants in poor condition, suffering from nothing but partial starvation, being treated with medicines and nostrums for debility, whilst their appetites are good, and they only require a sufficiency of fodder to effect a cure. It may truly be said that all ailments to which elephants are subject are directly or indirectly caused by insufficient feeding. Under-fed elephants become weak and unable to stand exposure; they cannot perform their work, and are laid open to attack by even such remote maladies as sunstroke and sore back through poor condition. The elephant, in common with all wild animals, goes to no excess in any of its habits, and there is no reason, except bad feeding, why the rate of mortality should be so high as it unhappily is amongst Government elephants in India. The actual work they have to perform is seldom arduous enough to affect elephants in health.

* Prepared from the seed of the *neem* tree, *Melia azadiracta.*

The amount of fodder required by an elephant is much greater than is usually supposed. The Government allowance in Bengal and Madras for an elephant of full size is as follows:—

BENGAL.	Lb.
Green fodder—viz., grasses, branches of trees, sugar-cane, &c., . . .	400
Or in lieu of the above, dry fodder—viz., stalks of cut grain, &c., .	240
MADRAS.	
Green fodder, ...	250
Or dry fodder, ...	125

But the amount of suitable green fodder which a full-grown elephant will consume in eighteen hours I have found, by numerous experiments, to be much greater than this—viz., between 600 and 700 lb. This is what a beast of average appetite will actually *eat*, excluding what it throws aside; and I have seen a large tusker eat 800 lb., or 57 stone, in eighteen hours. I lately experimented with eight females with *dhall* grass (a grass with stalks from five to ten feet in length that grows in water, and of which elephants are fond) for eight consecutive days upon cleared masonry stands, where the waste was collected and weighed. Commencing at 6 P.M., they ate an average weight of 650 lb. by 12 A.M. next day out of 800 lb., given as follows:—

	Lb.
At 6 P.M., ...	560
At 6 A.M., ...	240

800 lb. of the same grass stocked on an open grating lost by dryage—

In the first 24 hours, ...	40
In the second 24 hours, ...	120

So the total dryage in two days was 160 lb. This shows that the grass was not unduly wet. From 12 A.M. till 6 P.M. the above elephants were out bringing in fodder, and had pickings in the jungle. They also had 18 lb. of grain per diem.

800 lb. may be looked upon as the minimum weight of good fodder that should be placed before full-sized elephants per diem. This amount only allows a margin of 150 lb. for waste, so the fodder must be good, or 800 lb. will not be sufficient. A good elephant-load of fodder weighs 800 lb.; so as much as an elephant can bring in may be looked upon as necessary for his requirements. Smaller elephants will bring in quantities proportionately sufficient for their wants. I have never tried elephants exclusively

with dry fodder, but it is evident that the amount allowed in the Commissariat scales is quite insufficient.

The elephants in Madras and Bengal differ in no respect. They are frequently imported to both Presidencies from Burmah, and whilst those allotted to Bengal are allowed 400 lb. of fodder, similar animals in Madras are allowed 250 lb. But were either of these scales adhered to, the elephants would die in a few weeks. It is difficult to conjecture how they were fixed originally, but it is probable that these were the amounts intended to be purchased over and above what the grass-cutter could collect when free fodder was not obtainable in sufficient quantities. I found that in Bengal the present scale was in force prior to 1822.

Since representing the inadequacy of the above allowances to Government in official correspondence on the subject, I have been informed that experiments have been made in the Bengal Commissariat Department, in continuation of my own, which have proved that an elephant will eat 750 lb. of dry sugar-cane, which is more feeding fodder than grass, per diem, and that steps are being taken to remodel the fodder scale.

The following scale of cost of keep is for a female of full size in the Bengal and Madras Commissariat Departments respectively, per mensem :—

BENGAL.

	Rs.	As.
1 mahout,	6	0
1 grass-cutter,	5	0
18 lb. unhusked rice per diem, at 64 lb. per rupee,	8	7
Allowance for medicines, salt, &c.,	0	13
Fodder allowance, at 2 annas per diem,	3	12
Total Rs.,*	24	0

MADRAS.

	Rs.	As.
1 mahout,	9	0
1 grass-cutter,	6	0
25 lb. rice per diem, at 30 lb. per rupee,	25	0
Salt, oil, and medicines,	2	0
Fodder, average purchase per mensem,	6	0
Total Rs.,*	48	0

* The rupee is usually calculated at two shillings.

CHAPTER X.

ELEPHANT-CATCHING IN MYSORE.

COMMENCE ELEPHANT-CATCHING IN MYSORE—PLANS AT MORLAY IN 1873—FAILURE OF FIRST ATTEMPTS—CHANGE OF PLANS—COMMENCEMENT OF THE RAINS—VISIT OF A HERD—ITS MOVEMENTS—SURROUND THE HERD OF FIFTY-FOUR ELEPHANTS—EXCITING NIGHT-SCENES—THE SMALL ENCLOSURE—VISITORS TO CAMP—DRIVE THE HERD INTO THE ENCLOSURE—SHOOT A TROUBLESOME FEMALE—A WHITE CALF—CONDUCT OF HERD IN SMALL ENCLOSURE—OUR TAME ELEPHANTS—AMUSING MISHAP—A TROUBLESOME TUSKER—"JAIRAM" VANQUISHES HIM—CAPTURE OF A WILD TUSKER IN THE ELEPHANT LINES—ALLOTMENT OF NINE OF THE NEW ELEPHANTS TO HIS HIGHNESS THE MAHÁRÁJAH, AND TEN TO THE MADRAS COMMISSARIAT DEPARTMENT—SALE OF TWENTY-FIVE ELEPHANTS—PROFIT OF THE OPERATIONS TO GOVERNMENT—RESULTS TO MYSELF.

IT was in September 1873 that I arrived at Chámráj-Nuggar—a large village ten miles from the foot of the Billiga-rungun hills—commissioned to try and capture some of the herds of elephants which frequently left the hills and trespassed into the cultivated lands adjoining. I knew nothing of elephant-catching at the time, nor had I any men at command who did; but I knew where there were plenty of elephants, and I was well acquainted with their habits. Some of the Mahárájah's mahouts who were amongst my following had been accustomed to catch single elephants with trained females, and in pitfalls, but they had never heard of any one attempting the capture of a whole herd. It was said that Hyder had made a trial, a century before, in the Kákankoté jungles, but had failed, and had recorded his opinion that no one would ever succeed, and his curse upon any one that attempted to do so, on a stone still standing near the scene of his endeavours. Consequently all the true Mussulmáns who were with me regarded the enterprise as hopeless—though they judiciously kept that opinion to themselves.

It was owing to this general inexperience that the Chief Commissioner of Mysore had been reluctant to sanction the expenditure required for the attempt. The proposals originated entirely with me. I had been soliciting permission to make a trial for the past eight months, and it was only granted when the season for finding elephants in ground where it would be practicable to catch them—June to December—was far advanced. However, when I did get permission, I commenced the work with the hearty support of an officer of high influence in the province, a keen and experienced sportsman, and who warmly assisted my scheme. The Amildár, or head native official of the district, was an able and energetic person, and obtained for me the willing co-operation of the people required for carrying out the works I decided upon.

My first step at Chámráj-Nuggar was to send for my old sporting friends, the Morlayites, whom I questioned about the number of elephants in the jungles, their principal haunts and routes, and other particulars. I had not met these men for more than two years, when we used to hunt together; and though they were not very clean, I could almost have hugged them with pleasure at getting back to them and my old hunting-grounds; whilst, as I had always behaved well to them, they were delighted, and prostrated themselves in a body, declaring I was their father and mother, and that they had been as children bereft since I left them! I put them in good spirits by asking about such little grievances as Indian villagers generally imagine they have, regarding their lands, taxes, and so forth, and promised them that the Amildár would pay particular attention to anything that they had to represent if they rendered effective assistance in elephant-catching.

Next day I moved camp to Morlay, and occupied the hours between sunrise and sunset in tramping the jungles and examining places that seemed likely to afford facilities for circumventing elephants. I knew the whole neighbourhood well, so was able to decide upon a certain ford, marked A on plan, on the Honhollay river, at which to make an attempt. The river was here about twenty yards wide, but ordinarily with only a narrow and shallow stream flowing over its clean gravelly bed. In the rainy months heavy but short-lived floods sometimes rose twenty feet in a few hours. Wild elephants crossing from its east to its west bank used this and two other fords (the banks were not practicable except at these places), marked X, X on plan. They also retreated by the same routes. When on the west side of the river it was their custom to seek shelter in covers D or E, and we calculated that by stopping the two fords (X, X) we could drive a herd out of D or E across by ford A, which was indeed their favourite route.

Upon these considerations I marked out a kheddah at A, on the east

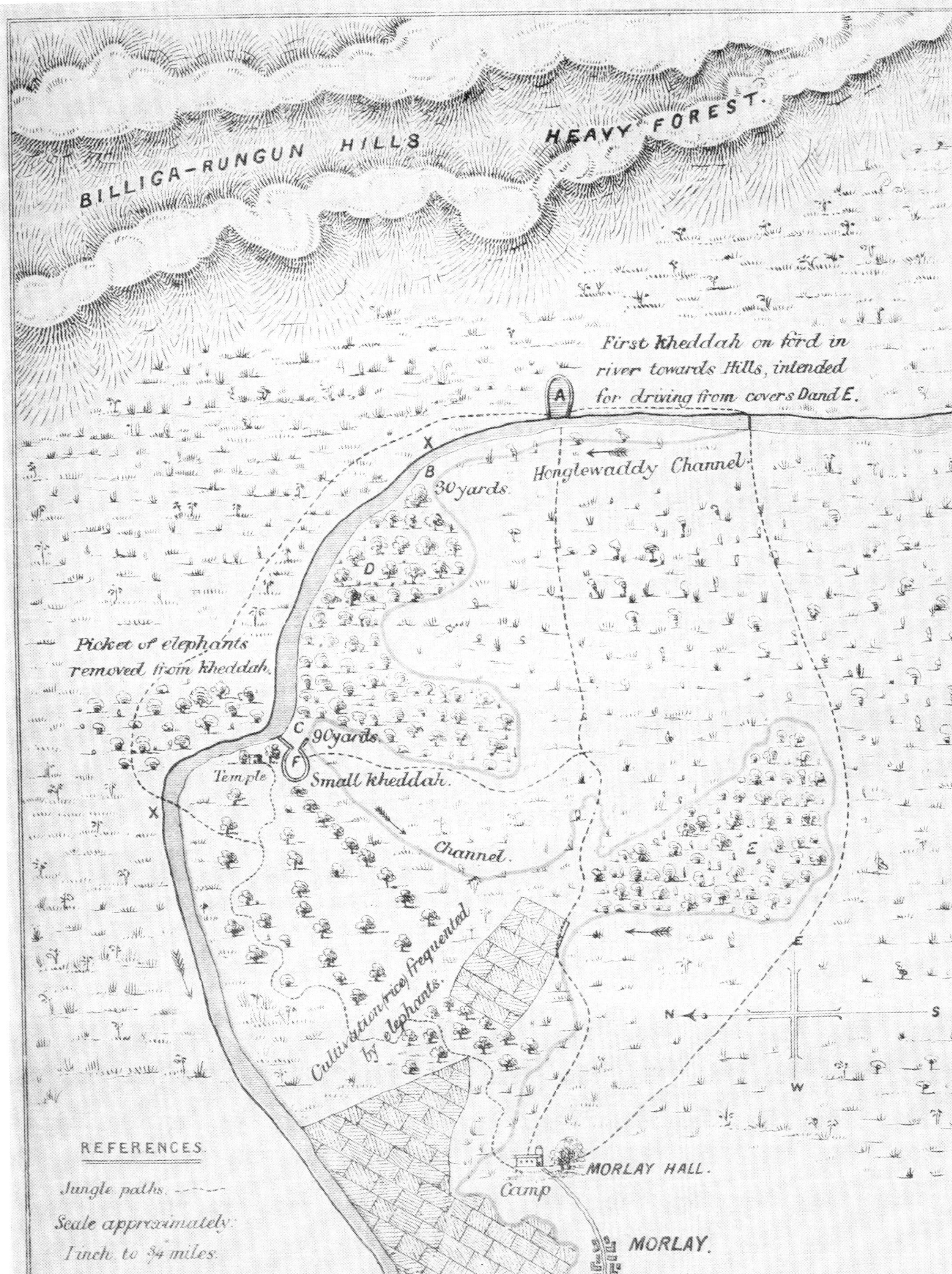
BILLIGA-RUNGUN HILLS
HEAVY FOREST.
First Kheddah on ford in river towards Hills, intended for driving from covers D and E.
A
X
B
30 yards.
Honglewaddy Channel
D
Picket of elephants removed from kheddah.
C
90 yards.
F
Temple
Small kheddah.
X
Channel.
E
Cultivation (rice) frequented by elephants.
E
N
S
W
REFERENCES.
Jungle paths
Scale approximately: 1 inch to 3/4 miles.
MORLAY HALL.
Camp
MORLAY.

bank of the river, consisting of a horse-shoe-shaped piece of ground surrounded by a trench. The trench was about five hundred yards round, and the entrance to the enclosed space was by the ford. The elephants would enter by the heel of the shoe, as it were, and would have to go some two hundred yards before they came to the farthest point, the boundary trench. The trench was eight feet wide at top, six at bottom, and eight feet deep (this I subsequently found was a greater section than is necessary to confine wild elephants), and in a few days it was finished, except where rock was met and had to be blasted. There were eight hundred men at work, whose wages were about threepence each per diem. They removed about one cubic yard per man per diem.

It was nearly a month before all was in readiness, as the removal of the rock was laborious work. The personal labour I spent on that enclosure, severe though it was, was not greater than the anxiety I had to endure. Some Job's comforters suggested that if one elephant fell into the trench the others would make a bridge of him and hie them back to the hills; others, that the gate which I had devised for closing the entrance, and which was hauled up on a single rope, to be cut away in the joyful moment when the stern of the last elephant cleared it, would be carried away like chaff before the wind by their backward rush! whilst a few did not hesitate to say that no elephants would approach a place bearing traces of new earth-work and the recent presence of so many work-people. I lived under canvas at Morlay, three miles distant, as the jungle was too unhealthy to admit of my camping at the work, and I frequently got drenched by the heavy September rains, which was not conducive to either comfort or health. I remained at the kheddah daily till late in the evening, and then rode to camp as fast as my pony could carry me, unattended, though there was the notorious man-eating tigress of Iyenpoor afoot, and many others of her race which I stood a chance of falling in with. They would not in all probability have interfered with me, but still it was exciting to my pony, who quite understood jungle-life, if not to myself. I was determined to make the scheme succeed if possible, not only from my love of adventure, and the necessity for executing what I had suggested to Government and undertaken to carry out, but from the desire to prove to several officials who considered the scheme to be the vision of a lunatic, that their croakings were rather the utterances of Bedlamites. Pleasantries appeared in the Bangalore papers regarding the probable effect the kheddah operations would have on the price of salt, which it was represented was being laid in by me in large quantities for application to the caudal appendages of any elephants I happened to meet with!

At last all my plans were completed. Fortunately the elephants had been absent from the neighbourhood up to this time—there were three herds which commonly frequented it—but on the 5th of November the trackers came in early to say there were about thirty elephants in cover D! Immediately messengers started to all the villages near, where orders had been given to the people to hold themselves in readiness to help in the great Government elephant-catching scheme. Still it was twelve o'clock before they collected. I fumed and chafed at the delay, and I am afraid some of the last to arrive did not find me in the best of humours. However, shortly after twelve I started with about five hundred of them—far too many, as I afterwards found—and when we approached the temple I ordered one body to the left, to station themselves along the north-east bank of the river; a second to the right, to cut the elephants off from communication with cover E; and a third, composed of the best men, chiefly Morlayites, to drive the elephants out of cover D. They were to begin to beat at the temple, and we hoped that the elephants would be kept straight for ford A by the guiding-lines of stops. I took my own station near the ford on the west side of the river, with the object of giving the elephants a final impetus forward as they approached it, and to guard the gate with my rifles when they had entered.

After the usual delay, inseparable from anything natives have to do, I heard the beat begin, half a mile distant, and presently five elephants approached the crossing of the river, but kept themselves concealed in the thick jungle between it and the Honglewaddy channel. I observed that they were looking back wistfully as if for their fellows, nor did the beaters follow them up as quickly as they should have done. After some time the five went back, whilst the shouts and shots of the beaters continued near the spot from which the elephants had been originally started. I did not like to leave my post at the ford; but at last, as no news came, nor was there any sign of more elephants approaching, I stationed a man, in whom I thought I might repose confidence, at the gate, and went with my rifles to see what was the matter. I found that the main body of the elephants had not left cover D, chiefly on account of numbers of the men forming the guiding-line on the south having left their places, and so confused the elephants by joining the beaters, and shouting in all directions, that they did not know which way to flee. They had therefore ensconced themselves in an extensive and almost impenetrable thicket of thorns, whilst the fiends in human shape who had spoilt all my plans were mobbing them in every direction, at a respectful distance, yelling at the top of their voices, and apparently quite oblivious of what the object to be attained was. I gesticulated to them to clear the side towards which we wished to make the elephants break, shaking my fist at them in a fury. The villains redoubled their cries, beating their sticks with heavy thuds on the ground; they thought I was angry at their not exerting themselves sufficiently! Talking was useless; a trombone could hardly have been heard in that din; so arming my gun-bearers with rattans, I sent them amongst the rascals, whom they quickly dispersed, and most of them bolted, and, happily, did not appear again.

I now made the best re-disposition I could of the Morlayites, and we managed at last to start a number of the elephants on the right road. Some of the best men and I pursued them, determined to catch even a small number rather than fail altogether, and they were going fast and straight for the crossing, when, just as they reached it, we at their tails, a sudden shot in front saluted them. A momentary halt and crush ensued; the leading elephants turned, the others followed, and back they came, heads down, tails twisted, going their best, and evidently oblivious of us and everything in their path. The river-bank was close at hand on our left, the channel on our right, whilst the herd almost filled the intervening space. I was maddened by the ill-luck and failure of our measures, and I determined if the elephants got back now it should be over my body; so, shouting to the men not to give way, I fired at and floored one elephant in the front rank. The beaters with me behaved very pluckily, some even throwing the blankets which they carried rolled up on their backs into the elephants' faces before making off. The fall of the leading elephant acted as a momentary check on the others, but they were resolved to be back to the thick cover they had left; so, swerving to their left, they bustled across the channel in mad haste, and with a prodigious amount of splashing, struggling, and roaring, gained the far side, and continued their flight, the wounded elephant amongst them.

The fatal shot that had turned the elephants, in the moment when success was all but grasped, had been fired by my trusty friend at the gate, who must have become frightened at their rapid advance. But the exact circumstances of the case are involved in mystery, as, when I went to have a little conversation with him, I found he had left his gun against a tree and had bolted, and I have never seen his face from that day to this!

The Morlayites now lost their heads, as every one else appeared to do on that memorable occasion. They pursued the retreating elephants with shouts and brandishing of clubs, and as the huge beasts again shuffled across the Honglewaddy channel to regain the cover, some of the boldest actually struck at them from the bank with their long bamboos, the blows sounding loudly on their broad croups. The elephants might have turned and rent them many times during the hunt, but they seemed to have been deserted by the intelligence and sagacity with which they are popularly accredited in as great a degree as the men were by common-sense, and to have no ideas beyond using their legs.

It was now evening. I was drenched with perspiration, bruised, scratched, and hardly able to speak for hoarseness. I threw myself down on an elephant-pad under a tree, lighted a cheroot, and applied myself to a review of the day's proceedings, as it was worse than useless to continue the hunt. This, then, was the result of my plans and pains. Things could not have looked more promising at the commencement of the action, yet in four hours the elephants had been terrified beyond hope of their returning to our side of the river for months, and my men demoralised by our failure. However, in the midst of discouragement there was something to be thankful for. No one had been killed, as might well have happened, and the attempt had clearly demonstrated the impossibility of succeeding with such untrained, though willing material. This was something gained; and as I conceived that greater eventual success might be evolved from our present failure, I did not feel greatly discouraged on a consideration of all the circumstances. I had had too many reverses in my sporting experience to be surprised at this one. The Morlayites had shown great pluck, and I believed if they were disciplined they would act more judiciously on another occasion. They also had seen how frightened the elephants were at them, and their confidence would rise in proportion. I had made the mistake of having too many men engaged. Elephants must, as the butcher says of beef-steaks in *Martin Chuzzlewit*, when Tom Pinch is trying to cram his purchases into his pocket, "be humoured, not drove." The collapse of my immediate hopes was certainly rather depressing, but reflecting that I probably felt it more at that moment than I should in a few hours, I mounted my elephant and rode home, followed by my chop-fallen heroes.

I had a long and earnest consultation with my right-hand men over the day's events round the camp-fire, when dinner and the soothing pipe combined to enable us to review them with some calmness; and long after I turned in I heard the trackers considering what we should do on the next occasion. Some of the Morlayites were again quite confident, and were agreed that if such and such things had happened that did not, and others had not that did, they would have been keeping a joyful watch over impounded elephants at that moment, instead of looking wistfully towards the dark and distant hills in which they had doubtless already found safe shelter. "Yes," said Márah, a cautious old hunter, "and if your aunts had had mustachios they would have been your uncles!"

During the next few days I hit upon a plan for the future which had the great advantage that few men would be required to execute it, and even undisciplined ones could hardly spoil it. This was to fortify cover D, so as to prevent the egress of elephants after they had once entered it, and to catch them in it, instead of trusting to a drive in open country.

The elephant season in the low country—June to December—was now over, and the herds had betaken themselves to the hills, but I commenced in January 1874 to put the cover in readiness, during the dry weather, for the coming rainy season. I employed a European overseer, Jones, to help me, and it was fortunate I had such assistance, as I was frequently prostrated during the hot weather by attacks of ague and fever, the result of the exposure I had unavoidably been subjected to for the past few months. I found leisure to superintend the building of a rough bungalow instead of living in a tent, and I also amused myself by shooting a few of the tigers in the neighbourhood. Amongst these was the Iyenpoor man-eater.

It will be seen by reference to the sketch-plan that the Honglewaddy channel approaches the river to within 30 yards at B. It then runs inland, owing to the levelness of the country, but again approaches to within 90 yards of the river at C, near the temple. The space (cover D) bounded by the channel between B and C, and the river, is about 50 acres in extent, and consists of a jungle of large trees, forest creeping-plants, and several strong thickets. In this retreat it had been the immemorial habit of herds of elephants to take shelter at certain seasons, and to issue forth at nights into the adjacent cultivated country. The north bank of the river was so steep that they could not cross at any point between fords X, X; whilst there were only five places where they could cross the channel on the west, as it was deep and had perpendicular banks. I, however, had the banks cut to a uniform vertical height of 10 feet, except at the crossings, to make sure of the elephants not getting out of the cover when once in. To barricade the channel crossings, each about 10 yards in width, cocoa-nut trees, which are exceedingly strong and light when dry, were kept in readiness; and to prevent the elephants escaping by passing up or down the river (past B and C), the bed was spanned at those points by barriers composed of five rows of heavy chains. As soon as elephants entered the cover (of their own accord), it would only be necessary to connect the channel and river at B and C by cross trenches to make the surround complete.

All was in readiness by May. After a few showers the early rains set in in good earnest, and on May 5th a large herd of elephants came down the hills into the low-country jungles. On the 19th five of them visited enclosure D during the night, and after feeding about returned to the herd, which was three miles distant. From this time till the 9th of June small parties visited the cover occasionally, but always returned to the head-quarters of the herd. This was very tantalising. We were kept constantly on the stretch; and each morning, until the trackers returned to camp, the villagers of Morlay who were to help were detained at home so as to be mustered at a moment's notice if required, whilst a man was stationed on the wall of the Hurdenhully fort to fire a small cannon I had mounted there, as a signal to other villagers to collect at Morlay in case we wanted more men. Tools for digging the trenches at B and C, baskets for carrying earth, ropes for securing the barricades, and provisions and cooking-pots for the multitude, were stored in the temple buildings. Special services were held daily by the Poojáree and trackers at that celebrated shrine, and the promises of gifts held out to Koombappah for success were sufficient to have moved the heart of even as stony a deity as himself.

On the 9th of June I was at a hill some six miles west of Morlay looking after a bear. The trackers had brought in their usual morning report before I left my bungalow, to the effect that the elephants were still at the foot of the hills, five miles from cover D; so, not expecting them to make a move during the day, I had sent the trackers back to their duty of surveillance, and with a number of men from Oomchwaddy was busy in the pursuit of the said bear, a female with a cub. It was afternoon, and I was seated on the top of the rocky hill, which rose some five hundred feet from the plain, amused by the chase of the bear by my men along the hillside below. The bear had broken wide of me when she was roused from a thicket, and I had not had a shot; but being encumbered by her cub, which was riding on its mother's shoulders after the manner of young bears, the old female could not get along so fast as to keep much ahead of my men, who terrified mother and cub so much by their hot pursuit that the cub fell off; and before it could follow its mother—being very young—a blanket was thrown over it and it was secured, whilst its mother held on for a cave close at hand, into which she fled.

This scene was enacting when I heard the distant boom of my old cannon on the fort-wall of Hurdenhully. I waited to hear it repeated. Yes, another shot! No mistake this time. There goes the third! Hurrah! That is the signal that the elephants are on our side of the river! The smoke of a fire lighted on the highest ground near Morlay—the sign that I was required at camp—now attracted my attention and that of the men with me, so down the hill we went pell-mell, thinking no more of the bear; and making the men fall in, I mounted my elephant and we started for Morlay.

We passed through Oomchwaddy and Hurdenhully, where the people were hastily collecting, and soon reached camp.

Here the lately despondent but now rejoicing trackers met us with the gratifying intelligence that the whole herd had made an unexpected move after mid-day, and had marched straight to the river, which they had crossed after bathing and drinking, and were now revelling in the succulent rushes and grass growing along the channel. Anxious though we were to begin, we agreed that it was too late to do anything that day, as the herd must be already scattered for the night's grazing, whilst the proper time to deal with them was when they were collected during the day.

I accordingly gave orders that no one should leave camp, but that all should be entertained "by Government," whose guests they were to consider themselves as having the inexpressible honour of being. Most of them were Oopligas and Torreas, both meat-eating castes (except as to beef); so I ordered my flock of sheep to be driven up immediately, and as I named the headmen who were to choose for their people, they made a dash amongst them and dragged out the sheep they preferred, amidst great amusement and comments upon their respective notions of mutton. These were speedily carried off and slaughtered, whilst another man of each group received cooking-pots, rági-flour, curry-stuffs, and tobacco, at the stores, where Jones presided.

What a night of pleasant anticipations and merriment it was! Everybody was happy, and we occasionally heard the trumpet of the elephants, fully three miles distant, as they fed and disported themselves about the river. I visited the various knots gathered round the fires dotted about the cleared plain before my bungalow, and said a few words to them about their conduct on the morrow. Agreeable fellows the rustics of Mysore are to entertain. They do not drink, and where the greatest dissipation is smoking or snuffing, there is no likelihood of quarrels or too noisy mirth. In this respect my Oopligas were a great contrast to the tame-elephant attendants, chiefly Mussulmáns, with a sprinkling of Pariahs, or low-caste Hindoos. When it was necessary to treat these for any special services, the only thing was to give them a few sheep and bottles of spirits—without which it would have been no treat—and to order them not to approach the camp till next morning. Their revels seldom concluded without a fight, though when the effects of the *bhang* they smoked, and their potations, passed away, they resumed the natural quiet demeanour of Asiatics.

Every one was astir betimes on the eventful 10th of June. I have caught a good many elephants since, and have witnessed many exciting scenes in the work, but I shall never forget the pleasurable anticipations

I experienced on this occasion. Every contingency that could be foreseen had been carefully considered; nothing had been left to chance. The men had had their respective posts allotted to them weeks beforehand, and we had even had a rehearsal, or review day, on which my tame elephants, under the direction of their mahouts, led by a Morlayite experienced in the ways of the wild ones, had represented a herd, whilst we took steps to meet their various moves. I had also practised the men in deer-hunts, &c., when I gave prizes in the shape of coloured handkerchiefs for turbans, as well as rupees, to those who distinguished themselves. I certainly felt that I now had a very different following to the undisciplined band that frustrated the first attempt. I had imbued them with some notions of obedience in executing instructions, whatever they might be; of working together; and of silence. The difficulty of getting natives to do anything without noise can only be fully understood by those who have had to deal with them. I considered it a triumph that I could march three hundred of them on an exciting expedition, without a whisper being heard. Despite all this I experienced a good deal of anxiety, now that the time for testing our arrangements had come; but I daresay this added to the pleasure of the occasion, as had the result been beyond doubt, where would the excitement have been?

At 9 A.M. we started for the temple. Early in the morning I had been joined by Major G., Deputy Inspector-General of Police for Mysore, and a keen sportsman, who happened to be encamped at Chámráj-Nuggar, and to whom I had sent word overnight. As Gaindcully, the elephant we were riding, swung along, followed by the long serpentine line of beaters in single file (the jungle-path being narrow), I felt proud of the comments my friend bestowed on my men, as he was in a position to appreciate the state to which they had been brought, having to drill and reduce natives to order for the ranks of the police.

When we reached the temple, the trackers, who had preceded us, informed us that all the elephants were not in cover D; some were scattered feeding on the upper side of the channel, and would have to be driven to join the main body. This was quietly effected by a handful of men, though a female with a young calf, an albino, gave us some trouble, threatening to charge. Had the men acted as of yore there would doubtless have been a scene, but by giving her time to retire safely with her charge we got her pounded into D with the others. Having ascertained that all the elephants were now in, all hands were engaged in barricading the crossings and cutting the trenches between the channel and river at B and C. To render this latter work easy I had previously had the trenches dug and filled in again, a small drain covered with flat stones being left at the bottom of each. Water was now admitted to these from the channel, whilst the end near the river was kept closed, and as the water had a head of some ten feet, it speedily blew up the superincumbent earth and scoured out the trenches to the depth and width required. It was past mid-day before we got all the elephants into the cover, and not a moment's rest did any of us get till 11 P.M. Captain C., of the Revenue Survey, came over from his camp at Surgoor, and Major G. and he helped to superintend the people. At one point the supply of tools was insufficient, and Captain C. was superintending and encouraging a body of men who were digging with sharpened sticks, and even their bare fingers! The elephants were very noisy in the cover, but did not show themselves. At every twenty yards three or four men were stationed to keep up large fires. These were reflected in the water of the channel and river, which increased their effect. We all had a most exaggerated idea of what the elephants might attempt, and the strength of our defences was in proportion, and greater than they need have been. I was kept on the move almost all night by alarms at different points, fortunately groundless ones. One tusker showed himself on the bank of the channel, but met with such a reception from firebrands and stones that he retreated in haste. The river was an advantage, as the elephants had easy access to water. The lurid glare of the fires, the gaunt figures of the lightly-clad watchers, their wild gesticulations on the bank with waving torches, the background of dense jungle resonant with the trumpeting of the giants of the forest,—formed a scene which words are feeble to depict, and that cannot fade from the memories of those who witnessed it.

By 11 P.M. the defences were thoroughly secured, and I had leisure as I stood by a log-fire with nothing but my trousers on (my flannel shirt and coat were drenched with perspiration, and were being dried before the blaze), a piece of bread in one hand, and a bottle of claret and water in the other, to reflect on our complete success so far. That the elephants could not now escape was certain, unless indeed they carried some of our barricades, which were, however, so strong as to be almost beyond their power. The men differed as to their number. I had seen about twenty; some declared there were fifty, but I could not believe this at the time. The number, however, was fifty-four, as we subsequently found. I tried in vain to rest. The excitement of the scene was irresistible, so I betook myself to walking round the enclosure at intervals throughout the night, followed by a man carrying a basket of cheroots, which I distributed to the people. The rest of the time I lay upon my cot, which my servant had been thoughtful enough to bring from Morlay with his cooking paraphernalia, enjoying the wildness of the sounds and scenes around, and soothed by cheroots and coffee. When the elephants approached the place where I was the guards thrust long bamboos into the fires, which sent showers of sparks up to the tops of the trees overhead, and they also threw joints of a bamboo-like reed into the flames, where they exploded with a sound as loud as pistol-shots.

The first crow of the jungle-cock was the most grateful sound I think I ever heard, as it showed our anxious vigil was drawing to a close. We knew that during the day the elephants would give us less trouble. My headmen now joined me from the points where they had been stationed during the night, and we set about considering the next step to be taken —viz., making a small enclosure or pound off cover D, into which to get the elephants confined. Of course this would take some time to carry out.

If driven from the east we knew the animals would pass between the temple and channel, at the west end of the cover, with a view to crossing the river below the temple, and regaining their native hills, which, however, they were fated never to see again. I therefore laid out a pound (F) of 100 yards in diameter, surrounded by a ditch 9 feet wide at top, 3 at bottom, and 9 feet deep. This was connected with the large cover by two guiding-trenches which converged to the gate. It was completed in four days by the personal exertions of the Amildár with a body of labourers, who worked with a will, as their crops had frequently suffered from the incursions of elephants, and they appreciated the idea of reducing their numbers. The last thing completed was the entrance-gate, which consisted of three transverse trunks of trees slung by chains between two trees that formed gate-posts. This barrier was hauled up and suspended on a single rope, so as to be cut away after the elephants had passed. The news of the intended drive attracted several visitors from Mysore. Tents were pitched in an open glade close to the river, and we soon had a pleasant party of several ladies, the cheery Deputy Commissioner of the district and his Assistant, two officers (Captains P. and B.) of her Majesty's 48th Regiment, M. of the Forests, and Captain C. and Major G., who had remained from the first day. The evening before the drive all assembled within view of the point where the elephants were in the habit of drinking at sunset, and were gratified with an admirable view of thirty-five of the huge creatures disporting themselves timidly in the water.

On the morning of the 17th, everything being in readiness for the drive, Captains P., B., and I proceeded with some picked hands to drive the herd from its stronghold towards the pound. We succeeded in moving them through the thick parts of the cover with rockets, and soon got them near to its entrance. A screened platform had been erected for the ladies at a point near the gate, where they could see the final drive into the enclosure from a place of safety.

The elephants, however, when near the entrance, made a stand, and refused to proceed; and finally, headed by a determined female, turned upon the beaters and threatened to break back down an open glade. P. and I intercepted them, and most of them hesitated; but the leading female, the mother of the albino calf, which had been evilly disposed from the beginning, rushed down upon me, as I happened to be directly in her path, with shrill screams, followed by four or five others, which, however, advanced less boldly. When within five yards I floored her with my 8-bore Greener and 10 drams; but though the heavy ball hit the right spot between the eyes, the shot was not fatal, as the head was carried in a peculiar position, and the bullet passed under the brain. The elephant fell to the shot, almost upon me, when P. fired, and I gave her my second barrel, which in the smoke missed her head, but took effect in her chest, and must have penetrated to the region of the heart, as a heavy jet of blood spouted forth when she rose. Probably one of the large arteries was cut by this shot. The poor beast moved off a few paces and halted, a stream of blood issuing in a parabolic curve from her chest, and making a loud gushing sound as a pool was formed in front of her. For some moments she swayed from side to side, and then fell over with a deep groan, to rise no more. This was a painful scene; the elephant had only acted in defence of her young; but shooting her was unavoidable, as our lives, as well as those of the beaters, were in jeopardy.

The next scene partook of the ridiculous. The herd had dispersed and regained its original position. The little albino calf, seeing P., screamed wildly, and with ears extended and tail aloft chased him. He, wishing to save it, darted round the trees, but was near coming to grief, as he tripped and fell. The result might have been disastrous had I not given the pertinacious youngster a telling butt in the head with my 8-bore. His attention was next turned to a native, who took to his heels when he found that three smart blows with a club on the head had little effect. After some severe struggles, in which a few natives were floored, the calf was at last secured to a tree by a native's waistcloth and a jungle-creeper.

While all this took place the beat became thoroughly disorganised. When the elephant had charged P. and me, our men had given way, and the herd regained its originial position at the extreme east end of the cover. After a short delay we beat it up again to the spot near the gate from which it had broken back. The elephants here formed a dense mob, and began moving round and round in a circle, hesitating to cross the newly-filled-in trench which had reached from the channel to the river, but which was now refilled to allow them to pass on into the kheddah. At length they were forced to proceed by the shots fired, and by firebrands carried through the paths in the thicket. The bright eyes of the fair watchers near the gate were at length gratified by seeing one great elephant after another pass the Rubicon. After a short pause, owing to a stand being made by some of the most refractory, the last of the herd passed in with a rush, closely followed into the inner enclosure by a frantic beater waving a firebrand. P. and I came up third, in time to save any accident from the fall of the barrier. C., who was perched on a high branch of the gate-tree, cut the rope, and amidst the cheers of all, the valuable prize of fifty-three elephants was secured to the Mysore Government.

I often think of the rapture of that moment! How warmly we "Sahibs" shook hands! How my trackers hugged my legs, and prostrated themselves to P. and B. An hour of such varied and high excitement as elephant-catching is surely worth a lifetime of uneventful routine in towns! Sore disappointment had been undergone by myself and men. Many tedious days and nights had we laboured against discouraging incidents and hardships. But all was forgotten in the success of that moment. We lost no time, however, amidst our self-gratulations, in thoroughly securing our prize. Guards were immediately posted round the kheddah, and my own tent pitched outside the gate; but the elephants gave no further trouble. The jungle inside was dense, and they kept so quiet that, large number though there was, we could scarcely see anything of them from the outside for some hours, until they began to move, when they soon trampled down much of the jungle. They never attempted to cross the trench. The most noisy animal of the herd was the little albino calf, which had broken its bonds during the second drive and made its way with the others into the kheddah, and which continued to roar lustily for its mother, and in pain at the kicks which were freely administered to it by the other elephants when it endeavoured to push its way amongst them. If the writers who have stated that female elephants suckle and tend each other's calves indiscriminately were but subjected to half the pummelling the unfortunate orphan underwent the first day and night in the enclosure, they would have but a poor opinion of indiscriminate suckling, I imagine.

On the day after the drive we commenced the work of securing the wild ones. Out of seventeen tame elephants belonging to the Mahárájah and Commissariat Department which I had in camp, ten of the most steady and courageous males and females were told off for work in the enclosure, and the rest to bring fodder for the captives. Water was supplied to them

Phototint.

H. N. Wright & Co London.

through bamboos across the trench, emptying into an improvised trough. As none of the mahouts had seen elephants caught before, except single ones, they were rather nervous about entering with but ten among so many wild ones. P. rode one pad-elephant in advance, and I another, to encourage the men. The wild ones all mobbed together when we entered, and showed great interest in our elephants. After some little time we separated a few from the herd, and a mahout slipped off under cover of our tame elephants and secured a noose round a young tusker's hind-leg. The tame elephants then dragged and pushed him backwards nearly to the gate of the kheddah, where we secured him between two trees. We afterwards found, however, that it was much easier to hobble each elephant's hind-legs, and then to let it fatigue itself by dragging them after it for some time before we finally secured it, than to proceed as we did at first.

In ten days, during which time the visitors remained, and we had a merry camp, we secured all the elephants. Calves were allowed to go loose with their mothers. The captives were led out of the enclosure by our elephants as fast as they were secured, across the river, and were picketed in the forest. Water-troughs were made for them of hollowed lengths of date-trees. These were pushed within their reach by a bamboo, and withdrawn with a rope to be again filled. Two men were appointed to each large elephant, and one to each small one. They made themselves shelters of boughs and mats just beyond the reach of their charges, and by constantly moving about them, singing to, and feeding them, many could handle their elephants in a few days. The elephants at first kicked or rushed at their captors (they very seldom struck with their trunks); but as soon as they found nothing was done to hurt them they gained confidence, and their natural timidity then made them submit without further resistance. There was a great variety of temperament observable amongst them. The small elephants, about a third grown (particularly females), gave the most trouble. The head jemadár ascribed it to their sex and time of life. "Wasn't it so with human beings?" he said. "How troublesome women were compared to men, who were always quiet!" He was a Mussulmán, and had several ladies in his establishment, so, as I was an inexperienced bachelor, I did not presume to question his dictum. One young elephant lost the sole of one foot with three toes attached after it had become loosened from her violence in continually kicking up the ground, and died soon afterwards. A mahout and I mounted a full-grown female on the sixth day after she was removed from the enclosure, without the presence of a tame elephant, which shows how soon elephants may be subjugated by kind treatment.

The ropes were changed from one leg to another every day, otherwise the wounds made by them would have been very serious. Whilst this was being done it was necessary for a tame elephant to stand near the wild one, as it became alarmed on seeing men on foot near. We were much troubled by maggots in the wounds of the new elephants. In a few hours after they were dressed they would swarm again. The animals kicked up sand and blew it upon their sores to keep off the flies; this sopped up the oil and dressings we applied, and the chafing of the ropes was much more severe when sand got under them. The mahouts used various substances, as lime, tobacco, the juice of certain plants, &c., to kill the maggots; but they were unfortunately all agents of an irritating nature, and though fatal to the maggots, were far from conducive to the healing of the wounds. I have since found camphorated turpentine a valuable remedy. On the present occasion, with a bucket of margosa oil (called also *neem* oil, most offensive in smell, and deterrent to flies) at hand, and a mop for applying it, the men managed in about a month to heal their elephants' wounds.

During the tying-up process in the kheddah several amusing incidents occurred. Active fellows would constantly cross it on foot with ropes or other things that were required, and at first they were pertinaciously chased by the wild ones. The men made for the protection of the tame elephants, and it was considered creditable to do this with as little hurry as circumstances would admit. The arena formed a centre of attraction to the on-lookers, as the theatre of a Spanish bull fight may do, and the men who showed the greatest coolness were loudly applauded. The elephants, however, soon gave up pursuing when they became accustomed to seeing people. The wild ones did not attempt to interfere with the men when they gained the shelter of the tame elephants. On one occasion a friend in the Forest Department, who was riding one of our elephants, was swept off, as well as the mahout, by an overhanging creeper, when their elephant was dragging a captive across the kheddah. Having but a confused idea of the points of the compass when they gained their legs, they rushed toward the nearest elephant for protection. It was a very fine animal, but unfortunately a wild one, which they mistook for a friend! The elephant was rather startled and did not take so prompt an advantage of their mistake as it might have done. They meanwhile made some remarkably good time towards the gate of the enclosure, which they reached in safety.

The largest tusker amongst the captives began to be troublesome a day or two after the herd was impounded. He would approach our elephants as if to measure his strength with theirs. A prod with a long spear in the head kept him off at first, but the novelty of that treatment wore away, so

I told the riders of our tuskers to set their elephants at him if he gave more trouble. Amongst them was one called Jairam, not taller than the wild elephant, and with the disadvantage of having blunt tusks; but he was of a most warlike temperament amongst his own kind, though remarkably gentle and good-tempered to his keepers and strangers. It had been necessary to restrain him hitherto from attacking the wild tusker, but I now gave his rider permission to gratify Jairam if the wild elephant required chastisement. Whilst we were at work that day in the kheddah I heard the clash of meeting tusks, and a tremendous scuffling behind me. I turned and beheld the valorous Jairam with the wild tusker's head jammed between his tusks, whilst he ran him rapidly backwards towards the trench, urged on by his delighted rider. The scuffling of even a pair of bullocks makes a considerable noise; that created by struggling elephants may be imagined. The tusker having got his head into chancery could do nothing but run back to clear himself. He fortunately managed to do this when just on the brink of the trench, and made his escape, pursued round the enclosure for some minutes by the gallant Jairam, who, amidst the plaudits of all, added to the tusker's discomfiture by administering some nasty prods behind whenever he could catch him. I sent for some money and rewarded the mahout before the spectators, as his position had been a highly dangerous one during the tilting-match. Mahouts are always pleased when their elephants deserve commendation, and Jairam had a double allowance of grain and a large bundle of sugar-cane that evening as a mark of his master's approbation. The wild tusker was thoroughly cowed by this encounter; and it was amusing to see the riders of the elephants told off to guard whilst the others were engaged in tying the captives, jockeying the late combatant round the enclosure when he did anything which afforded them an excuse for administering correction.

One great piece of excitement was the capture of a single male elephant in the elephant-lines. Unfortunately I was the only spectator amongst our party. I was just getting up at dawn one morning when a mahout rushed into my tent saying, "Wild elephant, wild elephant!" and away he went again. The word he used for elephant might mean one or any number, and imagining a herd must have come, and was threatening interference with our captives, I ran down to the elephant-lines just as I was, in my flannel sleeping-suit. I found the men unshackling three of our best females, and seizing spare ropes, and they now told me that a single male elephant was amongst the new ones picketed across the river. I jumped on to Dowlutpeary behind the mahout. We only had girth-ropes on her, no pads, and not even dark-coloured blankets to cover ourselves.

Crossing the river we saw some mahouts in a tree, who pointed to the jungle on the left, where we found the elephant, a fine tusker, but with the right-hand tusk missing. He was a young elephant, and would be a prize indeed. We all lay flat on our elephants' necks. Presently the tusker approached us, and my elephant's mahout turned Dowlutpeary round with her stern towards him, that he might be less likely to see us. He put his trunk along her back, almost to where I sat. I took the goad from the mahout, so as to job his trunk if he came too near me, but he seemed satisfied. Bheemruttee and Pounpeary, the other two elephants, now made advances to him under the direction of their mahouts, and he soon resigned himself unsuspiciously to our company.

He now led us through the lines, interviewing several of the captured elephants, whose position he did not seem to be able to understand, and then retired to a shady tree, as the sun had risen. I signed to the hiding mahouts to get the other tame elephants quietly across the river, but to keep them out of sight; and as soon as the elephant stood perfectly still, my mahout and Bheemruttee's slipped off, whilst Pounpeary's rider and I kept the three elephants close against the wild one to prevent his seeing the men. They had been at work tying his hind-legs for a considerable time, when he attempted to move and found himself hobbled! The critical knot had just been tied when he shifted his position! He was on the alert in an instant. Our elephants sheered off with great celerity, as he might have prodded them with his sharp tusk. The mahouts each threw a handful of dust into his face in derision before they retired, and now the fun began. Men came running from all directions with ropes, to the dismay of the tusker, who trumpeted shrilly and made off at an astonishing pace, scuffling along with his hind-legs, which were not very closely tied to each other, and which he could use to some extent. He rushed away through the low jungle, the whole of our elephants and men in hot pursuit. He was red with a peculiar earth with which he had been dusting himself, and formed a great contrast to the black tame elephants. Our tuskers were all slow (their pace might have been improved by an application of the Assam elephant-hunter's spiked mallet), and we did not gain on the elephant for nearly half a mile. The men on foot were running in a crowd alongside him to his intense terror. At last he turned into a thicket and halted, and we quickly surrounded him. Dowlutpeary and Bheemruttee again went in, and he was secured and marched back between four elephants in triumph. I sold him subsequently (for Government) for £175; had he had both tusks he would have brought double that sum. I gave the three mahouts who secured him £5 each—a small fortune to them—the moment the elephant was made fast, and said a few complimentary words upon their activity. I have always found that, in rewarding natives for any service, the value of a present is greatly enhanced by its being given on the spot in presence of their fellows: and the Canarese proverb, "Though the hand be full of money, there should be sweet words in the mouth," should not be forgotten; a few pleasant words go well with rupees.

The captured herd consisted of sixteen male elephants of different sizes, of which three were large tuskers—the highest was 8 feet 5 inches at the shoulder—and three *mucknas*, or tuskless males; thirty females,* full or half grown; and nine calves. Of the largest elephants nine were allotted, after careful selection, for the Mahárájah's stud, ten to the Madras Commissariat Department, nine died, chiefly young ones, and twenty-five of the least valuable were sold by public auction at Chámráj-Nuggar three months after capture, when most of them were tame enough to be ridden away. These latter brought an average price of £83, 8s. each, or an aggregate of £2085; and the total realised for the fifty-four (deducting deaths) was £3754, which, after deducting £1556, the total expenditure from the commencement of operations in 1873, left a surplus to Government of £2199. The elephants drafted into the Mahárájah's and Commissariat establishments were the most valuable animals, but were only credited to the Kheddah Department (by the orders of the Chief Commissioner) at the same price as the second and third rate animals sold for at auction—viz., £83, 8s. each. At least £100 per head more might have been added, when the surplus receipts would have been £4099.

The Chief Commissioner complimented me on the performance of my task in an order on the subject as follows: "The success that has attended Mr Sanderson's skilful and energetic arrangements in this matter is in the highest degree creditable to that gentleman, and the Chief Commissioner cordially congratulates him thereon, and will have much pleasure in bringing his excellent services in organising and carrying the same out to the favourable notice of the Government of India." The experiment having succeeded so well, the scheme was sanctioned for a further extended term, and the officiating Under-Secretary to the Government of India addressed the Chief Commissioner of Mysore as follows: "I am directed to state that his Excellency the Viceroy and Governor-General in Council is pleased to sanction the grant to Mr Sanderson of a bonus of £200, in acknowledgment of the skill and personal daring displayed by him."

Not long after this, I was deputed to Bengal on temporary duty for elephant-catching, leaving the work in Mysore in abeyance for some time, though

* This includes the female shot in the enclosure on the day of the drive.

my trackers and best men were allowed half-pay until my return. An account of the expedition which I undertook after elephants into the wilds of the Chittagong hill-tracts will be given in the next chapter. I have not caught elephants in Mysore since my return from Bengal in 1876, owing to the disastrous famine prevalent in Southern India, the cause of which, lack of rain, affected the fodder upon which we are dependent for maintaining newly-caught elephants. But everything is kept in readiness at Morlay for the continuation of operations as soon as affairs improve, and it will be strange if, with our extended experience, my Morlayites and I are not able to do even better than in 1874. The herds in Mysore are large and numerous. I calculate that there are at least 800 elephants in the jungles where catching operations can be carried on.

A few remarks on the breaking of newly-caught elephants may not inaptly close this chapter. As soon as a wild elephant is secured, two keepers are appointed to it, who commence, one on each side, to fan it with long branches, keeping out of its reach. At first the elephant is furious from fear, and attempts to strike or kick them. They keep up a wild chant, addressing their charge by any extravagant title they can think of, such as "King of a thousand elephants," "Lord of the jungles on the summit of mighty hills," &c. The elephant is well fed from the beginning, and it is a remarkable circumstance that they eat from the first. They do not seem to be able to break through their habit of constantly feeding—a wild elephant grazes or browses almost incessantly—and if an elephant refuses its food it is generally something more serious than alarm that ails it. A not uncommon idea that elephants are starved into submission is quite unfounded. In a day or two the elephant pays little attention to the men—being engaged on the choice fodder with which it is supplied when they are at work at it. They gradually approach till they can clap its sides, its legs being secured for fear of a kick, which might kill them on the spot. The elephant soon learns to take sugar-cane, fruit, &c., from the hand, and allows them to be put into its mouth, which all elephants prefer to taking food in their trunks. I found a small allowance of rice for each elephant useful, as a pinch can be wrapped up in grass, with a little sugar, and the constant feeding with such morsels forms a bond between the animal and its attendants. Girth-ropes are soon tied round its body, and under the tail as a crupper, and the men climb on to it by these. When an elephant once gives up striking at its attendants (which it generally does in a few days), it is very seldom that it subsequently does anything intended to injure them, unless terrified by haste or excitement in their movements. Nor are there any elephants which cannot be easily subjugated, whatever their size or age. The largest elephants are frequently the most easily tamed, as they are less apprehensive than younger ones.

The elephant should not be taught to kneel, nor be subjected to other unnecessary restraints, until well over the immediate effects of capture, say in four or five months. It may then be taken into the water, and the downward pressure of a pointed stick behind the shoulder near the spine will soon make it kneel to avoid the pain.

Elephants are taught to trumpet by the extremity of their trunks being tightly grasped between the hands, when they are obliged to breathe through the mouth, in doing which they make a loud sonorous sound. They are rewarded and made much of for this, and so learn to "speak," as it is termed, on an indication of what is required. In Dacca the Government elephants are particularly well trained, much more so than in the south of India. They are taught to collect their own fodder where it is plentiful, and to hand it up to the coolie on their backs, who packs it,—and many other useful services.

CHAPTER XI.

THE BENGAL ELEPHANT-CATCHING ESTABLISHMENT.

JOURNEY TO DACCA—THE GANGES—A TIGER ON BOARD A RIVER-STEAMER—APPEARANCE OF DACCA—MANUFACTURES OF MUSLIN, SILVER JEWELLERY, AND SHELL BANGLES—THE ELEPHANT DEPOT OR PEELKHÁNA—SYSTEM OF ELEPHANT-HUNTING—A TRIP UP A TRIBUTARY OF THE BRÁHMAPOOTRA—CAMP—PECULIAR ABSENCE OF ROCK IN THE GANGETIC DELTA—UNSUCCESSFUL SEARCH FOR WILD BUFFALOES—CHANGE MY GROUND—A LONG HUNT AND AN UNSUCCESSFUL FINISH—BETTER LUCK—BAG FOUR BUFFALOES—RETURN TO DACCA—DESPATCH ELEPHANTS TO CHITTAGONG—KHEDDAH PARTIES—ARRANGEMENTS FOR SUPPLIES WHILST ELEPHANT-HUNTING IN THE FORESTS—DIFFICULTIES OF THE COUNTRY—PROVISION DEPOT AT RUNGAMUTTEA—LEAVE CHITTAGONG FOR THE JUNGLES—CHOLERA IN CAMP—DESERTERS—THEIR PUNISHMENT.

I LEFT Mysore on September 1, 1875, for Bengal, and proceeded to Calcutta. Here I reported myself to the Commissary-General, and then left for Dacca, *viâ* Goalundo. Goalundo, the terminal station of the Eastern Bengal railway, is on the Ganges, 158 miles north-east of Calcutta. From Goalundo river-steamers leave for Dacca, and stations in Assam, about twice a-week.

The expectations I had formed of the beauty of the Ganges were woefully staggered. Instead of a clear rolling flood, I beheld an extremely muddy tidal river. Though Goalundo is, I believe, 140 miles from the sea, the tides reach far above it, and keep the river brackish, and in a constant state of muddy agitation. The Ganges at Goalundo appeared to be about two miles wide, and as the day was stormy there was quite a high sea running on its exposed surface.

The trip to Dacca from Goalundo occupies two days; the boats anchor at sunset, as the navigation of the river is difficult. In addition to carrying passengers, and a large number of coolies to the tea-estates in Assam and elsewhere, each steamer tows two huge goods-flats. Hides, jute, and tea are the chief cargoes from the interior to Goalundo. The flats are lashed on each side of the steamer, and the trio bears a ridiculous resemblance to a small hen with two large chickens under her wings. This arrangement of the flats is necessary, as in rounding corners, and steering between sandbanks, they would get aground if towed astern, and when going with the tide they would overrun the steamer when she slackened speed. The steamers are paddle-boats—I believe of 180 horse-power each. The current of the Ganges frequently runs at eight miles an hour, and none but powerful boats could make head against it. The machinery of the steamers is exposed, and seemed to be a never-ending source of wonder to the coolie emigrants on board.

Continuous rain had flooded the country contiguous to the river, and boats were to be seen moving under full sail in what appeared to be verdant meadows—in reality rice-fields, where the crop showed above water. Large numbers of the Gangetic porpoise (*Platanista gangetica*), a fish between six and seven feet long, disported themselves not far from the steamer. I tried several shots at them with my express, but though they appeared to roll in a deliberate manner, it was difficult to fire with accuracy, and quickly enough, to kill them. I hit one or two crocodiles when we came within reach of them.

The captain of the boat, who had spent many years afloat on the Ganges, told me of an instance of a tiger boarding his steamer when at anchor during the night. She was lying half a mile from shore, and towards morning some natives were engaged with a boat in laying out an anchor astern to prevent her swinging round with the tide. When they pulled back, a rope was thrown to them by a man on deck, and they brought their boat in close to the steamer's rudder. The deck of the river-steamers is only three feet above the water, and the rudder projects several feet from the sternpost for power in steering. A tiger, about two-thirds grown, that must, whilst swimming the river, have mistaken the anchored boat for an island whereon to rest, had taken up its position on the rudder. It was too dark for the men to see it, and in its fright at their coming so near, the creature sprang at the man in the bow of the boat, and from him at the lascar on board the steamer. It did them little injury, and took refuge somewhere on deck. The lascars awoke Captain H.; but as there were a great many coolies on board, and it was impossible to shoot without risk of killing somebody, he decided to wait till daylight. As soon as it was sufficiently light a search was instituted, and the tiger was found in the coal-bunker. He knocked over two or three inquisitive natives, ran along the deck, and jumped overboard in front of the paddle-wheel. As he did so Captain H. broke one of his hind-legs with a ball. The wounded beast then clambered into the wheel, but just as Captain H. was about to finish him he fell into the water, and was seen no more; the rapid current carried him under, and out of reach in a few moments. Somewhat similar instances have been known of tigers getting into native boats. I imagine such must have happened much as in this case, through the tigers seeking a rest during a long swim.

The approach to Dacca by water is striking. Some of the buildings of Mohammedan type which line the river in the native part of the town appear to be of considerable antiquity. At the ends of the streets which debouch on to the river clusters of boats are anchored, and an active trade goes on in fish, vegetables, grass for cattle, &c., all brought from the villages up or down the river. In the stream are anchored two or three Government steamers, belonging to the European officials for use on their tours of duty. At the southern end of the town are the Europeans' residences. They stand in green compounds, well back from the river, which is here bordered by a wide esplanade, the usual lounge of the evening. Here is situated the palatial residence of the Nawáb Abdool Gunni, C.S.I., whose liberality and benevolence are widely known around Dacca. The Europeans in Dacca are beholden to him for warm support in all their amusements—hunting, racing, balls, music, croquet-parties, &c.

Though Dacca is about a hundred miles from the sea, the country is so low-lying that the tides run up the river far above it. Its height above sea-level is only about ten feet.* For this reason the Europeans' houses are generally two-storeyed, which is unusual in India, and the upper one is mostly used, as the lower is frequently damp. Still Dacca is one of the most healthy stations in Bengal. This is somewhat strange, as the exhalations from the river about October and November cannot but be injurious to health. The stagnant water which has up to this time inundated the country adjacent to the river for a great distance above Dacca, finds its way into the main stream when it shrinks, and brings with it enormous quantities of decayed vegetable matter, floating islands of grass, drift-wood, &c. One day I saw a dead panther, floating so high out of the water that it was evident its decease had taken place some days before, pass my bungalow. I sent a boat after it, but the skin was useless, the hair coming off when handled. The animal had perhaps been drowned, as it bore no marks of having been shot. The stench from the river was sometimes so great as to awaken me during the night, and as the weather was too hot to admit of

* It was in the country lying between Dacca and the sea that the great cyclone wave occasioned such terrible loss of life on November 1, 1876. It is only its distance from the sea that renders Dacca safe from being similarly overtaken.

windows being closed it was rather distressing. When the river had run itself down to summer level it became almost stagnant, except for the flow of the tides. I well remember this from a dead pariah-dog making trips up and down with the flow and ebb for a day or two. Each time it passed there was a visible change for the worse. It looked larger than when last seen, and floated more jauntily high out of the water; nor was its colour improved by the loss of patches of hair. At last, after one or two unsuccessful attempts, I sent a bullet through it at a hundred and fifty yards, and put a stop to its ghastly trips.

Dacca is a populous native city (70,000 inhabitants) and a large and favourite civil station. A wing of a native regiment is quartered here. It was a place of great importance under the Moguls, but its former glory has in a great measure departed. Dacca used to be famous for its ship-building, and its fleet of eight hundred armed vessels, employed in guarding the southern coast against the ravages of Arracanese pirates. It was widely celebrated for its manufactures, amongst which muslin of incomparable fineness was one of the most noted. This is now difficult to procure. The best is only made to order, and costs about £1 per yard. A piece I had of twenty yards, and average width, weighed, if I remember rightly, six rupees (twelve shillings in silver). The native silver filigree work, in European designs, is superior to anything of its kind of English or Continental manufacture. A large trade is carried on in armlets for native women, cut from shells, brought by the native trading-boats to Dacca from the coast of Ceylon and other places. The cutting is effected with a huge semi-circular knife like a cheese-cutter, worked with both hands. A small circular-saw would do as much in an hour as twenty men in a day.

Dacca is the headquarters of the Bengal Kheddah, or Elephant-Catching Establishment. Its situation on a branch of the Ganges from which large supplies of water-grasses, suitable for fodder, are obtainable, and within two hundred miles of the forests of Chittagong, Sylhet, and Cachár, which abound with wild elephants, is perhaps the best for the purpose in Bengal. The Peelkhána, or elephant depot, is situated just outside the town, and covers an area approaching one quarter-mile square. It consists of an intrenched quadrangular piece of ground in which the elephants' pickets are arranged in long rows. At each picket is a masonry flooring, with a post at the head and foot, to which the animals are secured. The flooring is necessary to prevent them kicking up the earth. Along one side of the quadrangle is a shed several hundred feet long, in which the elephants can be kept during the heat of the day. There is also a hospital for sick elephants; houses for gear and stores; a native doctor's room for treating the attendants; a shelter for howdahs and ropes, &c. The depot is situated close to the river for convenience of bathing and watering the elephants, and also that fodder may be brought by boats.

Most of the elephants required for the service of the Bengal Government are furnished by the Dacca establishment. It is under a European officer, and a yearly exodus of all hands is made to hunt in the forest-tracts of Chittagong and Assam. The establishment contains fifty trained elephants or *koonkies,*—derived from the Hindoostan word *kumuk*, aid. These are all females. In addition to the permanent stud of koonkies, there is always a large number of new elephants undergoing training. When fit for service these are allotted to military stations as required. The hunting-party usually leaves Dacca about the beginning of December, and after working for three or four months (this season is selected as little rain falls), returns with the captured elephants about May. The training of these occupies the establishment till November, when the animals are despatched to Commissariat stations, leaving the establishment free to hunt again. The annual captures in Dacca for seven years prior to 1875-76 averaged fifty-nine elephants. I found from old records that from 1836 to 1839 inclusive, sixty-nine elephants were the annual average.

In the chapter upon the method of capturing elephants, I have mentioned the composition of a Bengal hunting-party. The expense of maintaining the full number of men of which it consists the whole year round would be so great that only the jemadárs and chief men are permanently employed, the coolies required being enlisted for two or three months annually, as required. This system of hunting has been pursued by the Bengal Government, and probably by former native governments, so long, that the people required for kheddahs are easily collected at Chittagong and other centres. Though many die at times from the effects of these jungle-trips, and some are killed almost every year by elephants, there are always plenty of volunteers for the work.

The permanent Superintendent of the Dacca Kheddahs having obtained furlough to England, I accepted the acting appointment for eighteen months, but I only held it for nine, as I was permitted to return to Mysore at the end of that period to continue kheddah operations there. And though I was under orders to return to Dacca for the last three months of my officiating term, to make another expedition into Chittagong in January 1877, the return of the permanent Superintendent before the expiration of his leave rendered my doing so unnecessary.

I took charge of the depot from Major C. in September, 1875. As we sat at a table under a shady tree in the quadrangle, with a roll of the elephants before us, they filed past, and all made their salutations. Those that had been caught but a few months were not all quite *au fait* at salaaming. Several baby elephants accompanied their mammas; others, a little older, were ridden by little boys, the mahouts' sons, who joined in the march past and seemed proud of their duty. There were 159 in all.

As there was little to do before the hunting season—December—beyond my daily inspection of the Peelkhána, and the continued training of the elephants, I decided to make an expedition up one of the tributaries of the Ganges to a place called Berramtollie, about forty miles above Dacca, where I heard there were a few wild buffaloes. These animals are not found in Southern India, so I was anxious to add them to my game list, and also to see the localities from which fodder was drawn for the elephants, the amount of which arriving at the Peelkhána astonished me, after the difficulty experienced in the matter of fodder in Southern India. I therefore despatched twenty-five elephants by land, to give them a little outing as well as myself, as it always does elephants good, and I followed by boat next day. There was a large choice of boats at the Dacca landing. My servant chose one about fifty feet long, having a comfortable cabin and a small room for boxes on deck. It only drew a foot and a half of water, and was propelled by eight rowers, with a steersman. The forward half of the deck was occupied by the rowers, the latter half by the cabin. Upon the roof of this the steersman sat, guiding the boat with a large oar lashed to the sternpost. In the forward-deck was a small square pit, which answered the purpose of a galley.

I left Dacca at six o'clock in the morning. The boat was narrow and sailed well, but only before the wind, as it had no keel. We soon turned into a tributary that led to a place called Kásimpoor, and here we had to take down the large sail as the breeze was against us. The main stream was about seventy yards wide, with a considerable current. The flood-banks of the river were not less than a mile apart, and were lined with groves of trees, palms, and jungle, with villages and fishermen's huts appearing here and there. Between these banks was one unbroken sea of the richest green imaginable, composed of rice-fields and extensive patches of broad-leaved rushes, the elephants' fodder. But little open water was to be seen except the main stream. When the river should run down in a couple of months, and confine itself within the main channel, the rice-crops now standing in three feet of water would be reaped. Throughout the day the boat was kept in dead water over the flooded land, and as it was not deep the men found poling more effective than rowing. I saw a number of boats loading with grass for the Peelkhána, and could now understand where the fodder came from. This supply only lasts, however, from May till November, or during the time of the inundations. When the water retires there is an end of the luxuriant growth.

In the afternoon we turned into a smaller tributary, and after following it for some miles we reached camp under a splendid banian-tree, so wide-spreading that the twenty-five elephants and their attendants found plenty of room under it without encroaching upon my camp. As a rule, trees of the order *Ficus* are not so fine in Eastern Bengal as in the south of India. This may be occasioned by the presence of water within a few feet of the surface, which prevents their roots striking sufficiently deep. This tree, however, was an exception amongst its fellows. In addition to the inferiority in the size of the trees, the massive granite temples and other buildings common in Mysore and other parts of Southern India are wanting in Eastern Bengal. There is an extraordinary absence of stone throughout the delta of the Ganges. There is not a single rock, not a pebble, not even a nodule of gravel, for a distance of four hundred miles from the sea. The most permanent building material is but indifferent brick; hence, nothing can lay claim to the antiquity which makes many remains in Mysore and other provinces so deeply interesting. For anything there is to be seen to the contrary, this part of the country might have been brought under cultivation within the last ten years.

After breakfast next day I took all the elephants, and went through a variety of grass and bush-jungle, occasional swamps, &c., in the hopes of finding buffaloes, but I felt very helpless through not having had any experience in the sport. I saw a few hog-deer (*Axis porcinus*) an animal not found in Southern India, but no buffalo. At last we found some marks, and I tried to track a solitary bull, but lost the trail in a mile. Oh for some of my Mysore Oopliga or Kurraba trackers! The country was wet, and tracking comparatively easy, and I saw no jungle that buffaloes could not be followed into—even on foot; but none of my men were adepts. At last we met some charcoal-burners who seemed likely fellows, and who told us the buffaloes grazed in the rice-fields at night, but retreated to jungles near a place called Rámpoor during the day. To Rámpoor we started accordingly, and on the way picked up a native (the villagers here were not unlike the Mysore Kurrabas and Shōlagas), and under his guidance the elephants tramped some miles of likely jungle, but without our seeing anything. Our guide, however, promised better things on the morrow, so we returned to camp. This kind of work is most beneficial to elephants, as they graze the whole of the time, finding a variety of fodder, and the exercise and change please them.

The return path to Berramtollie led through a sea of green rice-fields; occasionally skirted oases in the shape of mounds and rounded hills, all closely studded with beautifully straight, tall trees, with large leaves much like the cinchona; whilst several large sails moving steadily along up the nullahs intersecting the rice-fields had the appearance in the distance of immense white birds. When I got to camp I found an observant peon had marked a pea-fowl to roost in a tree not far away. It was a difficult light to shoot in, but I managed to bring it down with my rifle at sixty yards; and as I had fowls enough for my own consumption, I made the peon a present of it, with an exhortation to continued vigilance in such matters.

Next day all the elephants started for Rámpoor, and after breakfast I followed in my boat up a nullah, or natural canal, which was about twenty yards wide, four deep, and very prettily shaded with trees. The water was almost dead. We reached Rámpoor in the afternoon, and I went out with my friend of yesterday to examine the country. We saw new tracks of buffalo, but nothing else. Next day we again went through plenty of promising jungle, but though my conductor was eager to show sport, he was not an adept at the only method to attain his object with certainty—steady tracking. I therefore returned to breakfast, cogitating upon what to do next, when, just as I had finished, a man came in with news of some buffaloes having grazed in his rice-fields during the night. I scarcely felt inclined to go out again on such information, as the day was hot, and the villagers apparently incapable of finding the animals, but when the man was brought forward I saw at once that he was the right person at last. There was no mistaking him. The experienced sportsman can tell the genuine hunter at a glance. Whatever their race or colour there is a free-masonry amongst sportsmen, and though I could not speak a word of my new friend's language, I could have shaken hands with him at once. His appearance might not have been prepossessing to some. He had a very rough matted head of hair, and a string and a rag round his loins. But he was quiet and composed in his manner, though he threw the timid glances of his class, so familiar to me, around him; and his replies, through an interpreter, confirmed the confidence I felt in him. I at once ordered out five elephants, and gave my guide some tobacco, which delighted him. I regarded him as a brother come in the moment of my sore need.

Sending the elephants to a point two miles down the nullah, I was rowed to the same place in my floating house. I had no tent, but lived in the cabin of my boat. Mounting Tárá Ránee, I followed the new tracker and another man to their fields, where several buffaloes had grazed. There was a scarecrow in one corner, which presented a rather ridiculous appearance, as the buffaloes had grazed the crop quite short, except under its outstretched arm and about its feet. It was thus left guarding, with an appearance of great solicitude, about fifty stalks! The men carried the tracks from here in good style through jungle composed of bushes much like hazel, interspersed with fine trees; beds of a peculiar broad-leaved plant; and occasional swamps and long grass. The buffaloes—apparently eight or ten—had wallowed in a pool, and for some distance beyond the grass and bushes were whitewashed with mud from their brushing against them. When we had gone about three miles we found a pool only recently disturbed, and I dismounted, as from sundry signs similar to those I well knew in bison-shooting—such as the animals loitering and wandering, and more particularly (as the compass attached to my watch-chain informed me) from their having turned back towards the fields they had grazed, doubtless with the intention of visiting them again that night—I imagined they were not far ahead.

We were entering some thick cover when up they jumped, close on our right, and crashed away. I did not catch sight of them, but ran along the path they made through the grass and bushes. One—the bull no doubt—kept lagging behind, and breaking away again and again just before me; but the undergrowth was very rank, and though I ran nearly a mile I never saw him. I waited for my followers, and we resorted to tracking again. The men kept the trail very well for two miles, when we came to a serious check, caused by the buffaloes having met some charcoal-burners, at sight of whom they had scattered in all directions; and as the ground was not sufficiently soft to render the old bull's tracks very discernible from the others, whilst the locality had been recently much trampled, the finding the newest tracks, and picking out the bull's amongst them, occupied time. The men made many gestures signifying that the buffaloes must be far ahead, that we should not catch them up before sundown, and pointing to the position of the sun about seven in the morning, with much nodding and grunting in an assuring manner, by which I understood them to say we should make certain work of them in the morning. But I have so constantly found that when matters look least promising success is often close at hand, that I would not hear of giving in, and encouraged them to persevere by the well-understood pantomime of tapping the palm of the upturned left hand with the fingers of the right held in a suggestive manner together, as if passing coin into the said upturned hand. They grinned in an appreciative manner at this, and girt up their loins afresh, and by making a long cast we hit off the trail again. I saw my only chance was to ride the elephant close behind the trackers, as I could not see to shoot on foot in the grass. We expected a long hunt before we came up with our game this time, if we did so at all that day. I was looking round, admiring the jungle, when crash, crash, went the jungle close ahead, as the bull started suddenly and lumbered off! He had got our wind! Another few yards and I should have viewed him! I told the mahout to push on the elephant with all speed, the trackers leading at a run through the still bending bushes, when the wide-spreading, massive horns, and huge head of the bull appeared suddenly before me, staring at the elephant, and only thirty-five yards away! He looked as cool as if he had just risen from his lair. I clutched the driver wildly by his shaven crown to stop the elephant, and got a fair shot at the bull's chest with my 8-bore and twelve drams, but I could not see to put in the left for the smoke, and away the bull went. Well, he can't go far with that! and I heartily congratulated myself on getting so fine a specimen of a buffalo. I now dismounted, and we followed him. There was not much blood, but that often happens with thick-skinned animals. The internal bleeding would be the more severe, and I pressed on, with the trackers behind me now, as I thought our game might prove vicious if still on his legs when we came up with him. The blood, however, ceased shortly, and the trackers had to lead again. This was strange. The brute had also jumped a deep and somewhat wide grip—a last effort, no doubt. But no; he has gone on at a gallop on the other side! The end of the hunt was that we never saw the bull again, though we tracked him till dark. Had he been fairly hit with such a weapon as the 8-bore he could not have gone far. The ball must have made a flesh-wound of little importance, hitting him to one side in the shoulder instead of in the chest; and I daresay the old fellow is alive and well to this day, as I hope, seeing that I cannot have him!

We had a long tramp back to the boat through the dark and thick jungle. Apart from the loss of the bull, I felt it unfortunate that I should have made such a *début* amongst my new people. I feared the trackers' confidence in my shooting would be shaken; whilst the fifty hungry mahouts and grass-cutters in camp would hear of our ill-success with real grief, as they had been calculating upon steaks for supper. My gun-bearer, Jaffer, who had accompanied me from Mysore, had, I knew, recounted with his own additions his master's deeds in the shooting line there, and I felt that greater things had been expected of me. Well, it often happens that the sportsman gets animals to which he is but ill entitled, as far as having worked for them is concerned, and he must therefore set off these pieces of good luck against his unfortunate days.

Early in the morning we started, with three elephants following, to examine the rice-fields along the nullah. We found the track of two buffaloes quite close to the elephants' pickets, and after carrying them for two miles through undulating, grass-covered hills, and swampy bottoms, I saw a buffalo standing broadside on in a pool amongst long grass at the foot of a slope we were descending. I was riding a very fine elephant, Tárá Ránee—Queen of the Stars—at the time. The buffalo had not seen us, so, telling the mahout to keep the elephant steady, I sent a ball through its shoulders from the 8-bore, which dropped it on the spot. Immediately there was a great rushing about in the grass, and the herd—of which the two we had followed were members—consisting of about a dozen individuals, came trotting towards us, all covered with wet mud that glistened in the early sun, with their noses poked stupidly in front of them, not seeing where the shot came from, and undecided whither to flee. They nearly ran over the trackers who had not seen the buffalo when I did for the long grass, and who had gone several yards in front of my elephant before I fired. On seeing the elephants the buffaloes broke into a wild gallop, passing us to right and left, and within a few yards' distance. I bowled over one with my second barrel before they got level with us, and seizing my double 4-bore, I killed a third, and wounded a fourth behind us. I knew this one could not go far; and when we had examined the fallen ones, the trackers and I followed and came upon it, a large cow, lying dead. It was unfortunate that only one of these—the first one fired at—was a bull, and he was but an insignificant one; but the last-recovered cow had a splendid pair of horns, which, though less massive, are longer, and have a finer sweep and greater symmetry, than any bull's I have seen. They measure 9 feet 1 inch from tip to tip, outside curve, and across forehead.

The day was getting hot by this time and I returned to camp. On hearing of our success a number of men immediately started to cut up two of the buffaloes which had had their throats cut before they were dead, without which Mussulmáns will not eat any animal's flesh. On their return, with elephants carrying the meat of the two huge creatures, the camp was shortly festooned with meat cut into long thin strips for drying in the sun. The surplus was to be taken to Dacca for the men's wives and little ones. I told off two men to preserve a quantity of meat for the mahouts who had been left at Dacca, and though it would only give them a taste each, Indian sporting dependants all like to have a share in the products of their master's hunt.

I spent two or three days in this neighbourhood, not so much for shooting as to see the country. I took the whole of the elephants out for a few hours every day, marching in an extended line as if beating, but moving slowly so that they might feed. They were a very fine lot, and their men seemed willing and active fellows, and though I could not talk to them as they spoke Bengalee, we got along capitally by signs, and the aid of an interpreter when necessary. The latter was a rather complicated way of conversing, as I had to speak to Jaffer in Canarese (not his language more than my own), who translated into Hindoostánee to a Bengalee who understood Hindoostánee. This was similar to an Englishman's telling a German in French what he would communicate to an Italian who understood German!

After my return to Dacca I made an interesting trip into the Garrow hills in Assam, of which I shall give a short account further on. In November I despatched 79 elephants of previous years' capture to Barrackpoor, they being sufficiently trained for service; and I then started 80 elephants to Chittagong, 154 miles by land, to proceed by slow stages, with a view to commencing the catching-operations of the season. I followed by sea from Calcutta on December 13th, but I had previously to recall 30 of my 80 elephants to assist in driving the covers near Goalundo, where his Royal Highness the Prince of Wales and party intended to make their *début* in pig-sticking. Arrived at Chittagong, I found that the two jemadárs whom I had sent a month beforehand to collect two kheddah parties had made all preliminary arrangements, and it only remained for me to advance the men two months' pay, and to make arrangements for the provisions we should require when beyond the reach of civilisation.

Chittagong is a district situated in the north-east corner of the Bay of Bengal. It is divided into two tracts, of widely differing character,—viz., the coast district (2700 square miles), well cultivated and populated, and producing a large surplus stock of rice for exportation; and the hill-tracts (6800 square miles), inhabited by but a few rude tribes, and clothed with dense jungle. From the latter tract immense supplies of wood for boat-building and household purposes are drawn by the inhabitants of the coast district, by way of the Kurnafoolie river, which forms a highroad into the hills, as it is navigable almost to its source, as are also its tributaries. In these hills wild elephants abound, and the locality has been one of the chief hunting-grounds for the supply of these animals to Government for about a hundred years, and probably long before that to former native Governments. The professional elephant-catchers are all Chittagong men, and their skill in their profession is unrivalled. The hillmen never engage in the work.

I had decided, upon the advice of the most experienced men, to work near the head-waters of the Chengree (*vide* map) and Myanee rivers, but I found it most difficult to obtain any exact account of the distances and various obstacles to be encountered in so wild a country. The head-men had all been there before, but no European, as the former Kheddah Superintendents seldom went beyond Rungamuttea, the most advanced civilised outpost in that direction. As to the maps available, the chief points and general lie of the country only had been settled by triangulation. Regarding details it was stated, "Nearly all the hills in this district are covered with impenetrable jungle; the subordinate streams and hill-features have therefore been sketched."

I was determined to explore the country in person, as the chance of being first into a new field is one seldom to be had nowadays, and is certainly not to be neglected; and the inability to obtain any exact account of what was before us added considerably to the pleasure of the expedition from my point of view. All accounts agreed as to the Chengree and Myanee being accessible to small dug-out boats nearly to their sources, some two hundred miles from Chittagong following their courses; and on this means of transit I arranged our provisioning. The boats, or canoes, used for conveying the rice, salt fish, &c., required for the people, were procured in Chittagong, and carried about seven hundredweights each. They drew eight inches of water when loaded, and could be dragged over shallows and fallen trees conveniently. I engaged sixty, with three men to each, at 24 rupees each boat and crew *per mensem*, and free rations to the men. This flotilla proceeded up the Kurnafoolie to Rungamuttea, the frontier police station. I visited this place, making a pleasant trip in a small paddle-steamer obligingly placed at my disposal by the Commissioner of Chittagong, and arranged a depot there, and had it stocked with two months' provisions. I placed this under a European named Wilson, a clerk in my office. He remained at the Rungamuttea depot during our trip into the wilds beyond, and carried out the very arduous duty of keeping us duly provisioned, and maintaining communications, most satisfactorily. The amount of provisions required for the two kheddah parties and tame elephants' attendants was a little over seventeen hundredweights *per diem*, so that the commissariat arrangements required no little attention and forethought.

The two jemadárs did not recommend that the hunting parties should proceed to their ground by the same course as the stores—the rivers—but proposed that we should march across the hills from Chittagong until we struck the Chengree, where one party might await the arrival of boats from Rungamuttea, and work in the valley of the Chengree, whilst the other crossed the watershed into the Myanee valley, to be similarly supplied by boats up the Myanee. Having ascertained that a place called Rájamáka-

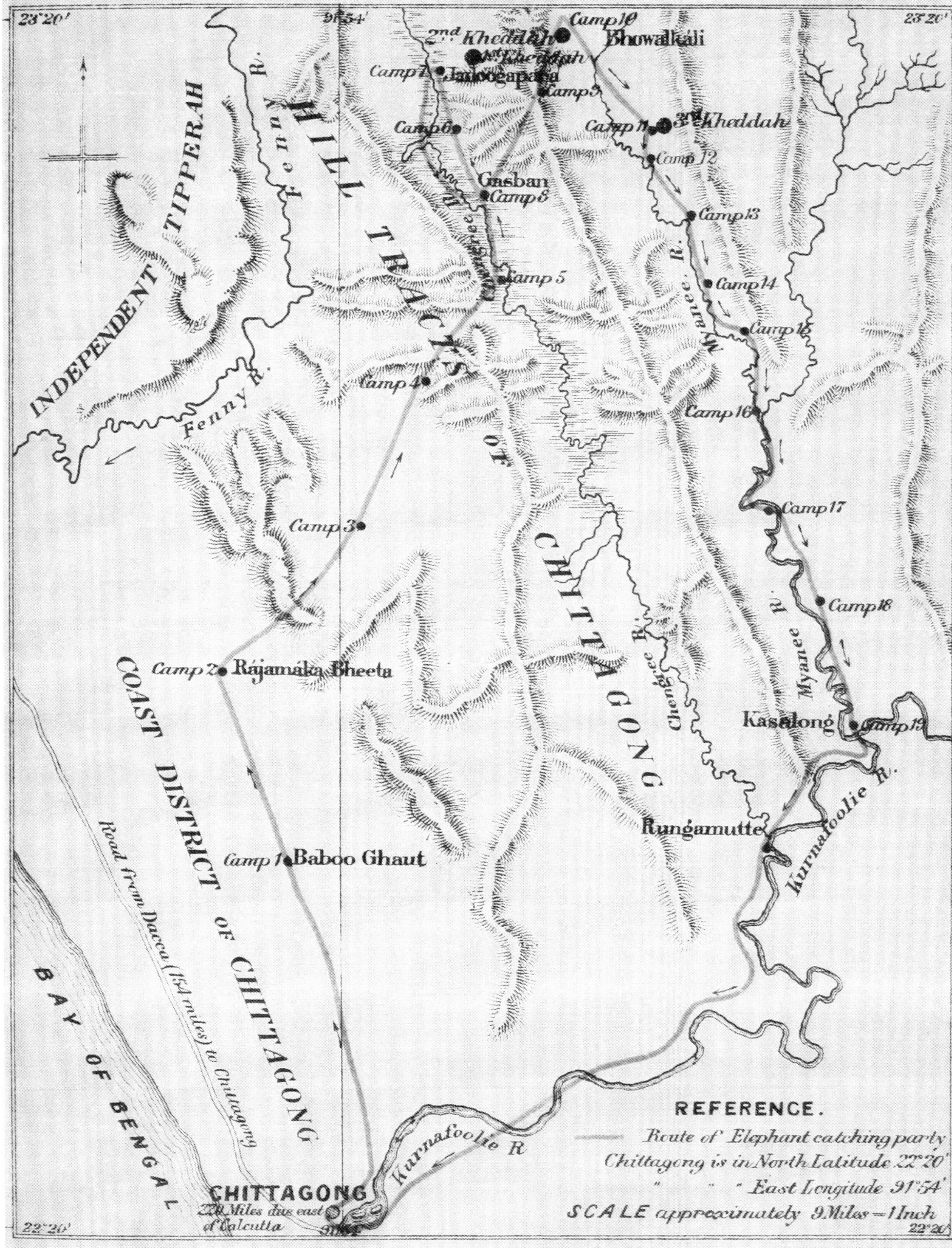

23°20'
91°54'
23°20'
Camp 10
Bhowalkali
2nd Kheddah
1st Kheddah
Camp 7
Jaloogapara
Camp 9
Camp 11
3rd Kheddah
Camp 6
Camp 12
Gasban
Camp 8
Camp 13
INDEPENDENT TIPPERAH
Fenny R.
HILL TRACTS OF CHITTAGONG
Camp 5
Camp 14
Myanee R.
Camp 15
Camp 4
Fenny R.
Camp 16
Camp 17
Camp 3
Camp 18
Chengree R.
Myanee R.
Camp 2
Rájamáka Bheeta
Kasalong
Camp 19
COAST DISTRICT OF CHITTAGONG
Kurnafoolie R.
Rungamutte
Camp 1
Baboo Ghaut
Road from Dacca (154 miles) to Chittagong
BAY OF BENGAL
REFERENCE.
Route of Elephant catching party
Chittagong is in North Latitude 22°20'
" " " East Longitude 91°54'
SCALE approximately 9 Miles = 1 Inch
Kurnafoolie R
CHITTAGONG
220 Miles due east of Calcutta
22°20'
91°54'
22°20'

Bheeta—camp No. 2 on map—would be a convenient point from which to make a start, it being the last civilised place in the coast district, I ordered the kheddah parties to be assembled there by the 27th December.

I left Chittagong, a pleasant station notwithstanding all that is said of its unhealthiness, and its sociable little community of Government officials and tea-planters, on 26th December 1875, and reached Báboo Ghât by evening, doing the chief part of the journey in the small steamer before-mentioned, which took me up a tributary of the Kurnafoolie, not marked on map. Elephants met me at the furthest point the steamer, which only drew two feet, could reach, and took me, my servants, and effects, to camp. I found that cholera had unfortunately appeared amongst the attendants of our elephants. Sergeant Carter—the only European who accompanied me on this expedition, and who had marched with the elephants from Dacca, whilst I went by sea—reported that one man out of three attacked had died, and that one of the others was in a critical condition. This intelligence marred in no small degree the pleasure of our start, as I foresaw that if cholera—which was showing itself here and there in the villages in the coast district—broke out in our party, the whole undertaking might end in failure. I spoke to the native doctor attached to the establishment regarding due care in treating and segregating the suffering men, and ordered Sergeant Carter to march at three in the morning, so as to reach the next camp before the sun was hot, which was advisable for both men and elephants. I followed with my own camp at 6 A.M., and after marching through the level, highly-cultivated country that constitutes the coast district, we reached camp No. 2, seventeen miles, about 11 A.M.

Rájamáka-Bheeta is a small village on the border of the immense jungle which extends without a break from Chittagong for hundreds of miles north and east through Tipperah and the Looshai country, and south through Arracan and Burmah. I found the two kheddah parties mustered here as agreed upon, each 370 strong. The rest of the day of arrival, and next day, I was occupied in superintending the taking of the names and places of residence of the coolies, for identification in case they deserted, which the jemadárs informed me they frequently did. It was necessary to give them two months' pay in hand to leave with their families, and I learned it had become a practice with many, as no one but the jemadárs had accompanied them into the jungles hitherto, to remain only until one capture of elephants had been effected, and then to desert. This was an easy method of making from fifteen to twenty rupees, as they were fed the while, and with luck some elephants might be caught almost at the outset. I had the men arranged in lines, and whilst inspecting them a crier preceded me, proclaiming at the top of his voice, and occasionally beating a tom-tom to insure attention, the awful pains and penalties to which deserters would render themselves liable. This kept the men in check to a great extent, though when we had been out about fifteen days, ten bold spirits ran away. I determined my words should not be unfulfilled, and immediately promised ten active mahouts five rupees each if they succeeded in catching any of them. The runaways had a start of twelve hours, and were not likely to loiter by the way, but the pursuers followed without rest for a day and night, traversing the dense jungles with torches, and succeeded in catching eight of them just at the outskirts of the jungle. These they brought back pinioned, and with leading-ropes round their necks. I held an imposing torch-light court-martial upon them when they arrived. The jemadár strongly urged the advisability of hanging them there and then, and cast his eye about for a likely overhanging bough to which to suspend them "in a row" as he said. I believe they really thought I should act upon his recommendation; but after much consideration I allowed mercy to prevail, and gave them a severe punishment instead of the capital one! This much reduced the inclination to make off, and the few others who did decamp before the end of the expedition were brought from their distant homes by the police to Rungamuttea, where the political officer gave them two months' imprisonment with hard labour for stealing the Government provisions which they had taken with them, and which formed the only ground upon which they could be criminally convicted. Almost all the kheddah men were rascals of various degrees, as it was only this class who cared to take such dangerous and irregular employment; and though I thought none the worse of them for their antecedents, as they did their duty manfully, strict discipline was necessary to prevent their evil proclivities from interfering with the success of our work.

CHAPTER XII.

AN ELEPHANT-CATCHING EXPEDITION INTO THE HILL-TRACTS OF CHITTAGONG.

ENTER THE HILL-TRACTS—ENDURANCE OF THE MEN—MY CAMP ARRANGEMENTS—ORDER OF MARCH—FIRST NIGHT'S ENCAMPMENT—PRECAUTIONS AGAINST MALARIA—SECOND DAY'S MARCH—HILLMEN—ENCAMPMENT—ELEPHANTS COLLECTING FODDER—COOKERY IN THE JUNGLES—THIRD DAY'S MARCH—A DIFFICULT CLIMB—QUICKSAND—AN ELEPHANT ROLLS DOWN A HILLSIDE—CHARMED DUCKS—A FALSE ALARM—REACH THE CHENGREE RIVER—NEW YEAR'S EVE—JUNGLES—CANES—REMARKABLE CREEPERS—NOVEL FISHING—SUDDAR ALI SURROUNDS A HERD OF ELEPHANTS—KOOKIES—THEIR CRUELTIES—MARCH TO JÁDOOGAPÁRA—THE STOCKADE—THE DRIVE—CAPTURE THIRTY-SEVEN ELEPHANTS—A FEMALE ALMOST TAKES ME IN REAR.

ON the 29th December I stood at the edge of the jungle at Rájamáka-Bheeta, whilst the men entered in single file, each salaaming and crying Allah! Allah! by way of invoking luck. The matchlock-men led the van, firing *feux-de-joie* with a few rounds I had given them from the magazine to celebrate the commencement of our enterprise. Each coolie carried a springy bamboo lath across his shoulder, with a basket at each end, through which the bamboo passed. These baskets contained fifteen days' provisions, as it was uncertain when we might meet the provision-boats coming up the Chengree; and should we fall in with elephants on our way a halt would be necessary. Each man's rations weighed 33 lb., and as the head-men and matchlock-men made their gangs carry their rations as well as their own, and each had a few cooking-pots, the weights were over 40 lb. per man. With this they marched for several days from morning till night, in hilly country, often in the beds of streams, and through bamboo-cover and long grass, under a broiling sun. The men were generally of miserable *physique* according to our notions, but they had the patience and endurance of mules. On the third day of marching I saw several of them with raws on their shoulders, caused by the pressure of the bamboo; still they kept on with wonderful pertinacity, partly induced by the promise of extra tobacco and the prospect of a speedy return to their homes if elephants were captured soon, but chiefly by the *esprit de corps* of the two parties, whose head jemadárs, Gool Budden and Suddar Ali, each strove to outmarch the other, and to get to the hunting-grounds first. In this Suddar Ali, who was a younger man than Gool Budden, succeeded, as he left his party under a lieutenant, and with a few of his men outstripped the main body by doing nearly forty miles a-day. He was rewarded by finding a herd of elephants in the valley of the Chengree before we arrived; and when the men came up on 2d January, after five days' marching, he at once surrounded it; whilst Gool Budden had to march over the Kálamoin range—a terrible job—into the Myanee valley, and did not find elephants till the 7th.

When I started for these unexplored wilds I never expected to escape fever, and possibly a necessity for a speedy return to open country; consequently I cannot speak too thankfully of the health our whole party enjoyed. We fortunately left cholera behind us; and though towards the end of the two months a few of the men were down with dysentery, we only lost four during the trip, including one killed by an elephant. I had provided myself with every comfort and convenience, and amongst other things I had reason to congratulate myself on possessing before the trip was over was a tin of 100 lb. of ship's biscuits and a keg of salt Bengal humps and tongues. I had an ample supply of tin provisions, plenty of books, and comfortable camp-fittings. I also had tents and everything as comfortable as possible for my servants—Madrassees—who had accompanied me from Mysore, and who comprised a head-servant, a cook, a table-servant, and four Bengalee peons. My trusty henchman Jaffer—my factotum for many years—of course accompanied me, in charge of my shooting and fishing gear. I had a most energetic lieutenant in Sergeant Carter, who was blessed with the constitution of an elephant. He was the only European besides myself in the hunting party, Wilson remaining at the Rungamuttea depot after making one trip up the Chengree with the first instalment of provisions. No amount of work ever distressed Sergeant Carter; and after the longest days he used to sit up with a very modest allowance of Commissariat rum and an ample supply of tobacco, far into the night. In fact, as far as I can say from personal observation, he may never have turned in at all, as I always left him sitting by the fire before his tent, and found him there early in the morning when I got up for coffee!

Having seen the last man into the jungle on the morning of the 29th, my tent was struck, the elephants loaded, and we marched at 7 A.M. I halted the column for a moment as we left the camping-ground to shoot some jungle-fowl (*Gallus ferrugineus*) which were pecking in the recently-reaped rice-fields. I determined that I must have blood on starting on such an expedition, so I hunted them into a thick bush from which an elephant dislodged them, and down came the two cocks in a cloud of feathers. This species does not occur in the south of India; it is almost identical with the common red domestic fowl of Bengal villages, though somewhat smaller.

Our order of march throughout was for me to lead the column of elephants on my riding-elephant — the coolies being always well ahead of us, as they usually started some hours before—and for the sergeant to be the last man of the column. Several elephants carried tents and supplies; my servants and dogs were disposed upon others; the native doctor surmounted his pills and instruments on the back of a third; and three carried coops of fowls and ducks, which cackled loudly when they were bumped against trees and thickets.

The first day we marched till 5.30 P.M., ten and a half hours, about twenty-five miles. In some places we followed the beds of shallow, gravelly streams, very shady and pleasant. The jungle was occasionally open forest, and the marks of sámbur (*Rusa Aristotelis*) were exceedingly numerous; but from 11 A.M. till we halted, our route was through one unbroken stretch of grass, the path leading over small round hills, the grass being everywhere upwards of ten feet in height. This was country which had been cleared and cultivated at intervals from time immemorial, relapsing for a few years into waste. In the distance, a long and regular line of blue hills, the Bhangamoora range, bounded the horizon before us. Our goal was beyond this, as no elephants were to be found in the grass-country which extended to the hills. The Chengree lay between the Bhangamoora range and the next, the Kálamoin. Our course all day was N.E.

I was glad, on ascending a saddle about five o'clock, to see the advanced-guard encamped in a green valley where the grass was short, embosomed in hills, and just before me. The smoke of the fires already started was filling the valley with a soft blue haze, whilst a busy hum rose from the throng. I descended the hill, and found a good camping-place some two hundred yards from the men; and as the baggage-elephants came up one by one with tents, &c., and deposited their loads, they were shackled and turned loose on the sides of the hills for half an hour's grazing before being secured for the night. They had fed throughout the day's march, and only required a little fodder to make them comfortable.

My first care on reaching the ground was to start half-a-dozen men for firewood, whilst I took others with me carrying kettle, water-pots, wash-hand basin, saucepan, and all available vessels, to secure a supply of clear water for cooking and drinking for myself and servants before the small stream which ran through the valley should be disturbed by the thirsty elephants. This done, I sounded the assembly on my cornet for Sergeant Carter, who was not yet in sight, to let him know that the day's march was over, and he soon came up with the last elephants.

The valley was very damp, and after dinner I had a fire kept up for half an hour in the tent; and though I turned in amidst the smoke, it was better than a cold raw atmosphere. I believe that, with a small fire kept up in or near the tent all night, and of course mosquito-curtains, and a cot at least three feet from the ground, a person may sleep in the most malarious swamps or jungles with safety. As the miasma is carried up, or annihilated, in the warm atmosphere, I have frequently done so without ill effects. In unhealthy jungles I make it a rule to keep within the influence of the camp-fires after sunset, and in the mornings until the jungles are warmed by the sun, when possible.

December 30, 1875.—To-day we marched from 7.30 A.M. to 3.30 P.M. The coolies got off at 4 A.M. The country was more difficult than yesterday, and we only did about sixteen miles. Here we caught up the coolies, and found such a good camping-ground that I ordered a halt. With so many men and elephants, for whom space, water, and fodder were necessary, it was not every place that offered facilities for camping. The country to-day was all grass and a little bamboo, but closer and steeper than yesterday. The few villagers we saw were Hill Arracanese and Chuckmas, and had strongly-marked Indo-Burmese features. I noticed a breed of fine white fowls and several geese in the two or three villages we passed. All the houses were raised upon bamboo platforms about ten feet from the ground, a good protection against malaria and dampness.

Our encampment this evening was better situated than yesterday. My tents and the sergeant's occupied a small hillock covered with short grass, rising in the centre of a narrow valley. The coolies were comfortably squatted on the level ground along the stream, where they erected grass huts as a protection against the soaking night dew. The view up to the closing of the valley, a vista of about half a mile, was unique. Several small rounded hillocks, like the one my tent occupied, rose from the level ground; spurs ran out from the sides of the hills enclosing the valley, here only about three hundred yards wide; and the stream wound a tortuous course around these and the hillocks. The spurs at their lowest points were covered with a rich green grass, whose silken tassels, two and a half feet in length, of a silvery or ashy grey, raised themselves on graceful stalks over the broad level of green leaves, themselves ten to twelve feet in height. Higher up the sides of the valley the tassel-grass was replaced by the graceful wild plantain, whose broad, emerald-green fronds, some drooping, some shooting up to a height of twenty feet, contrasted effectively with the dark-green feathery leaves of the bamboos.

The elephants were scattered in all directions, gathering their night's fodder, pulling down branches, bearing over with a fore-foot and uprooting the succulent plantain, or reaping the long grass with their trunks with a swishing sound. The attendant of each stood upon its broad back, laying the fodder evenly across as the patient and sagacious animal collected and handed it up. This was work which suited the elephants, who grazed at leisure, and only handed up of their abundance when adjured with more than usual earnestness to *tull* (in elephant language, to "hand up"). Towards nightfall they came in, moving mounds of green, the mahout or grass-cutter perched upon the evenly-balanced load, singing blithely. My dogs were lying upon the tent-sacks, whilst I sat by the fire amusing myself by watching the preparations for dinner. The cook is busy near a small trench over the fire, in which two or three pots and saucepans are simmering in a row. A duck is roasting on a bamboo spit over a pan of charcoal, a saucepan-lid being ingeniously propped sideways underneath it to catch the gravy, whilst avoiding the fire, and basting goes on merrily. My interest in the operation is of a complacent nature, as I know the bird will shortly appear, as nicely browned, as correctly stuffed, and as neatly served, as it could be in headquarters.

One or two chickens which have got out of the rough jungle-coop are going about "wee-weeing" mournfully as night closes in and thoughts of jackals affright them. They are not to be overlooked! they are objects of tender solicitude, and will be wanted before many days, either for curry or "*ishtew*" (stew!). E'en now the cook's minions make insidious advances towards them, seize them, shrieking, and thrust them into the basket amongst their fellows, where they shortly settle down and are at peace.

And now for dinner. What a blessing it is to have a good Madras cook in Bengal! The roast duck forms one of the few cases in life where reality does not fall short of anticipation; the curry could not be mistaken, even by an idiot, for the less spicy productions of the *artistes* of the leading Presidency; and I am not required by my *chef* to contemplate any of the culinary audacities which Bengalee *bobbachees* (as cooks are there called, Heaven help them!) designate as puddings.

The evening is chilly, and the mist gathers heavily, so a seat close to the fire and a thick overcoat are both pleasant and necessary adjuncts to the post-prandial cheroot. The light from the hundreds of small cooking-fires in the valley produces a strange effect. Some of the elephants are picketed between me and the nearest blaze, and are thrown into strong, weird relief in the fog. The hum amongst the tired men is gradually decreasing, and before I turn in, the whole encampment, except that where stand the elephants, is comparatively quiet.

December 31.—This day's march, though only thirteen miles, was a very trying one; it, however, landed us at our goal, the Chengree stream. We started at 7.30 A.M. with a tremendous ascent of a spur of the blue hills I had noticed ahead at the commencement of our march, and found that the enchantment of the distant view vanished on closer acquaintance. The hill-side was covered with long grass, which, when trodden down by the leading elephants, made a slippery foothold for the rest. As the huge beasts toiled up the almost vertical acclivity in a long straight line, zigzagging being impossible, I thought what the effect would be should one slip and roll down; recovery would have been impossible, and the whole line behind would have gone like nine-pins.

The view from the top of this hill was uninteresting. Before us were higher hills, covered with nothing but long grass, with a few bamboos in the hollows; behind us all the fine trees had been *joomed* * off the country.

We now descended nearly as deep a valley on the far side as the one we had left, and then kept along the bed of a shallow stream. As we rounded a corner I saw the ground shake under the elephants before mine. This was a peculiar kind of quagmire occasionally met with, over which, though the surface bends, animals may often pass in safety; but when it once gives way it is rapidly broken up in all directions. It is, fortunately, seldom deep enough to be dangerous. My mahout pushed my elephant on in the hope of getting over safely, as we were light, shouting to the men behind to take another line; but the surface had been too much tried already, and when we were almost over, through the elephant went, sinking to her girths. An elephant never gets flurried in situations where a horse would struggle and make matters worse; and by resting a portion of her weight on her curled trunk upon the firmer surface in front, she managed, after much surging and rolling about, to get through it.

In a mile more we caught up the coolies who had preceded us some

* *Jooming* is the method of cultivation common to all jungle-tribes, and consists in cutting down and burning the timber, the ground being relinquished after the one or two crops have been obtained from it, the fertilising effect of the ash having worn out by that time.

Phototint H. d. Wright & Co London

Chumna's Roll

hours. About five hundred were resting at the foot of a steep ascent, in which was a pass where they could only go in single file, and which took much time to get over. I saw we should be kept for hours if this were the only way up, but I felt assured that the opposite side of the spur, round which the nullah wound, must be at least as easy as this; so leaving Sergeant Carter and half the following to get up by the first route, I took all the elephants and the rest of the men along the nullah and round the spur, where we put the elephants at the steep ascent, the unloaded ones taking the lead and breaking down the bamboos and long grass. After a tedious climb under a hot sun, we reached a level saddle on the top at twelve o'clock; at the same time Sergeant Carter brought up the last of his detachment.

The men now preceded us along the narrow saddle, whilst the elephants rested to cool and feed after their climb, and we followed in an hour. The saddle was exceedingly narrow, and obstructed with bamboos and the ever-lasting grass, and a mishap occurred in the worst part, which, fortunately, was not as serious as it might have been. One elephant, Chumpa, was leading, mine being second at the time, when a large portion of earth over which she was passing suddenly gave way, and with a bellow of fright poor Chumpa slid down some yards, and then rolled over and over five distinct times down the steep grass hill, and just stopped short of a deep ravine at the bottom. It was a terrible sight to see an elephant, toes up, making such rolls. The mahout saved himself by jumping off when the earth slipped, and clinging to the grass. I sprang from my elephant instantly. As Chumpa made no sound when she got to the bottom I feared she must be killed. There was a great smashing of pots and pans during her roll, for she carried the native doctor's effects, amongst which were his live-stock, consisting of eight ducks.

Looking down the long lane in the grass I was relieved to see Chumpa getting on to her feet; her gear was left half-way, the girth-ropes having broken. Her mahout, like many natives when suddenly confronted by danger or difficulty, had quite lost his senses, and now commenced to beat his mouth, and cry that his elephant was dead. I gave him a box on the ear (Lord Lytton's Minute on the Fuller case had not been written then) that sent him flying down the slippery lane after his elephant, which he nearly reached before he pulled up. I followed, holding on by the grass, and we tried to soothe the poor beast after her fright. She did not seem hurt, and we got her on the path again with some trouble. I had often passed precipitous places on elephants with my legs dangling over vacuity. I made a mental note of this occurrence, and decided in future to turn the other way, so as to be able to jump on to *terra firma,* not into space with an elephant after me, in case of a roll.

Poor Chumpa was not seriously hurt, and in a month was quite well again. Astonishing to relate, four out of the doctor's eight ducks were found scathless; a few dabs of blood and feathers amongst the fragments of pots and pans along the line of descent led to the conclusion that the others had been crushed, but no piece of them was ever found large enough to enable any one to swear to their exact fate.

A certain amount of obscurity also shrouded the last moments of the survivors of this mishap. Some days subsequently I heard Jaffer and certain mahouts confidentially advising the doctor to have nothing to do with such evidently uncanny ducks, saying that they would not eat them if they were theirs—not for any consideration. They suggested their being allowed to swim away down the Chengree, on the banks of which we were then encamped, that not only might the danger that would assuredly attend eating them be avoided, but also such harm as would in all probability result from their continued presence in camp. Their representations seemed to have some effect on the doctor, and though he did not agree to release the ducks, he evidently had superstitious qualms about eating them. These would probably have given way when provisions became scarce, but before that time the ducks vanished in a mysterious manner. The doctor, who was exceedingly tall and lanky, beguiled a few hours of each morning by letting them out for a swim, he watching their aquatic gambols from the bank with tender solicitude. One morning whilst he was thus engaged a mahout came in haste to say his services were required in the elephant-lines at some distance. The doctor accompanied him, as the case was represented to be urgent, leaving his ducks disporting themselves near a bend of the stream below camp. When he returned from attending the case, which turned out to be much less serious than was represented, he proceeded to collect his ducks. He shortly, however, returned, looking very blank. They had vanished. He had sought them far and near, on the water and in the jungle, but no trace of them was to be seen. No one could tell him anything of them. Jaffer even asked him what he could expect of ducks that had survived a roll down a precipice on an elephant. They were evidently not subject to the ordinary conditions of their kind, and he advised the doctor to be thankful that they had taken themselves off instead of anything untoward happening to anybody. Suspicions were afterwards sought to be cast upon Jaffer and my special riding-elephant's attendants by the store-weighman, a friend of the doctor's, who declared that he saw them dining particularly well the night after the ducks were lost, and who stated his belief that duck formed part of their *menu*. Jaffer retorted that as he (the weighman) was a Bráhmin he could not possibly know what cooked duck looked like, unless, indeed, he had had some hand in their disappearance, and had been thus unjustifiably varying his vegetarian diet! At any rate, as to the circumstantial evidence against himself and messmates, the witness must have mistaken some curried pumpkin they were having for duck. Jaffer could scarcely, however, hear the subject mentioned without smirking, as if some savoury recollections stole over him!

At 2 P.M. we reached a place where the coolies were encamped; but as it was said the elephants could, before dark, reach the Chengree river, towards which we were now descending, I ordered them to push on. After making some terrible descents, which no beast of burden but an elephant could have managed, and from the paths down which we were obliged carefully to remove the pieces of wild-plantain stems strewn about by the leading elephants, lest we should have an accident to which the slipping of an alderman on a piece of orange-peel would have been a trifle, we got into a stream forming an easy roadway till we came to a fallen trunk of a tree about six feet from the ground, and which barred further passage. Its removal required the united strength of as many elephants as could get at it together. In striding over it as it lay, my elephant made such a lurch that I was thrown off the *chárjama* (riding-pad) into the stream.

After reaching the level ground at the bottom of the valley the jungle was much better, being fine heavy timber, clear of undergrowth and the abominable grass. Here a great uproar occurred in the rear of the column: elephants trumpeted, mahouts shouted, and the jungle crashed. Some one raised an alarm that a solitary tusker had attacked the females, but running back with my heavy rifle I learnt that it was only a new elephant, captured two years before—and which we had brought with us, with two or three others, to learn kheddah work—which had taken fright at something she saw or heard, and, after communicating her excitement to the other elephants near, had bolted and thrown her mahout. A couple of elephants gave chase and she was soon brought back. We shortly reached the river, at which I was very glad, as this meant that our chief hardships of marching were at an end. It would be impossible to exaggerate the difficulties of the past three days' marches, or to overestimate the great usefulness of our elephants. Poor, good beasts! their patience and docility under the annoying conditions of having to climb steep hills, and force their way through thickets under a hot sun, were admirable.

The river Chengree at the point where we struck it, probably about 100 miles above Rungamuttea, and perhaps 60 from its source, was only fifteen yards wide, and two feet deep. It was very muddy for a hill-stream. This was not the effect of rain, of which there had been none for some weeks, but seemed an inseparable condition of all the streams here, as they flowed through alluvial soil void of rock.

The Myanee, sister river to the Chengree, is a somewhat larger stream, and flows between the Kálamoin and Dalamoin ranges. We eventually worked east to the Myanee, and floated all our baggage down it to Rungamuttea on our return march.

New Year's Eve !—There were no means of celebrating the occasion. I was too hungry and tired to wait even for a special dinner to be prepared; so, consoling myself with morosely thinking that in sleeping the mystic hours away I should probably be more sensibly employed than many of my friends, I turned in and slept soundly till morning.

January 1, 1876.—It was excessively cold this morning, and foggy till some time after sunrise. Gool Budden and Suddar Ali's parties passed our camp about 8 A.M.,—Gool Budden's men to cross the Kálamoin range into the Myanee valley, Suddar Ali's to surround the elephants spoken of before, which were now about 28 miles further up the Chengree. I decided to remain where I was (camp No. 5 on map), and await Wilson's arrival with the provision-boats up the Chengree, and then to act as circumstances might require.

The jungle was very fine along the Chengree, being open forest of huge timber and giant creepers, with here and there patches of canes, the beautifully glossy, dark-green, serrated leaves of which, like giant ferns, shone in the morning sunlight. Nothing can be imagined more graceful or beautiful than a cane-bush (the ordinary cane of commerce). It often grows in extensive plots, but frequently in single plants, as a creeper running up trees, and crowning them with graceful plumes. The cane requires a moist, rich soil. There are several varieties: one makes the best walking-canes, another is used for basket-work, a third for the rattan of chair-bottoms, &c. Several of the men of our party were adepts at canework, and they made me many nice and useful articles of camp furniture.

Of all prickly things in creation the cane is perhaps the foremost, very different in its natural state to the smooth, but still pungent, implement of our school-days' recollection. It grows of all lengths, often above 200 feet; and both stem, leaves, and tendrils are covered with horrible thorns. The leaves are several feet long, serrated, and very graceful. Its fruit hangs in clusters of about fifty berries, each being the size of a cherry, and of a bright cream colour, with a singular appearance of being carved from wood. They are edible. Inside the skin is a sweet pulp surrounding the stone. The cane itself contains a large quantity of water throughout its length. I cut twenty-two feet off one of about three-quarters of an inch in diameter, and by simply blowing through it obtained half a tumblerful. The roots, and sprouts when just above ground, make a good vegetable. To prepare the cane for commerce, the rough peel, studded with thorns, is merely stripped off, and the cane is ready for use.

One remarkable product of these jungles is a parasite creeper generally about as thick as a man's arm, and looking like a dried stick. It hangs from trees, its leaves and young shoots being up amongst the foliage. If slashed through in one place only there is no result; but if another slash be given above, thus admitting air, a cupful or so of water gushes from the lower cut; the water seems quite drinkable. All along the river were a great many tracks of sámbur; fruits of different kinds attracted the deer. I found the morning's track of a solitary elephant whilst rambling in the neighbourhood of camp. Jungle-fowl (*Gallus ferrugineus*) were plentiful, as well as the black khálege pheasant; also the beautiful peacock pheasant (*Polyplectron chinquis*).

January 2.—Yesterday some of the mahouts, when out collecting fodder, discovered an old course of the river, in which was a pool of water full of fish. The pool was about 150 yards in length, 50 wide, and 6 feet deep. It evidently only had communication with the river during floods, and was isolated at other times; shady trees overhung it, and it was a most perfect preserve. I saw large fish of the carp tribe sailing about in it, and some monsters like pike. I decided forthwith to have fish for dinner.

A rod could not be used for the trees, nor could a fish have been played for the weeds, so I decided on another plan, which would furnish fun to the whole camp and fish for everybody.

It may not be generally known that fishing is one of the many useful acquirements of the elephant. Such, however, is the case; and without the aid of ours on this occasion, many a fine fish, which was shortly to be made as salt as was Lot's wife, might still be gliding about in that retired jungle-pool.

I had twenty-five elephants mustered without their gear, and all the spare men, who in great glee provided themselves with hastily-improvised bamboo spears, baskets, knives, &c., and we put the elephants in line at one end of the pool, two or three delighted attendants on the back of each. The elephants advanced down the pool in close order, enjoying the bath, and making the water surge as if a paddle-steamer was on it. Their feet stirred up the thick mud at the bottom, and I knew this would soon make the fish show themselves.

When the elephants had traversed the pool twice, some large heads appeared for an instant on the surface, then vanished. "Give them another turn" I shouted to the men, and I shortly joined the line on my pad-elephant. Large fish now came to the surface in sad strait, unable to stand the stifling mud, and glided gloomily about with their nostrils above water.

Now the fun began in earnest. The elephants separated as their mahouts gave chase to particular fish, and generally very soon transferred them to their baskets after chopping their heads off with their *daos.* Having a spear with a sharp blade nine inches long I bagged more than any one else, as I could strike the fish further off: they sometimes sank just as the men got within reach with their shorter blades. Their heads could be taken off with one slice with the spear, when they invariably floated at once; but if struck in the middle they sank, owing to the air-bladder being cut. A sort of cod-looking fish (one of the genus *Silurus,* I believe, scaleless, thin, deep, and silvery, with long feelers) which I cut in two behind the shoulders, closed its jaws upon the mahout's finger when he put it into its mouth to pick up the head portion, and hung on like a bull-dog for some seconds.

In following fish that, though in distress, were sufficiently conscious of danger not to let us get very near, the elephants exhibited much sagacity, abstaining (of course at a hint from their mahouts) from blowing under water or making any splashing. They enjoyed themselves immensely. My men were very noisy over their share of the sport, and it was highly amusing to watch the chases by several elephants at once of any particularly fine fish that was in a bad way. The men stood up on their elephants, and often several darts were made at once at an unfortunate fish, which one would triumphantly hold aloft, impaled through and through. Several men fell off and were half-choked in the mud, which, when dried, coated them over like whitewash. I believe, at least I hope, that had the shade of old Izaak watched us he would have forgiven us under the circumstances.

In getting into the pool at a new place where the water was deep and the bank straight my elephant entered carelessly. One elephant had just gone in before, but by kneeling and sliding in, whilst "Neelmony" stepped boldly over. In putting down her fore-feet she nearly turned a summersault; her head went right to the bottom I think; the mahout was under water, and I was up to my knees, with the elephant's hind-quarters somewhere about the back of my head!

The best fish I bagged was 7 lb. in weight; the generality were under 2 lb.; my total bag was 72 lb. I found that not one of the large pike-like fish that we had seen basking near the surface, and which the men called *gajál,* had been bagged. They evidently escaped by burying them-

Photoprint H. M. Wright & Co. London

Fishing in the Chengree Valley.

selves in the mud, and were not affected like the carp species. The discovery of this peculiarity caused my men much grief, and some who told me that those fish had "only one bone in them," and that "all the rest was meat," were quite depressed. I think they almost felt inclined to punch a small elephant coolie's head who provokingly showed, with both his outstretched arms, how long some were that he had seen.

On the 4th January news came from Suddar Ali of his having surrounded the elephants he had gone after on the 1st. The provision-boats had not come up yet, so, as I was getting anxious, I despatched two men on a raft down the Chengree to meet them; and leaving Sergeant Carter with the bulk of the elephants to bring on the supplies when they arrived, I started on the 5th at 7 o'clock to join Suddar Ali, and marched with six elephants till 4 P.M., about twenty-one miles, when we camped. The jungle for the most part of the way—our path skirted the Chengree—was fine open forest that had never been cut, except near a large *Jooma* settlement called Gásban, which we passed about 12 o'clock. The trees were so tall, and the shade so high and close, that nothing more than a skull-cap was necessary, the sun being unable to penetrate the dark forest.

Soon after starting we heard a solitary elephant in the cover by the path-side; he squeaked and trumpeted on winding our elephants, but did not show himself, having winded us also.

In this part of the hills there were very few inhabitants; Gásban was the only settlement for many miles round. The people of the hills are all called *Joomas* by the dwellers in the plains; but this is a term which merely signifies people who cultivate by *jooming*, or clearing forest-land for a year or two, and then abandoning it in favour of fresh land. The people were of several tribes—viz., settlers from Arracan, Chuckmas, Mugs, Tipperahs, and to the east the dreaded Kookies, or Looshais. Of these castes the Chuckmas appear to have more claims to be called aboriginal to the Chittagong hills than the others, though the Kookies (Looshais) are aboriginal in the eastern portion. I write under correction however, as I knew nothing of the languages and could not learn much from the people, of whom, moreover, we saw very few except at Gásban.

The one thing about which there seemed no doubt at all was, that the Kookies terrified the rest out of their seven senses, or had done so till recently, by occasional raids to the westward, when they are represented to have put to the sword everybody but such women as they carried off into captivity. It resulted from this that large tracts had been abandoned from time to time by the Joomas, when the Kookies, who seem to be a fine, warlike race, were hard upon them. Within the last few years, however, the establishment of Rungamuttea and Demágiri as frontier police posts, constituting a guard between the troublesome Kookies and the tribes to the west, has given confidence to the latter, and the hill-tracts will probably be better populated soon. A European political officer and a police officer live at Rungamuttea, and another police officer at Demágiri, and these maintain amicable relations with the Kookies. It is the Kookies' annual custom, I was informed, to have extensive raids of two, three, or four thousand men forming a single party. This raiding is done in the cold weather, from December till the early rains; and their "outing" may be regarded as something equivalent to them to the run to the lakes or seaside in summer amongst us. As they are an independent tribe they are merely requested to confine their pastimes within their own limits, and not to trespass on British territory as formerly. Infraction of this rule caused the Looshai campaign of 1870-71. It is said that the Kookies occasionally eat enemies slain in battle; but the Joomas are so terrified at the very mention of a Kookie that they perhaps exaggerate.

The Kookies do not appear to be troubled with more feelings of humanity than savages generally, as Gool Budden told me that when elephant-catching some years back, further north, a party of his scouts met several Kookies at a ford, carrying off girls from a Tipperah village which they had attacked. To prevent their running away, five or six girls were strung together by a strip of cane passed through a hole pierced in their left hands. By this simple method one man could take care of a good many of them. The scouts had no guns, and the Kookies made off with their unhappy captives. Gásban, the village I had passed on the Chengree, had been cut up by Kookies about 1852, but, being well within protected limits, was now flourishing again. The houses were all of bamboo, and raised high from the ground.

January 6.—Marched from 7 A.M. till 10 A.M., seven miles to Jádoogapára, where, it is said, once on a time stood a large Jooma settlement, till one fine morning a sudden yell on all sides at daybreak announced the Kookies, and no one escaped to tell the tale! I could not see a trace of the village; but the structures of the hill-people are not of a very permanent order. I left my tent to be pitched on the river-bank and started on foot to the place, two miles distant, where the elephants were surrounded. I was very much pleased and surprised at the amount of work Suddar Ali's men had done, and its business-like look. The kheddah, or stockade, into which the elephants were to be driven, was constructed of a circle of stout uprights 12 feet high, placed so close together that the hand could scarcely be introduced between them, and well backed with forked uprights and cross-beams, the whole being lashed together with strips of cane.

The guiding-wings, of similar construction, had also been completed, and the finishing touches were just being put to the work; the whole was concealed in thick jungle on an elephant-run, and the new wood-work was screened with cane-leaves. Everything was in readiness, and Suddar Ali said he would, if allowed, try and drive the elephants in at once. I left it entirely to him, as I had not seen elephants caught before by this plan, and knew nothing of it practically. Suddar Ali requested that I would take up a position near the entrance to the approach to the gate, and give the herd the final rush in, whilst he led the beaters.

I stood behind a large tree at the end of the left guiding palisade, with a couple of heavy rifles, one loaded with blank cartridge, one with ball. In a couple of hours the elephants were driven, without much noise, to within a quarter of a mile of the trap, the stops on each side keeping them straight for the stockade when they bore too much in any direction. The beaters being now well together and the flanking lines closing in, the final driving commenced with a great shouting and popping of guns, and the terrified herd came on through the jungle, their rapid passage making a quickly-increasing rushing sound, like the approach of a storm.

I had reconnoitred the ground beforehand, and found that there was a stream flowing through clayey soil across the line of approach, 100 yards in advance of my post. The ground was level for several yards on each side of the stream, and the clay deep and holding.

The sound of the elephants coming through the jungle beyond the stream was suddenly changed to a loud swishing noise as they rushed through some high reeds bordering it, and immediately after a loud squelching and splashing ensued, with sounds as of the drawing of gigantic corks, as the terrified monsters struggled in mad haste to extract their legs from the deep mud.

Gaining my side, they came on at a slapping pace through the thinner jungle, some carrying creepers which had been torn down from the trees on their heads, and all doing their best, with their ears thrown forward, and their tails straight out behind. One huge beast halted suddenly for a brief instant, almost touching the tree behind which I was standing, to listen. Ah! those terrible sounds! The kink which signifies demoralisation pervaded his tail, and he "wildly urged on his mad career." I ran from behind the palisade, and with a "yoick to 'em" and a couple of blank charges under the last elephant's tails, I pursued them down the run. It was only fifty yards; their panic was complete; after a momentary crush at the gateway the last huge stern passed in with a rush, and down came the gate! Several active fellows drew heavy bars across, which effectually secured it against being driven outwards.

I bethought myself just at this moment of the cries of an elephant which I had heard behind the others, and, thinking some might have been left behind, I faced round. It was lucky I did so, as I found myself confronting a large female with two calves of different ages, which were coming down the drive not forty yards from us! They were advancing hesitatingly, as a perfect Bedlam had been let loose about the stockade when the gate fell, everybody closing in to repel any attempt on the palisades. The big elephant was evidently doubting whether to keep to the line her companions had taken, or to make off back into the jungle.

The men at the gate escaped through the palisades without delay, but as it was a squeeze through I preferred taking my chance where I stood to being taken in rear when in the embarrassing position of getting under a low rail on all fours. I had my 8-bore rifle with twelve drams and hard bullets in each barrel, so thought myself capable of meeting her. The elephant now stopped and hesitated, though threatening an attack. She kicked up the dust with her fore-feet, and trumpeted shrilly, but at this moment some one poked her in the face with a long bamboo through the side palisades. She turned and went slowly and dejectedly away, and we saw no more of her.

Inside the stockade the poor terrified beasts, thirty-seven in number, were crowding each other into the smallest possible circle, each trying to keep as far as possible from the lighted torches that had been thrust through the palisades at short distances all round. Every stick of small jungle was quickly demolished in their struggles. As one was forced out of a good place in the circle by some stronger animal it rushed madly round the writhing mass, tail and ears cocked, trumpeting shrilly with fear, and again plunged headlong in. Each *débutant* was loudly cheered by the delighted coolies perched on the high stockade all round.

One or two of the elephants soon began to get over their first panic, and some of them advanced to an examination of the trench and palisades. This was *nuts* for the men, whose delight was now crowned in the opportunity of letting off blank charges literally against the heads of the huge beasts, from which the boldest recoiled as if shot.

CHAPTER XIII.

AN ELEPHANT-CATCHING EXPEDITION INTO THE HILL-TRACTS OF CHITTAGONG—(*continued.*)

A GHOSTLY NIGHT VISITOR—SECURING THE WILD ELEPHANTS—RÁDHÁPEARY—A VICIOUS FEMALE ATTACKS ME—DANGEROUS POSITION—NARROW ESCAPE—RETURN TO GÁSBAN—MEET A FELLOW-COUNTRYMAN—JOOMA ETIQUETTE—LIQUOR—WE DINE AT A JOOMA CHIEF'S—NEWS OF GOOL BUDDEN'S SUCCESS—MARCH INTO THE MYANEE VALLEY—A HILL VILLAGE—TREAT SOME PATIENTS—A GRAND CHASM—REACH BHOWÁLKÁLI—THIRTY-TWO ELEPHANTS CAPTURED—A MAN KILLED—A PORTION OF THE HERD GIVES TROUBLE—WE ARE OBLIGED TO LET THEM GO—AN ELEPHANT PAYS ME A MIDNIGHT VISIT—ATTACKS MY TENT—THE GUARD PUNISHED—SHOOT THE ELEPHANT—COMPLETE A KHEDDAH IN TWO DAYS AND CAPTURE THIRTEEN ELEPHANTS—JUNGLE-PRODUCTS—COMMENCE RETURN-MARCH TO RUNGAMUTTEA—YOUNG ELEPHANT KILLED BY A TIGER—I SHOOT THE SPOILER—WEIGHT OF A TIGER—SHOOT A TROUBLESOME TUSKER—LOST IN THE FOREST—CHORUS OF ELEPHANTS—A HILL-DOG—HIS SAGACITY AND ATTACHMENT—REACH RUNGAMUTTEA—SAD MISHAP—THREE ELEPHANTS DROWNED—JOOMAS EATING ELEPHANTS—MARCH TO DACCA—STATEMENT OF CASUALTIES.

HAVING seen all made safe, and fires lighted round the stockade, I returned to camp. It was intensely cold during the night, and towards morning the falling dew pattered so heavily from the broad-leaved trees around that I thought it was raining. I got up to look out, when I saw the grey form of an elephant of large size, but with poor tusks, standing silently in the foggy moonlight not more than thirty yards distant. He looked like a spectre waving its ghostly arm, as he pointed his trunk in the direction of the tame elephants and the tents by turns. I watched him for some time as he stood listening intently, till he moved noiselessly away in the direction of the tame elephants. He doubtless belonged to the captured herd, and was attracted to camp by the presence of the elephants with us. During the whole of the time we were out we were constantly visited by these roaming tuskers, of which more anon; and it was wonderful that they never meddled with the men who were sleeping under small huts of boughs, or even on the open ground, near their elephants. Some of the tame elephants were found to be in calf almost every year after their jungle-trips and the clandestine visits of these stray males.

Next day I went to the stockade, and in the afternoon Sergeant Carter arrived with six elephants carrying ropes and provisions, the boats having come up the Chengree under Wilson to camp No. 5 the day I left. As there were still some hours of daylight the mahouts proposed to secure some of the captured elephants within the stockade, especially two or three that had given a good deal of trouble during the night. We therefore opened a gap in the stockade and took in the six elephants barebacked, with a rope-tier holding the binding-ropes seated behind each mahout. I rode the first elephant, a very fine and powerful female named Rádhápeary. All catching-elephants of good courage evince the greatest relish for the sport of securing their wild companions, and Rádhápeary quite trembled with eagerness as she stepped inside and faced the wild ones. She was an old hand at it, as well as at *mélé shikár*, or noosing, in Assam.

Our six elephants formed abreast before the gap until it was securely closed again, when we advanced towards the wild ones. They formed up and showed much excitement at the sight of our elephants. A few came forward to interview us, and touched ours with their trunks. I was driving Rádhápeary myself, sitting as mahout on her neck, with a rope-tier behind me. Some of the men had spears, but I had only the iron driving-goad in my hand.

We pushed our elephants on with the intention of cutting off a few wild ones from the main body, and whilst doing this I got in advance of the others, and became separated from them. Some of the wild elephants were rather impertinent, and each tame one was engaged in driving any back that opposed it, when I heard a shout of "Sahib! Sahib!" from the men perched on the stockade, and on turning saw a large wild female, an old, tall, and raw-boned beast, coming straight at me from behind with her trunk curled and her head up. She was on my near side, and in another instant was upon me, but not before I had slipped round on the off side of my elephant's neck, and had driven the goad into her open mouth as she came down on my left thigh with her jaws. She fortunately had only one tush, which was broken and blunt. She did not attempt to seize me with her trunk, but to pummel me. This is the females' invariable plan of punishing each other; they put their chins on to the backs of their opponent, and bore and strike with their tushes. Cases have occurred in the kheddahs of mahouts being killed through timid tame elephants giving way under the pain and sinking down, when, if the driver has been thrown off, the wild ones have trampled him to death. This is, however, very uncommon, and few wild female elephants offer any resistance to the tame ones. Such a case as the attack upon me has never, as far as I can learn from mahouts who have seen hundreds of elephants caught, been known. It is an astonishing fact that the rider is hardly ever attacked. The mahouts use no concealment, going mounted into the stockade in their ordinary dress, and though their elephants may be surrounded by wild ones, any of which could by simply raising its trunk drag the men off, they are never molested. If it were otherwise, entering the stockade would be more dangerous work than it is. However, in my case the solitary exception I have known to the rule occurred.

After boring for a second or two on my thigh, and upon Rádhápeary's head, the elephant drew back, and I sat upright, thankful at escaping with a mere pummelling, when, almost before I became aware of her intention, the fiend came straight at me again. Over I went, only leaving my leg across the elephant's neck, and again I was severely bruised; the driving-hook was jerked out of my hand, and had it not been fastened by a cord to the elephant's neck-rope I should have lost it. Again I recovered myself, when the elephant came at me once more, pummelled my leg soundly, and drew blood from Rádhápeary's head.

When I sat up my breeches and flannel shirt had been torn almost to rags, and I believed my left thigh was broken, as it might well have been by the weight of the elephant's jaws. I had hardly a moment's time for thought, however; there was the determined beast but a few feet off, and I saw she was going to renew the attack. Her pertinacity was wonderful. I felt that I was doomed. I could not expect to escape many more such assaults. I should be unseated, when certain death awaited me as I was in the midst of the crowd of wild elephants. I felt perfectly cool, however, as long as I faced the danger and was engaged in defending myself. I calculated the chances against myself without a shudder. Most persons who have been in similar dangerous positions doubtless have felt this calmness, and I believe that men are often spared the bitterness which we are wont to associate with violent deaths when they are overtaken whilst facing a danger which their minds are engaged in resisting. Dr Livingstone mentions the same feeling when he was in the jaws of a lion. Who can doubt the difference between death to a man in action, and to a helpless prisoner?

I clutched the goad again. Forward went the elephant's ears and she was already in her stride, when a spear passed my head and stabbed her deeply in the temple, and in another instant Issamuttee, one of our elephants, struck her with her head like a battering-ram, full on the shoulder, and almost knocked her over. I was saved just in time. All our elephants had been engaged with some of the wild ones, and had not been able to help me, but Issamuttee's rider, a mere boy, called Choonoo, had got his elephant free and had arrived just at the critical moment. I should say that Rádhápeary had been occupied whilst all this went on in facing a young tusker who seemed inclined to try his tusks upon her, and had she not kept head on to him he doubtless would have done so; so she had been unable to pay attention to the attacking female, whom she could have overpowered in a moment had she been free to do so. Wild elephants are soon overawed by the pugilistic attainments of tame ones. The females in the herds have few contentions amongst themselves: when they do quarrel they chiefly punish each other by biting off the ends of one another's tails. Consequently when they are set upon and pummelled scientifically they soon give in. Rádhápeary was a long, heavy, and powerful elephant, of the highest caste of *koomeriahs.* Her courage was equal to her strength, and her science to both. She and another female actually killed outright a large *muckna,* or tuskless male, on one occasion, by the squeezing and heavy battering they gave him. The great point of science in a tame elephant in contending with others is to overreach them by holding the head high. This is equivalent to the P.R. movement of getting an opponent's head into chancery. If the wild elephant were allowed to have its head above the tame one's the mahout might be knocked off.

I was obliged to leave the inside of the stockade after this misadventure, as I felt sick and feared I might faint from the pain in my thigh. I was not seriously hurt, but had a long cut and abrasion from the elephant's tush from the hip nearly to the knee. The surface became rapidly extravasated, and I was stiff and lame immediately. Rádhápeary's mahout now took my place, and the troublesome elephant having been driven into a corner by the tame ones was soon secured. She never gave any more trouble, and when tamed was as quiet as the rest. When she was tied up the mahouts begged leave to be allowed to thrash her well! This was quite a native's idea. I respected the poor beast for her courageous defence, and forbade her being molested.

I had a bad night, as I could only lie on my right side, and in the morning was unable to walk. However, I had a mattress put on Rádhápeary's pad on to which I was hoisted, and was soon inside the kheddah again, though unable to take part in the catching. All our elephants had arrived by this time—fifty in number—and they made short work of the wild ones. Their hind-legs were hobbled and thick ropes put on their necks, when each was marched off by two tame elephants, one before and one behind, to our camp at Jádoogapára.

It would take up too much space to relate our operations at Jádoogapára in detail, so I will pass on.

On January 15th we marched back to Gásban with the captured elephants, and here I met a countryman, P., the political officer stationed at Rungamuttea. The meeting of Livingstone and Stanley in Central Africa was a trifle—to us—to this "forgathring" in one of the uttermost corners of the earth! I found P., who was a model frontier officer, squatted in a hut with the noble savages around him, trying to impress upon them some notions of Government dues, and taking a friendly pull at their liquor now and again. The Joomas hospitably invited me, through P., who had some knowledge of their language, to a drink of the beverage which had been provided for the assembled council. There was a pot of it holding several gallons and occupying an honourable position in the centre; across the mouth of the vessel was a thin slip of bamboo level with the liquor. From the slip of bamboo a small piece of stick depended about a quarter of an inch, and P. told me that Jooma etiquette required that the imbiber should lower the liquor by suction through a hollow reed till the dependent slip cleared the surface, when he was considered to have duly shown his appreciation of the brew. The liquor was prepared from fermented rice and fruits, and was very good, being something like cider. P. and I smoked and chatted till evening, when we looked at the new elephants, and then dined in P.'s up-stair hut. A clay hearth on the floor admitted of our having a fire. I slept in my tent, where the thermometer stood at 32° next morning, though the elevation was probably under 100 feet above sea-level.

Next day I accepted an invitation with P. to breakfast at the house of one of the Jooma chiefs. He gave us some good pork curry (we had seen the animal which furnished the wherewithal being pursued by Joomas with gleaming knives the evening before, who, as soon as they caught him, cut off his head almost before he had time to squeal), and a sort of pudding. We ate with our fingers off leaf-platters. I daresay any one at all fastidious might have had some qualms regarding the cleanliness of the cooks who prepared the repast, and I was amused at P.'s frequent apologies for his friends. However, I was not less of a jungle-wallah, accustomed to chumming with the noble savage, than himself, and felt quite at home. After breakfast I played some tunes on my cornet, and P. struck up on a tin whistle, which greatly pleased the Joomas.

P. departed with his dug-out boats next day down the Chengree towards

Rungamuttea, and I started on the 20th to cross the Kálamoin range to join Gool Budden. He had captured thirty-two elephants unassisted, but the rest of the herd had not been enclosed in the stockade, and were still at large within the circle of coolies. In eight hours' marching from Gásban with ten elephants, about sixteen miles, through bamboo and tree jungle, pretty clear and fairly level, we reached the top of the Kálamoin range. Here there was a small village, where I had a granary cleared out, and slept very comfortably. It was 10° warmer on the mountain-range than in the valleys, and the fog in the morning was all below us. The view of the valleys filled with the motionless white vapour, the hill-tops showing through it like islands in a sea of milk, was very beautiful.

I did a little doctoring before starting in the morning. A child of a few months old had been terribly burnt on the back, from the nape of the neck to the hips, through getting its little shirt on fire when left alone in a hut some days before. I melted Holloway's ointment and applied it, and gave the father a piece in a leaf to use again, as occasion required. I am afraid to say much in praise of the above useful compound, lest I should appear in advertisements in connection with the world-famed salve, and lay myself open to the suspicion amongst my readers of being in collusion with the great piller of the medical world. I may, however, say that in wild countries nothing is more convenient or effective for wounds of all kinds, from a cut finger to sore-back in an elephant. For a man suffering from phthisis I could only recommend a change to the warm plains out of the jungle, which of course he would not take, so I might have kept the advice to myself; and I was obliged to decline altogether to treat a blind girl. Her father was anxious I should try, as he said she was "such a fine girl, otherwise he would not have troubled me!"

I walked down the opposite side of the range rifle in hand in advance of the elephants. I saw no signs of game except the prints of a tiger. The jungle was open bamboo and large timber. At the bottom of the slope flowed a shallow stream with a firm gravelly bottom, and we kept along this for some distance till it joined a larger stream, when I mounted my pad-elephant and led the way. The bed of the large stream formed the most easy road for passing through a high range which we had to cross before reaching the Myanee vale.

Owing to the remarkable absence of rock in the Chittagong hills, in common with almost the whole of Eastern Bengal, whether hill or plain, the river had a very gentle flow, having cut its way down to so easy a gradient in the soft soil that further erosion had practically ceased. On each side the banks rose to about five hundred feet in height, and as nearly perpendicular as the nature of the earth admitted. Scarcely a beam of sunlight, except at mid-day, could penetrate the abyss, and the cold at this early hour was intense. Both sides of the gigantic cleft were clothed with wild plantains, the beautiful broad leaves of which, ten feet in length and two wide, were of an almost transparent emerald green. Orchids of various kinds, especially a gorgeous yellow one like laburnum, but fuller; tree-ferns; and across the ravine just above our heads, the overlacing of creepers—a peculiar feature in Eastern forests,—were wonderful to see. There were few birds, and the only signs of game were the tracks of the tiger I had seen the print of further back, and which had come by the gorge, and those of wild elephants that had used it some days previously. Gool Budden's party had cut some of the trunks of the trees lying across the stream which had impeded the elephants that carried their provisions.

We marched for three hours along this stream. The men were ordered not to talk or sing to their elephants; such sounds seemed impious intrusions on the grand silence that prevailed. The murmur of the stream and the plashing of the line of elephants were the only sounds which broke it. I felt cold even with a thick overcoat and rug, and the unfortunate mahouts, who were lightly clad and not particularly appreciative of the beauties of nature, were doubtless glad when we left the grand cleft for the more open jungles warmed by the sun. By evening we reached Gool Budden's camp on the Myanee, at a place called Bhowálkáli, after one of the most varied and pleasant marches I remember.

The portion of the herd which he had caught, numbering thirty-two animals, was a very good lot, containing few old or small ones. About twenty-five elephants (the remainder of the herd) which refused to enter the stockade with their fellows were still at large in the forest within the original surround. Gool Budden had been engaged in making another stockade at a fresh point; this was now ready, and in it we hoped to impound them. The men had mismanaged the tying of the elephants already captured, and had caused the dislocation of one fine beast's hind-legs at the hock—or, more properly speaking, knee-joint, as an elephant has no hocks—and a similar accident to one hind-leg of another. This was through their being left in the enclosure with their legs tied to trees during the night instead of being removed from the stockade. Elephants are very mischievous, and sometimes display the trait observable in many other animals of ill-treating such of their fellows as are in distress, particularly if suffering from wounds or accidents. These two poor elephants had been butted by the others and knocked over, their hind-legs, which were braced close up to the trees, being wrenched out of joint by their fall. The sufferings of one which could not rise were too horrible to witness. The hunters, like all natives of India, had never thought of terminating its sufferings. Many natives would not hurt the meanest insect, as to do no killing is a portion of the creed of some castes of Hindoos; but that it might be merciful to put an end to suffering in many cases they cannot, apart from their disinclination to take life, understand. The poor beast had given birth to a still-born calf, and had been in this terrible position for two days before I arrived. I immediately ended her sufferings with my rifle; but the other one, which did not seem very bad, and of the exact nature of whose injuries, whether sprain or dislocation, I was not then certain, was kept tied up in an easy manner. She was a magnificent animal—one of the finest we caught during our trip—and she marched about fifty miles on our return down the Myanee valley. The swelling at the hip abated a good deal, when I was able to see that it was really dislocated. The elephant had marched so pluckily, though dragging the leg, that the jemadár and I had had doubts of this hitherto. I ordered her release (though the jemadár offered £30 for her as a speculation of his own), together with a very old female which it was useless to take out of the jungles. I believe that though the injured elephant will be permanently lame she may live for many years in her native haunts. Her liberty was a poor, but the only, return we could make for the injury to which she had so unfortunately been subjected.

We tried for some days to drive the elephants still remaining at large into the kheddah but were thoroughly beaten. One man was trampled to death by an enraged female, from which I also had two narrow escapes, flooring her in each attack with my rifle; and as the attempts became highly dangerous to the men, I ordered them to relinquish the surround and take a few days' rest to recover from the fatigues of night-watching. During the time we were here a most extraordinary adventure happened to me, in having my tent pulled about my ears during the night by a wild elephant. I fear some of my readers may think it almost past belief, and I have felt doubtful about relating it; however, I will narrate what occurred.

A large space had been cleared in the forest on the bank of the Myanee for securing our new elephants, and for the convenience of our large camp. With the elephants from Gásban, which had been marched to our present camp, and our tame ones, we had over a hundred altogether. At the encampment (No. 10 on map) the Myanee flowed from north to south; our camp was on the west bank. The Myanee was joined at this place by a smaller stream from the north-west; my own and servants' tents, as well as the sergeant's and native doctor's, were pitched in the angle of junction, on the north side, and separated from the main camp by the smaller stream. Its banks, and those of the Myanee, were both very steep, except at the point of junction, where wild elephants had made a path across. This was now obstructed by our tents. Two or three single wild elephants had been wandering about the neighbouring jungles since we came, attracted by the large gathering of their fellows. One or two occasionally found their way into the elephant-lines: we had, with our tame elephants, caught two large females and a young male that came amongst our captives in broad daylight.

On the night of the 27th of January, I was awakened by the sudden crash of an elephant just inside the cane-jungle on the river-bank, within twenty yards of my tent. I jumped up, turned up the kerosine lantern that was burning on the table, and held up the tent-door. The light frightened the elephant and it made off; it had evidently come with the intention of crossing the stream by the accustomed path, and had been startled by the tents. Next night I was again awakened by an elephant—perhaps the same one—close at hand. I shouted at it as I lay in bed, but instead of making off I heard it step forward and seize my small bathing-tent, which was about twenty yards from mine, and a tearing and flapping sound followed as the brute tore it up. This was more than I could stand, so jumping out of bed, I seized my rifle and threw up the tent-door. I saw the white canvas being tossed up and down, but before I could make out the elephant against the dark jungle it dropped the tent and retired. It was just one o'clock. I thought the beast might return, so ordered two tame elephants to mount guard between my tent and the jungle till morning.

Next day I found the small tent had been torn in two; one half had tusk-holes through it, and the other bore the impression of a large muddy foot. As I thought it just possible that the elephant might take it into his head to visit my tent next night, I had the jungle cleared away for sixty yards beyond my tent, and told the men to picket two newly-caught elephants at the edge of the jungle: these we expected would give some notice of the approach of any other elephants. I also had Rádhápeary stationed close to my tent, and six men told off as a night-guard. My tent was nearer to the jungle than any of the others. I usually sat by a fire, between my tent and the servants', after dinner, and to-night I heard an elephant, probably my visitor of the night before, squeaking in the jungle about a quarter of a mile away. The guard remarked it, so thinking nothing more about it I turned in. I made the grand mistake of having the guard and fire between my tent and the next, instead of between me and the jungle.

I seemed to have slept for a long time when I was awakened by the corner of the tent nearest the jungle, and just above my head, being gently shaken. The tent was single-poled, twelve feet square, and secured by numerous ropes all round. I thought of the rogue instantly, and was out of bed in a twinkling, not even waiting to untuck the mosquito-netting which I always use as a precaution against malaria as much as against troublesome insects; I made a considerable rent in it in my haste. The faculty of becoming thoroughly awake, physically and mentally, at a moment's notice, is one acquired by persons accustomed, as dwellers in tents in Indian jungles frequently are, to occasions requiring its exercise; and as I sleep lightly, the motion of the tent, though very slight, instantly aroused me. Now that I was on my feet, rifle in hand, my first impulse was to shout; but imagining it might be some of the men outside who had touched the ropes, and that a hullabaloo inside would be rather ridiculous if that were the case, I hesitated. At this moment the tent shook again, very gently. I peeped through the door on the opposite side, where the guard was. The old story! All still; the fire reduced to a few smouldering embers—the men lying in a row near it, like corpses in their winding-sheets, stark and still! Rádhápeary was round the tent to my right, but I could not hear her moving. Just then the same gentle twang of the tent-rope in the corner over my bed shook the canvas, and I heard an elephant breathe. I now thought it must be Rádhápeary who had got loose, and in moving about was touching the ropes. I could hardly imagine that a wild elephant could be so near me, but I still hesitated to shout, believing that if it were a wild visitor I might only provoke an attack. However, as I heard nothing more for a minute or two, I called Rádhápeary gently by name, and was just going to open the door and look out cautiously, when there was one ponderous step forward, a tremendous smash, cracking of ropes, and tearing of canvas, and the whole end of the tent was driven in upon my bed. I knew who it was now, and shouted at the brute at the top of my voice. I would have given him both barrels through the tent could I have seen how he was standing, but his tusks had only come through the upper fly, the inner one being pulled down by his foot placed upon the side-wall of the tent to which it was attached, so I could see nothing of him. I expected to see his tusks or head through the tent in another instant, and reserved my fire. I was under no apprehension for my own safety. The other door was at my back, and the steep river-bank just beyond, down which I could have jumped if necessary, and no elephant could have followed; and with so many ropes I knew the tent could not be upset bodily. I only thought of making sure of the intruder by waiting till I saw the outline of his head, when I would have given him both barrels of my heavy rifle, and left him to enjoy the further demolition of the tent with what zest he might. What a novelty it would have been to bag an elephant inside one's tent at 1 A.M.!

After the first crash the elephant drew back. The small ropes in the eyelet-holes which laced the side-walls of the tent to the inner fly had all given way, and the side-walls on the sides nearest the elephant fell outwards. The unexpected flood of light must have startled him, as whilst I looked for the reappearance of his head he was already making off, a fact of which I only became aware when I caught sight of his hind-legs vanishing from the circle of light. I determined he should not depart without a souvenir of his visit, and, stooping, I fired through the open side of the tent after him, but, as I afterwards found, without hitting him.

By this time every one in the camp was up and piling wood on the fires, alarmed at the disturbance. The jemadár and some matchlock-men came from the elephant-lines with torches to see what had happened. We found that Rádhápeary had been lying down fast asleep, or she would have given some signal of the tusker's approach. His attack on the tent was not prompted by viciousness, but by the spirit of curiosity and mischievousness which are such strongly-marked characteristics of wild elephants, and which leads them to upset telegraph-posts, trample new road-embankments, pull up survey tracing-pegs, and to similar acts. I once heard a detachment of elephants playing with a long chain which we had left over night in the jungles, evidently pleased with the clinking noise it made. The presence of so many elephants encouraged this one's daring approach, and seeing my tent he had ventured upon an examination of it. My speaking inside led to his attack upon it.

I now took into consideration the case of the rascally guard, which ended in their getting a dozen as sound cuts each with a rattan as one of Gool Budden's lieutenants could administer. They belonged to his party of kheddah men, and he reviled them in Chittagong Billingsgate as the lascár whacked away, saying they were pigs and sons of pigs, and guilty, like their fathers, mothers, and every one of their relatives, of every species of immorality, in addition to the immediate neglect of duty for which they were being chastised. We had some great scoundrels amongst our two kheddah parties, but the jemadárs were stern disciplinarians and maintained fair order. It was rather too bad that when every one had been working hard all day except these lazy scoundrels, who had nothing to do but prepare for night-work, they should sleep while we were being pulled out of bed by wild elephants. One rascal had the audacity to tell me that he was watching most assiduously, but that "the elephant made such a rapid advance from the jungle, with one trumpet and three strides, that he had not even time to shout before the mischief was done!" As I turned in again and rolled myself in the blankets (the thermometer stood at 42°), I felt a pleasing conviction that he and his brother rogues would not, at any rate, lie on their backs again that night, should they relinquish themselves any more to the seductions of repose.

I hardly expected to see the elephant again; but just as I was getting up at daylight one of the men ran in to say the brute was making his way towards us through the jungle close by. I ran out and could hear the crackling of branches near the two elephants which were picketed on the edge of the jungle, and in a few minutes the tusker stepped out near them, and looked towards us. Now was there a hurrying to and fro in camp; the cook forsook the coffee he was preparing for me, and the Bengalee lascárs their hookahs. The movement had a decided tendency towards the other side of the small river between us and the main encampment, and the native doctor's long and lank form was conspicuous in the van. The tusker was a fine elephant, nearly nine feet high, but with poor tusks for so tall an animal. He stood looking quietly towards us, and evinced no intention of meddling with us again. He was a dangerous brute to have about, however, so I walked towards him, rifle in hand. I expected him to come on, when, if I failed to stop him (I was using my double 8-bore rifle, with twelve drams of the new No. 8 pebble-powder in each barrel), I had the river-bank on my right, to jump down which would have placed me in safety. When I was within forty yards the elephant turned suddenly to his right into the jungle. I had not time for a clear head-shot, so I gave him one barrel behind the shoulder, whilst the left took him too far back. The trackers followed him for about thirty miles, when they found him dead on the bank of the Myanee, and extracted his tusks. They did not return to camp for three days, owing to the difficulties of the country.

On January 28th our provision-boats arrived from Rungamuttea, and the men said a herd of elephants had crossed the river the night before in view of the boats, and about fifteen miles below our camp. All hands were quite rested now, and in an hour's time Gool Budden's party had started, the men marching along the river-bank by the elephant-paths, whilst their provisions and tools were floated down on bamboo rafts. I followed next day, and the trackers having found the herd on a tributary stream to the Myanee, the surround was commenced and completed without trouble. The stockade was then begun without delay, the coolies working all night in cutting the requisite poles and young trees for building it, and by afternoon of the 31st all was in readiness. The surround was not large, and the situation of the kheddah between two hills was a good one, so we managed to drive the elephants in at the first attempt. There were only thirteen, but seven of them were tuskers, three of these being very large. The two that form the subjects of illustrations of the *koomeriah* and *meerga* castes of elephants were among them, and were photographed for me by a friend when I reached Chittagong.

The kheddah had been made small to save time and we were now afraid that so many tuskers might force the stockade, so all hands were set to work to construct a second barrier in support of the first. This consisted, like the inner one, of uprights twelve feet high, about six inches in diameter, and supported by sloping props, the whole laced together with strips of cane. However, we might have saved ourselves this trouble, as the tuskers made no attempts upon the stockade. One female became troublesome after dark, and large fires were lighted all round, whilst men stood ready with lighted bamboo torches to repel her charges. She was certainly a most determined beast, and would have formed a fine subject for a Landseer or a Weir as she stalked round, occasionally standing with one foot poised in irresolution, as the points where she was seen to meditate an attack bristled with torches and sharp bamboos. Two or three times she strode across the narrow trench along the foot of the barricade, and thrust at it in a way that made it bend and shake for some distance on each side of the point of attack, but from the toughness and pliability of the structure it was never in danger. It was not until she had been severely burnt, and had also in turn injured one of the men by striking the torch he was holding into his face, that she desisted. I lodged three ounces of No. 4 shot in her cranium, fired at about a yard's distance, during her charges at the barrier. I sat on the stockade under shelter of an overhanging bough, watching the elephants until far into the night. The scene was a very wild one. The huge beasts impounded in so small an enclosure, the crackling and blazing fires all round, lighting up the trees to their topmost branches, and the ready shouts and challenges with which any of their movements were met by the watchful hunters, formed so exciting a scene that sleep was out of the question. The largest tusker kept the other males in a state of great disquiet. When he made the round of the kheddah at a slow, majestic pace, the commotion amongst his juniors was tremendous; and though keeping out of his way, they made vicious prods at the ones smaller than themselves. He, however, behaved most magnanimously, only punishing the next largest to himself if he fell in his way, but never going after him in a malicious manner. Had he done so he could certainly have killed him in such a confined enclosure. One of the tuskers was hurled against the barricade by a larger animal; the guards applied their lighted bamboos to the unfortunate beast while down in the trench as a hint to him not to do it again!

We secured these elephants without mishap, though some of our females showed great reluctance to working amongst so many tuskers. The men took care to cause no uproar in the enclosure, as, had the large tusker moved about rapidly, the others might have overwhelmed men and elephants in their endeavours to keep out of his way. When he was tied up he made tremendous though silent struggles to free himself, using every muscle of his giant frame in the endeavour to break his bonds. He continued to do so for several hours without intermission, when he desisted, and never afterwards renewed the struggle. This is invariably the case with the best-couraged elephants. If their first attempts fail they submit with dignity, whilst small animals hardly worth the catching will frequently fight for days, and injure themselves by useless struggling against the inevitable.

Having now captured eighty-five elephants, the marching of which out of the jungles would be a sufficiently arduous task, I ordered every one to collect on the Myanee where the stream near which we had caught the last elephants joined it, and here we formed a large camp (No. 12). The wild elephants were arranged in rows amongst the trees, two men being appointed to each to supply them with fodder and water, and to doctor their wounds. The spare men were employed in cutting fodder, which the tame elephants, as also the boats and rafts, brought to the encampment. The weather was delightfully bracing, with intense cold at nights.

I now had leisure to shoot, fish, and roam about the jungles. The forest along the river was particularly fine, and free from grass and troublesome undergrowth. It was evident from the marks on the trees that the river overflowed its banks to a considerable depth during the monsoon rains. The reason of this is that the dry-weather channel is very tortuous, so the floods take a straight course, cutting off the angles round which the stream now meandered. The spits of land subject to these inundations were overlaid with rich alluvial soil, in which one of the plants (*tára*), on which we fed the elephants, grew in great abundance. It is, I believe, a species of wild arrowroot. It has a succulent, triangular stalk, as thick as three fingers; the leaves are broad, and upwards of a foot in length. Many plants were ten feet in height. This fodder was easy to cut and convenient to stow on the elephants' backs, and was greatly relished by them. I have not seen it out of Bengal.

A remarkable product of the jungles was a sort of monster apple. It grew in great abundance on a handsome tree, like the horse-chestnut, but larger. Each tree had several hundred fruit on it, and at least one out of every hundred trees in the forest was of this kind, in full bearing. The fruit was green, with red and yellow tints on the ripest side, juicy, but very fibrous and sour. I observed that all wild animals ate it, so I ordered the cook to make a tart, though the minion expressed his fears that it might not be "good for master's body!" It required plenty of stewing, and a large amount of sugar, but was excellent from its fine acid flavour, and I had it almost daily.

It was astonishing that no one was ever injured by the falling of these large apples. They were tolerably securely attached, but still many did fall, and as the average weight was a pound and a half, they might have killed any one on whose head they had alighted. On one occasion an elephant shook a creeper that ran to the top of one of these trees, and brought a shower of fruit down, which made all who were near run for their lives, whilst a few came with heavy thuds upon the back of the author of the disturbance.

I found nothing to shoot but sámbur-deer and jungle-fowl (*Gallus ferrugineus*), squirrels of two kinds, and the black tailless hoolook monkey of the gibbon family (*Hoolook hylobates*). On the 8th February I started Sergeant Carter in advance on our return-march to civilisation, with sixty-two of the new elephants in charge of twenty-two tame ones, whilst I remained until the 13th, keeping the more troublesome and powerful animals to form my batch. The route to Rungamuttea was down the Myanee valley, as the river was low and formed an easy means of egress from the hills, whilst the country was too steep and jungly for a direct line. In some places we marched in the forest along the bank; but owing to cane-thickets and deep ravines which joined the Myanee, we usually found it more advantageous to keep to the river-bed. We were about a hundred and thirty miles from Rungamuttea, following the course of the river. It was not more than eighteen inches deep for the first few days' marches, with a firm gravelly bottom, and as the day grew warm when the sun was high it was a pleasure to the elephants, tame and wild, to be tramping in it.*

We must have presented a wild and picturesque scene as we filed down the stream. The largest elephants were secured between two or three tame ones. Some tame elephants had several half-grown wild ones fastened to them, which they kept under strict discipline, pummelling and kicking them

* The camps marked on the map are those I occupied in common with the elephants. They also made several additional halts.

if they attempted to walk in advance. On each tame elephant's pad its attendants had stowed their cooking utensils, spare ropes, and such small articles of cane-work (footstools, baskets, &c.) as they had made in their spare hours, and were taking to Chittagong to sell. Each had a long spear in his hand with which to keep the wild ones in order, if necessary. The small calves marched loose alongside their mothers. Behind the elephants came a fleet of our provision-boats carrying the rations. We usually marched from about 7 A.M. till 12, perhaps ten miles daily, when a halt was made; the elephants were secured in the forest on the bank of the river; and the people cooked their breakfasts. I always sent a boat with my tent and servants in advance of the elephants; they could reach the intended camping-ground by 10 A.M., so everything was ready for me when we arrived.

But I am anticipating, as two incidents occurred at camp No. 12 after Sergeant Carter left which may be worth mentioning. One was a tiger killing a young elephant, and my shooting the spoiler; the other, the shooting of a wild elephant in our elephant-lines.

The day after Sergeant Carter marched, two men returned with a note from him to say that a tiger had killed and partly eaten one of the young elephants of his batch close to his tent during the night; that he had ordered the carcass to be left undisturbed, and had proceeded on his march. Never having seen such a case before, I mounted an elephant and proceeded to the place.

The young elephant, a calf about four and a half feet high at the shoulder, and weighing probably six hundred pounds, had been standing just within the jungle off the encampment when seized, and was within twenty yards of the other elephants and of the sergeant's tent. Its hind-legs only were hobbled, as, being very quiet, it had been allowed almost since its capture, a fortnight before, to roam about the camp thus secured. The tiger had seized it by the throat as a bullock is seized; there were no other marks on any part of the body, and it had only been dragged a few yards. A large quantity of flesh had been eaten off both hind-quarters. As I did not know at what hour the tiger might return to his kill, and as sitting up all night in the jungles—the thermometer had been at 38° that morning—was not to be thought of, I returned to camp (it was now 4 P.M.), intending to try and find the tiger in the morning.

Next day I went to the carcass with a single pad-elephant and some men, whom I left at a distance whilst I took the elephant to the kill to reconnoitre. The jungle was continuous open forest, except on the river-bank, where there was a dense patch of thorny cane-thicket. I had calculated that I should probably find the tiger in this place after his meal. The carcass had been dragged about ten yards, and more of it had been eaten. I had scarcely remarked this when the mahout pointed quietly to the tiger lying down about fifteen yards to our left near the carcass. He was blinking at us in a good-humoured way, evidently happy after his meal, and thinking our elephant but one of the numbers he constantly saw in these uninhabited forests. He had a prominent ridge of hair on his neck, and a fine ruff round his face. I lost no time in putting an express bullet into his brain. He was a powerful, big, and old brute, measuring exactly nine feet in length, and weighing 349½ lb. As there were no inhabitants in that part of the hills, I suppose lying down close to his prey, even in the open forest, was this tiger's custom. As to his killing the elephant, there were no cattle anywhere in the hills, and all the tigers there were purely game-killers; and as by lurking on the outskirts of herds of elephants a stray calf doubtless occasionally fell in their way, I daresay this was not the first time this tiger had supped off young elephant. I have heard of what appears to be a well-authenticated case in Assam, of a tame elephant of full size, when hobbled and turned loose in a river-bed to graze, being attacked by a tiger, and severely bitten and mauled before its cries attracted the keepers, who were at a distance. In this case large pieces of flesh were torn from the elephant's thighs, and the tiger's object was evidently to make a meal of it, as it perceived it was in difficulties, being hobbled.

The shooting of the tusker in the elephant-lines occurred as follows: Whilst the elephants were at Gásban the mahouts had attempted to tie a tusker one night, as he visited the new elephants frequently, only disappearing with the dawn. He had followed us from Jádoogapára, and was in all probability the elephant I saw on looking out of the tent during the night of the 6th January. The mahouts had failed to secure him, and had thoroughly alarmed him, and though they subsequently tried various plans, he had grown too wary to be caught. When the elephants marched to Bhowálkáli he followed, and remained with us there, accompanying us to camp No. 12. He had become so accustomed to the sight of men by this time that he rarely left the elephant-lines, and did not molest the people who moved about. We might have caught him had we tried hard, but three of our females would have been required to march with him, whereas they could take charge of six wild females, which were better adapted for our purpose than one tusker; consequently he was not interfered with. But he now began to be troublesome, chasing the tame elephants when they went for fodder, and on more than one occasion nearly causing accidents amongst the men. One afternoon I was casting some rifle-shells when a mahout came to say the elephant was in the lines, and was interrupting work; so I loaded one of the shells—a copper-bottle—with detonating powder, and went after him. I found him stalking about amongst the new elephants, and the men hiding; so, getting within four yards of his tail, I whistled. As he turned I fired the shell into his temple and dropped him dead.

On the 13th of February my detachment of elephants marched from camp No. 12. On the 17th we found two dead elephants, both young ones, of Sergeant Carter's detachment, in the river-bed. The Myanee was deeper at this part than it had been higher up, and the exposure and fatigue of marching through water almost covering them had been too much for the youngsters. They were lying on a spit of sand; loathsome masses of maggots. They had died on the 10th; and as the wash caused by the elephants passing sent wavelets over the spit, the maggots floated off in tens of thousands, and the still water all along the banks was soon filled with them. As we camped two hundred yards below, on the same side of the river as the carcasses, the men could scarcely get water for some time without maggots in it.

On the 19th the morning was overcast and it thundered, whilst a fresh came down the river, showing it had been raining in the parts we had recently left. The river was too deep for marching, so I ordered a halt for that day, and in the afternoon, after a heavy shower, took my rifles and went in search of game. There were marks of bison (*Gavœus gaurus*) and sámbur, but I was unfortunate enough to see nothing larger than jungle-fowl and monkeys, until coming home we heard a single elephant feeding in thick cover. However, we could not get a sight of him. On ascending a piece of rising ground, from which we could see over a portion of the forest, and whence we expected to be able to make out the direction of the camp, we found ourselves altogether at a loss. There was no prominent landmark —nothing but level forest. The sun had been heavily obscured the whole day. I had no compass with me, and my three gun-bearers held diametrically opposed opinions as to the direction of the cardinal points. Here was a pretty fix. The gloomy and dripping forest was fast becoming dark; there were no paths; wild elephants were numerous; and we could not even agree upon the direction we ought to take!

I remembered at this time a piece of advice Sir Samuel Baker gives in his *Rifle and Hound in Ceylon*—namely, to make one's self as comfortable as possible when thus lost, and to wait till some one comes in search, instead of straying further and increasing the difficulties; so we set to work to make a fire. But this was not an easy matter. Everything was dripping wet, except a letter I had in my pocket—a letter from a lady, which was only sacrificed under the exigency of our rigorous circumstances—and we had great difficulty in getting any more substantial materials in the dark. At last the men collected a sufficiency of the dry inner bark of a tree, and the chewed fibres of wood from elephants' dung, and by shooting a piece of rag out of my rifle into my pocket-handkerchief hung on a branch, we got a light. A cheerful blaze soon sprang up, and I fired a couple of shots. In a few seconds a perfect chorus of elephants' cries, about two miles distant, broke the stillness, as the mahouts in camp made their animals "speak" (as they term it) in answer to our signal. There was every description of note from the stentorian lungs of the huge animals, from the shrill trumpet to the sustained tremulous growl. We could even distinguish the voices of several individuals—Tárá Ránee, Mohungowry, Issamuttee, &c. Whilst waiting for the relieving party, sitting round the cheerful blaze, and congratulating ourselves in having succeeded in starting it, a sudden puff of gunpowder in its midst made us all jump up. On examining into the cause, I found that an 8-bore cartridge loaded with ten drams had fallen from my pocket in the darkness before we kindled the fire, and had now gone off on the ground, but the bullet remained on the spot, whilst the cartridge-case was only moved a few inches. I judge from this that a cartridge going off in a sportsman's pocket would do him no harm beyond setting his coat on fire. An elephant and men with torches soon arrived, and we reached home safely.

A faithful dog that I had picked up at Jádoogapára accompanied the party, and showed great delight at finding me. He was a hill-dog belonging to the Joomas, and had strayed from a party of them who came to see the elephants. He was of a bright rufous colour, with a bushy tail curling over his back, and had a sharp, intelligent face. He was about a year old. The first time I saw him was one day playing with two fox-terrier puppies and my bull-bitch Lady, which accompanied me on my trip, and I could not but admire the amiability he displayed when I threw tent-pegs at him to drive him away; so I finally made friends with him. Though he had been brought up entirely amongst natives he would have nothing to do with any of my men thenceforth, and always remained close to my tent. At the same time he never came in unless specially invited, nor pushed himself forward in any way. He never fought with the others for food, but would sit patiently by and take without greediness whatever was left or given to him. His sagacity and attachment to me were extraordinary. On one occasion, intending to shoot by the way, I had started in a boat in advance of the elephants down the Myanee, having sent "Jooma," as I called the dog, to be tied up where he could not see me start. He was let loose when the other boats and elephants started half an hour later, and not finding me, he plunged into the river instead of going in a boat as usual, evaded all attempts to stop him, and swam down stream, running along the banks where they admitted of it. We were floating quietly down with the stream, looking for game, when a distant yapping attracted our attention, and I saw a small object, from which the voice proceeded, coming down the river. This was Jooma's head as he swam. We waited for him, to his great delight; he had followed us for eight miles. I subsequently took him round by Chittagong and Calcutta to Dacca, and thence to Mysore, where he is now happy with my other dogs, a thousand miles from the land of his birth.

I reached Rungamuttea on the 24th February. The elephants had been marched by land latterly, as the river was deep. The only incident that occurred worthy of note was the drowning of one of our new elephants, and two of our best tame females, near Rungamuttea. We had left the Myanee above its junction with the Kurnafoolie, and were marching by land, but owing to the lie of the country we had to cross the Kurnafoolie occasionally. It was very deep, and the elephants had to swim. One morning whilst crossing where it was about eighty yards wide and thirty feet deep, in a gorge through a saddle in the hills, a tusker, which was secured between two tame ones—one in advance of, and one behind him—sank like a stone, probably from being seized with cramp from the coldness of the water, and dragged the two females with him. Their mahouts tried in vain to slash the ropes through: they had barely time to save themselves by swimming. Anything more sudden or unexpected I never witnessed. One elephant appeared again for a brief moment—at least about two feet of her trunk did: she waved us a last farewell, when all was still, save the air-bubbles which continued to rise for some time from the calm, deep pool. Every one who witnessed it was shocked. The drivers of the elephants yet to cross hesitated; we could not but believe the unfortunate beasts would come up again. Their mahouts sat down and cried like children over the loss of the faithful beasts they had tended for years.

Elephants are such excellent swimmers that I cannot understand how it was that the two tame ones were unable to gain the shore, which was only thirty yards distant, by towing the drowning wild one. When they floated we found that they were in no way entangled; and it was not owing to snags catching the ropes, nor to any under-current, that they were drawn down. One of the tame ones—Geraldine—was a great favourite of mine, and she and the other were worth £300 each. The tusker was worth £600, so the money loss to Government was considerable.

Next morning I went in a boat to examine the bodies. The news of the occurrence had spread, and I found about two hundred Joomas from villages near assembled on the banks of the river, with a flotilla of dug-out canoes and rafts. They had baskets and knives of every description, and were awaiting the arrival of some one in authority to give them permission to take the elephants' flesh, which they eat. They were like vultures watching a carcass until it is sufficiently decomposed to allow of a commencement being made. In the centre of the pool floated three leaden-coloured objects. These were our poor elephants. Their buoyancy was such that three men could stand on each without submerging them. The Joomas towed them ashore, and cut off their fore-feet for me, for making into footstools in remembrance of them; and I then gave them permission to fall to, which they did with such a will that by next morning at the same hour not a vestige of the elephants remained. The boats and rafts had been laden with flesh, and even the bones had been broken into pieces and carried off to boil into soup (elephants' bones are solid and have no marrow). It was well the bodies could be turned to account instead of being left to pollute the air and water, as would have been the case in most parts of India, where natives will not eat elephants' flesh.

Arrived at Rungamuttea, my chief labours were over. The trip had been very successful, and we had concluded our operations very expeditiously. Mahouts and grass-cutters came from Chittagong or volunteered from amongst the kheddah men, and every new elephant was entered in a roll and brought on to the strength of the Commissariat Department. They were then divided into lots of twenties under jemadárs, and the whole number, with the tame ones, proceeded by gentle marches *viâ* Chittagong to Dacca, a distance of 200 miles, under the supervision of the sergeant. Only two died on the way; the rest reached Dacca on 5th May. All the Europeans in the station assembled to see the cavalcade of about a hundred and thirty elephants arrive. Some calves had been born, but they had all died. Most of the new elephants carried their mahouts and their baggage. All but a few of the quietest were still attached to the tame ones, lest they should take fright and cause accidents. Arrived in the Peelkhána, or elephant-stables, a picket was allotted to each, and their systematic training was commenced. They would be fit to march to the military station of Barrackpore, near Calcutta, at the end of the year, whence they would be allotted to the different military stations, and applied to light work in about two years.

I left Dacca for Mysore in June '76, but I have recently heard of these elephants from the Commissariat Department. Sixteen died in the first year, which is not a high rate of mortality for newly-caught elephants, and others would probably die before they were fit for active service. This shows how great a number of elephants is required annually to keep up the strength of the Commissariat Department even in one Presidency. The full strength of the elephant establishment in the Lower Commissariat Circle of Bengal is nominally 1000, and the annexed table shows the number which died in one year, and may be taken as a fair annual average. Many entered in the table, particularly in the Barrackpore, Dacca, and Assam columns, are newly-captured animals, and a considerable proportion of these are milk calves.

I had expected to work the kheddahs in Bengal at the commencement of 1877, but circumstances arose which prevented it. Such operations as were conducted were but partially successful, owing to cholera breaking out amongst the kheddah men, and to the ravages of the great storm-wave which caused such terrible loss of life in Chittagong and the tracts along the north-east portion of the Bay of Bengal in November 1876. These causes rendered it difficult to collect men for the work, or to obtain fodder, and only thirty-six elephants were caught.

[TABLE.

STATEMENT OF CASUALTIES AMONGST COMMISSARIAT ELEPHANTS IN BENGAL IN 1874-75.

Causes of Casualties.	Stations at which Casualties occurred.																		Total.
	Dinapore.	Barrackpore.	Fyzabad.	Dacca Khed-dahs.	Assam Khed-dahs.	Peshawar.	Bareilly.	Gowhatty.	Lucknow.	Debrugarh.	Saugor.	Hazaribagh.	Fezpore.	Agra.	Chakrata.	Mooltan.	Shillong.	Sibsaugor.	
Falling into traps,	...	...	...	...	...	...	...	...	...	...	...	...	...	...	...	...	...	1	1
Lurza,	2	...	...	1	...	...	1	...	...	...	...	...	...	...	1	...	...	...	5
Diseases of the stomach,	1	2	...	1	...	1	...	...	...	...	...	1	...	...	...	...	...	...	6
In giving birth to calves,	1	...	...	...	2	...	...	...	...	...	...	...	...	...	...	...	...	...	3
Zahirbad,	...	5	4	8	7	...	...	1	1	...	...	...	...	...	...	...	...	...	26
Fever,	...	1	1	1	...	...	...	...	...	1	...	...	...	...	...	...	...	...	4
Injuries received,	...	...	...	2	1	...	1	...	...	...	...	...	...	...	...	...	...	...	4
Congestion of the brain,	1	...	...	...	...	...	...	...	...	...	...	...	...	...	...	...	...	...	1
Apoplexy,	1	...	...	2	7	1	...	...	...	...	...	...	...	...	...	...	...	...	11
Dysentery,	...	...	...	...	3	...	...	...	...	...	...	...	...	...	...	...	...	...	3
Colic,	1	...	...	...	1	...	...	...	1	...	...	...	...	...	...	...	...	...	3
Vomiting,	...	...	...	...	...	...	1	...	...	...	...	...	...	...	...	...	...	...	1
Inflammation of the lungs, bowels, &c.,	1	...	...	2	...	2	...	...	...	...	...	...	...	...	...	...	...	...	5
Escaped,	...	...	...	...	4	...	...	...	...	1	...	1	...	...	...	...	...	...	6
Internal diseases,	...	11	...	...	...	1	...	...	...	...	1	...	...	...	...	1	...	1	15
Debility,	...	...	...	11	1	...	...	...	...	...	...	...	...	1	...	...	...	...	13
Drowned,	...	3	...	1	...	...	...	...	...	...	...	...	...	...	...	...	1	...	5
Cold,	1	...	...	...	...	...	...	...	...	...	...	...	...	...	...	...	...	...	1
Destroyed,	...	...	...	...	...	...	1	...	...	...	...	...	...	...	...	...	...	...	1
Total,	9	22	5	29	26	5	4	1	2	2	1	2	...	1	1	1	1	2	114

CHAPTER XIV.

RIFLES AND CAMP-MANAGEMENT.

GENERAL REMARKS — HEAVY RIFLES — OPINIONS OF SIR SAMUEL BAKER AND THE LATE CAPTAIN JAMES FORSYTH UPON RIFLES—HEAVY GAME—LIGHT GAME—4 AND 8 BORE RIFLES—HEAVY CHARGES—BATTERY FOR INDIAN SPORT—EXPRESS RIFLES—OBJECTIONS TO THE EXPRESS FOR HEAVY GAME — SHELLS — CAMP - ARRANGEMENTS — MALARIAL FEVER—PROBABLY ONLY CONTRACTED AT NIGHT — PRECAUTION AGAINST MALARIA—NECESSITY FOR SLEEPING OFF THE GROUND—CAMP-FIRES—TEMPERANCE—BOILED AND DISTILLED WATER—INDIAN SERVANTS.

THE reader who has done me the honour to follow me thus far, will be aware that my recitals have been confined hitherto chiefly to sketches of jungle-life in the parts of India I have had experience of, and to the natural history, capturing, and training of elephants.

Before passing to other animals, and the more purely sporting portion of my narration, I propose to offer a few remarks upon rifles, and on the medical portion of camp-management. I can look back to having lost so many animals when a beginner—animals toiled after without grudge, and the loss of which, through the ineffectiveness of my rifles for the work in hand, cost me pangs at the time which only the young sportsman can understand; and I have suffered so much from the malarial fevers that are the most dreaded enemy the sportsman has to contend against in campaigns into the localities where large game is to be found,—that I hope my experiences may save some from similar disappointments of the chase, and from the shiverings of ague and burnings of fever that I have endured, and which may be averted with knowledge and care.

There is perhaps no subject upon which more frequent discussions arise amongst sportsmen than that of the best rifles for game. The matter really admits of no great latitude of opinion, nor is it men who have had much experience that differ. The conflicting views are held by those who speak more from theory or a limited experience than extensive practical knowledge. There are two well-known sportsmen, amongst others, whom every one will admit to be thoroughly qualified to speak on the subject,—namely, the late Captain James Forsyth, Bengal Staff Corps, author of the *Sporting Rifle and its Projectiles* (which I strongly recommend to any young sportsman who has not read it); and Sir Samuel Baker, whose experience with large game is unrivalled. Both advocate the use of the heaviest rifle the sportsman can manage upon all sorts of game. Yet it is not unusual to hear men express a decided opinion to the contrary, generally conveyed in the formula, "A 12-bore is big enough for anything." Sir Samuel Baker says that such should rather say, "I cannot carry a heavy gun," or, "I cannot shoot with one," than speak against them on principle.

All the world over animals are divisible into but two classes considered as objects for the rifle, and for each class a distinct rifle is required. The first consists of such ponderous beasts as the elephant, rhinoceros, buffalo, and bison, whose hides are tough and whose bones are massive. The second comprises tigers, bears, and all descriptions of deer and smaller animals; these may be termed the soft-bodied class. For the former a ball of immense smashing power is necessary, otherwise it may be arrested by powerful bones and muscles before it can do sufficient damage; for the second class, whose bodies do not offer a quarter the resistance of those of the larger quadrupeds, a different kind of effect—that of the express or explosive bullet—is the most advantageous, because it can be produced by a rifle of a more manageable description than one required to effect as great results with a solid bullet.

I have generally found men who do not use or understand heavy-game rifles make one or other of the following remarks on examining them: "What a weight! who could carry that?" or, "It must kick fearfully!" It will be understood that, as regards the first objection, such pieces are only taken in hand by the sportsman when actually firing at game, and are at other times carried by his attendants. I may also say that the weight seems very much less under the exciting circumstances in which such pieces are generally used than when they are handled in cold blood. As regards the kicking, their weight being proportionate to the charge of powder used, they recoil little more than an ordinary 12-bore.

It is sometimes argued that hundreds of large animals have been bagged with 12 or 14 bore rifles, or even smaller weapons. True: but how many more have escaped or have been consigned to die lingering deaths, that would have been secured with heavier metal? A 14 or 16 bore, with 4 drams of powder, is sufficient to kill even an elephant if a fair shot can be had at his brain. But suppose the elephant to be rushing through a tangled break or long grass, when only a hurried and indistinct shot can be had at him, the smaller gun would be useless unless its ball reached his brain, whilst the heavy projectile would floor or stun, even if it did not kill him. A rifle for heavy game should be capable of meeting these contingencies—not be adapted only for picked shots and bright moments.

A few years ago 12-bore rifles (1½-oz. ball) were more generally used perhaps than any others for general shooting, but the introduction of the express has led to their very general supersession for sport with the lighter class of game. I think all experienced sportsmen are agreed that 12-bores are too insignificant for use upon the heavy class, and that they form a half-and-half weapon, neither one thing nor the other—wanting the accuracy, handiness, and killing power of the express, and the smashing effect of a large bore—and are weapons which we may well dispense with in the present day. Some sportsmen—not very keen ones—like a 12-bore on the ground that it gives them, within the compass of one weapon, a better chance with both classes of game than a large-bore or an express; that is, they seek to adapt one piece to widely different uses. As well might a man hope to find combined in the same horse the speed of a Derby winner and the power of a Suffolk Punch! The only description of shooting for which a 12-bore is still useful is at beasts of the lighter class which may happen to be seen but indistinctly through masses of twigs or other obstructions. The express bullet is not always to be depended upon for covert-shooting. Its conical form leads to its being easily deflected from its course. I have frequently found no further traces of an express bullet after a shot fired through thick cover, where a spherical ball would certainly have reached its mark. But shooting through thick places, even in an Indian jungle, is decidedly exceptional.

Sir Samuel Baker recommends the use of a four-ounce (No. 4) ball for very heavy game. That even this ball, projected by 12 drams of powder, will frequently fail to floor an elephant, or to put a bison or buffalo *hors de combat* at once, I have proved; yet men who have never used them will argue against such heavy weapons as unnecessary.

I at first killed several elephants with a No. 12 spherical-ball rifle, with hard bullets and 6 drams of powder, but I found it insufficient for many occasions. I then had a single-barrelled C. F. No. 4-bore rifle, weighing 16½ lb., and firing 10 drams, made to order by Lang & Sons, Cockspur Street. A cartridge of this single-barrel, however, missed fire on one occasion and nearly brought me to grief, so I gave it up and had a No. 4 double smooth-bore, C. F., weighing 19½ lb., built by W. W. Greener. This I have used ever since. I ordinarily fire 12 drams of powder with it. This is as far as man can go with powder and lead, if I except Sir Samuel Baker's half-pound shell-rifle, the "Baby;" and though the above gun has failed me once, as I will hereafter relate, it usually effectually settles any difference with an elephant.

I have another favourite weapon, a No. 8 double rifle, firing 12 drams, and weighing 17 lb., also by W. W. Greener. As may be imagined it has enormous penetration, and is very accurate. I have stopped and killed charging elephants with it, but I prefer the 4-bore for certain occasions in elephant-shooting. The illustration shows the relative and actual sizes of balls of the different calibres above mentioned. Gauge means the number of spherical lead balls to the pound.

No. 4. (Four oz.) No. 8. (Two oz.) No. 12. (One and a half oz.) ·500. ·450. (Express.)

NOTE.—Eley's No. 4 cartridges do not take a bullet of much over 3½ oz. A breech-loading 4-bore, therefore, carries a bullet only a little larger than a muzzle-loading No. 5.

Heavy-game rifles are, of course, only taken in hand when the game is met; the sportsman could not carry them far himself. Any man of medium strength will find himself capable of handling a 17 to 20-lb. rifle, and of firing 12 drams with spherical ball, under the excitement of elephant-shooting. As regards recoil, it is not serious with such weighty guns. A friend of mine, the well-known "Smooth-bore" of Madras, once fired at a tusker with my No. 8 double rifle and 12 drams. I usually keep the left barrel of heavy pieces on half-cock, as the jar to the left lock in firing the right barrel is very great. "Smooth-bore" did not think of this, and we afterwards found that the left barrel had also had its fling at the tusker. My friend had fired 24 drams and a pair of 2-oz. bullets almost simultaneously, but said he did not feel any severe recoil!

All rifles for elephants and heavy game should be double-barrelled, as they have to be made as heavy if single to withstand the recoil, and the danger of a miss-fire is a fatal objection to single-barrelled weapons. It is evidently useless to have a light large-bore, as the recoil of such a weapon precludes the use of a charge of powder proportionate to the weight of the ball. A recent writer on Indian sport speaks of "a powerful 6-bore (2⅜ oz.) rifle, burning 4 drams." About three times this charge would be more nearly what such a rifle would require. A big ball before a light charge of powder is as useless as a heavy sword in the hands of a weak man.

Were I asked my opinion as to a battery to be taken out to India I should recommend a ·450 express* as the sportsman's own weapon—the one to be always in his hands, whether tiger-shooting in the jungle or antelope-stalking in the plains; and a heavy rifle of No. 8 gauge, to burn up to 12 drams of powder, and weighing between 16 and 17 lb., for anything larger than tigers. Of course if the sportsman can afford a pair of the latter weapons so much the better. If he intend to shoot elephants—and the day may come when elephant-shooting will be allowed again in India—he should have a still larger double rifle or smooth-bore. I should recommend a No. 4. I have, for my own part, become so thoroughly impressed, after giving them a fair trial, of the indispensability of heavy rifles for large game, that I disposed of a pair of pet 12-bores I had, and with which I had killed many big beasts, in favour of a double 4, a double 8, and a double express. Without something of the cannon kind, game of the ponderous class cannot be brought to fighting quarters with even a moderate degree of safety or effect. The sportsman will have to follow the ignominious plan of popping at them from safe places, or, however boldly he may encounter them, he will find small weapons entail constant disappointment. With really heavy metal he feels that confidence and power to overcome the hugest beasts which constitute the chief elements of pleasure in following and facing them.

I am decidedly opposed to the use upon buffalo, bison, and such animals, of the express rifle of either ·500 or ·450 bore (equivalent to 38 and 50 spherical gauge). The express is essentially a rifle for soft-bodied animals, and is not adapted for use on those with thick hides and massive bones. Though bison have not unfrequently been killed with the express, a return of the beasts wounded and lost for each one bagged would, as far as the experience of my friends and myself goes, be a terrible document. Sir Samuel

* Messrs Lang & Sons, 22 Cockspur Street, are now building for me a ·450 express, to burn 5¼ standard drams. The advantages which will be secured by this unprecedentedly large charge will be apparent to those who understand that most admirable weapon the express. About 4½ drams is the largest charge that has been used hitherto in the ·450. Powder-measures supplied by various gunmakers differ considerably, and often bear about the same proportion to the standard measure as the reputed quart does to the imperial. It is advisable, therefore, to have a guarantee from gunmakers as to the actual amount of powder which their cartridges are capable of holding.

Baker says: "A hollow bullet fired from an express rifle will double up a deer; but it will be certain to expand upon the hard skin of elephants, rhinoceros, hippopotami, buffalo, &c., in which case it will lose all power of penetration. When a hollow bullet strikes a large bone, it absolutely disappears into minute particles of lead, and of course it becomes worthless."

Two sportsmen, Captains E. and P., perhaps the best shots in Southern India, if the Bangalore rifle-meeting performances are a test, who have shot in the Billiga-rungun hills with me, have, after ample experience, denounced the use of the express on bison. On one occasion P. fired six times at a bull with a ·500 express and hollow bullets: the sixth shot, which was in the head, killed it; but the others, which were all accurately placed behind the shoulder, beyond sickening the beast failed through want of penetration. E. fired eleven shots amongst bison with both solid and hollow hardened bullets, with unsatisfactory results: one bull that was dropped, and again floored whilst struggling on to his legs, and left for dead whilst E. pursued the herd, got up, and was never seen again. If a *solid* hardened bullet be used with an express, the principle of the weapon, and the cause of its immense efficiency on soft-bodied animals, are lost, and the rifle becomes merely a hard-hitting small-bore. No one will dispute the sporting truism that "a good big 'un is better than a good little 'un;" and both theory and practice sufficiently show that a hard-hitting large-bore, before which the largest bones are as those of chickens, is the proper weapon for heavy game.

My experience of shells has been too limited to allow of my saying much on the subject. What I have seen of them has led me to discard them myself as unnecessary, but I do not wish to condemn them. I have found Forsyth's swedged shells fairly effective in a 12-bore rifle; but Mr W. W. Greener advised me against having them for an 8-bore he was making for me, on the ground of their not possessing sufficient stability for a large-bore and heavy charge. He recommended a steel-core bottle-shell in preference. I tried three Forsyth's shells, which I made and loaded carefully myself, with the above rifle (No. 8) and 6 drams of powder, at a target forty yards distant. Two of these flew into two pieces each; these pieces struck three feet apart, and effectually frightened me from trying any more experiments. I think that with the express—which acts like an explosive bullet—for the lighter class of game, and with heavy solid spherical bullets (the only reliable bone-smashers) for the heavier class, sportsmen will find themselves able to do without shell-rifles of a calibre between the two.

Supposing the young sportsman to have provided himself with an efficient battery, I will now proceed to make a suggestion or two for his camp-management.

It will be unnecessary for me to enter into details about equipage. Excellent hints on the subject of tents and kit may be found in many books on Indian sport, and in others devoted entirely to the subject. The great principle to be borne in mind in making arrangements for jungle-life is, that the sportsman should make himself and followers as comfortable as possible. Any amount of hard work may be done by all during the day if they have dry clothes and a comfortable dinner and bed at the end of it. Roughing it when there is no necessity—and there seldom is nowadays in India—is a mistake which only the inexperienced fall into. There is rarely any reason why a sportsman should sleep without sheets, drink out of a tin pot, or dine off a box, though these are merely discomforts. In matters actually affecting the health of the party in jungle localities, it is suicidal not to know what are the precautions to be observed, or to neglect them.

Malarial fever is the great obstacle with which the sportsman in Indian jungles has to contend; but, though it is a dread reality, it is at the same time made more of a bugbear to the inexperienced than it need be. Miasmatic air, from its heaviness, lies and travels close to the ground, and it is probably not active during the day when the jungles are warmed by the sun. Cold and dampness are its great auxiliaries. It appears to be taken into the system by inhalation, and it is supposed the poison also exists in water contaminated by decaying vegetable matter. As evening closes in there is a raw feeling in the air in the jungles which the sportsman must perceive is inimical to health. Some jungle-tribes build their houses on platforms ten feet high, knowing by experience the advantage to health in being thus elevated. But as a moving camp cannot take this precaution, the miasma about the sleepers must be destroyed or dissipated. This is to be done by keeping up fires to windward. The pestilential exhalations are thus carried up in the current of lighter air, or are consumed. Small tents of thick material should be used for master and servants, as they are warmer than large ones. At night the jungle-people in each camp, or some of the sportsman's own men, should keep up a fire as close as possible to the tents, and so placed that the warm air from it may blow over them. Whilst within its influence it is impossible that malaria can touch the sleepers. Let the sportsman but go out of the circle of the fires during the night, and he will feel how cold and raw the air is compared to that within their genial influence.

Every one must sleep well off the ground. The sportsman's cot should be at least three feet high—raised by forked uprights if necessary—and he should sleep within mosquito-curtains.* For his servants, if nothing else

* In some parts of India the nights are so sultry, even in the forests, that this would hardly be possible. It is doubtful, however, if miasma is abroad in such a temperature.

is available the tent-sacks should be stuffed with straw or dry grass; these will raise the men above the dampness of the ground. Servants are excessively careless, and unless the sportsman see after them himself they will take no precautions on their own account. All rank vegetation close at hand should be cleared away, by burning if possible, and the camp should be situated on as high and dry ground as can be found, but must not be exposed to high winds.

The sportsman should invariably change his clothes and boots if wet from rain or perspiration the moment he comes in; not go out earlier, nor remain out later in the evening, than necessary; and have his meals as regularly as possible. It is a good plan to take something, if only a few biscuits, with one, as in the heat of the chase one may lose the men who carry the luncheon-basket. Temperance in the use of liquor is of course absolutely necessary. Everything that tends to debilitate the system renders it liable to the effects of malaria. The sportsman whilst undergoing unusual exposure and hard work can ill afford to be careless in any respect. One frequently feels so well with the pleasant exercise and excitement of a jungle-trip that there is a tendency to excess or heedlessness.

I always have the water for my own and servants' cooking and drinking boiled and cooled before using. I have been almost exclusively a water-drinker for years, and believe that no one need be afraid of any water if this precaution—or better still, distillation—be adopted. A small still is easily carried about, and the water of any puddle can then be used. The plan of putting brandy into water to kill the deleterious matter is admitted to be perfectly useless. If out early or late, a cheroot is an excellent precaution against breathing the miasma which is prevalent at those hours, or a torch of dried bamboos carried in the hand will effectually dispel the cold air. Exposure to dew must be particularly avoided.

Some sportsmen take two or three grains of quinine daily whilst in feverish localities. It may do good and can do no harm, but it can be of little avail without every precaution in other respects. I was amused on one occasion by two friends who came to my camp for bison-shooting. They were imbued with a wholesome dread of fever, and had brought with them a large bottle of medicine, in the averting powers of which they placed much reliance, and with which they frequently refreshed themselves. They went to the top of the Billiga-rungun hills, and in the heat of the chase after bison stayed out in the jungle two nights, sleeping in improvised shelters hardly sufficient to keep off the dew, without a fire, and on the ground! I had been unable to accompany them; but when they returned and told me of their doings, and of the constancy with which they had applied themselves to their medicine, I assured them that all the quinine mixture in the world would not counteract exposure such as they had undergone. They returned to their station in a great fright, and had hardly got there before they had such severe fever as almost sent them both to England. It is thus that fever often comes to be made the spectre it is to the inexperienced. One gets it through reckless carelessness, and speaks of the deadliness of the jungles he visited, whilst he might have lived in them in safety for a month with proper care. I presume malarial fevers are similar in most parts of India, and that the following observations, though made particularly with regard to Mysore, will apply equally elsewhere:—

Fever in Mysore is of two kinds: that prevailing at certain seasons in open country, where there are no jungles within many miles, and which seems due entirely to the sudden variations of temperature attendant on the changes of season; and the more noxious kind, similar, but more severe, in its symptoms, contracted in jungle localities, and apparently the result of miasma or poison arising from decaying vegetable matter. These fevers are very seldom fatal to Europeans, except the latter in aggravated cases; but they are most difficult to shake off, recurring at varying stated periods, often for many years. They debilitate the system, and may bring into prominence any other weak point the patient has.

Amongst natives, on the other hand, malarial fevers are exceedingly fatal. Far more succumb to them every year than to cholera and small-pox put together. As fever, however, is insidious in its working, and is not infectious, it causes little alarm, and comparatively little is heard of it. It appears to be owing to the greater natural strength of the European constitution that Englishmen withstand, or throw it off, where natives succumb. Nursing in the stages where the patient is inclined, through prostration, to do nothing but die quietly, also puts to right those who, if left as the native frequently is without suitable nourishment and attention, would fare little better than he does.

Fever is most prevalent about the commencement and end of the rainy season. The alternations in temperature are then considerable, and the winds in the open country are chilly. In the jungles, the decaying vegetation is stirred up by light rains which are insufficient to wash it away. The jungles are most healthy during the hot weather, when the undergrowth has been burnt. This burning is the grand destroyer of all malaria, and the sportsman may tramp the then begrimed forests in perfect safety.

Fever generally shows itself in a week or ten days after the person has been subjected to the influence that has caused it. It begins with lassitude headache, loss of appetite, and pains in the limbs. Severe shivering fits follow, generally accompanied by vomiting. After a few hours of this, more or less, a hot fit, equally intense, commences, at the end of which the patient probably perspires freely (if steps have been taken to induce this great desideratum in fever treatment). The attack is then over for the time. It may recur the next, second, or third day. I have had perhaps as much experience of fever as any one, before I understood how to avoid it, and may briefly illustrate its course in my own case. Ten years ago I had my first attack. I was prostrated, with intervals of delirium, for a week, and had to take two months' leave of absence for change of air. For about three years fits occurred at gradually lengthening intervals, and of decreasing severity. They were induced by much exposure to the sun or night air, over-fatigue, or irregularity of any kind. I subsequently contracted fresh attacks, but these did not take such hold upon me as the first. One may become to some extent acclimatised to fever, as one never can to exposure to the sun.

Though I think I might almost set up as a medical practitioner if I only had fever cases to deal with, as my experience in treating myself and followers has been of an extensive character, I will not lengthen my remarks by going into that subject. Should a sportsman unfortunately contract fever, he will find admirable directions, in small compass, for self-treatment, in the medical portion of a small work entitled the *European in India.*

I may add one suggestion which, if I remember rightly, is not contained in the book referred to, that the vapour-bath, made with a vessel of boiling water placed under a chair, upon which the patient sits, the whole being enveloped in a thick blanket, will be found a valuable addition to the other treatment, and soon steams the chills of fever out of the sufferer's bones.

A word for Indian servants, than whom there probably are not better in the world for camp-life. How delighted one's "boys" are when "going shooting" is the word! They are cheerful and willing under great discomforts, and with few appliances make their master as comfortable in the jungles as in headquarters. The manner in which a good camp-servant will serve up dinner, from soup to pudding, is astonishing. His cooking-range is but a shallow trench in the ground, in which is the fire, and over which the earthen pots simmer, the whole sheltered perhaps from a howling storm by a tree or a few mats. The sportsman soon finds that, if only from motives of convenience, it is necessary to look to his servants' welfare. Englishmen in India are, as a rule, very kind to their servants, who become warmly attached to good masters' interests; but for want of forethought young sportsmen's followers are sometimes subjected to discomforts which do not arise from want of humanity, but of knowledge. For my own part, having resided so much amongst natives—often not seeing a European for months together—I feel that sport would not yield me one-half the pleasure it does if my people did not enjoy it with me, and feel interested in their master's success. It would be unpleasant to think that they disliked my trips into the jungles, and probably with reason, if they were to be exposed to danger of fever. A rig-out of warm clothes and a blanket at intervals, with a small travelling allowance to compensate for the extra expense they are put to for their food, keep servants healthy and contented. If the marches are long, the sportsman's means of transport—usually carts in Southern India — should be increased for the servants' convenience. Long foot-marches on cold nights or hot days soon knock up domestics accustomed to life in comfortable quarters.

CHAPTER XV.

ELEPHANT-SHOOTING.

GOVERNMENT PROHIBITION REGARDING ELEPHANT-SHOOTING—THE TRUE KING OF BEASTS—PECULIAR EXCITEMENT OF ELEPHANT-SHOOTING—DANGER OF THE SPORT—THE WILD ELEPHANT'S MODE OF ATTACK—STRUCTURE OF THE ELEPHANT'S HEAD—THE BRAIN—THE BEST SHOTS—GUNS FOR ELEPHANT-SHOOTING—SIR SAMUEL BAKER'S OPINION—SHOOTING ELEPHANTS BEHIND THE SHOULDER—THE FORMER METHOD OF SHOOTING WITH "JINJALLS"—THE ELEPHANT'S CHARACTER AS AN ANIMAL OF SPORT—CIRCUMSTANCES UNDER WHICH THEY USUALLY ATTACK MAN—HOW TO FIND THE TUSKERS IN A HERD—THE ALARM-SIGNAL—ELEPHANTS' RUSHES—DANGER OF SHOUTING AT ELEPHANTS—A COURAGEOUS FEMALE IN THE CHITTAGONG HILLS—KILLS A MAN—CHARGES MY RIDING-ELEPHANT—FLOOR HER—ANOTHER CHARGING FEMALE IN KÁKENKOTÉ—SINGLE ELEPHANTS—THEIR HABITS—ELEPHANTS LYING DOWN—THEIR SKILL IN RETREATING—HOW TO FOLLOW WOUNDED ELEPHANTS—DANGER OF SHOOTING ROGUE ELEPHANTS NOT GREATER THAN ATTACKING HERDS—TAKING OUT TUSKS—DEAD ELEPHANTS—NATIVE IDEAS ABOUT THEIR FLESH IN MYSORE—IN CHITTAGONG—PREPARING FEET FOR FOOTSTOOLS.

AS of late years the shooting of elephants, except dangerous ones, has been prohibited throughout India and Ceylon, I have felt doubtful about writing on the subject. But it is certain that in a few years the interdiction will have to be relaxed, as elephants are being preserved without corresponding measures being taken for their reduction by capture. Information on the subject may then be of some interest, so I propose to add my quota to what has already been written regarding this grandest of all field-sports.

Who that has seen the wild elephant roaming his native jungles can deny that he is the King of Beasts? Sir Samuel Baker says, "The king of beasts is generally acknowledged to be the lion; but no one who has seen a wild elephant can doubt for a moment that the title belongs to him in his own right. Lord of all created animals in might and sagacity, the elephant roams through his native forests. He browses upon the lofty branches, upturns young trees from sheer malice, and from plain to forest he stalks majestically at break of day 'monarch of all he surveys.'"

What possible claim can the lion, or in India the tiger, lay to the royal title? Is the elephant not as infinitely their superior in every good quality of mind as he is in physical strength. Let them enter the lists against him; at one spurn from the foot of their suzerain, behold the claimants flying through the air with half the bones in their bodies broken!

It is difficult to define the exact elements which make elephant-shooting the supremely exciting sport it is; but its danger, and the necessity for the exercise of the sportsman's personal qualities of perseverance, endurance, and nerve, are prominent ones. The best trackers can only bring their master up to the game, when everything depends on himself. The size of the noble beast which is the object of pursuit; the fine line of country through which the chase always leads; and the fair stand-up nature of the encounter when the game is met,—all tend to elevate elephant-shooting above all sports with the rifle.

Let us compare it with the much-vaunted pursuit of the tiger. In Southern India at least, the latter sport is chiefly conducted from trees, towards which the beaters drive the tiger. After disposing and instructing his men, the best sportsman can do no more: he is entirely at their mercy; and even if he bags the tiger, it is only a piece of straight shooting at a large mark that he can pride himself upon. Any one who possesses influence and can obtain plenty of beaters may make a much longer score than better men not similarly circumstanced, though without possessing other personal qualifications than that of a cranium thick enough to stand the power of an Indian sun whilst perched in a tree at mid-day. Tiger-shooting is no criterion of a sportsman's attainments. Many men have bagged their fifty tigers who never succeeded in stalking an old stag sámbur. Then, if the game is not bagged, there is nothing to compensate the sportsman for his ill-luck and exposure. His only solace is in abusing his beaters; his very night's rest is embittered by the thought that if it had not been for "that rascal" who did something or other that he should not have done, he would have had *another tiger*—hollow glory—to add to his account.

What a different picture does elephant-shooting present! The sportsman's knowledge of woodcraft and of the habits of his game are constantly in requisition; the skill of his wild jungle-trackers is a never-wearying matter for admiration; the beauty and diversity of the scenery through which he passes, by lake, hill, and stream; the constant excitement kept alive by the fresher and fresher signs of the noble game ahead,—make it a sport worthy beyond all others of the true sportsman. Even if unsuccessful, the pleasures which have attended the day's pursuit surely compensate to a great extent for an empty bag. As the elephant-hunter bares his brow to the cool evening breeze on the hills in which the hunt has probably terminated, he finds pleasure in reflecting that he has done everything possible to insure success, and that, though he may not have attained it, he has done more—he has deserved it.

On the authority of the greatest of ancient or modern Nimrods, Sir Samuel Baker, elephant-shooting may be pronounced to be the most dangerous of all sports if fairly followed for a length of time. Many elephants may be killed without the sportsman's being in any peril; but if an infuriated beast does attack, his charge is one of supreme danger. This danger, however, has this charm, that though so great unless steadily and skilfully met, it is within the sportsman's power, by coolness and good shooting, to end it and the assailant's career instantly by one well-planted ball. In other sports the danger, though less in one way, is greater in others. Thus a leopard hardly bigger than a tom-cat may jump out of a bush and claw the best sportsman; and though it may not do him mortal hurt, the most skilful may be unable, through the unfair nature of the attack, to avoid undergoing the indignity.

The wild elephant's attack is one of the noblest sights of the chase. A grander animated object than a wild elephant in full charge can hardly be imagined. The cocked ears and broad forehead present an immense frontage; the head is held high, with the trunk curled between the tusks to be uncoiled in the moment of attack; the massive fore-legs come down with the force and regularity of ponderous machinery; and the whole figure is rapidly foreshortened, and appears to double in size with each advancing stride. The trunk being curled and unable to emit any sound, the attack is made in silence, after the usual premonitory shriek, which adds to its impressiveness. A tiger's charge is an undignified display of arms, legs, and spluttering; the bison rushes blunderingly upon his foe; the bear's attack is despicable; but the wild elephant's onslaught is as dignified as it seems overwhelming—and a large tusker's charge, where he has had sufficient distance to get into full swing, can only be compared to the steady and rapid advance of an engine on a line of rail. With all this the sportsman who understands his game knows that there is a natural timidity in the elephant which often plays him tricks at the last moment. It is not difficult to turn or stop him with heavy metal, and if knocked down, he never, I believe, renews the attack.

Before the sportsman can hope to succeed in elephant-shooting he must have a thorough knowledge of the structure of the head, and of the position of the animal's brain. To gain this he should examine a skull sawn vertically into halves, and, if possible, compare it with a living elephant's head; these steps will fix the prominent internal and external points in his mind.

Internally (fig. 1), it will be seen that the cranium consists of light cellular bone of very open construction. The walls between the cells are as thin as note-paper. The cells differ in size: the largest has a capacity of about two wine-glasses. There are no powerful bones, except one knob in front; a walking-stick may almost be driven through an elephant's skull from the sides. The only vital portion of the head is the brain; this lies low and far back. In a very large male elephant, say nine and a half feet at shoulder, its extreme length horizontally is twelve inches, and vertically six inches. Its shape is somewhat oval.

It will be evident, on an examination of the skull, that if the brain be missed by a shot no harm will be done to the animal, as there are no other vital organs, such as large blood-vessels, &c., situated in the head. It thus happens that, in head-shots, if the elephant is not dropped on the spot he is very rarely bagged at all. A shot that goes through his skull into his neck without touching his brain may kill him, but it will take time. I have never recovered any elephant that has left the spot with a head-shot. The blood-trail for a few yards is generally very thick, but it often ceases as suddenly as it is at first copious. Elephants are sometimes floored by the concussion of a shot, if the ball passes very close to the brain; large balls frequently effect this. No time should be lost in finishing a floored elephant, or he will certainly make his escape. Many cases have occurred of elephants which have been regarded as dead suddenly recovering themselves and making off.

The three chief shots at the elephant's brain are: the front (or forehead) shot; the side (or temple) shot; and the rear (or behind the ear) shot. The illustrations of heads in different positions will assist to explain them.

Should the sportsman and the elephant be standing on tolerably level ground, and the elephant be facing the sportsman with its head in its natural position, a shot in the centre of the forehead towards the top of the bump at the base of the trunk, and about three inches higher than a line drawn between the eyes, will be instantly fatal. (Fig. 2.)

Should the sportsman be to one side of the elephant, at right angles to it, a shot directly into the ear-hole, in a line to pass through the opposite ear, or anywhere within the blank space indicated in fig. 2, will be instantly fatal. To obtain the indicated space, draw lines from the top and butt of

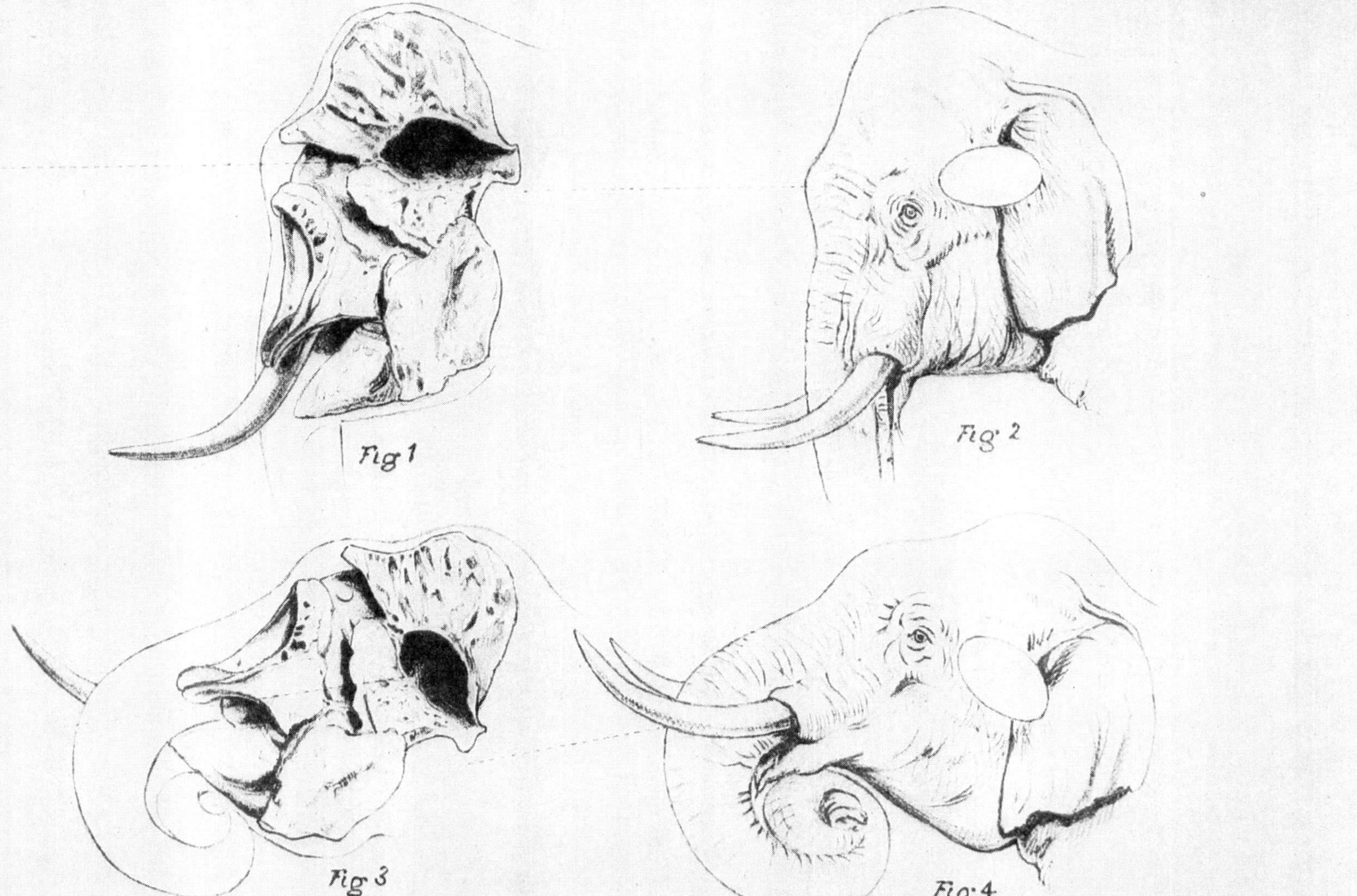

Phototint

H. M. Wright & Co London

Diagrams shewing the position of the Elephant's Brain

the ear to the eye; join the top and butt of ear by a vertical line as a base to the triangle. Of the triangle thus formed, about one-third of the area from the base is fatal. A shot nearer the apex will pass in front of the brain, if delivered at right angles with the elephant's course.

The shot behind the ear is in the hollow just over the large bump or swelling at the junction of the jaw and neck. It must be taken at about an angle of 45° with the elephant's course, from behind. When an elephant changes his position from any of those indicated above, the lines to the brain are of course altered. Thus an elephant charging with his head held high will have to be aimed at, from in front, a foot or so lower than when at rest as in fig. 2; and if taken at a half-face for the temple-shot, instead of at a right angle, the ball must enter nearer the apex of the triangle indicated in fig. 2 than for a right-angled side-shot.

The shot requiring most accurate calculation is the shot to kill a charging elephant from in front. Figs. 3, 4, show the position in which the head is usually carried in attacking; it is only lowered when the object of offence is within a few yards. To reach the brain the bullet must pass through about three feet of curled trunk, flesh, and bone; and sometimes the most powerful rifles, even a 4-bore and 12 drams, will not effect this. It is thus occasionally impossible to kill an elephant if the head be held very high, but very heavy rifles will generally either stop or floor him, or at least give him such a shock that he is glad to take himself off. I have known a female elephant to be killed by a shot through the roof of the mouth, that being the line to the brain from lower ground, when the head is held very high, and the elephant is coming down-hill. It is a fortunate circumstance, however, that elephants do not always hold their heads in this all but impracticable position.

I have never seen an elephant elevate its trunk in charging as it is commonly represented to do. It is always so careful of that organ that, if it imagines there is any danger, it keeps it coiled up. The trunk, if upraised, would obstruct the animal's sight to a great extent, and no useful purpose would be met by the position. It would be more reasonable to suppose it outstretched towards the object of attack; but it is never, in my experience, carried otherwise than tightly coiled.

There can be no two opinions amongst those who have had experience in elephant-shooting as to the description of guns required in the sport. A very small bore, with sufficient penetration to reach the brain, will kill an elephant as efficiently as one of greater calibre, if its ball be lodged in the vital spot. Elephants have been bagged with 12 and 16 smooth-bores and 3 drams, and with the ·500 and ·450 (spherical gauges Nos. 38 and 50) expresses, with solid hardened bullets. But these have been picked shots. As the sportsman cannot always hope for such, light guns should not be trusted in. It is not uncommon, however, to hear those who have made lucky shots, or have heard of their being made, decry heavy weapons as unnecessary burthens. The young sportsman, however, will do well to turn to the opinions of those really capable of advising on the subject. Sir Samuel Baker, after a life's experience with elephants and other heavy game, recommends "a single-barrel rifle to carry a half-pound projectile, or a four-ounce, according to strength of hunter." I have adopted a modification of the latter—viz., a double-barrelled 4-bore, which is no heavier than a single would have to be made to carry the charge of powder; it is smooth-bored. This affords the extra safety and execution insured by a double-barrel; and as it is only used at close quarters, a smooth-bore is sufficiently accurate, and offers a great advantage over the rifle in reduction of friction in the projectile.

If it is astonishing with what light weapons elephants may sometimes be killed, the shocks they withstand on occasions are equally surprising. I have fired a No. 4 spherical ball, driven by 12 drams of the strongest powder, through elephants' heads on three occasions without even staggering them. The narrowest escape I ever had in elephant-shooting was through failing to even stop an elephant with my No. 4.

Sir Samuel Baker, in his *Rifle and Hound*, gives an instance of an elephant's taking four shots with a 4-bore and about an ounce of powder, whilst making repeated charges, before being bagged. My humble experience has satisfied me that even the biggest balls and largest charges of powder that can be employed are not always effectual in stopping a charging elephant; and until an effective explosive shell is invented for the purpose, it appears that such contingencies as the above must be expected to occur now and then. An elephant may be killed by the temple-shot with even a 14-bore smooth-bore and 3 drams, but there is as much difference in the power required to kill by a picked shot, and to stop a charging elephant, as there is to move a locomotive at rest, and to arrest it when at full speed. Men who can "do anything" with a 10 or 12 bore (occasionally heard of) are to be envied; but ordinary mortals will do well to equip themselves against heavy game with weapons to compensate as far as possible for their inferior attainments. In my humble opinion, the largest possible guns that can be used should be used upon all kinds of big game.

Indian elephants are seldom shot behind the shoulder, and though I have killed them thus with my 4-bore, I think it a pity to do so. It would be cruel to fire at them there with smaller bores. When an elephant can be approached to within a few yards, and dropped on the spot, it is hardly sportsmanlike to take a long shot, and risk wounding the animal uselessly.

The guns called *jinjalls* with which elephants were shot by natives in former days, are simply small cannon, fired from a tripod-stand. Two which I have weigh 45 lb. each, and carry a round bullet of nearly half a pound. The charge used was about half a pound of powder; native powder is not very strong, however. The guns are of native iron, the admirable softness of which alone prevented their bursting. A hunting-party consisted of four men—two to carry the gun slung on a pole, one the stands, and the fourth —the captain—to track, lay the gun, and to fire it. When the elephants were standing listlessly in thick cover at mid-day the gun was placed on the stands at about three feet from the ground, and directed anywhere on an elephant's carcass. It was fired with a touch-match, which gave the hunters two or three seconds to get away. It was usually fired within thirty yards' distance. The match being applied, every one ran for their lives, as the gun, being overcharged for its weight, always flew back several yards, and broken limbs were not unusually the result of failing to get clear. Elephants seldom escaped when wounded, and active hunters are said to have bagged five or six occasionally in a day. As a reward of £7 per head was paid for them by the Madras Government, this was a lucrative employment. There is no doubt that if this slaughter had not been prohibited years ago, the number of elephants would have been very much diminished at this day, and a continuation of it might soon have brought about their practical extinction in parts of Southern India.

The elephant's character as an animal of sport has been variously represented. Sir Samuel Baker considers it savage, wary, and revengeful; Sir Emerson Tennent, the reverse. Both these views are, I think, extreme, and I apprehend that the truth lies between them. Though the elephant has little in his nature that can be called savage or revengeful, unless he is maddened by wounds or ill-treatment, he is certainly neither imbecile nor incapable, as Sir Emerson Tennent would have us believe, when he says, "So unaccustomed are they to act as assailants, and so awkward and inexpert in using their strength, that they rarely or ever succeed in killing a pursuer who falls into their power." Sir Emerson Tennent was not a sportsman, and apparently, from his writings, never in his life encountered elephants when roused to anger, which must be taken into consideration in accepting his view of the matter.

In their wild state, if a single elephant, or a herd, discover the approach of man at a distance (by their sense of smell), they almost invariably move off; but should a man suddenly appear within a few yards of them, he will be charged perhaps oftener by elephants than by any other animals. But in this case the elephant's position is analogous to that of a timid man, who, with a stick in his hand, is suddenly confronted by a cobra. He would naturally strike at it in self-defence, though he might be glad to let it pass if it crossed his path at some distance.

The elephant's whole character is pervaded by extreme timidity, and to this, rather than to deliberate daring, must be ascribed much of the charging when a herd is suddenly encountered. I consider it decidedly exceptional for any elephant, in a position where it has time for reflection and the option of retreat, to attack a man. Solitary elephants, which have occasionally made themselves troublesome by killing passers-by on main roads, have invariably been animals that have become accustomed to man, through their habit of frequenting fields and the neighbourhood of villages, and which, through being constantly molested by watchers, have become morose and dangerous. There have been notable instances of these elephants becoming both suspicious and revengeful, as stated by Sir Samuel Baker. In usually retreating before man, the wild elephant shows no inferiority in courage to other jungle animals, as they all retire from his intrusion. In jungles where elephants are not harassed, they are eminently unsuspicious and inoffensive.

My own modest experience in elephant-shooting rests upon only about twenty elephants bagged. I lost several others when I first commenced, however, and I have had a good deal to do with troublesome animals, whilst driving them into the kheddahs, so that I have seen more of elephants under excitement than merely on the occasions when I have shot them. I may also say that most I have bagged have been picked ones, some of them proscribed as notoriously troublesome and dangerous animals, or they have been determined beasts met with in the herds whilst engaged in the capture of their fellows. I cannot understand any person's wilfully shooting female elephants, except as in Ceylon, where their numbers at one time had to be thinned, as they were becoming too numerous. Females, no doubt, give as good sport as males—in fact, they are always the first to charge; but they carry no trophies, and the sportsman with any romance in his nature will let them pass if only in consideration to their sex.

The art of approaching elephants successfully, and of picking out the particular animal wanted amongst a large body, requires practice. When a large herd is grazing in detachments, as a large herd always does, each separate group has to be examined for the tuskers, and the sportsman is likely to be winded, and the alarm given, before the search is successful, unless he knows his work. In a small herd the difficulties are less, but as a rule the tuskers are not so fine as those with larger herds.

When feeding, elephants will usually be found to be heading steadily in a certain direction; the rear-guard should then be examined for the tuskers, as they seldom go in front. The most ordinary precaution will enable the sportsman and his gun-bearers to move about within a few yards of them, if in cover, as long as they keep the wind, which is the one thing needful to observe in stalking elephants. It is seldom that they cannot be approached to within ten yards for a shot. When herd elephants are at rest, they dispose themselves in scattered squads in close contiguity. There is then nothing to distract their attention as they doze, and they are more liable to observe danger than when engaged in feeding. On the least alarm they close up, and if their fears seem well founded they make off, and the best tuskers, which are probably near (but are seldom found amongst the females), may escape without being seen. It is consequently often advisable to use patience and to remain at a distance till the herd is again at graze—say after three o'clock in the afternoon—rather than approach elephants in cover during the day. I have never seen a tusker undertake to cover the retreat of a herd; they take a line of their own invariably when danger threatens.

The alarm of the presence of man is usually communicated by the elephant that discovers it by a peculiar short, shrill trumpet, well understood by the others, and which the sportsman will soon learn to distinguish amongst all the other sounds made by elephants. All stand perfectly still at this signal for some minutes, when, if they make up their minds that the alarm is well founded, they close up and move rapidly off. At other times, if the elephant that perceives danger discovers that it is very near, it moves off quickly without a sound. The alarm is at once taken by all the others, and a beginner in elephant-shooting may find that the whole herd has been gone some time before he is aware that he has even been discovered. If attacked, the stampede of a herd is overwhelming: whilst running, some of the elephants often trumpet shrilly in alarm and anger; and if hard pressed, females with young calves will turn upon their pursuers without hesitation.

It occasionally happens that elephants mistake the quarter from which danger comes, and during their rush to escape, the sportsman may be placed in great danger. When a herd stampedes it is impossible to tell for a moment, amongst the crashing of bamboos and tearing down of creepers from high trees, which way they are making, if they are hidden in dense cover. The best thing to do on all occasions is to stand still against a tree or bamboo-clump; to run is to risk being tripped up, and perhaps to be left sprawling in the elephants' path, or to provoke a chase if they are close behind.

Elephants are poor sighted, and so intent on making off when thoroughly startled, that I have been almost brushed against without being discovered. The rapidly advancing line of huge heads and cocked ears, bobbing spasmodically up and down as the elephants come rushing on, levelling everything before them, is a trying sight at first, requiring some nerve, and the reflection that they are escaping, not charging, to stand. If circumstances ever occur to make a run unavoidable, the pursued sportsman should always take down-hill, and choose the steepest places at hand, as elephants fear to trust themselves on a rapid descent at any great pace; up-hill, or on the level, a man would be immediately overtaken in rough ground.

When a shot is fired at a herd unaccustomed to firearms, the whole frequently mass together and stand huddled in a heap, shrinking at each shot till the smoke and smell alarm them. There is no doubt that, in such cases, they believe the noise to be thunder close at hand; the firing of heavy charges may easily be mistaken for the almost simultaneous flash and crash often heard in storms during the early rains. It is undoubtedly from the same belief that tigers not unfrequently return to eat at a carcass shortly after a shot has been fired at them by the ambushed native shikárie. Unless they believed the noise to be something else than firearms, it is evident they would not come back again.

When a herd of elephants makes off, they go at a great pace for a short distance, but do not maintain it long before they settle into a fast walk, which they often keep up for ten or fifteen miles, if they have a wounded elephant and no young calves amongst them. The sportsman should run after them at once, as an ordinary runner can generally keep near them for two or three hundred yards, if the ground be fair.

When elephants are close at hand, standing in indecision, no one should shout to turn them. A charge by one or more of them is almost sure to be made if they are suddenly startled in this particular manner. I have seen, and myself experienced, several instances of the danger of this. In Chittagong, whilst driving elephants into a stockade on one occasion, they approached the guiding-line of beaters too closely, when a man who was behind a small bush shouted at them within thirty yards. A female at once charged him; the man fell, and with the pressure of her foot on his chest she split him open, killing him on the spot. This elephant had a very young calf, from solicitude for which she became a perfect fury. I was lame at the time from the effect of a pummelling I had had a few days previously from a wild elephant, so was riding a tame one during the beat. The beaters on foot could not approach the elephants for fear of this particular female, so I rode towards her, when she charged my elephant. I fired my express rifle pistol-fashion in her face, as she came on the off-side and I was astride on the pad and could not turn. This shot sent her off, but on further pressing she again came on, this time from the front, when I rolled her over with the No. 8 and 12 drams in the forehead. This shot was too high, however, and she got up and made off, and eventually made good her escape.

In my early days at elephants I was once following four in the Kákenkoté jungles through a swamp of grass twelve feet high; I thought one was a tusker I was in search of. I kept within twenty yards of their tails in the lane they made, till at last, seeing they were all females, I thought to have some fun with them, as I had always seen elephants run away on the few occasions I had disturbed them, and I rashly gave a loud shout. They turned and curled their trunks up, but did not retreat. I saw I had caught a Tartar; however, I gave another shout, throwing my sun-hat towards them at the same time. At this moment one hidden in the grass to my left front uttered a piercing scream, and rushed down upon myself and gun-bearers. She could not see us, nor we her, till she burst out ten feet in front of me into the path. I had just time to give her my Lang 4-bore and 10 drams in her face, without any particular aim. This fortunately dropped her; but she got up as quickly as she went down, and, to my relief, turned and made off with the others. This elephant charged solely on the provocation of a shout.

The most interesting branch of elephant-shooting is the pursuit of single male elephants—either those which are quite solitary, or herd-tuskers when wandering apart from their companions. The latter usually join their herds by eight or nine o'clock in the morning, and great expedition must be used to overtake them before that time, as the noise they make whilst feeding guards the sportsman against stumbling on them unawares, and a close and favourable shot can usually be obtained. Purely solitary elephants cease feeding by ten o'clock; they then generally stand listlessly in some thick cover, usually bamboo, or under a tree in high grass; or they lie down in such places and rest. When lying down they snore, but not loudly; the sound coming through the long trunk has a metallic sound. They occasionally raise the ear that is uppermost and let it fall with a loud slap on the neck; this sound is quite distinct from the flapping of the ears when the beast is standing up, and is well known to elephant-trackers.

The habit of lying down to rest is much more common amongst elephants, wild and tame, than I have found people even with some acquaintance with them suppose. All wild beasts lie down during the day, and not unfrequently at night, and it is not easy to guess how the notion arose that elephants do so less than others. All tame elephants, except a few timid individuals that are nervous about the stray cattle, pariah-dogs, and jackals that often prowl round their pickets, lie down to sleep. The idea prevailed in old days that elephants had no joints and could not lie down. A good estimate of the calibre of a wild tusker may generally be arrived at by the impression of his tusk in soft soil. One that will admit five fingers in the groove is well worth following; his tusks will be over 60 lb. the pair.

In single-elephant shooting, a very remarkable circumstance, which the sportsman should be aware of as occurring in their retreat, is, that all noise often ceases after the first headlong rush of a hundred yards or so, and the novice may suppose the elephant has stopped, whereas he has merely subsided into a quick, noiseless walk, and though a person be close at hand, the brushing of the boughs against the beast's tough sides will scarcely be heard. I have lost more than one elephant through advancing cautiously when I thought the wounded beast had stopped, whilst he was rapidly putting himself beyond the reach of pursuit. The noiselessness with which a whole herd also makes off on occasions when it suspects danger and seeks to avoid observation, is equally astonishing.

A plan I always pursue in following wounded elephants if they cannot be overtaken in the first burst, and have to be followed far, is to send two jungle-men ahead on the track, and to follow with my gun-bearers a hundred yards behind. This is the safest plan for the trackers, as they can creep silently on and see or hear the elephant before he perceives them. An advance can then be made with a knowledge of the position of the enemy; but for all to approach together in the first place is likely to give the elephant warning, and he may do damage before his proximity is suspected. In all encounters with wild beasts it is more than half the battle to strike the first blow. I have seen all but the most plucky trackers scatter and flee before an unexpected attack by a wounded wild animal; the effect is that of a surprise, and the success is with the side that effects it. A Shōlaga was killed on the Billiga-rungun hills some years ago when out with two sportsmen; an ambushed tusker (wounded) suddenly rushed out, the trackers fell, and one was trampled to death on the spot. Had they been sent forward to make their own observations this would not have happened.

As to there being any greater danger in shooting rogue elephants than herd-tuskers, as is usually supposed, I have much doubt. In the first place, in single-elephant shooting the having only one animal to deal with is an immense advantage. There is little danger of being run over by accident, as in a mob; and it will be found that, in charging, single elephants, though perhaps more liable to attack in the first place, are not more determined than members of herds. A female with a young calf is infinitely more likely to attack a man, and to do so persistently, than nine-tenths of male elephants. If some solitary animal, which has been accustomed to lord it over field-watchers and helpless travellers, is met, the unexpected novelty of a battery opening upon him is likely to disconcert him, and, like all bullies, he is demoralised by a reverse. A man-eating tiger is not more dangerous to hunt than any other; and in my experience, and from all I have heard, rogue elephants, when the tables are turned on them, are not more determined than others.

When a tusker has been secured, his tusks may either be hacked out, or left for about ten days, when they can be drawn out without much trouble. If the tusks are to be cut out, the flesh along the nasal bones up to the eye must be removed and the tusk-cases split with a hatchet, but the tusks are usually somewhat blemished in the process. The best pair of tusks I ever bagged were 4 feet 11 inches and 5 feet respectively in length (when taken out), 16½ inches in circumference at the gums, and weighed 74½ lb. the pair.

A dead elephant is soon a disgusting spectacle. The carcass swells to an enormous size, the legs on the side which is uppermost becoming stiff, and projecting horizontally by its distension. Many hundreds of vultures collect on the neighbouring trees, or fight for a seat upon the carcass, awaiting the time when they shall be able to make a commencement. This is not for at least six days, when the carcass bursts, and collapses with rottenness. By this time it is crawling with millions of maggots, and has become whitewashed with the droppings of the filthy but useful birds. The spot resounds with the buzzing of innumerable flies, and the stench is so great as to be easily perceivable at half a mile to leeward. Wild hogs not unfrequently feed upon the carcass, as I have seen by their tracks; and I think it is not unlikely, as stated by natives, that tigers do so occasionally.

When the vultures are able to commence, the carcass is reduced to a pile of bones and a heap of undigested, masticated grass (the contents of the stomach), in a few hours. Large though the amount of flesh is, it is soon disposed of by the hundreds of ravenous birds, whose croaking, hissing, and flapping, as they feed and fight, may be heard for a considerable distance. If the stench is overpowering before the carcass is devoured, it is almost worse when the birds have left. The whole neighbourhood is pervaded with the most pungent odour of guano, and the site of the recent disgusting feast is trampled into a puddle by their feet.

In Mysore even the lowest classes of natives, who have no objection to carrion, will not eat the flesh of the elephant. They imagine it to be very heating, and believe that many of the vultures which feed on it die. In cutting up an elephant they think it necessary to oil their hands and arms, believing the blood will cause serious skin affections. It was not till my men had seen me at work up to my elbows, and unoiled, that they would dispense with the precaution. In Chittagong the hill-people were glad to get elephants' flesh, and always carried away every morsel of those that died during our hunting operations. One, which I had had covered with earth, as it died inside one of the kheddahs, and would have interfered with our work, was exhumed after we left and eaten by the Joomas.

Elephants' feet make unique footstools ; the fore-feet being round, are better adapted for this purpose than the hind, which are oval. The feet should be cut off a few inches below the knee, and the bones and flesh must be taken out. This is hard work, and strong knives are necessary. It facilitates the operation to slit the foot down behind, and sew the cut up afterwards; but this is not absolutely necessary, and is better avoided if possible. The feet should, when cleaned, be well rubbed inside and out with arsenical soap, and folded away for convenience of packing. They will keep in this state till the sportsman's return to headquarters, when they must be softened by many hours' soaking in warm water ; they are then to be rubbed again with arsenical soap. After this they should be placed in the sun, filled with sand, and all loss by shrinking prevented by frequent ramming. When thoroughly hard and dry the sand must be removed and the feet stuffed with coir. The nails should be scraped till quite white, and the skin should be covered with a coating of lamp-black. Both skin and nails should then be varnished, and the top of the foot covered with panther's skin, or with velvet or other material, secured round the edge by large-headed brass or silver nails, and a velvet band. Small feet make good cheroot-boxes for the table with a mahogany tray inside, partitioned off for different sizes, and a mahogany or silver lid, surmounted by a small silver elephant to lift it off by. They can also be made up into tobacco-boxes, ink-stands, small boxes for a lady's table, &c.

CHAPTER XVI.

INCIDENTS IN ELEPHANT-SHOOTING.

CAMP AT POONJOOR—WANT OF RAIN—MOVE CAMP—A TIGER IN A SHŌLAGA'S HUT—SHŌLAGA TRACKERS—A TROUBLESOME COUGH—FIND ELEPHANTS—MANŒUVRE TO GET A SHOT—KILL A TUSKER—I NARROWLY ESCAPE AN INGLORIOUS END—JUNGLE-TRACKERS—MY YOUTHFUL TRACKER GORRAVA—THE DIFFERENCE BETWEEN HITTING AND BAGGING—PERSEVERANCE—THE KÁKANKOTÉ ROGUE—HIS HABITS—KILLS TWO TRAVELLERS—KÁKANKOTÉ—THE CUBBANY RIVER—FOREST—KURRABAS—THEIR HABITS, FOOD, APPEARANCE, DWELLINGS—GARROW AND CHITTAGONG WILD TRIBES' DWELLINGS—KURRABAS' METHODS OF CATCHING WILD ANIMALS—THE FLYING SQUIRREL—ETHNOLOGY OF THE KURRABAS—OLD POOJÁREE—JUNGLE TRIBES' FEAR OF ELEPHANTS—I REACH KÁKANKOTÉ TO HUNT THE ROGUE—NEWS OF HIM—TRACK HIM—HEAVY RAIN—FIRE AT THE ROGUE—WILD ELEPHANTS' RUSHES—THE ROGUE ESCAPES—MELANCHOLY REFLECTIONS.

IT was in July 1870 that I had obtained ten days' leave of absence, which it was my intention to devote to a bear and bison shooting expedition at Poonjoor. I had already sent on my tents and servants from Mysore, and on the day before my leave commenced I managed to be at Atticulpoor, on the extreme limit of my district, so as to commence shooting without loss of time. I spent the day in casting bullets and making other preparations, and in viewing with pleasant anticipation the Billiga-rungun hills, stretching before me in a grand blue line. The day was delightfully cool and cloudy, and the highest peaks were often hidden in the mists. With my glass I could see a mass of rocks away on the left, twenty miles distant, where I had captured a pair of tiger-cubs two months before; also the valley where I had shot my first bison, and other places endeared to me by similar recollections.

Having taken some coffee and biscuits early next morning, I jumped into my trap with my guns, which the horsekeeper held whilst I drove, and started to Poonjoor. The road was very rough, often merely a track, but I had a fiery Pegu pony and a light and not valuable dog-cart, so we lost no time by the way. I saw large numbers of pea-fowl and jungle-fowl, and a few jackals, but no large game. At Poonjoor I found my old sporting companion, Bommay Gouda, awaiting me. I could have hugged the old fellow; how I envied him for living always in the jungles! My tents were ready pitched, and breakfast on the table, so it did not take long to make a start in search of bison. Bommay Gouda could hold out no very bright prospects of sport, as he said there had been a deficiency of rain, and the bison and bears were in the hills, where it was impossible to get at them without a well-organised expedition.

We walked about, up hill and down dale, for many hours without seeing anything, and returned in the evening rather disheartened. During our ramble we saw the prints of a stag sámbur that had been pursued by a tiger; this had occurred some days before, after a night's rain. The tiger had evidently failed in the chase. Every bound of both animals was twelve or fifteen feet. There were numerous tracks of elephants, but they were forbidden game.

It was evidently useless remaining at Poonjoor, as game was scarce, so by Bommay Gouda's advice I made arrangements to march next morning to Yerlsáriga, a Shōlaga hamlet five miles along the foot of the hills. At daybreak Bommay Gouda led the way to our new ground, through fine forest, in which we crossed picturesque streams; these, though shallow, were clear and rapid, and formed frequent small cascades. My shooting-tent and camp-equipments were carried by men, and I selected a spot to pitch my habitation under a tree close to the Shōlagas' huts. These dwellings are very snug and neat: they are only about five feet high inside, and seven feet in length and breadth; the door is three feet high and two wide.

The Shōlagas turned out of a couple of houses for my servants, who made themselves very comfortable. I may here mention that two years after this time a tiger was shot in one of these two huts by Bommay Gouda. The animal made its appearance near the village in the middle of the day, whereupon many of the Shōlagas fled into their huts, the others into the jungle near. The tiger showed no intention of molesting the people, and composed himself under a cart which two Mussulmáns had driven to Yerlsáriga to load with bamboos. As he seemed inclined to remain there for an indefinite time, one of the Shōlagas ran to Poonjoor for Bommay Gouda, who had an old matchlock. When Bommay Gouda arrived he took a deliberate shot at the tiger, but missed, and the animal betook himself into one of the huts, which was open and untenanted. A Shōlaga very boldly shut the door with a long bamboo, and by making a hole through the wattle-and-dab wall Bommay Gouda got another shot and killed this strangely-behaved tiger. There is no doubt that it was suffering from some disease or hallucination which rendered it oblivious to what was going on. It was described as being apparently stupefied. I have known somewhat similar cases of wild animals being found in an unconscious and incapable state in the jungles.

Bommay Gouda had with him a good Shōlaga tracker and his son by the time I had pointed out the camping-ground, and we set out. The Shōlaga reported bison as scarce, bears more so (owing to want of rain), but elephants, he said, were numerous, and gave them trouble in guarding their little plots of cultivation from their nocturnal visits. There seemed to be little hope of sport except with elephants; and as they were evidently very destructive, I determined to put in force the clause of the prohibition against shooting them, which provides for cases where they are a burden to the cultivators, and I gave the word "Forward!" to the delighted Bommay Gouda. He had been an elephant-hunter in days gone by, and was thoroughly imbued with the peculiar enthusiasm of the sport. He always said, "*Ánay byárté, dhoré byárté*" (elephant-shooting is the sport for gentlemen). So tremble, ye elephants, wherever ye are, for men are on your tracks whose eyes would not miss the print of the tiniest deer.

The Shōlaga and his son, a lad of fourteen, led the way towards a dense belt of jungle three miles distant, where they said the elephants were generally to be found. I rode a pony until we got within a mile of the place; we then advanced cautiously. Presently, in crossing a sandy nullah, the trackers pointed to the tracks of what appeared to me to be about half-a-dozen elephants, but they explained that there were between forty and fifty, and that the prints had been made early that morning. In tracking, nothing is more difficult to a novice than to estimate with even approximate accuracy the number of individuals in a herd of elephants. Sometimes they travel in single file (when marching any distance), and the uninitiated might be excused for believing that but a single elephant had passed, where fifty would be nearer the number; and, on the other hand, a small herd will, by feeding for some time within a small area, often leave signs which lead the inexperienced to suppose that a much larger number has been there. Experienced trackers can tell pretty accurately at a glance how many animals the herd contains.

I always fortify myself with breakfast or luncheon before going into action—one does not know when one may have an opportunity of getting anything again that day; so whilst I was laying in some cold fowl and bread-and-butter, the trackers took their snacks of rági-bread. This viand is not more seductive to the taste, nor pleasant to the eye, than an old shoe-sole, but it is the common travelling food of the working classes in Mysore, when they have not time to prepare a regular meal.

Bommay Gouda, who had the ordering of the attack, now sent on the two Shōlagas, whilst he, myself, and Jaffer, who carried my second rifle, followed. The men with the tiffin-basket and pony were left behind, with orders to join us when they heard shots. We had only gone a short distance when a faint trumpet away to our left attracted our attention. The elephants were in the cover where the Shōlagas expected to find them, so we hurried on with less caution, as they were at some distance. I found it necessary to send the old Shōlaga tracker back to join the men with the pony, as he began to be troubled by a cough, which I knew from considerable experience of natives would break out at the most inopportune moment. I found out subsequently, in other hunts, that the old fellow was always similarly afflicted when we got near formidable game! He confided to me, after we had been longer acquainted, that he was not so active as he once was, and that he mistrusted his powers of escaping from an elephant by flight; and as his duty was really over when he brought me and my gun-bearers up to game, I gave him standing permission to fall back before fighting commenced, which proved a panacea for his malady.

The elephants were in a thick piece of jungle through which a sandy nullah wound its way; it was about fifteen yards wide, quite dry, with high banks. Hiding ourselves on the side from which we approached, we heard the elephants feeding in the thick jungle on the opposite bank. The branches of trees were bent down now and again, or an occasional trunk was raised to reach the tender leaves, but as it was nearly mid-day the elephants were quite hidden from view. Occasionally a squeak of pleasure from the young ones, or deep grumblings from the big ones, were heard. I had never been near wild elephants before, and I felt the pleasurable excitement that attends a young sportsman's first encounter with new and formidable game.

We sat in cover for some time, hoping the elephants would make a move, but they seemed inclined to rest in their cool retreat, and showed no signs of emerging from it for some time. At last I could no longer restrain my wish to see an elephant in his wild haunts, so whispering to Jaffer to keep near with my second rifle I got quietly into the nullah, and walking noiselessly over the soft sand, brought my head to the level of the opposite bank. I peered through the bushes; it was much easier to see under than through them, and my eyes were immediately greeted with the sight of the legs and feet of several elephants. One was within eight yards of me.

Drawing myself up behind a small tree, I stood on the bank with my rifle ready. I could just distinguish the head of the owner of the nearest pair of colossal understandings. Suddenly it struck me that the elephant was watching me, as its head was turned in my direction, and I expected to hear a shriek and a rush forward. I kept my rifle to my shoulder, intending to fire both barrels, and if I failed in flooring it, to jump down into the nullah, and with the second rifle stand on the opposite bank. However, as I waited, my heart thumping against my ribs, the huge head swung lazily to one side and back again, showing the half-closed, dozing eye. The elephant was a female. As my intention was to get a tusker I left her in peace, and getting quietly down, delighted with my first close peep at wild elephants, I regained the other bank, intending now to wait till the herd should move into better ground. Jaffer, though a plucky fellow, had, like his master, never seen elephants till now, and was not sorry to be relieved of his duty of standing in the nullah with the second rifle, as he was afraid some of the herd might come up it and take us in rear.

We sat down and held a long consultation, when presently it struck us that the elephants were very quiet, and when Bommay Gouda and I reconnoitred their late position we found that they had moved off. It is remarkable how quietly a herd of elephants will slip away, and how little trace they leave of the passage of their huge bodies. These must have obtained a slant of our wind; but as this herd* was constantly in the habit of visiting cultivation, near to the habitations of man, it did not go far.

We followed immediately, and shortly entered thinner jungle, interspersed with large trees, where we came up with the elephants marching sedately along, a few of the young ones wandering to right and left as food tempted them. It was now about three o'clock in the afternoon and near their feeding-time. They looked so different from tame elephants: instead of being black, as the latter are from frequent washing, they were reddish, owing to the dust with which they had covered their bodies. I scanned them eagerly for a male elephant in vain, till the gleam of a pair of tusks through a bush caught the quick eye of the lad Gorrava, and presently out stalked a tusker! He was not a large elephant, and by any but a young hunter might have been passed unmolested, but his tusks settled him as my victim.

It was very difficult to approach this particular elephant, as the herd was now scattered to browse, and whilst avoiding one we were liable to be

* I captured these elephants in June 1874, as related in Chapter X., within a mile of the place where I encountered them on this occasion.

seen or winded by another. However, at last we got to the banks of the ravine to which the elephant had by this time made his way. We were here nearly discovered by a small female which came from behind us, and was apparently intending to cross the nullah near us; she luckily, however, turned off, or we should have been seen or winded, and the whole herd would have been alarmed. Following the main body, in which was the tusker, along the bank of the nullah, we reached a large tree with an open space in front. The nullah bounded the space on the opposite side, and on the right and left; in fact, we and the elephants were on a tongue of land surrounded by the nullah, excepting in the direction from which we had come. About thirty elephants were collected here, and amongst them was the tusker. There were four or five other smaller tuskers, but none worth shooting. They sauntered about unsuspicious of danger, caressing each other affectionately, and enjoying their fancied security. At last they made a move to cross the nullah ahead, where a steep path about five yards wide led down into it and up the other side. I saw that this was the place to cut off the tusker, but the difficulty lay in preventing stray elephants taking our wind and giving the alarm. As the herd jostled each other in the narrow passage I was delighted to see the tusker loiter behind, and he entered the pass amongst the last. I now ran quickly across the open space, about fifty yards in width, and entered the path at the heels of the rear-guard. Nothing could be seen but seven huge sterns in a line as their owners walked down the incline to cross the nullah. I was within ten feet of their tails, but quite lost to all sense of danger in the excitement of the moment. I had read and re-read Sir S. Baker's delightful tales of elephant-shooting in Ceylon, till I fancied the sport was much easier, much less dangerous, than I subsequently found it to be.

I kept my eye on the tusker who was in the middle of the line, and was wondering how I was to get a shot at his brain, when, as luck would have it, some vegetable attraction overhead tempted him, and he raised his head to reach it with his trunk. I had beforehand fixed the fatal spot in my mind's eye, and catching sight of his temple I fired. For a moment I could see nothing for the smoke, but heard a tremendous commotion amongst the elephants that were in company with the tusker. Stepping a little aside, I saw their huge heads all turning towards me, their ears outspread, and their trunks curled up in terrified astonishment. Being a novice in the sport, I felt for the moment that I was in real danger. Jaffer was at the top of the pass instead of being at my heels, for which I afterwards gave him a severe lecture. I stood my ground however, determined if any of them charged to fire at the foremost and to run to Jaffer for the second rifle; that failing, the case would have been rather bad. However, charging was far from their thoughts; right about, quick march, was more to their fancy; and with shrieks and trumpets away they went, some to the right, some to the left, joined by the whole herd in one headlong race up or down the nullah. But my tusker remained stone dead upon his knees! The triumph of such a success, attained unassisted and in my first inexperienced attempt, quite transported me. Oh that one could retain the freshness of one's first conquests in subsequent enterprises! Of what account were toil, expenditure of all my spare cash, danger undergone, and past ill-luck, in that blissful moment? My game had been outwitted by careful stalking and a due admixture of caution and adventuring of our persons. The whole herd was now in flight. I had succeeded beyond my wildest hopes!

My bullet had reached the tusker's brain, and in sinking down he must have been supported by the bodies and legs of the elephants between which he was wedged in; thus he still remained on his knees though quite dead. He retained his kneeling position for some minutes, when by the gradual subsidence of his carcass he heeled over, and fell heavily on to his side. I narrowly escaped being crushed between him and the bank as he sank, just springing out of the way in time. It would have been a fine thing indeed if, after bagging my first elephant, I had fallen a victim to the collapse of his carcass!

As a rule, jungle-tribes only know the country thoroughly well in the immediate vicinity of their dwellings, but within this limit every path, pool, salt-lick, and favourite cover, is familiar to them. They can thus usually tell where an animal will be found at any hour. Hence it is most desirable to have them with a party whilst hunting in their respective localities, as they are often able to save time by leaving the trail and leading the sportsman by a more direct route to the place where the animals he is in quest of are. It was for this reason that Bommay Gouda had brought the old Shōlaga and his son along with us. The son had a pleasant and intelligent face for a Shōlaga—they are generally hideously ugly—and I took a fancy to him at once. Young though he was he tracked the elephants skilfully, and behaved boldly. And now, eight years later, Gorrava is one of my favourite jungle-men, and is employed in the kheddahs. We are *confrères* against the bears, bison, &c., and many a good day's work have we done "since first we met." Gorrava is tall, lithe, and active, with the lightest step, the quickest eye, and the best judgment of the many good trackers I know. That confidence between a sportsman and his hunters, so essential to good and enjoyable shooting, has long been established between us. I have perfect trust in Gorrava's ability to work out any trail, whilst he knows that I never fire at random, and thereby render futile the care he has taken to bring me up to game.

Much judgment, only to be acquired by experience, is necessary for success in large-game shooting. When an animal is suddenly pointed out to the young sportsman his first idea is that it will vanish in another moment, and his impulse is to fire at any part of it visible. Thus, though most jungle-shots are within fifty yards, and it is not difficult to hit an animal at that distance, some sportsmen are as often unlucky as successful in eventually getting it; for there is a great difference between *hitting* and *bagging*. Unless the ball of even the most powerful rifle be well placed behind the shoulder, or in the head or neck, a stricken beast will frequently travel for miles; and through the intervention of night, or a heavy shower that obliterates its tracks, it may be lost. It is more sportsmanlike even to let a doubtful opportunity pass than to make a hurried and uncertain shot, which too often but leads to wounding and losing game. Moreover, nothing discourages a really good tracker more than having random shots fired at animals which he has been at the trouble of following for miles, and which one moment's coolness would have brought to bag. Much more of the difference between successful and unsuccessful sportsmen with large game is due to knowledge of such points, and to self-control, than to their respective attainments as marksmen. Glaringly uncertain chances should never be taken. Useless firing disturbs the jungle, and an occasional success is a poor recompense for frequent disappointment. Men who constantly blame their "bad luck" may be fairly regarded with suspicion. Things fall out unfortunately at times, but as a set-off, equally bright moments are not uncommon. Such a thing as constant bad luck to the persevering and thoughtful sportsman—even though a tyro—I need hardly say there cannot be.

One of the most useful lessons of the sportsman's pursuits is to teach him the value of perseverance. The successful hunter must always be a determined one. All such can count in their experiences many triumphant chases, made so by persistence when all hope had apparently vanished. Another half-hour's pursuit has frequently changed what without it would have been a blank day into a red-letter one. Such successes are those which are most highly valued. What satisfaction would there be in catching a fox in a mile? or in hearing a young lady say "yes" the first time one asked her?

The next elephants I went after were four solitary animals, on different occasions, of which I bagged two and lost two. They were all individuals which were destructive to villagers' crops, and which I obtained permission to shoot wherever and whenever I met them. I then sallied forth after the Kákankoté rogue, a really dangerous animal, which had taken possession of about eight miles of the main road between Mysore and the Wynaad country. He at first did nothing more than alarm travellers by frequently appearing on the road. But after some time he took to chasing persons, and at last killed two men within a few days. This was reported by the Amildár, or native official in charge of that part of the country; and I was soon at Kákankoté, intent on slaying the brute.

Whilst *en route* to the rogue's neighbourhood I met some travellers, one of whom was cut and bruised about the head and face. It appeared he had fallen into a gravel-pit by the roadside upon a false alarm being raised that the rogue was coming! At the entrance to the jungle I found two native policemen had been stationed to warn travellers to proceed only in parties, and men were sent with them to beat tom-toms and sound horns till they were safely through. I dismounted from my pony and marched with my carts from this outpost to Kákankoté—eight miles—which we reached without seeing the rogue.

Kákankoté is a small hamlet of half-a-dozen huts, forty-nine miles from Mysore, on the road to Wynaad. It has a traveller's bungalow used by occasional sportsmen. The Cubbany river runs close past Kákankoté, and for sixteen miles the main road skirts its north bank through the heavy forest. Thus animals which come from the interior forests lying to the north, to drink at the river, are obliged to cross the main road; and in the height of the hot weather (March, April, and May), when the pools in the forests are dried up, whole herds of elephants resort to the river to bathe and drink, usually from five in the afternoon till eight in the morning.

The jungle around Kákankoté consists of teak and other heavy timber and bamboos. It is inhabited by a few scattered Kurrabas, a wild race, but first-rate assistants to the sportsman in quest of large game. These wild men of the woods care little for money; if supplied with rice, *arrack* (native spirit), and tobacco, while in the sportsman's camp, they are quite content; and a *cumbley* (blanket), as a reward for special services, may be added at the end of the trip. A more wretched set of human beings than Kurrabas it would be difficult to imagine. Their unvarying dress in all weathers is a small piece of dirty cloth round the loins, though the extremes of heat and cold in the jungles at different seasons are great; and during the monsoon months the rain is almost incessant. They cultivate small patches of grain, just sufficient for their bare necessities. The labour entailed by their method of cultivation is very great. The jungle has first to be cleared and burnt, and the ground dug up by hand; the crop must then be guarded day and night from elephants and other animals. It not unfrequently happens that single male elephants refuse to be driven from these clearings by the firebrands and other methods adopted for frightening them. In such cases very little grain is left for the unfortunate proprietor. Of more importance to the Kurrabas than their grain-crop are several descriptions of edible roots and wild honey. Of the former they have eight kinds; two of these are very good, being not unlike sweet potatoes.

The men are usually of poor *physique*, the women squalid and ugly to an astonishing degree, and the children frequently sickly, and subject to great mortality. It is pitiful to see many of the latter, with thin legs, glazed skins, and distended stomachs, the outward signs of diseased spleens —the result of malarial fevers and bad water.

I believe the one fact of the dwellings of jungle-people in Southern India—at least the Kurrabas and Shōlagas in Mysore—being built on the ground, is sufficient to account for their miserable condition. The miasma which causes jungle-fevers is said to be heavy and to hang close above the surface, for which reason it is unsafe to sleep on, or close to, the ground in malarious localities. The Kurrabas and Shōlagas do not understand this; and their children, from their short stature, live more in the unhealthy stratum of air than adults. This may partly account for the greater proportion of sickness among them. In the Garrow and Chittagong hills in the north-east and east of Bengal the jungle-tribes live in large and well-constructed houses raised eight or ten feet from the ground on bamboo supports. In front of each is a verandah or platform for the children to play on, and in which their parents sit when idle; the whole is reached by a ladder, and is of such simple construction that any jungle-man can build himself a house in two or three days, with no other tool but his axe. Thus the people sleep well above the reach of malaria, and are kept dry and comfortable in all weathers, instead of grovelling on the damp ground, as do the Kurrabas and Shōlagas.

A probable reason of the Kurrabas and Shōlagas living in such plight as they do may be that in former times they were liable to disturbance by every one who entered the forests, and not being numerous or warlike, they avoided annoyance by flight. Consequently the custom of such light structures, which might have to be abandoned at a moment's notice, has become established, and that being the case, none of them now think of making any change. The Kurrabas have no weapons for killing wild animals, but they take a few deer in pitfalls dug near their plots of cultivation. They are skilful at catching the lungoor monkey (*Presbytis priamus*), the flying-squirrel (*Pteromys petaurista*), and the Malabar squirrel (*Sciurus malabaricus*). They use a net for the purpose, of stout twine made from the fibre of certain barks, not unlike a butterfly-net in shape, but much longer in the bag, and without a handle or hoop at the mouth. This net, held open by twigs, is placed upon a thick branch, and is fastened to it by a cord about six feet long, which passes through the meshes round the mouth, in place of a rigid ring. Thus, when a squirrel or monkey runs along the limb of the tree it enters the net, which at the least disturbance falls from the branch, when the throttle-string effectually closes the mouth, and the Kurrabas climb up and secure the prize. They show great skill in anticipating the line the animal will take when driven, as they must set the net in a distant tree and drive the prey towards it. They have another plan with the flying-squirrel when they do not want to take it alive. This beautiful creature is about three feet and three-quarters in length, of which the tail is one-half. It is nocturnal in its habits, usually living in holes in trees during the day, at a considerable height from the ground. The Kurrabas strike the trees with their axes; this starts the squirrel, and if further alarmed it launches itself out towards the next tree, spreading the membrane which extends from the fore to the hind feet along its sides, and which enables it to take these flights. It does not flap this parachute or wings, but merely sails in a downward direction. It can cover distances of fifty yards or more, starting from the top of one tree and reaching the trunk of the next close to the ground. It then runs up the trunk and repeats the flight. It cannot change the direction of its flight after it has once launched itself; and the Kurrabas take advantage of this peculiarity by posting one of their number behind the trunk of a tree to which they force the squirrel to fly, and who, as it alights, generally manages to kill it with his axe-handle. It is a very gentle and timorous creature. It is called "flying-cat" by the Kurrabas; and when sitting in the fork of a tree, the parachute membrane being then closed and invisible, it is more like a grey cat, both in size and colour, than one of the squirrel family. When launched off for a flight it is about twenty inches in length (excluding its tail), and twenty-four in breadth, across its extended membrane.

I cannot state exactly to what era or race the Kurrabas may be supposed to belong, but I imagine they are a purely aboriginal people. The theory sometimes advanced that such wild people are the descendants of persons who have been obliged to flee to the jungles in comparatively recent troublous times, can hardly, I think, be substantiated in their case. Probably in all but the very earliest ages the jungles of India have had inhabitants, and the Kurrabas may be as ancient as any. They have peculiar but not unpleasing features. Their hair is frequently curly, somewhat like the wool of a negro: this is an essential point of difference between them and the Hindoo people of the open country. Still the Kurrabas have no separate language, but talk Canarese with a peculiar intonation. They worship jungle-spirits, elephants, tigers, certain trees, &c. A peculiar difference between them and the wild tribe of the Billiga-rungun hills—the Shōlagas—is, that the Kurrabas eat the flesh of the bison, whilst a Shōlaga will not even touch the dead animal. Eating the flesh of the cow being abhorrent to the Hindoos, it would appear that the Kurrabas belong to the earliest races of Southern India, distinct from the Aryan or Dravidian people who overspread the country from the north, and probably brought the observance with them.

I always collected a number of these poor aborigines in my camp on my shooting expeditions, and though all of them were not engaged in tracking, I had the pleasure of their society when the day's work was over. There was rice, curry-stuff, tobacco, and a tot of grog at night for each, of which they much approved. Amongst the Kurrabas at Kákankoté was one old man, their *Poojáree,** or hereditary priest and head-man. This ancient of the woods held the rather extraordinary but convenient idea in a tracker, that, in virtue of his sacred office, he could not be killed by a wild elephant, and he would lead the way after a wounded or evilly-disposed one where the other Kurrabas were reluctant to go. I did not attempt to pervert him from his convictions, but always took care to support him with my heavy rifles, to prevent his being convinced of the fallacy of his views, and trampled into a pancake, at the same moment. It is a remarkable fact that jungle-people are ordinarily more afraid of wild elephants than of any other animals. I have known many who had little fear of tigers, bears, or bison, and yet dreaded being called on to track elephants. This is from no superstitious fear, but probably has its origin in the size and formidable appearance of, and the noise made by, elephants when roaming at large in their native wilds.

The Kákankoté rogue was well known to the Kurrabas by his large size and dark colour, and the upward curve of his short tusks. He had also lost more than half his tail whilst fighting—a common mutilation amongst elephants. The day I arrived at Kákankoté to hunt him I despatched two parties of Kurrabas to ascertain his whereabouts. In the evening they returned; the Poojáree's party had found recent marks at a pool, and had followed them till sundown. The rogue was then within half a mile of the same pool, and feeding towards it with the evident intention of drinking

* The illustration is a reproduction of a pencil sketch made on the spot by a friend, and is a most faithful portrait of old Poojáree.

Phototint H. M. Wright & Co. London.

An Esteemed Friend.

there again during the night ; so everything was got ready for following him on the morrow.

Next morning I had just risen, an hour before daylight, when news of him was brought in by two Kurrabas, who had left him standing in their clearing close to the main road, feeding on the rági crop which they had been guarding. They had started at 4 A.M., and after making a circuit to pass the elephant, had come five miles through jungle infested by wild animals, with only a torch of dry bamboo, to give me the information. As soon as it was daylight we set off down the main road for the Kurrabas' clearing, where we found that not only the rogue, but another elephant also, known by the Kurrabas to be a *muckna,* or tuskless male, and a frequent companion of the rogue's, had grazed about for some hours. They had left at daylight, crossing the road into the forest to the north of it.

My battery consisted of three breech-loading rifles—viz., a single C.F. spherical-ball No. 4-bore, by Lang & Sons ; a double C.F. No. 12 Forsyth's spherical-ball rifle, by W. W. Greener ; and a double 16-bore rifle, by Purdey. The two Kurrabas were to track, and Jaffer and another man carried my spare rifles.

About nine o'clock we got up to the elephants. They had by that time located themselves in thick cover for the day. It would have been difficult for us to move about in such stuff; and escape by flight, if attacked in it, would have been impossible. After some recent experience I had had with an elephant in a somewhat similar place, I thought it unadvisable to follow the pair into their stronghold, so we sat down to wait till they should quit it of their own accord. It began to rain heavily, and the noise made by the downpour on the broad leaves of the teak-trees was so great that we could not hear the elephants breaking branches, though they were close at hand. We sheltered ourselves from the pouring storm as well as we could, cowering at the foot of a large tree, and keeping a look-out lest the elephants should come in our direction.

The rain continued without intermission for six hours. The sandwiches I had brought with me for breakfast were reduced to pulp. I was wet to the skin, and it was no easy matter to keep even the cartridges dry. I was amused at the Kurrabas' attempts to keep themselves somewhat less moist than they would otherwise have been. They tacked three or four broad teak-leaves together with thorns, so as to form a rude hat ; this kept a portion of the heavy droppings from the trees from their shoulders as they crouched on the ground, hugging themselves in their shivering arms.

At last the rain ceased, and wiping the rifles as dry as possible we proceeded to look for the elephants' marks. They had fed close to us for some time during the rain, but had moved off two hours ago. Their marks were all but obliterated, and the tracking was slow in consequence. The bamboos showered drops of water upon us as we brushed against them, and the low-lying places had been converted into a succession of pools by the recent deluge. After proceeding about a mile we heard the pair feeding in a hollow amongst thick bamboo-cover, which, however, hid them from view. They were moving slowly forwards, breaking a branch now and again, but heading steadily towards the clearing they had left in the morning. The regular, slow, crunching sound made by their grinders as they chewed the tough wood and leaves, was the only interruption, except the occasional crash of a bough, to the stillness of the dark and gloomy afternoon in the deep forest. The cover they were in was too thick to be entered with any degree of safety; whilst the tusker's notoriety—though in reality he was no more dangerous before a sportsman's rifle than any other elephant—made us observe extra caution. We followed the slowly advancing pair, keeping parallel with them outside the cover in the open tree-forest. At last they came near the edge, and I saw their heads indistinctly amongst the bamboo-fronds. Ordering Jaffer and Bettay Gouda (the other gun-bearer) and the Kurrabas to keep behind a thick bamboo-clump, I took my 4-bore rifle and crept forward for ten yards—which brought me to within thirty of the elephants. The muckna first passed slowly along, keeping inside the cover, and then the tusker. The latter gave me but an indistinct shot, which I, however, thought it advisable to take, as evening was drawing on apace; so I fired from a rest on a white-ants' hill behind which I knelt. The ground was wet and slippery, and I made a scramble in gaining my feet, which rather delayed me in getting back to the bamboo-clump for my second rifle. I glanced over my shoulder as I reached its shelter. Horrors! both elephants were close behind me, their heads bobbing spasmodically with the pace at which they were shuffling along; they were actually coming through the heavy curtain of smoke which hung in the damp air like a fog behind me! I thought we were doomed, at least to a race for our lives—and a race against an elephant is one which admits of no doubt as to the winner; but almost in the same instant it flashed across me that the elephants could not possibly have seen me and commenced a simultaneous chase so instantaneously. No—it was clear they were running away; so collaring Jaffer and Bettay Gouda, and pressing them close against the bamboo-clump to prevent their moving, I waited in breathless anxiety. The two Kurrabas had looked out and seen the elephants coming; and without more ado—thinking we were discovered—they now started off before the monsters, almost under their trunks, doubling like hares, without even looking behind them. The elephants passed the bamboo-clump like a pair of runaway locomotives, and thence went off at full speed in different directions, not heeding the Kurrabas, and utterly scared by the suddenness of our attack.

What an instantaneous transformation of scene in that dark and silent jungle had the drawing of a trigger effected! The change from placidly browsing elephants to madly fleeing ones, from hiding Kurrabas to men going for dear life, was as ludicrous as it was sudden; and when the runaways came back after their unnecessary display of agility, we all had a quiet laugh over the occurrence. Bettay said that for his part he considered it was in consideration of some good deeds that he must have done in his former life,* that he had been favoured to witness so goodly a sight.

As often happens in shooting big game of all kinds, especially elephants, which are generally attacked at very close quarters, these two animals had set off instantly on the terrible alarm, without waiting to ascertain the nature of the danger, or whence it came. They had even rushed through the cloud of smoke in their headlong flight. The intentions of wild animals are often misinterpreted by the inexperienced, and a precipitate flight of this kind in the direction of the sportsman may be construed into a determined charge.

The rogue had a very moderate pair of tusks, as I found some months afterwards when I killed him; but of course they appeared to us to be splendid specimens now we had lost him! I had aimed too high, as I was then but imperfectly acquainted with the structure of an elephant's head, and the ball had passed above the brain. There was a thick blood-trail, in two distinct lines, showing that the bullet had gone through the elephant's cranium; but it did not continue far, as is usually the case with wounded elephants.

I think I never in my life felt so disappointed. I had left Mysore in the hope of speedily returning in the proud *rôle* of the successful rogue-slayer. Myself and men had been drenched to the skin, and starved all day, in persevering in the chase—circumstances which, though cheerfully overlooked during the excitement of the hunt, now forced themselves unpleasantly upon our attention. I suddenly recollected how hurtful a thorough drenching is in a malarious locality, and how extremely likely to be followed by an attack of jungle-fever. To add to our discomfiture we were miles from home, to reach which our powers of walking and wading would be severely tried. Life had suddenly become a blank! I should never smile again!

How astonishing are the changes of mood induced by surroundings! Seated by the camp-fire a few hours later, after a bath, a good dinner, and

* The Hindoo idea of a former state of existence.

a drop of hot whisky-and-water to correct the effects of the day's ducking; with a Trichinopoly cheroot under way, my companions of the day and other Kurrabas of weight in jungle matters around me, and the cheerful blaze lighting up the forest overhead; I took a much more hopeful view of existence than I had so recently done, and believed it was possible I might yet be happy. The men had had their meal (it is advisable in jungle-trips to leave some of the companions of the men who accompany their master at home to cook; otherwise, after a hard day, they may be too tired to do it for themselves, and may fall asleep without eating anything); permission to smoke had been accorded to all (natives are too respectful to smoke before their superiors without invitation); and even the reticent Kurrabas had found their tongues, and were now discussing the chances of finding the elephant on the morrow. More can be learned of the simple nature and ideas of jungle-tribes, and of their feelings and customs, as also of the habits of their fellow-inhabitants of the forest, the wild beasts, by the camp-fire than at any other time. Often has some passing allusion attracted my attention to matters which direct inquiry would never have elicited. Investigation amongst jungle-men must be carried on in a desultory way, and at fitting times. Any prolonged mental effort soon fatigues their untutored minds. A Kurraba is as quickly tired by a steady course of questions as the most brilliant conversationalist would be if set to push his way through the jungles in which the Kurraba travels from morning till night without fatigue.

The next day we followed the tusker's track for many hours, but he had travelled rapidly, and evidently without being seriously affected by the shot. As I have already stated in the preceding chapter, elephants are rarely recovered when merely wounded by a head-shot. If they are not killed on the spot the sportsman may usually spare himself the trouble of following them, as in one night they travel a distance which will take him two days to cover.

But happily "hope springs eternal in the human breast," and I left Kákankoté comforting myself with the prospect of another hunt and better luck shortly. The Kurrabas promised to let me know when they next heard of the rogue. He was now off into Coorg, and was not likely to show himself again in his old haunts for some time.

CHAPTER XVII.

INCIDENTS IN ELEPHANT-SHOOTING—(*continued*).

SECOND EXPEDITION AFTER THE ROGUE—HE KILLS A KURRABA—WOUND HIM—A CHASE—KILL HIM—HOW TO MAKE FIRE WITH TWO STICKS—ROLL THE ROGUE'S CARCASS OVER—CUT OFF HIS HEAD—PLACE HIS HEAD ON VIEW BY THE ROADSIDE—THE ROGUE'S IMPERTINENT FRIEND THE MUCKNA—TAKE HIM DOWN A PEG—MY BEST TUSKER—AN EXCITING HUNT—LARGE TUSKS—WOUND HIM—THE PROVERBIAL STERN-CHASE—ENCOUNTER HIM AGAIN—FURTHER PURSUIT—KILL HIM—REFLECTIONS—SHOOT AN ELEPHANT IN A PIT BY ACCIDENT—A SPORTING PARSON—THE GARROW HILLS—NARROW ESCAPE FROM A TUSKER—SIR VICTOR BROOKE AND COLONEL HAMILTON'S BIG TUSKER—A COMMON ELEPHANT-SHOOTING STORY—ELEPHANTS' POWERS OF GETTING OVER WOUNDS.

FIVE months after the incidents related in the last chapter I again found myself at Kákankoté on a second campaign against the rogue. He had temporarily deserted the neighbourhood, as anticipated by the Kurrabas, after the rough usage he had been subjected to, but had now returned, evidently not improved in temper, and had marked his arrival by killing a Kurraba, a relative of one of the trackers I had with me on our late expedition. The Kurraba was surprised when digging roots in the jungle, but would probably not have been caught had he been alone. Two youthful aborigines were with him, and it was after putting them up a tree, and in attempting to follow, that he was pulled down and torn limb from limb by the elephant. The Kurrabas who found the body said that the elephant had held the unfortunate man down with one fore-foot, whilst with his trunk he tore legs and arms from their sockets, and jerked them to some distance. Under ordinary circumstances an elephant has no chance of catching a Kurraba; they dodge in the underwood like rabbits, and are out of sight in a moment.

It was on Christmas Day, 1872, that I started with the Kurrabas for a pool in the jungles near Kákankoté, where they said we should be pretty sure of finding the rogue's tracks, as most other water-supplies were very low, whilst at this one he could both drink and enjoy a pleasant mud-bath. The morning was cold, with a raw fog. Our party consisted of six Kurrabas, my two gun-bearers, and myself. Four Kurrabas were to track, and the other two to bring the pony and luncheon-basket at some distance behind us after we took up the trail. I left instructions for half-a-dozen men to follow us later in the day with knives, axes, ropes, &c., and to wait at a certain place in the jungle, to be sent for in case we should bag the elephant. Our path lay for a mile and a half along the main road. The miserable Kurrabas preceded us, taking long pulls at the cheroots I had given them. They kept the smoke in their mouths for some time, and then expelled it slowly through their nostrils, so as to lose none of its flavour. Even along the main road they moved with the quiet apprehensive air natural to all jungle-men.

We soon turned off into the forest. The cheroots were extinguished and stuck behind their possessors' ears for future use, and when we reached the pool the night's tracks were carefully examined. The rogue had drunk there about three o'clock in the morning. In the vicinity of the pool was a large patch of bulrushes and grass ten feet high. He had entered this, and it was some time before the Kurrabas could carry the tracks through to the other side. The difficulty of tracking in this high grass was very great. It was not only dry and withered, and trodden into lanes by old elephant-paths in all directions, but the elephant had passed through it some hours before, and the fog and dew had since settled on all the paths alike, and obliterated the indications of their respective dates. Elephants have a great fancy for keeping to each other's old tracks, and when all are dry alike, or alike covered with dew, the wits of the best trackers are tried to keep up the track at a sufficient pace to reach the game in moderate time. There is great pleasure in watching the working out of a difficult trail. The man who sends out to have elephants found for him, and then goes and shoots them, loses, in my opinion, much of the real pleasure of this grandest of all sports.

After leaving the long grass the trail led through easier country. The elephant had pushed along at a good pace. Our great object was to reach him before 10 A.M. Up to that time we might expect to find him feeding in open forest, but later in the day he would be sure to be in the thickest places, where the difficulty and danger of attacking him would be increased.

We carried the track through open forest, bamboo - covert, and long grass till 12 A.M., when we came regularly to fault, as the thickets we were now in had been much trampled a month before by herd-elephants, and the rogue had wandered from one path to another in a most puzzling way. I have much too great an opinion of the Kurrabas to suppose they would not have worked out the trail sooner or later; but at this moment the rogue relieved us of all further trouble as to tracking, by trumpeting, or rather squeaking, in some high grass about two hundred yards back on the track we had just come! This illustrates the necessity of sportsmen and their followers observing the greatest caution, and never speaking or moving without circumspection, after entering the jungles. One cannot tell where any animal may or may not be. Here was a case: the elephant had wandered about, and had finally lain down close to his tracks, but in thick cover. His original track led past where he now was, and we had all passed him within a few feet unknown to him and to ourselves. Had my party been advancing incautiously, thinking that as the trackers were ahead the elephant must be so also, where should we have been had he suddenly burst into our midst? Such an attack is sure to demoralise one's men, and some accident would have been pretty nearly certain to occur in the confusion. Fortunately the wind was all right, and we had passed him without being either seen or heard. The sound he now made was merely a squeak of caprice as he got on to his legs after his mid-day snooze.

When the rogue trumpeted my men were greatly excited. Here we were face to face with the man-slayer! They could hardly speak, but I knew this was not from fear; often when more of a novice I have felt the same. It is excessive excitement, with, of course, a certain amount of apprehension. This all vanishes when the game is actually at the end of one's rifle, and I saw it was the same with Bettay and Birram, my gun-bearers, when we subsequently got up to the elephant. I gave them a minute or two to get cool, told them to stick close to me, and to mind not to clink the guns together, and then ordered the Kurrabas to advance.

Old Poojáree, who was always ready for dangerous work, now took the lead. We pushed through dangerously thick stuff, where I expected to hear the elephant's war-trumpet every moment, and to have him burst out on us; but fortunately we had the wind, and the unconscious monster stood unaware of the fact that enemies were at hand.

We were within ten yards of him before we could make him out, and he then only appeared as a dark mass in the young bamboo and grass in which he was standing. There was fortunately a good breeze blowing, which made sufficient noise amongst the branches to cover our approach; but it was impossible to get near enough, even with this advantage, for the head-shot in such thick stuff. I therefore decided to give him the 4-bore behind the shoulder, if I could only make out how he was standing; but there was a difficulty about this, as even his feet were hidden in the undergrowth, so that though we stooped and looked along the ground we could get no clue to his position. As luck would have it, however, he at this moment raised his trunk to reach a bough overhead. I saw his temple, and seized my 12-bore, intending to reserve the 4-oz. in case the first shot did not kill him; but before I could draw a sight on him his head was again hidden. Fearing that if I delayed any longer a slant of wind might discover us, I took the 4-oz. and fired at where I now knew his shoulder was. The report and smoke from 10 drams in such thick cover were tremendous. The elephant remained montionless for an instant after receiving the shot, when, with a wild scream and tremendous crash away he went, fortunately not in our direction, as there was nothing thick enough to shelter us, and we might have been run over by accident. As soon as I could reload the 4-bore we raced after him. The grass and bushes on both sides of his track were covered with blood, and my hands, face, and gun became sticky with it as we ran on through the grass. We had only gone about two hundred yards when the Kurrabas stopped short, and with the one word "*ánay*" (elephant), vanished. There was the elephant sure enough, standing about twenty-five yards from us in an open space amongst grass up to his shoulders, and facing us. The 4-bore had taken him about halfway up the left shoulder, and his lungs must have been damaged, as blood was gushing from his mouth; this accounted for the state of the grass and bushes we had passed through. He must have stopped through being choked by the bleeding, and hearing us running behind him, had faced round to receive us. As the Kurrabas vanished he came a few steps forward with a grunt, and again stopped.

He certainly was a sight to give a novice in elephant-shooting a "turn." Blood was gushing from his mouth, covering his chest, fore-legs, and trunk. His twinkling eye showed he meant mischief; his head was held high; his trunk curled between his tusks; and one foot was planted boldly in advance, ready for a forward movement. I and my gun-bearers were still within the cover and concealed; so, taking immediate advantage of his halt for a steady shot, I aimed between his eyes, and dropped him dead with the 4-bore. We found this bullet afterwards in his neck, it having gone through the brain and about fifteen inches of muscle behind.

Our delight at this speedy and fortunate termination to our hunt may be imagined. I jumped on to the fallen monster's side, which was six feet from the ground as he lay. We had certainly overthrown him by some boldness; we had brought the pursuit to a speedy conclusion by pushing up to him even in a disadvantageous and dangerous position.

The two Kurrabas with the pony and luncheon-basket now came up; and the party with knives and ropes, who had heard the shots, were not far behind them. Whilst my men were cutting off the feet I had some tiffin and a cheroot; and the Kurrabas also applied themselves to their half-finished weeds of the morning, discussing with great relish the events of the day's sport. One of the Kurrabas made a light for us with two dry sticks in a few minutes. The process is as follows: A notch is cut in a stick as thick as one's little finger; this is laid on the ground and held down with the toes, the notched side being uppermost. The end of a stick about fifteen inches long, and as thick as an ordinary lead-pencil, held vertically, is now inserted in the notch, the end being first rudely sharpened. This is made to revolve rapidly between the hands, under considerable downward pressure. The sticks soon commence to smoke at the point of contact, and a brown charred powder is worked out at the notch. In about a minute the friction kindles a spark in the powder, which is then taken up, placed in a piece of rag with a handful of dry grass or leaves, and blown into a blaze.

When I had finished tiffin we set to work to roll the elephant over, as I wanted to see the shoulder-shot, which was underneath. This we effected by working at one leg at a time with ropes and props. After a couple of hours of indescribable labour we rolled the huge mass over. On examining his head I found the marks of my unsuccessful shot of some months previous. This was a good Christmas-day's work; and though I had no roast-beef, and no plum-pudding, what did that matter? had I not enjoyed the noblest sport to be had in the world? Tigers and so on are all very well, but give me a rogue-elephant for real sport.

We went back to the carcass next day, and after immense labour succeeded in severing the head from the body. A path was cleared from the main road for a bullock-cart, and we levered the head into it, and brought it in triumph to Kákankoté. I had it put down by the roadside for two days, during which time it was on view to the passers-by, after which some Holoyas (low-caste Hindoos) were set to work to cut off the flesh. I had the skull preserved complete, and the feet prepared for subsequent conversion into footstools. The rogue was a large elephant, but with poor tusks, only three feet eleven inches in length each when taken out, ten inches in circumference at the gum, and weighing 22½ lb. the pair. They were much curved upwards, which was one of the peculiarities by which he was known. Two-thirds of his tail were gone; the sore at the end of the remaining portion was alive with maggots; and as his tail at this point was as thick as a man's calf, the agony which the poor brute must have endured was enough to account for his savageness.

As I had shot the rogue on the second day after my arrival, and I intended staying eight days more, I now turned my attention to searching for other single elephants. There were no herds in the jungle at that time of the year; the herds leave the vicinity of Kákankoté about October, and betake themselves to the lighter jungle bordering on the heavy forests. Here the grass is not so overgrown, and is consequently more palatable, and the cover is not so thick as to distress the calves, which are chiefly born towards the end of the year.

The muckna, the late rogue's friend, was the only single elephant now in the jungles, and as the Kurrabas said he was always ready to chase them if they met him, I thought it well to give him a lesson. I did not wish to kill him, as he had no trophies, but merely to impress upon him the fact that man was sometimes a dangerous creature to meddle with. The day after shooting the rogue we followed the muckna, and the two leading trackers, who were fifty yards in advance of myself and gun-bearers, nearly stumbled on him lying down in some long grass. The elephant gained his feet in a moment, and with a tremendous crackling of bamboos emerged into the open forest about sixty yards from us, head erect, ears cocked, and squeaking continuously as he looked about for the disturbers of his rest. I was just about to give him a shot through the head, but above the brain so as not to kill him, when one of the trackers who had found his way out of the long grass ran to the bamboo-clump behind which my men were sheltering. I was standing in the open to the left of the clump in grass up to my shoulders. The muckna heard or saw the movement in our direction, and at once came towards us. When within forty yards I gave him the 4-bore high in the forehead. This staggered him, and with ears pressed closely to his neck, and tail lowered, he made off in a manner more hasty than dignified. We all shouted derisively at the collapsed and retreating combatant, and I daresay the lesson made him a wiser elephant. I have seen him recently in the same jungles, and having heard nothing more to his disadvantage, hope he has become a reformed character.

There were no other single elephants at this time in the jungle on the Kákankoté side of the Cubbany. The Kurrabas, however, said that they had heard that there was one in the Baigoor forest on the other side of the river, but that they knew no particulars about him, as other Kurrabas lived there, whose duty it would be to afford us information. As this seemed to be the only other beast we were likely to meet with, I despatched four Kurrabas with two days' provisions to see what they could learn of him, and applied myself to fishing and deer-shooting till their return. On the second evening two of them returned to say that they had found the single elephant's tracks; that he was an immense beast, as shown by his footprints; and that the other two Kurrabas were following him with several Kurrabas of the locality. It is always necessary for trackers to see an elephant if trophies are the sportsman's object, as the animal may turn out to be a muckna, or tuskless male.

Next day, not expecting news till evening, I was wandering in the forest, accompanied by three or four Kurrabas, when we came on the fresh trail of an elephant. It had evidently been made during the night, but by what elephant we could not conjecture. There was no single elephant but the muckna left in the Kákankoté jungles now that the rogue was shot, and it was incredible that the former could have remained about the place after the treatment he had received so lately. Whilst we were discussing the matter in low whispers, beyond which the voice should never be raised in the jungles—there is nothing to gain and everything to lose by audible talking—we heard a light rustling sound approaching. In an instant we were all under cover of some close young bamboo-coppice, as it was as likely to be the elephant as anything else, when who should appear but our party of Kurrabas from the other side of the river, following the trail eagerly, all with their eyes upon the ground, and dripping from crossing the river. As they came close to where we were hidden I made a sudden movement among the bamboos. If a nod is as good as a wink to a blind horse, a rustle is as effective as any greater demonstration to a Kurraba, and there was an instantaneous, though quiet, scatter amongst them. A whistle brought them together, when they said that this was the elephant from the Baigoor forest; that they had followed him for the two preceding days without seeing him, as he was restless and kept constantly on the move; that he had crossed the river during the night; and they added the gratifying intelligence that he had very large tusks, the prints of which they had seen where he had lain down in soft soil. They had also brought me the diameter of his footprint (the fore-foot) on a slip of bamboo, which, on applying to a steel tape which I always carry in my pocket for measuring game, I found to be exactly eighteen inches. As twice the circumference of an elephant's fore-foot is his height at the shoulder, this gave nine feet five inches, which is very tall even for a male elephant; and when I shot him I found he was nine feet seven inches. Sometimes the foot measurement is an inch or two out, but very rarely, and the difference on this occasion probably arose from mis-measurement of the footprint.

The Kurrabas were all very keen in the pursuit, and I encouraged them by saying it was clear the elephant had come to where I was to meet his death. They all assented with nods and grunts to this predestinarian view, and added in Canarese that it was evidently his "*hanay burré*," or the "writing on his forehead" (his fate).

We pushed rapidly along as the trail was comparatively fresh. At places where the elephant had stopped to feed—in moving from one part of the country to another elephants generally march pretty steadily, merely grazing by the way—the Kurrabas immediately spread to find where he had gone on again. This was much more expeditious than following each footstep, as it may be necessary to do with only one or two trackers. A low note, in imitation of the Indian wood-owl, a sound which would alarm no animal that heard it, immediately announced the fact when a tracker hit off the track, and we were seldom delayed from the direct line for more than a minute or two. I was relieved at the commencement of the hunt of the rifle I ordinarily carried by one of the Kurrabas, and I now took off my coat, as the day was warm even in the shady forest, and we were frequently running. The elephant had several hours' start of us, and was heading towards the Coorg jungles, where he would be beyond our reach. Between 7 and 10 o'clock A.M. we must have gone twelve miles; and this exertion, despite the interest of the chase, was beginning to tell upon me. There was a stream some little distance ahead, and we entertained high hopes that the elephant might rest near it during the day.

As we pushed quickly along like a pack of hounds down the finely-wooded and gentle slope, at the foot of which the stream ran, we found the elephant had begun to loiter and feed about, and finally, on the bank of the stream, he had devoted at least two hours to demolishing a bamboo-clump, the leaves and twigs of which form a principal part of the elephant's food. The appearance of a bamboo-cover after a herd of elephants has fed in it is remarkable. Roughly speaking, there are two kinds or varieties of bamboos. One description—the small bamboo—grows to about thirty feet in height, and usually in small clumps, each bamboo about an inch and a half in diameter. The large kind—the giant bamboo—grows in clumps sometimes twenty paces in circumference, the individual stems in which are occasionally seven inches in diameter. This bamboo is hollow, the wood being half an inch thick. The elephants pull the bamboos down with their trunks, and holding the stem under foot, strip off the young shoots and foliage. The stems are split open by the pressure of their feet. The crackling and crashing noise made by elephants feeding amongst bamboos is very great; and they reduce the clumps to such disarray, bending them at about ten feet from the ground, but not detaching them, that it is difficult to move through the cover after them. The bamboos are left lying at every conceivable angle from the different clumps, interlaced across the spaces between, and twisted into every shape.

When we reached the almost dry bed of the stream we observed a *nelly* tree (*Phyllanthus emblica*) overhanging the bed on the far side, under which the elephant had stood for some time, picking up the acid fruit, of which elephants and other herbivorous animals are fond. He had remained here until an hour before. He would not be likely to travel fast, even if he kept moving, during the heat of the day. So, much encouraged, and refreshed by a hasty drink of water, we scrambled up the bank in his tracks, at a place where no one who has not seen what a wild elephant can do would imagine it could ascend, and then spread to find which direction he had taken. He had wandered about a good deal, and his tracks were confused. At this moment, from in front of us, and about a hundred and fifty yards distant, came the pleasant sound to the ears of weary trackers of a breaking bamboo! The elephant was not alarmed; this we knew by the character of the sound; and as we all collected again, I held up a handful of powdered dry leaves to see how the wind blew. Such as there was was favourable, and taking my gun-bearers, Jaffer and Birram, and two of the best Kurrabas, we went towards the elephant. The other trackers climbed trees to be out of harm's way. All wild animals are liable to return by the path they have come, if suddenly alarmed, and it is by no means safe for followers to remain on the track when a wounded beast is on foot.

When we were about forty yards from the elephant the Kurrabas suddenly pointed him out; they whispered eagerly, "*Bhoopa! kombu nōrdu!*" (what a monster! look at his tusks!) He was certainly a magnificent beast. He stood with his hind-quarters against a tree, toying listlessly with a bamboo, and looked even larger than he really was, from standing on rising ground. I almost trembled with eagerness when I saw the prize! His tusks were twice as large as any I had ever seen before. I dreaded losing him. His head was in full view, but the distance was rather too great for a certain shot at the brain. What if I lost him as I had done the rogue some months before!

I dared not contemplate such a thing, so taking aim at him behind the shoulder, about half-way up the body, I fired the 4-bore, loaded with 10 drams of powder and a hardened lead-and-quicksilver bullet. This shot took him about a foot too far back, as I afterwards found. With a shrill scream of pain away the elephant went over the rising ground. We ran to the top, hoping to hear him fall, but he was soon out of hearing. The other men joined us, and we explained what had occurred; then dividing the trackers into two parties, four of whom were to go in advance, and the rest to come with me behind, we began with care, and at a much slower pace than we had brought the hunt to this point, the really dangerous work of following the wounded tusker. We did not think it possible he could go far.

We followed him, however, for three miles, and I shall never forget the terrible dread we had of losing him. There was but little blood, and I felt afraid to look at my men; for was I not conscious that I deserved reproachful looks? I ought to have got nearer to the elephant and made sure work of him on the spot, instead of behaving like a novice. However, I could not believe that he would escape in the long-run with that leaden pill in him. There was a fallen tree in the path about four and a half feet in girth, and some two miles from where I shot him; he had got over this considerable obstacle, when we thought if he had been very bad he would have gone round it. My men exclaimed "*Ayyo! ayyo!*" (alas! alas!) at this evidence of his strength.

After going for about three miles, our hopes sinking with every step, we came up with the leading trackers, who were halted in consultation at a spot where the elephant had at last fallen or lain down. This revived our spirits considerably; we felt certain our quarry could not now escape, and from lamenting my men changed their tune entirely, and began to praise a god—Mástee—who was reverenced as the presiding spirit of these jungles, and to whom they had been promising cocoa-nuts, and latterly even a sheep, for his assistance.

We had hardly renewed the hunt when a breaking bamboo was heard ahead, and one of the leading trackers ran back to say that the elephant was just before them, but that the jungle was close and difficult to shoot in, and that the others would send back word when he got into better ground. Before long the signal was given, and I, Jaffer, and Birram, went forward with the best Kurraba—a curly-pated young fellow called Bussava. We were soon only forty yards behind the elephant, which was walking slowly along through open forest, interspersed with a few bamboo-clumps. The grass was a little too long, being up to our necks, and rather dry and noisy, so we kept our distance, hoping for a chance of closing in better ground. The elephant seemed almost exhausted, as I observed he panted heavily. I felt a pang at the suffering which the cruelty of giving him a body-shot was occasioning, and I resolved never to shoot another elephant except in the head. To steal up to within ten paces, and drop an elephant dead before he is aware of danger, is the poetry of the sport; to kill him by body-shots the prose. The latter is certainly more dangerous, as following and again encountering wounded elephants is likely to lead to a fight; but the cruelty of subjecting so grand and harmless a creature to unnecessary pain must make every sportsman shun it.

The elephant at last stopped, and in another moment was swinging round, the picture of rage. He had got our wind, and I have no doubt would have charged back in another moment, but as he showed his full broadside I fired at his shoulder, as he was too unsteady to afford me a certain head-shot. There must have been something the matter with my 4-bore, for it kicked most unmercifully, and nearly sent me on my back; but it did more for the elephant, as it knocked him completely over like a rabbit. This shot, I subsequently found, struck him high in the shoulder.

The elephant quickly regained his feet, whilst I endeavoured in haste to withdraw the exploded cartridge of the 4-bore, which was a single barrel. The heavy charge of powder had so expanded it that I was unable to extract it, whilst the elephant made across to our right. Seizing my 12-bore Greener rifle, which was loaded with 6 drams and hardened bullets, I ran to get a side-shot, but was rather startled by the elephant's suddenly pulling up and facing almost directly towards me. I took two rapid shots right and left at his temple, but failed to floor him. He only recoiled at each shot, but still stood his ground. I do not believe he was looking for us, but that he was utterly stunned and stupefied by the heavy blows he was receiving. I took my last spare rifle (16-bore Purdey) and fired a third unsuccessful shot. I now only had one loaded barrel, and I reserved it, as I expected every moment that the elephant would discover us. We were behind a tree, and I determined if he charged to let him get to within a couple of yards of the muzzle before firing, when by a general bolt we might have escaped in the confusion. I admired the conduct of my second gun-bearer, Birram, a young and promising pupil in the gun-bearing line, who, though quite new to this style of work, was on his knees at my feet behind the tree, trying with his teeth to extract the 4-bore cartridge, paying all his attention to his duty, and not even looking at the elephant. At last he got the cartridge out, and I rammed in another, at the moment that the tusker started off again at a swinging pace. In hurrying after him I fell over a log in the grass, and as I was running as fast as I could, and carrying a 16½-lb. rifle, I got a heavy fall. For the moment I felt quite stunned, and imagined half the bones in my body must be broken. As I lay sprawling I thought how I should fare if the elephant turned upon me! I could not after this carry my own rifle, and had some difficulty in hobbling along at the pace the trackers went.

The elephant had changed his course from the line he had been steering before the second encounter, and was now heading back again towards

Kákankoté. The hunt had been north hitherto; it was now to the south-east. Kákankoté was six miles distant. I drew the Kurrabas' attention to this, and said that the tusker evidently knew we should have to convey his tusks and head to the bungalow presently, and that we should never be able to manage it if he was so disobliging as to die far off. This sally pleased these simple aborigines, who have the imperturbable good-humour and easily-excited risible faculties of wild tribes generally.

We were astonished at the distance the elephant still went—about four miles. He had also kept up the pace, as we saw by his footprints. The recent encounter seemed to have acted as a refresher to his flagging energies. However, we felt certain of him; and this part of a hunt, when the result is no longer doubtful, and whilst excitement and anticipation are still at their height, is the quintessence of a sportsman's enjoyment.

We at last came to the stream on the banks of which we had encountered the elephant about three hours before, and at nearly the same spot. He had crossed it after drinking at a pool under the bank, which I knew would soon affect him seriously, with his body-wound; but still he had ascended the bank where it was very steep, and up which I found considerable difficulty in following, as my right leg and left shoulder were painful with my fall. But this was the gallant beast's last effort. The Kurrabas had foretold the probability of our finding him near the stream, as he would have to ascend rising ground if he still held on on the other side. Moreover, indications had not been wanting in the last few hundred yards that his bolt was nearly shot.

The leading trackers shortly found him close ahead, and came back to say that he appeared quite done. Bussava, my two gun-bearers, and I again advanced. The elephant was standing near a salt-lick to which elephants, bison, and game of all kinds, were in the habit of resorting to eat the earth, which is impregnated with soda. He was facing a perpendicular bank into which he had driven his tusks, and now stood leaning upon them in his weariness. Poor beast! I crept up to within fifteen yards, and killed him with the 4-bore through his brain. He rolled heavily over, and our hunt was ended.

After the momentary exultation was past, I thought regretfully of the noble life which I had sacrificed to afford the pleasure of a few hours' mad excitement. The beast to whom nature had given so noble a life; which had roamed these grand solitudes for probably not less than a hundred years; that may have visited the spot on which it now died half a century before Waterloo was fought, and which but for me might have lived for half a century more,—lay bleeding and still quivering before me, deprived of its harmless existence to gratify the passion for sport of a youth hardly out of his teens. Nor had it had a fair chance. I had not faced it boldly and killed it in open fight. It had not even seen its enemies, nor had a chance of retaliation. Trackers from whom escape was as impossible as from blood-hounds had been urged in pursuit; the most powerful weapons which science could place in the hands of a sportsman, against which any other animal of creation would have gone down at once, had been used for its destruction. Could I congratulate myself greatly on my achievement? The forest around was indescribably grand. No sounds but those of Nature fell on the ear. The trees were of immense proportions, and to their huge stems and branches numbers of ferns and orchids of different kinds clung. Their trunks were moss-grown and weather-beaten. The undergrowth consisted of ferns up to our shoulders. Truly an elephant has a noble nature, and one may almost believe he delights in the wild places he inhabits as much for their beauty as for the safety they afford. He wanders from stream to hill-top, rubs his tough hide against the mighty forest giants, and lives without fear, except of man, his only enemy. What a bloodthirsty creature the self-constituted lord of creation is! Though impressed with the wild beauty of the creations of Nature around him, how his heart jumps at the sound of the game which he has doomed to destruction! and with Nature only as a witness, how he fearlessly raises his impious hand against her creatures!

Despite these and similar somewhat sad reflections, which must come upon all sportsmen at times, I cannot look back upon this hunt but as one of the most interesting and exciting I ever had. Its length, the alternations of hope and misgiving as to the result, the final success, and the trophies I won, make it stand first in my memory.

This was the largest elephant, and possessed of the best tusks, of any I have ever shot. The following are his measurements:—

			Ft.	In.
Vertical height at shoulder,			9	7
Length from tip of trunk to tip of tail,			26	2½
Tusks	Each showing out of gum,		2	4
	When taken out	right,	5	0
		left,	4	11
	Circumference at gum,		1	4½
	Weight	right, 37½; left, 37		74½ lb.

Of course I was very liberal to the Kurrabas and others on this occasion. To give an idea of the expense of such a trip, I add a list of what I disbursed amongst them. The rupee is counted at two shillings:—

	Rs.
Present to nine Kurrabas, ...	36
Cumbleys (blankets) to do., ...	15
Present to my gun-bearers, ...	30
Holoyas for cleaning the skull, ...	3
Warm clothes for servants, ...	20
Two carts to Kákankoté, ...	20
Tobacco, arrack, and rice, ...	20
Sundries, say	6
Total, . .	150 (£15)

One remarkable incident that happened to me in the Kákankoté jungles on another occasion was the accidental shooting of an elephant in a pit. I was following a herd at the time, and had sent two Kurrabas ahead on the trail, when one of them came running back, gesticulating frantically, and said an elephant had fallen into a pit, and was just getting out. Away he went again, I trying in vain to understand from him what had occurred, until he pointed ahead into the long grass and said, "There, there! shoot him, shoot him!" Not knowing what to make of this, except that there was an elephant somewhere in the grass, I ran on, and almost fell into an old disused pitfall, which now contained an elephant. His head was a little above the level of the ground. As I stepped quickly back he threw his fore-feet on to the bank, and tried to reach me with his tusks. The whole occurrence was so sudden and unexpected, and his rush so startling, that I instinctively pulled the trigger of my 4-bore rifle from my hip as I stepped back; there was no time to bring it to my shoulder. The shot went through the base of his right tusk and buried itself deeply in his neck. He fell backwards, but recovering himself, he commenced dashing his head with great violence against the sides of the pit in his stupefaction. I therefore took a light gun from Jaffer and killed him. The shot from the 4-bore was a mortal one, and sparing him was merely prolonging his agony.

The elephant's getting into the pit had apparently occurred as follows: The herd had passed about two hours before. The pit was one of a number of old disused ones, scattered throughout the jungles, and was not now even covered in for elephant-catching. It had not been used for many years, and the overhanging lemon-grass half hid it from view. The tusker, not perceiving it, perhaps when gambolling with his companions, had fallen in. The herd had immediately fled in alarm, as elephants always do; and when the Kurrabas came upon the elephant trying to clamber out they thought he was on the point of succeeding, and by their excitement led me to the hasty action which resulted in his death. He would have worked down the bank of the pit with his tusks, and made his escape in a few hours, as it was only seven feet deep, but had I known how he was circumstanced of course I would not have fired at him. It was a strange combination of accidents, the elephant's falling into the pit to begin with, and his meeting his death at my hands in such an untoward manner. I could but agree with Jaffer's view of the case, that it was his *kismut*, or fate.

We had a fine example upon this occasion of the effects of fear—the power of the senses over the physical faculties. One Kurraba, who was much afraid of elephants, peered into the pit with a nervous air which amused my gun-bearers, and Bettay, who was standing near, gave him a sudden push into it and on to the dead elephant. The Kurraba's fear knew no bounds. He rushed at the most difficult side of the pit, attempted to scramble up, fell back when he was just at the top, tried again, falling down upon the elephant as before, and in his desperation I believe would not have succeeded in the next five minutes, when one instant's coolness would have released him. He screamed as if he were possessed, and when some one hauled him out he ran away for fifty yards before stopping. This little incident, from its suddenness and ridiculousness, caused much amusement, and the Kurraba was made the butt of a good many pleasantries for the rest of the day.

I once encountered a rather unexpected fellow-sportsman in the hunting-field. My tent was pitched at Poonjoor, in the middle of a fine open plain, on the bank of the Honhollay river. As I rode into camp on my arrival I observed three small tents, like gipsies' wigwams, half hidden amongst the dense and rank undergrowth on the edge of the jungle bordering the plain. On inquiry I was informed that these more picturesque than convenient tenements belonged to a clergyman and two half-caste police inspectors who were chaperoning his reverence on a shooting expedition. They were from the Madras district of Coimbatore, which runs close to Poonjoor. Poonjoor was an unfrequented spot, and I was surprised that any one should have found their way there but myself; nor was my astonishment lessened when I learnt that the reverend gentleman and his assistants had shot an elephant the day before, and were now gone forth to bring in his tusks! This was more than a sporting layman could bear with equanimity, particularly as elephant-shooting was prohibited in Mysore, and we who lived in the country were obliged to content ourselves with very little of it. I therefore felt this poaching and clerical outrage quite a personal grievance.

As I was enjoying the beauty of the scenery around camp half an hour before sunset, and forming hopes of the morrow's sport, watching the changing light on the cliffs before me, and upon the smooth and rounded grass-hills of the higher ranges of the Billiga-runguns, my tranquillity was disturbed by seeing his reverence with his coat off, dragging an elephant's ear in one hand, whilst he carried three feet of its trunk over his shoulder, across the plain towards his tents! This was maddening! I felt that I met him at a serious disadvantage, and I am afraid I approached his lowly tenement in a wrong spirit; it had to be such an extremely humble one, as I had nothing to set off against his tusker!

However, I found him as pleasant a companion as he was a keen sportsman. He was chaplain to the Madras Railway Company, his duty being to visit the various employees at stations along the line where there were no facilities for public worship. My wicked feelings regarding the elephant vanished in his genial society; and when I learnt some time afterwards of the disasters which followed his trip—of his having got severe jungle-fever, the effects of the damp encampment he had chosen at Poonjoor; and that, when on a trip to the Neilgherries to dispel its effects, he had got married, and had been obliged to sell off his battery,—I felt none of the delight which I am afraid I might have experienced at Poonjoor could I have contemplated his future reduced condition.

The narrowest escape I ever had in elephant-shooting happened more than a thousand miles from the scene of the above adventures. It occurred in the Garrow hills, whilst I was in temporary charge of the Elephant Kheddah Establishment in Bengal in 1875-76. Before relating it I will venture to give a short account of these hills, as they are practically a *terra incognita*, even to Europeans in India, not a hundred of whom have ever visited them. The duty which led me into the hills was a prospecting expedition for the elephant-catching establishment. I had with me nine elephants for travelling. The large number in the stud at Dacca enabled me to select good ones, with which I was able to move comfortably and fast.

The Garrow hills are situated on the north-eastern frontier of Bengal, and are bounded by Nepaul on the north, and Assam on the east. They are some 4000 square miles in extent, or four times the area of the Neilgherries. They have only been subject to British rule since 1868; prior to this they were independent and unexplored territory. The lawlessness of the Garrows, who made raids into the low country of Bengal from time to time, eventually necessitated their being placed under supervision. For this purpose an armed police force entered the hills in 1868, and established the present small hill-station of Tura. The hills are now under the Chief Commissioner of Assam. A deputy commissioner, police officer, and surgeon reside at Tura, which boasts of three wooden bungalows, a rough-and-ready style of jail for peccant Garrows, and a compact block of police huts. It has water "laid on" from the hills above, and neatly-cut walks and rides through the woods near.

Until 1870 this distant abode of the British Lion was defended by a stockade, the palisades bristling with sharp fire-hardened bamboos, whilst the neighbourhood was pleasantly *panjied.* The uninitiated may imagine that this *panjieing* is some ornamental arrangement of the grounds, so I must explain that *panjies* are not a device for the attraction, but for the discouragement, of visitors. They consist of bamboo spikes driven into the ground, almost level with the surface, the earth being scraped away round each so as to form a cup. Hundreds of these are laid in every direction; grass, falling leaves, &c., soon hide them; and if trodden upon they inflict fearful wounds. A place strongly *panjied* is quite safe against night attack or general assault, and can only be approached by a person knowing the locality, or after the *panjies* shall have been disposed of in detail.

The Garrow people are not tall, but are well built, and both men and women have open, good-natured countenances. They are warlike and constantly at variance amongst themselves, feuds between different villages being kept up for many years. They have a passion for human heads, and are in the habit of decapitating their enemies. When a village has possessed itself of the head of a member of another, there is no peace between the two communities until the loss has been adjusted by a head from the original offenders. Open fighting is not resorted to so much as stealth. For this reason Garrows seldom venture abroad but in well-armed parties. They believe that a decapitated person cannot be at peace in the next world until they have got another head for him from amongst his murderers. Consequently a sacred obligation rests upon his friends to procure him one. It may be soon, or not for years, but it must be got in the end. When a long interval of time intervenes, they are accustomed to say that their friend in the next world will have a "very long neck!" Much has been done by the British Government since taking over the hills to put a stop to this practice, and it is now only in vogue in villages distant from Tura, and which are still little influenced by British power. I learnt from Captain Williamson, the Deputy Commissioner at Tura, that if the skulls collected by contending villagers be destroyed, the feud must, by the Garrows' usages, cease, and that he had had an immense number burnt at Tura in presence of the parties interested, though there was no doubt they were but a small portion of the heads still in the possession of the Garrows.

For dress the men wear a strip of cloth round their loins, and the women merely a band of cloth about a foot in width and just long enough to meet round the hips, where it is knotted by the upper corners on the right-hand side. This perilous species of petticoat is occasionally weighted by the punctilious with four or five rows of beads along the lower hem. The women are well made, and one or two of the younger ones I saw were decidedly pretty. They wear large bunches of brass rings, 3½ inches in diameter, in their ears; this gives a stiff carriage to the head. One beauty, who permitted me to count her ornaments, had thirty-two rings in each ear. I weighed some spare ones; they were sixteeen to the pound. The lobes of their ears were distended in consequence, though the weight is partly sustained by a string across the head. The holes through their ears are frequently large enough to admit of three fingers being inserted together, and one fair one had the lobe of one ear torn through; this, strange to say, is considered a point of beauty amongst them. What tortures will not the softer sex all the world over inflict upon themselves in gratification of their vanity! Agonies from which strong men would recoil are nothing to them.

The jungles in the Garrow hills differ widely in character from anything to be seen in the south of India. There is a scarcity of heavy timber, owing to immemorial *joom* or *dhaya* cultivation (the felling of heavy forest and sowing for one or two seasons); consequently, in the absence of shade, grass fifteen to twenty feet high, creepers, canes, and undergrowth of all kinds, flourish apace. There is a large amount of bamboo in the hills, but it is of an inferior kind. There are few places where anything like stalking can be done; consequently, though game is plentiful, it is not a desirable hunting-ground. The game comprises wild elephants, a few rhinoceros, buffalo in the lower valleys, bison, bears, sámbur, barking-deer, two kinds of pheasants, jungle-fowl (*Gallus ferrugineus;* the common grey jungle-fowl of Southern India—*Gallus sonneratii*—is here unknown); the hullook, or tailless black monkey (and at least two other species); and a few minor animals.

The hills are well suited for elephant-catching; the herds are large, numerous, and undisturbed, and the supply of water and fodder unlimited. There would be some little difficulty about labour at first, as the low-country people fear entering the hills, evil spirits and fevers being supposed to be somewhat prevalent. I therefore decided on this occasion not to commence kheddahs in this locality, but it will probably be one of the most important elephant-fields for the supply of the Bengal Commissariat hereafter.

Having made all the inquiries I desired, I commenced my return-march to the plains of Bengal. This was in October 1875. During the first day's march I passed two large herds of elephants; one probably contained eighty individuals. Next morning I was walking in advance of the baggage-elephants when we heard elephants feeding in a valley to our right. The jungle was tolerably feasible here, so I determined to have a look at them to form an idea of their general stamp, and what fodder they were most intent upon, and other particulars. My gun-bearer, Jaffer, who had accompanied me to Bengal from Mysore, and an experienced mahout to examine the elephants, accompanied me, with a heavy rifle in case of accidents. The herd consisted of about fifty individuals, and after examining them for nearly an hour at close quarters, merely keeping the wind, we turned to rejoin the pad-elephant on the path.

Just then a shrill trumpeting and crashing of bamboos about two hundred yards to our left broke the stillness, and from the noise we knew it was a tusker-fight. We ran towards the place where the sounds of combat were increasing every moment: a deep ravine at last only separated us from the combatants, and we could see the tops of the bamboos bowing as the monsters bore each other backwards and forwards with a crashing noise in their tremendous struggles. As we ran along the bank of the nullah to find a crossing, one elephant uttered a deep roar of pain, and crossed the nullah some forty yards in advance of us, to our side. Here he commenced to destroy a bamboo-clump (the bamboos in these hills have a very large hollow, and are weak and comparatively worthless) in sheer fury, grumbling deeply the while with rage and pain. Blood was streaming from a deep stab in his left side, high up. He was a very large elephant, with long and fairly thick tusks, and with much white about the forehead; the left tusk was some inches shorter than the right.

The opponent of this Goliath must have been a monster indeed to have worsted him. An elephant-fight, if the combatants are well matched, frequently lasts for a day or more, a round being fought every now and then. The beaten elephant retreats temporarily, followed leisurely by the other, until by mutual consent they meet again. The more powerful elephant occasionally keeps his foe in view till he perhaps kills him; otherwise, the beaten elephant betakes himself off for good on finding he has the worst of it. Tails are frequently bitten off in these encounters. This mutilation is common amongst rogue-elephants, and amongst the females in a herd; in the latter case it is generally the result of rivalry amongst themselves.

The wounded tusker was evidently the temporarily-beaten combatant of the occasion, and I have seldom seen such a picture of power and rage as he presented, mowing the bamboos down with trunk and tusks, and bearing the thickest part over with his fore-feet. Suddenly his whole demeanour changed. He backed from the clump and stood like a statue. Not a sound broke the sudden stillness for an instant. His antagonist was silent, wherever he was. Now the tip of his trunk came slowly round in our direction, and I saw that we were discovered to his fine sense of smell. We had been standing silently behind a thin bamboo-clump, watching him, and when I first saw that he had winded us, I imagined he might take himself off. But his frenzy quite overcame all fear for the moment; forward went his ears and up went his tail, in a way which no one who has once seen the signal in a wild elephant can mistake the significance of, and in the same instant he wheeled round with astonishing quickness, getting at once into full speed, and bore straight down upon us. The bamboos by which we were partly hidden were useless as cover, and would have prevented a clear shot, so I stepped out into open ground the instant the elephant commenced his charge. I gave a shout in the hope of stopping him, which failed. I had my No. 4 double smooth-bore loaded with 10 drams in hand.

I fired when the elephant was about nine paces distant, aiming into his curled trunk about one foot below the fatal bump between the eyes, as his head was held very high, and this allowance had to be made for its elevation. I felt confident of the shot, but made a grand mistake in not giving him both barrels; it was useless to reserve the left as I did at such close quarters, and I deserved more than what followed for doing so. The smoke from the 10 drams obscured the elephant, and I stooped quickly to see where he lay. Good heavens! he had not been even checked, and was upon me! There was no time to step right or left. His tusks came through the smoke (his head being now held low) like the cow-catchers of a locomotive, and I had just time to fall flat to avoid being hurled along in front of him. I fell a little to the right; the next instant down came his ponderous fore-foot within a few inches of my left thigh, and I should have been trodden on had I not been quick enough, when I saw the fore-foot coming, to draw my leg from the sprawling position in which I fell. As the elephant rushed over me he shrieked shrilly, which showed his trunk was uncoiled; and his head also being held low instead of in charging position, I inferred rightly that he was in full flight. Had he stopped I should have been caught, but the heavy bullet had taken all the fighting out of him. Jaffer had been disposed of by a recoiling bamboo, and was now lying almost in the elephant's line; fortunately, however, the brute held on. I was covered with blood from the wound inflicted by his late antagonist in his left side; even my hair was matted together when the blood became dry. The mahout had jumped into the deep and precipitous nullah to our left at the commencement of hostilities.

How it was that I did not bag the elephant I cannot tell. Probably I went a trifle high, but even then the shock should have stopped him. He was, I believe, unable to pull up, being on a gentle incline and at full speed, though

Phototint. H. M. Wright & Co. London.

A Hard-headed Tusker.

doubtless all hostile intentions were knocked out of him by the severe visitation upon his knowledge-box. Had I done anything but what I did at the critical moment there is no doubt I should have been caught. I felt as collected through it all as possible. The deadly coolness which sportsmen often experience is in proportion in its intensity to the increase of danger and necessity for nerve.

Jaffer and I picked ourselves up and pursued the retreating tusker. He was now going slowly and wearily, and we were up with him in two hundred yards from the scene of our discomfiture, but in such thick cover that it would have been folly to have closed with him there; so, as we had the wind, we kept about thirty yards behind him. Unfortunately the bamboo-cover was extensive, and in about a quarter of a mile he joined the herd without once emerging into the open, as we had hoped he would, and afford us another chance. The herd had only gone about two hundred yards at the shot, and were feeding again; and as I feared that following the tusker would only bring us into collision with other elephants, we abandoned the chase and returned to the pad-elephant. Had I only had my Mysore Shōlaga or Kurraba trackers with me we should no doubt have recovered the elephant.

In Chapter VI. I have referred to the very large tusk of an elephant shot in the Billiga-rungun hills by Sir Victor Brooke and Colonel Douglas Hamilton, some years before I first shot there. For the following interesting account of their adventures with this elephant I am indebted to the pen of Sir Victor. The tusk referred to is, I believe, the largest on record for an Indian elephant.

"In July 1863, Colonel Douglas Hamilton and I were shooting on the Hássanoor hills, Southern India. We had had excellent sport, but until the date of the death of the big tusker, had not come across any elephants. Upon the morning of that day, in the jungles to the east of the Hássanoor bungalow, we had tracked up a fine tusker, which, partly from over-anxiety, and partly, I must confess, from the effect on my nervous system of the presence of the first wild bull-elephant I had ever seen, I had failed to bag. About mid-day I was lying on my bed chewing the cud of vexation, and inwardly vowing terrible vengeance on the next tusker I might meet, when two natives came in to report a herd of elephants in a valley some three or four miles to the north of our camp. To prepare ourselves was the work of a few seconds. As we arrived on the ridge overlooking the valley where the elephants were, we heard the crackling of bamboos, and occasionally caught sight of the back of an elephant as it crossed a break amongst the confused mass of tree-tops upon which we were gazing. Presently one of the elephants trumpeted loudly, which attracted the attention of some people herding cattle on the opposite side of the valley, who, seeing us, and divining our intentions, yelled out, "*ánay! ánay!*" (elephants) at the top of their voices, in the hopes no doubt of receiving a reward for their untimely information. The effect of these discordant human cries was magical; every matted clump seemed to heave and shake and vomit forth an elephant. With marvellous silence and quickness the huge beasts marshalled themselves together, and by the time they appeared on the more open ground in the centre of the valley, a mighty cavalcade was formed which, once seen, can never be forgotten. There were about eighty elephants in the herd. Towards the head of the procession was a noble bull, with a pair of tusks such as are rarely seen nowadays in India. Following him in direct line came a medley of elephants of lower degree—bulls, cows, and calves of every size, some of the latter frolicking with comic glee, and bundling in amongst the legs of their elders with the utmost confidence. It was truly a splendid sight, and I really believe that while it lasted neither Colonel Hamilton nor I entertained any feeling but that of intense admiration and wonder. At length the great stream was, we believed, over, and we were commencing to arrange our mode of attack, when that hove in sight which called forth an ejaculation of astonishment from each one of us. Striding thoughtfully along in the rear of the herd, many of the members of which were, doubtless, his children, and his children's children, came a mighty bull, the like of which neither my companion, after many years of jungle experience, nor the two natives who were with us, had ever seen before. But it was not merely the stature of the noble beast which astonished us, for that, though great, could not be considered unrivalled. It was the sight of his enormous tusk, which projected like a long gleam of light into the grass through which he was slowly wending his way, that held us riveted to the spot. With almost a solemn expression of countenance Colonel Hamilton turned to me and said, 'There's the largest tusker in India, old boy; and come what may you must get him, and take his tusk to Ireland with you.' It was in vain I expostulated with my dear old friend, recalling my morning's mishap, and reminding him that in jungle-laws it stands written—'Shot turn and turn about at elephants.' It was of no avail. 'You must bag that tusker,' was all the answer I could get.

"It took us but a short time to run down the slope, and to find the track which swept like a broad avenue along the bed of the valley. Cautiously we followed it up, and after about a quarter of a mile came upon the elephants. They were standing in perfect silence around the borders of a small glade, in the middle of which stood the great tusker, quite alone, and broadside on. He was about fifty yards from us, and therefore out of all elephant-shooting range, but the difficulty was to shorten the distance. To approach direct was impossible, owing to the absolute want of cover, so after some deliberation we decided on working to the right, and endeavouring to creep up behind a solitary tree which stood about twenty yards behind the elephant. When within ten yards of this tree we found, to our annoyance, a watchful old cow, who was not further than fifteen yards from us, and to our right, and had decided suspicions of our proximity. To attempt to gain another foot would have been to run the risk of disturbing the elephants. Seeing this, and knowing the improbability of our ever getting the bull outside the herd again, Colonel Hamilton recommended me to creep a little to the left so as to get the shot behind his ear, and to try the effect of my big Purdey rifle, while he kept his eye on the old cow in case her curiosity should induce her to become unpleasant. I should mention that we now, for the first time, perceived that the old bull had only one perfect tusk, the left one being a mere stump, projecting but a little beyond the upper lip. I accordingly followed Colonel Hamilton's suggestion. At the shot the old bull, with a shrill trumpet of pain and rage, swung round on his hind-legs as on a pivot, receiving my second barrel, and two from Colonel Hamilton. This staggered the old fellow dreadfully, and as he stood facing us Colonel Hamilton ran up within twelve yards of him with a very large single-bore rifle, and placed a bullet between his eyes. Had the rifle been as good as it was big I believe this would have ended the fray; but though its shock produced a severe momentary effect, the bullet had, as we afterwards ascertained, only penetrated three or four inches into the cancellous tissue of the frontal bones. After swaying backwards and forwards for a moment or two, during which I gave him both barrels of my second rifle, the grand old beast seemed to rally all his forces, and rolling up his trunk, and sticking his tail in the air, rushed off trumpeting and whistling like a steam-engine. Colonel Hamilton followed and fired two more hurried shots, while I remained behind to load the empty rifles. This completed, I joined my friend, whom I found standing in despair at the edge of a small ravine overgrown with tangled underwood, into which the tusker had disappeared. For some little time I found it difficult to persuade Colonel Hamilton to continue the chase. Long experience had taught him how rarely elephants when once alarmed are met with a second time the same day. At length, however, finding that I was determined to follow the tracks of the noble beast until I lost them, even should it involve sleeping upon them, my gallant old friend gave way and entered eagerly into a pursuit which at the time he considered almost, if not absolutely, useless.

It would be tedious, even were it possible, to describe all the details of the long stern-chase which followed. After emerging from the thorny ravine into which the elephant had disappeared, the tracks led over a series of extensive open grassy glades, crossed the Mysore-Hássanoor road beyond the seventh milestone, and then followed the deep sandy bed of a dry river for a considerable distance. At length, when about nine weary miles had been left behind us, we began to remark signs of the elephant having relaxed a little in his direct onward flight. His tracks commenced to zigzag backwards and forwards in an undecided manner, and finally led down a steep grassy slope into a densely-matted thorny jungle, bordering a small stream at its foot. I was the first to arrive at the edge of the thicket, and without waiting for my companions, who were out of sight, followed the tracks cautiously into it. I soon found that it was almost impossible to track the elephant any further. The entire thicket was traversed by a perfect labyrinth of elephant-paths, and on each path were the more or less recent footprints of elephants. Giving up the idea of tracking for the moment, I was on the point of commencing a further exploration of the thicket, when a low hiss attracted my attention, and looking round I saw the native who had accompanied us beckoning to me and gesticulating in the most frantic manner. Upon going to him he pointed eagerly in front of him, and following the direction of his finger my eyes alighted, not upon the elephant as I had expected, but upon Colonel Hamilton, who from behind the trunk of a small tree was gazing intently towards the little stream which ran not more than thirty yards from where he was standing. With the greatest care I stole up to his side. 'There he is in front of you, standing in the stream ; you had better take him at once or he will be off again,' were the welcome words which greeted my ears. At the same moment my eyes were gratified by the indistinct outline of the mighty bull, who, already suspicious of danger, was standing perfectly motionless in the middle of the stream, which was so narrow that the branches of the low bamboos on its banks nearly met across it. The distance—twenty-seven yards—was too great for certainty, but there was no choice, as even if the elephant had been utterly unaware of our vicinity, the tangled, thorny nature of the dense jungle surrounding him would have rendered it impossible to have approached nearer without discovery. As it was, the perfect immobility of all save his eye, and every now and again the quickly-altered position of his tattered ears, showed undeniably that the chances of flight and battle were being weighed in the massive head, and that there was no time to lose. Covering the orifice of the ear with as much care as if the shot had been at an egg at a hundred yards, I fired. A heavy crash and the sudden expulsion of the stream from its bed ten or twelve feet into the air followed the report, and I have a dim recollection of my old friend hugging me the next moment in his delight while he exclaimed, 'Splendid, old boy! he's dead; and the biggest tusker ever killed in India!' But our work was not yet over. With one or two tremendous lurches from side to side the old bull regained his feet, but only to be again felled by my second barrel, and this time to rise no more. The shades of evening were closing in fast, and a long journey lay between us and home, so we had but a few moments to admire one of the grandest trophies it has ever fallen to the lot of a sportsman to secure."

There is a common elephant-shooting story which one frequently hears in India, of sportsmen having been overtaken by infuriated elephants which have endeavoured, but failed, to pin them to the ground, a tusk entering the earth on each side of them, whilst they have escaped without injury. I have never heard any one say the occurrence had happened to himself, but men have been named—generally Major somebody—as having undergone the agony. Why unfortunate majors should always be selected as the victims is not easy to understand. I think the popular idea of a major is a man arrived at an age when a rubber and a cheroot, or a game at billiards, is more congenial diversion than foot-racing with wounded elephants, and of a figure which would not fit easily between a pair of tusks. Were a slim sub-lieutenant substituted as the hero, the story would be robbed of a certain amount of its improbability. Then why the victim should be robed in a jacket of spotless white—as sometimes the more daring versions affirm—it is difficult to conjecture. It is certainly not a suitable colour for jungle-shooting, though it answers well in the story, as it shows plainly to the horrified listener the blood which has trickled from the wounded monster's forehead on to the unhappy major's back!

My readers may rest assured that no major who was ever prodded at by an elephant lived to become a lieutenant-colonel. It is almost a physical impossibility that a man could be got between the tusks, on the ground, without the elephant's kneeling or treading on him; and as the elephant uses its ponderous fore-feet in addition to its tusks in disposing of an enemy, nor major nor other man would be likely to escape a deliberate attempt at scotching him.

The manner in which wild animals, especially herbivorous ones, recover from severe wounds, which in India always become fly-blown in a few hours, is worthy of remark. Some flies deposit their young alive as very small maggots. I have known many people doubt this fact. Indeed I myself could scarcely believe it at first, but I found the fact was well known amongst natives, and I have often observed maggots produced in this manner. The parent fly deposits as many young maggots as would cover a shirt-button. When first produced the young are about a sixteenth of an inch in length, but they grow with wonderful rapidity.

When an animal's wound is fly-blown it constantly rubs the part against trees, and an elephant blows mud or dust upon it. Carnivorous animals excepted, very few, I believe, die of putrefaction of their wounds, though I have known bison and elephants have unhealed wounds for upwards of a year. It is marvellous how they manage to keep them clean. I have seen a mass of maggots as large as an egg which had fallen from an elephant's wound where he had rubbed against a tree.

CHAPTER XVIII.

THE INDIAN BISON (GAVÆUS GAURUS).

DISTRIBUTION IN INDIA—APPEARANCE—HEIGHT—SIZE OF HORNS—GREGARIOUS NATURE—FOOD—CHARACTER—HABITAT—SUBJECT TO MURRAIN—INDIAN CATTLE DISEASES—BISON-CALVES—SOUNDS MADE BY BISON—FLESH—THE BISON AND MITHUN OR GAYAL OF BENGAL COMPARED—NEVER BROUGHT ALIVE TO ENGLAND—MY OPPORTUNITIES OF OBSERVING BISON—PROBABLE AGE ATTAINED BY BISON—SOLITARY BULLS—THEIR DISPOSITION—THEY CARRY THE BEST HEADS.

THE Indian bison (*Gavæus gaurus*), or the Gaur, is undoubtedly the finest species of the genus *Bos* in the world. It differs in appearance from the American bison, commonly called Buffalo (*Bison americanus*), in being larger, in having no shaggy hair on the neck and shoulders, and in other essential particulars of form; whilst it lives entirely in dense forests, especially those of hill-tracts, instead of on open prairies like the American bison.

The bison is distributed throughout India and the countries immediately to the east of the Bay of Bengal wherever the conditions necessary to its existence—viz., heavy forests of large extent, and hilly country—are found. It prefers high elevations, from 2000 to 5000 feet, but is found also in the low country. I have shot bison within three miles of the coast in Chittagong, at an elevation of under 100 feet. The bison is not found in Ceylon, but is stated by Jerdon* to have existed there sixty years ago, and to have become extinct. It would be interesting to know to what cause this is to be attributed, if true,—as the wild elephant, the bison's almost invariable contemporary, still flourishes in the island.

The prevailing colour of the bison is a dark coffee-brown amongst the cows, which deepens to black in mature and old bulls. The legs from the knees downwards, as also the forehead, are of a dirty white colour, whilst inside the thighs and fore-arms the hair is of a bright chestnut. The head is

* The accuracy of this statement seems doubtful.

somewhat short and square for the size of the animal, particularly in the bulls. The eye is a peculiar feature, the pupil being a pale slaty blue and very large, which gives a solemn appearance to the animal when at rest. The ears are broad, and are like those of the deer tribe rather than the *Bovidæ.* The neck is short, heavy, and immensely powerful.

The bison has no hump above the level of the dorsal ridge, but there is an exuberance of flesh in the bulls immediately over the shoulders. The dorsal ridge runs with a slight rise backwards to about the middle of the back, and there ends abruptly with a drop of nearly five inches in large animals. The quarters are plump and the tail somewhat short.

The largest bulls stand eighteen hands (six feet) at the shoulder, and according to Elliot, as quoted by Jerdon, even six feet one and a half inch. I have never myself shot them above eighteen hands fair vertical measurement. The animal when standing certainly does not look its height. The hide of old bulls is frequently almost devoid of hair on the quarters, and after a sharp hunt gives out an oily sweat. In this peculiarity the bison differs from domestic cattle, which never sweat under any exertion.

The cow is considerably lighter in make and colour than the bull, and is more active. The horns are more slender and upright, with more inward curvature, and the frontal ridge is scarcely perceptible. In young animals the horns are smooth and polished; in old bulls they are rugged and indented at the base, and massive and worn at the points.

In old bulls the vertical form of the cows' and younger bulls' horns is replaced by a much more horizontal growth. The largest bull that I have shot had horns which measured as follows:—

	Ft.	In.
From tip to tip, round the outer edge and across the forehead, . .	6	2
Across the sweep, ...	0	33
Circumference of horn at base, well clear of forehead, . . .	0	19
Between tips, ...	0	19

Horns are seldom found larger than the above in all their dimensions.

The bison's appearance is a strange admixture of that of the genera *Bos* and *Bubalus.* In Canarese, and, in some localities, in Hindoostánee, the bison is called the jungle-buffalo. The old bulls with almost hairless hides, and both sexes as to their white foreheads and stockings, and the peculiar habit of holding their noses almost horizontally when staring at any strange object, closely resemble the buffalo. Their legs, too, are short, and their carcasses are heavy, which further assists the likeness. I found some difficulty in getting my Mussulmán shikaries to eat bison at first, though their throats were duly cut, as they regarded them as buffaloes, which many Mussulmáns in Southern India do not eat; but I did not find this prejudice regarding buffaloes existing in Bengal.

Bison seldom form herds of more than thirty or forty individuals; the general number is about twelve. I have, however, seen a collection which, I believe, contained not less than one hundred. It was at the commencement of the early rains whilst pasture was still limited, and this gathering was very temporary. One bull holds undisputed sway in each herd, the other males being younger animals incapable of disputing his authority. On the leading bull's strength declining with age he is ousted by more youthful rivals, and thenceforward *invariably*, I believe, leads a solitary life, unless he is able to force himself for a season into a herd whose chief is in worse case than himself. I have never found a really aged bull with a herd.

I will first treat of the habits of herd-bison, and then of the solitary bulls; the latter are noble beasts, and well entitled to a special notice.

Herd-bison are shy and retiring in their habits, and retreat at once if intruded upon by man. They avoid the vicinity of his dwellings, and never visit patches of cultivation in the jungle, as do wild elephants, deer, and wild hog. The bison is thus an animal which would soon become extinct before the advance of civilisation were the latter rapid, or were the jungles which he roams limited in extent; but his exemption from serious diminution, except in isolated positions, is secured by the existence of the continuous jungles of the Western Ghâts and other forest-ranges.

Bison, though found in the low-country jungles, are very partial to high and well-wooded tracts, and their activity in hilly ground is astonishing. A herd scrambles up a steep hillside almost with the facility of a troop of deer, or thunders down a slope into the thicker cover of the valley, when alarmed, at a rapid trot or free gallop.

The food of the bison—as of the wild elephant—consists chiefly of grasses, and only in a secondary degree of bamboo leaves and twigs, the thick and succulent tuberous shoots of the bamboo which appear during the rains, and of the bark of some trees, particularly one known in Canarese as "Nelly" (*Phyllanthus emblica*). Bison feed till about nine in the morning, or later in cloudy and rainy weather; they then rest, lying down in bamboo-cover or light forest until the afternoon, when they rise to graze and drink; they also invariably lie down for some hours during the night.

Although certainly quick in detecting an intruder, bison can scarcely be considered naturally wary animals, as they seldom encounter alarms in their native haunts. Unsophisticated herds will frequently allow several shots to be fired at them before making off, and even then probably will not go far. But if subjected to frequent disturbance they quickly become as shy as deer, and if alarmed by the approach of man they retreat without loss of time. In localities exposed to frequent intrusion they are found only in small herds, and when startled retreat rapidly, and usually put a considerable distance between themselves and the apprehended danger before stopping.

I have never known a case of herd-bison attacking man, except such individuals as were wounded, and, being pursued, found themselves unable to escape. Even these more often die without resistance than otherwise. The character of ferocity sometimes given to bison by sportsmen is entirely foreign to their character, and can only have arisen in the hunters' own fears which have led them to mistake for an attack what is really the bewildered rush of a herd misled by fright into the very danger they aim at avoiding.

The habits of bison and wild elephants are very similar in many points. Their requirements in food and cover being almost identical, the same causes influence the movements of both. They are frequently found feeding together; each are inoffensive and tolerant of the close proximity of the other. The remarks upon the habits of wild elephants in Chapter VI. may be applied with a few modifications to the bison.

Both seek the deep and ever-verdant valleys, watered by perennial streams during the hot months, or from January to May, where they are safe from the jungle-fires which sweep the drier localities. With the early rains of April and May a plentiful crop of succulent young grass springs from beneath the black ashes, and the bison and elephants then roam forth to feed and enjoy their emancipation from the thraldom of the season of scarcity. About September the grass in hill-ranges has become so coarse, and the annoyance from insects during continued rain so great, that the herds move into more open country, and especially into forest-tracts at the foot of hill-ranges where suitable cover exists. Here the grass is seldom more than two or three feet high, whilst it is as many yards high on the hills, and there are comparatively few insect-pests. The herds have here to be content with somewhat light cover, they usually lie up in bamboo-thickets, and if seriously alarmed retreat at once to the hills.

Almost the only divergence in the habits of bison and wild elephants occurs here. Whilst the former timidly confine themselves to the forest, the elephants roam in herds or singly far out into open and partly-populated country.

When in the low country the bison frequently visit the spots known as salt-licks, where a peculiar kind of earth is found, usually of a greasy consistency when wet, and of a dull-grey colour, of which all wild animals eat considerable quantities at intervals, more commonly in the wet weather.

Natives assert that tigers, and the *Felidæ* generally, eat this earth. I have never myself seen traces of their doing so, though I think it probable, as my dogs would frequently eat it. I do not know of any of these salt-licks existing at a great elevation in hill-ranges; they appear to be found chiefly, if not entirely, in the low-country jungles, below 3000 feet.

It is whilst in the low country that bison sometimes suffer from cattle diseases through feeding in jungles used by infected domestic cattle. These epidemics are exceedingly fatal. The three most dreaded are called in Canarese: *Dod-róga*—The great sickness; *Kei-by-róga*—Foot-and-mouth disease; *Cheppay-róga*—Shoulder-blade disease. The following are the symptoms of each:—

Dod-róga.—The beast coughs once, the ears immediately droop, it stands listless, and will not graze. The coat becomes staring, violent purging commences, the evacuations being mixed with bloody mucus; there is much running at the nose and mouth, and the beast drinks to excess. Flies deposit their eggs about the mouth, eyes, and ears. It becomes rapidly weak and staggers. In from two to four days death generally ensues: some may live for a week. No effectual remedy is known. Of beasts attacked not more than about ten per cent recover; those in best condition are the chief sufferers; old and poor cattle occasionally survive an attack. Beasts that have once been attacked are said never to have the disease again. It is highly infectious. Calves drinking infected beasts' milk die. The stench from infected cattle is intolerable. The lowest castes of Hindoos (Holoyas and Mádigas), and also wild hogs, eat the flesh of the dead cattle, without any ill effects; but tigers will not touch it, or even, it is said, kill beasts suffering from the disease. Infected herds are frequently driven into jungles where tigers are known to be, as it is superstitiously believed by the natives that if the tiger can be got to kill a beast the disease will leave the rest. It is probable that the disease is on the wane when the tiger recommences killing amongst them. The tiger, doubtless, discriminates between infected herds and those not infected by the stench of the former.

This disease prevailed among the bison in the Billiga-rungun hills in 1867, and the Shōlagas estimate that it killed two-thirds of them. I saw many of their remains when I first shot in the hills in 1869. Just as I was leaving India—in April 1877—it again broke out amongst them, and I have no doubt has decimated them. It was introduced, on the latter occasion, by the famine-stricken cattle driven to the jungles for pasture when there was none elsewhere.

Kei-by-róga.—In this disease the mouth of the infected animal becomes sore, frothy, and suppurates, and thus renders grazing difficult. The beast is observed to limp and lick its feet, which are found to swarm with maggots—the hoof having suppurated and become loose. Frequently the hoofs drop off. It is generally severe for a month. It is much less fatal than *dod-róga;* like that disease it is most destructive amongst young animals in good condition. Perhaps twenty-five per cent of beasts attacked die. There is no known remedy, but a collar of pieces of wood is occasionally put on to prevent the beast licking its feet. Infected cattle are also kept standing in puddles as a preventive against maggots. I have shot bison suffering from this disease.

Cheppay-róga is confined to beasts under three years of age, especially calves, and is invariably fatal. Beasts quite well one day will be found to have a shoulder or hind-quarter swelled and puffy in the morning. The affected part feels spongy to the touch, and the beast limps. The stomach also swells. Death follows within six or eight hours. The flesh of the dead animal looks black and inflamed.

The bulk of cow-bison calve in September, a few in April and May. The bison-calf when very young resembles the calf of the domestic cow, the colour being a reddish brown, and the future white of the forehead and legs showing but indistinctly as a leaden tinge. The cow-bison separates from the herd when her calf is born, and keeps it in one place for about four days, feeding near it till it is strong enough to accompany the herd, which remains in the locality, and which she then rejoins with her offspring. The habits of bison and elephants differ in this respect: the female elephant does not separate from the herd; the latter remains with her for about two days after her calf is born.

The bison utters three distinct sounds. The first is hardly like any uttered by the *Bovidæ*, and closely resembles a common sound made by elephants. It is used by bison to call each other at a distance, and can be heard for about a mile in favourable ground. It may be described as a sonorous bellow. The second is a low "moo," indicative of apprehension or curiosity. I heard this from several cow-bison once when they discovered two Shōlagas and myself creeping on hands and knees towards them in grass about three feet high; they probably supposed us to be tigers, as they stood their ground for half an hour, within forty yards, till I got a chance at, and killed, the bull. The third sound is the loud whistling snort of alarm with which they dash off when frightened. I have also heard a bison, held by bull-dogs, roar like a common bull.

The flesh of the bison is somewhat coarse, but is well flavoured. Steaks cut from along the dorsal ridge behind the shoulders are the best. They should be cut thick and grilled when fresh from the animal, with a plentiful dusting of black pepper, which process makes them tender. If the animal is allowed to get cold, or the steaks are cut thin, or are over-cooked, they will be as tough as leather. I have eaten steaks from the oldest bulls, cut out and cooked almost before they had given the last quiver, and found them excellent. The marrow-bones are those above the knees and above the hocks; the shin and shank bones are almost solid.

In Mysore, except the two lowest castes, Holoyas and Mádigas, who eat any dead cattle, and the Kurrabas of Kákenkoté, no Hindoos will eat the flesh of the bison; this is because it is, in their opinion, the same as their sacred cow. As Mussulmáns require the throat to be cut before it is dead, it is seldom bison-beef appears in their *menu*, as few people care to approach a dying bison whilst any doubts remain regarding its demise.

The bison has never been domesticated in Southern India, though I believe it could be under the same circumstances under which it, or its very near relative the *gayal* or *mithun* (*Gavæus frontalis*), is kept in captivity in the countries to the east of the Bráhmapootra, Assam, Tipperah, Chittagong hills, &c. But it is certain that it could never be kept out of its natural wilds, and its domestication would not thus be of much practical value. A strain might possibly be obtained by crossing it with domestic cattle, and by toning down the first result with a further infusion of domestic blood, animals might be produced which would live in the plains, and the bison's enormous strength would be a gain in its progeny. But to a people like the ordinary natives of India such considerations or experiments are of no interest.

No bison-calf has ever, I believe, reached England alive; and though they have been kept for a year or so in India, they have not survived much longer away from their natural wilds. The domesticated individuals which I saw in the Chittagong hill-tracts were in their native forests; they merely returned to the villages at nightfall, where they were fed with a little salt, the only tie between them and their owners. They were not secured or housed, but lay about on the village green, and at dawn they were off again to the jungles. Any that were required for milking were detained a few minutes, and then followed their companions. They had no attendants in the jungles. The hillmen informed me that they kept them chiefly for the sake of killing one occasionally for meat at feasts. These animals were thus feral to all intents and purposes, except in their having no dread of man. They seemed very peaceful in disposition. I was assured by the hillmen that they would not live more than a few months in the plains of

Bengal. Under similar conditions there is no doubt the bison would live, and probably breed with domestic cattle, upon his own forest ground in Southern India.

I believe the distinction between the bison and the *gayal* was made by Cuvier, or Blyth; and Dr Jerdon has quoted them. The difference is, however, exceedingly slight, and from the sportsman or general observer's point of view the two animals are to all intents and purposes identical. Were it not that I should be setting my opinion against that of the above-named eminent naturalists, I should say the animals are the same, and that the distinction has been founded on a comparison of the wild individuals in the one locality, and the domesticated and impure race in the other. The name *gayal* is merely the local native name in Bengal.

When in the hill-tracts of Chittagong I saw numbers of domesticated *gayal*, and examined them closely. Jerdon says of this animal: "The *gayal* or *mithun* (*Gavæus frontalis*) is found in the hilly tracts to the east of the Burrampooter, and at the head of the valley of Assam, the Mishnee hills and their vicinity, probably extending north and east into the borders of China. It is domesticated extensively and easily, and has bred with the common Indian cattle. It is a heavy, clumsy-looking animal compared with the bison, *the wild animal similarly coloured and with white legs.* It browses more than the bison, and, unlike that, it has a small but distinct dewlap. The domesticated race extends south as far as Tipperah and the Chittagong hills, and northwards has been seen grazing in company with the yâk, close to the snows. It is better adapted for rocky and precipitous ground than the bison."

The points which Jerdon here notes seem slight divergencies on which to found a distinction between two animals, when it is seen that the following essential points exist in both: the dorsal ridge ending abruptly in the middle of the back; the peculiar light-blue full pupil of the eye; the unmixed brown colour of the hide, with chestnut inside the thighs and on the abdomen; the white forehead and legs; similar horns.

In the alleged points of difference there seem to be none that may not be the direct result of the bison's (or *gayal's*) domestication. Heaviness and clumsiness of appearance might follow partial curtailment of the wanderings of the wild animal, whilst its browsing more than the bison of Southern India might be caused by local differences in pasture. I cannot imagine any animal better adapted for rocky and precipitous country than the bison; but if the domestic *gayal* is so, that, too, may be a peculiarity arising from the nature of the country. The chief point of difference seems to be in the *gayal's* having, it is said, a small dewlap which is wanting in the bison. This may have happened to be a peculiarity in certain specimens, and probably caused by crossing with domestic cattle; but, even if peculiar to the whole species in the north-east of Hindoostán, it is not a more essential difference than that of male elephants in Ceylon being almost all tuskless, though identical with the elephants of continental India, amongst whom a tuskless male is a rarity. I venture to think that, unless the comparison is made between a wild *gayal* and a wild bison, and some distinction is then established, the very slight difference, if any, that exists between them may be put down to partial domestication alone.

I was determined to see a wild *gayal* for myself when in the Chittagong hills, and I was fortunate enough to shoot an old solitary bull, a very good specimen. The pursuit of this animal occupied me four days; the dryness of the ground, and the inexpertness of the trackers, made the hunt a difficult one. I can state that there was not one single point of difference in appearance or size between it and the bison of Southern India, except that the horns were somewhat smaller than what would have been looked for in a bull of its age in Southern India.

I have enjoyed the best opportunities of observing bison in Mysore when mounted on an elephant. As bison and elephants constantly feed together, the presence of an elephant causes them no alarm, nor do they observe the rider if he use ordinary precautions to conceal himself. Whilst some of the herd are lying down peacefully chewing the cud, or affectionately licking each other's ears and cheeks, others are grazing, or browsing on the young shoots of bamboo. The characteristic placidity of their disposition is here seen to advantage; and I have often wished for a pencil, and the ability to use it, rather than the murderous rifle, that I might carry away with me a representation of these scenes. I have often left the poor beasts undisturbed.

I should think it probable, judging from the cases of two or three Bráhminee bulls I have known of, which had entire liberty, the choice of fields to graze in, and no work under the yoke, that bison may live to about fifty years of age.

SOLITARY BISON.

Unlike solitary elephants, individuals amongst which are frequently young males biding their time till they are able to appropriate a herd, solitary bison are always, as far as my experience goes, old bulls, and invariably scarred with healed cicatrices showing the fights they have been engaged in in their declining days.

The morose and savage disposition frequently ascribed to these solitary animals is rather a traducement of them; and though jungle-people are occasionally killed by them, these mishaps arise rather through the circumstances under which the solitary bison is often met, than from any change of disposition ascribable to his banishment from the circle of his companions. In a herd of bison some individuals are generally standing up, and perceive the approach of an intruder; but with a solitary bull it not unfrequently happens that, whilst lying in long grass which hides him, a jungle-man in search of honey or roots approaches his lair unawares. The bison perhaps imagines that it is a sámbur or other animal moving through the grass, and does not rise till the man is nearly upon him, when he jumps up with a suddenness of which such a huge beast would hardly be thought capable, and seeing an intruder almost within horn's reach, rushes at him to dash him from his path. I have not known any instance of an unwounded solitary bison attacking man except under the above circumstances. A gentleman was killed on the Pulney hills in 1874, but this was through incautiously following a wounded bison into thick cover. In the above case the beast went on at once after killing his victim in his rush. Only in one case that I know of has a wounded bison turned and gored his victim. I do not even think the solitary bull is more dangerous when wounded and followed up than a member of a herd. I have seen both die without resistance, and both gave some trouble.

The solitary bull invariably carries the best head, and is a more noble object of pursuit than herd animals. After having shot a good many bison I have latterly given up firing at herds altogether, in favour of old bulls. In a herd it is always difficult to secure the leader, unless he is a very prominent animal, and even then there are always so many wary cows that the herd may be off before there is time to pick out the bull. It is only the novice who cares to shoot herd-bison; any one who has killed a fair number must have the instincts of a butcher to continue the useless slaughter of these fine beasts. The solitary bull is the noblest of his race, and his pursuit can never, I imagine, pall on the most successful hunter.

CHAPTER XIX.

ADVENTURES IN BISON-SHOOTING.

ENJOYABLE CHARACTER OF THE SPORT — SPORTING KNIVES — HEAVY RIFLES — VITALITY AND ENDURANCE OF BISON — HOW TO APPROACH BISON — ONE OF MY FIRST ATTEMPTS — MY ALLY H. — CAMP AT YEMMAY GUDDAY — FLOORED WITH FEVER — MY TRACKERS FIND BISON — I WOUND A BULL — FOLLOW HIM NEXT DAY — A LONG HUNT — BROUGHT TO BAY — KILL HIM — FINGERS BEFORE FORKS — MARROW-BONES — HONEY — BAG ANOTHER LARGE BULL — CAPTURE TWO TIGER-CUBS — ACCOUNT OF HOW P. AND I SLEW THE HANAY-KERRAY BULLS — ANOTHER OLD BULL — A FOUR DAYS' HUNT — PERSEVERANCE REWARDED — THE GREAT MOTHER.

AFTER elephant-shooting there is, perhaps, no sport with the rifle to be compared to bison-stalking. Whether herds or solitary bulls are the object of pursuit, the chase leads through the finest country, generally the forests of deep valleys at high elevations. It affords ample scope for the exercise of woodcraft and sportsman-like qualities, and gives a great amount of healthful exercise and excitement. An early start must be made to find the animals before they lie down for the day, so the sportsman enjoys the varied pleasures of a mountain view at early morning, when the air is cool and invigorating. This starting at break of day is not very safe work, perhaps, as far as malarial fever is concerned; but what recks the young sportsman of that? The pursuit is vested with peculiar interest for him; he hopes to get a head which shall throw the trophies of his friends into the shade; and a pleasurable smack of danger adds to his anticipations as he thinks of the stories he has heard of bison-charging! Then, too, he hopes to have better luck than to get fever. Didn't Brown and Robinson of his regiment shoot at Bandipoor for ten days, which every one tells him is a "safe" place for fever, but neither of them had a touch?

The trackers must be first-rate for good bison-stalking; and until the game is ascertained to be near, it is a good plan to allow two to go on a hundred yards ahead, whilst another follows leading Nimrod and his gun-bearers. In this way less caution is necessary in advancing, and the sportsman may amuse himself by looking about him instead of having to give heed to every step, an exercise which becomes irksome if continued for many miles. Several men carrying luncheon-basket, &c., who are not required for fighting purposes, can then be included in the following, but for all to advance together is likely to spoil sport. I have a most excellent pony which has saved me many miles of walking after bison before I had elephants. An elephant is, of course, the best animal to have with one, as in addition to riding it, spoils can be brought home from places where they would otherwise be inaccessible.

A good set of common wooden-handled butchers' knives is indispensable. The ordinary so-called shikár knife is generally useless for cutting up and skinning a large animal. It is too thick for the purpose, and too short in the blade, and in cutting deep it becomes a case of forcing a thick wedge in where a thin one is sufficient. Shikár knives are seldom made of sufficiently soft steel to be sharpened readily. They may do for stabbing; but for such purposes as cutting branches, or flaying a beast, there is nothing equal to the butcher's knife, about a foot long in the blade, and two inches wide, and under an eighth of an inch thick. It may be taken for granted that butchers use the style of knife best suited for their work, and it certainly differs widely from the common shikár knife. A sportsman may be fairly judged from his knives; if he cannot take the field without begirding himself with a young hanger he may be safely set down as a tyro. For defensive purposes a knife is very seldom required, as either from his position or the suddenness of an attack a man can rarely use it on an animal, whilst nineteen out of twenty sportsmen might hamper themselves with one all their lives and never have occasion to draw it. All but beginners soon discard such articles, and let their followers carry more effective implements. The labour entailed in even cutting off a bison's head without proper knives is very great.

Heavy rifles are absolutely necessary for good work on bison. I prefer No. 8 with 12 drams of powder. I have only lost one bison I ever hit with mine of this calibre. Many bison have been killed with a 12-bore and 4 drams; but an immense proportion of those fired at with such rifles have been wounded and lost, many to die a lingering death. The vitality and endurance of wounded bison are at times quite startling. I used a 12-bore spherical-ball rifle and 6 drams with hard bullets for some time, but I lost many bison, and never succeeded in flooring them as can be done with an 8-bore. Even when wounded with the latter I have known bison hold on for long distances and take many shots. When one or more in a herd are wounded, and the herd makes off, it is very difficult to follow the wounded animals if the herd scatters, unless there is a strong blood-trail—which there seldom is with bison wounded with small-bores, as their thick hide closes over the wound. With an 8-bore a decided effect is soon produced, and the wounded beast will probably be found lagging behind before he has gone far. The chagrin and disappointment of the young sportsman who has worked for hours to get a shot at bison, and then sees them go off when wounded with small-bores, as little damaged apparently as if he had been using a pea-shooter at them, may be imagined. To give an idea of how a wounded bison will hold out sometimes I will relate a single instance, out of many similar ones I have seen. I wounded a solitary bull with my 12-bore spherical-ball rifle and 6 drams, hitting him rather too far back behind the shoulder, one evening. Next morning we found a large quantity of coagulated blood where he had lain down during the night, and we put him up in thick cover a mile further on. We thought he would not go far, seeing how much blood he was losing, and how soon he had lain down after being wounded; but we followed at a rapid pace from 8 A.M. till 2 P.M., when I gave in, and the trackers kept on till dusk, without catching him up, and we never saw him again. On this occasion the wound bled freely, and I think I am within the mark when I say I saw more than a gallon of blood from first to last on his trail.

When the bison are ascertained to be near, the sportsman should advance with one or two good trackers and one gun-bearer only. The herd may be found grazing unsuspectingly, if the advance has been carefully managed, or a huge head and horns suddenly come into view, staring with a pair of startled eyes at the intruders, and the next moment a loud snort alarms the herd and they dash away. In any case, whether a shot has been fired or not, the sportsman should run after bison without delay. Perhaps only one animal has seen the danger, and the others often go but a few yards before they pull up in hesitation. Bison have a formidable appearance when thus roused, but they are not dangerous in reality. They do not travel as fast as they appear to do from the noise they make, and several shots may almost always be obtained by a good runner.

An old solitary bull is always to me such a treasure that I take great pains after it, and with such keen trackers as Gorrava and Bommay Gouda it is seldom one escapes; for a long time I have not lost one that we have been after. I will commence the two or three incidents I shall relate in bison-shooting with an account of one of my first attempts.

In May 1870, when the young grass was springing after the early rains,

I got ten days' leave of absence, and paid my first visit to the bungalow on the Billiga-rungun hills. I little thought how pleasantly the lines were to fall to me hereafter, and that I should be engaged in work which now constantly takes me to the locality, and all over the hills. There was a country-born European living in a room in the bungalow in those days, in charge of an experimental Government Cinchona Plantation, and he proved himself very obliging. He (H.) was a young fellow with the constitution of a bison, and he seemed to enjoy life, though his pay was but Rs. 40 a-month, and he lived miles from everywhere. He shot a deer or two occasionally with a dangerous old blunderbuss he possessed—regarding which we entered into an early arrangement that it was never to be fired when I was near—and thus he was able to obtain a little meat. He procured fowls and milk from the low-country villages.

As there appeared to be no bison close to the bungalow, according to the accounts of the Shōlagas whom H. collected for me, I decided by their advice to take my tent and servants to a place called Yemmay Gudday (bison-swamp), and I asked H. to come with me. We started early, the Shōlagas carrying my things, whilst H. packed his effects in a blanket and shouldered them himself. This I thought a good trait, as his class are usually above doing much for themselves.

We arrived at Yemmay Gudday—a low-lying valley embosomed in hills—and found a good site for the tent. This was hardly pitched when I had a severe attack of ague and fever, from recent exposure to the sun in the low country, and could not go out that day. I had a pan of burning charcoal placed under my bed (though it was then mid-day, and the tent very warm), all my spare blankets and clothes piled upon me, and drank scalding tea. Still my teeth chattered as if I had been in my night-shirt on a cold winter's night. I could not sleep, and in the morning, though the fever had left me, I was too weak to attempt walking, so sent H. out with the Shōlagas to find what bison there were near.

In the afternoon a Shōlaga brought word that they had found a herd within two miles of camp. This was too much for me, so I was helped upon my pony, which a man led, and away I went. We were soon met by H. and a tracker who said the bison were in a small cover only a hundred yards away. I dismounted and took the 12-bore spherical-ball rifle which I used in those days, loaded with 6 drams of powder. I quite forgot my weakness for the moment.

We were near the cover when with a sudden stampede the herd, of about twelve, rushed out in single file (having winded us), and made up a slope on my left, thirty yards distant.

The leading animals were all cows or young bulls; two fine black bulls, a perfect pair, brought up the rear. I waited to see if there were any better ones to come, but as there were not I gave the last a ball through his ribs, but rather too far back; and with a second shot, broke his off hind-leg at the hock-joint, in which I afterwards found the ball sticking, though fired with such a large charge of powder. He kept on, and I sank down too tired to give chase, my ears singing through weakness and the heavy discharge of the rifle. The trackers followed the bull for about a mile, when they rejoined us, and we returned to camp. As he was on three legs we felt certain of finding him in the morning, even if the body-shot did not kill him before that time.

Next morning I felt comparatively well again; I had slept soundly all night, and felt strong enough to walk some distance. It is astonishing how quickly the feeling of languor induced by fever and ague frequently leaves one.

We took up the bull's tracks from where the Shōlagas had left them last evening. Further on he had left the herd and lain down by himself—a good sign. We followed fast till we got to a suspicious patch of long grass, in a dip, and one of the trackers climbed a few feet up a small tree to see into it; at least he *walked* up the tree with his hands and feet, as natives do not climb as we do. I have often astonished jungle-men by swarming up trees which, owing to their being thick and smooth, and offering no foot-hold, they could not themselves climb. One of my elephant-hunting Kurrabas once said, "We have often thought what was to become of Budhi (the Incarnation of Wisdom—myself!) if an elephant chased us; but we see it is we who will have to look out for ourselves, not our lord!"

The tracker immediately signed that the bull was lying down in the grass, and at this moment he jumped to his feet a few yards off. I could only see the tips of his horns, and he could not make us out. No one stirred, or he would doubtless have charged, being so close, and in a few seconds he turned and made off. It was fortunate he did not charge the sapling the tracker was on; had he done so, the latter would have been shot out of it like an arrow from a bow.

The bull now took to some elephant-paths, but the grass was short, so we could follow without wasting time in precautions. In going down a hillside one tracker stepped aside and thrust his arm into a hole in a tree, from which, amidst a swarm of small bees, he drew several pieces of honey-comb in layers; these he broke up and we all ate some, and left the rest on our track for the men who were following with ropes, &c. At last we caught up the bull in a fine open wood; he was about sixty yards away, and was making off when I gave him both barrels of my 12-bore. On receiving these he changed his mind at once; the poor beast was driven to the last extremity of pain and rage; he evidently felt that further flight could avail him nothing, and back he came towards us to within twenty-five yards, snorting with fear and pain. I was behind a tree which forked near the ground, through which he could see me but could not get at me; so I reloaded my discharged rifle, without using my spare one, whilst the bull stood where he was. I then gave him both barrels in the chest and dropped him to his knees, but he rose again apparently quite bewildered. Before I could fire he turned and got into a swampy place from which he could not extricate himself on three legs, so I walked close up behind him and brained him between the horns. This bull had come about six miles on three legs.

There was a nice stream flowing through the dark wood, and as the luncheon-basket was brought up, with a towel and a dry flannel-shirt, I soon made myself comfortable. I invited H. to have some luncheon, which he consented to after some pressing. He took his plate to some distance, and I noticed he soon discarded his knife and fork in favour of his fingers; he said he preferred "fisting it." Natives of all degrees in India use their fingers alone in eating, and most poor Europeans and half-castes follow the custom of the country.

We cut out some steaks and the marrow-bones and returned to camp. At night we roasted the bones in the camp-fire, and mixing red pepper and salt with the marrow, scooped it out with bamboo-spoons, and ate it with some toast I had reserved for such an occasion. I managed half a bone with some difficulty, as the marrow was exceedingly rich, but H. not only ate the other half, but had both the other bones! I could not have believed it possible had I not seen something similar in Shōlagas eating a cupful of honey without being sick.

I was struck by the simplicity of H.'s camping arrangements at night. In lieu of a tent he stretched his blanket over a horizontal stick on two forked uprights, one end of which gipsy arrangement he plugged up with thorny bushes, perhaps to prevent tigers dragging him out! whilst his legs and boots sticking from the other formed a prominent feature after he retired. I offered him a corner in my tent, but he preferred his own tenement. Poor fellow, he was very contented with his style of life, and I think he enjoyed the trip with me; I gave him a bottle of beer every night, and other things which he never got in his solitary life.

I bagged one other splendid old bull during this trip, a solitary animal, and as large a one as I have ever shot. I have since tried, without success,

Phototint

H. M. Wright & Co. London

Bull Bison.

to outdo this feat of my griffinage. The measurement of his horns are given in the preceding chapter. The Shōlagas and I also found two fine young tiger-cubs amongst some rocks whilst looking for bears, and as we ascertained that their mother was away hunting for something for supper, I got down into the cave where they were and collared them, with the assistance of a bull-terrier—old Boxer. I handed them up to H. and the Shōlagas, who wrapped them up in *cumblies* (blankets) and made off with them. We cast many furtive glances behind as we fled; I had had little experience then; I ought to have left the cubs and watched for the mother's return.

From this time till I was settled at Morlay in 1873, I went after bison whenever I had a chance. Since I commenced elephant-catching, and have now innumerable opportunities for sport, I have confined myself entirely to old solitary bulls.

I once had a memorable bison-hunt with a friend, Captain P., of H.M.'s 48th Regiment. We jotted down the following account of it at the time:—

"THE HANAY-KERRAY HILL BULLS."

"Four o'clock, sir," said our faithful henchman J., as he entered our shooting-tent, followed by our servants with hot chocolate and toast. We jumped out of our beds, and after doing justice to the light refreshment, lit our cheroots, mounted the pad-elephant, and started with our followers, who had been marshalled ready in front of the tent by the invaluable J. It was no ordinary shooting expedition upon which we were bound. We had heard of a pair of bull-bison that had been seen the day before by our jungle-people near a swamp in the Billiga-rungun hills, at the foot of which we were encamped; and as wild elephants are numerous in the hills, frequenting the same ground as the bison, we anticipated little difficulty in approaching them with an elephant.

Our preparations for the day were on a scale worthy of the occasion. In addition to a couple of the best hillmen as trackers, several others followed us with hatchets, ropes, and skinning-knives in case of our hunt proving successful, whilst a luncheon-basket of fair dimensions led the van. Nothing could be more enjoyable than the ride through the jungles in the early morning. Not a breath stirred the towering bamboo-clumps beneath which our path lay, and whose feathery branches were reproduced in fantastic shadows by the bright moonlight on the ground beneath, now yellow with their fallen and withered leaves. Pea-fowl uttered their discordant cry whilst yet securely perched in the high trees; and sámbur and spotted-deer, with a warning bark, dashed away into the thickets as we passed. The first grey tinge of approaching day was just overspreading the eastern sky as we commenced the ascent of the hills by an elephant-path; an hour and a half of climbing brought us to the entrance of a valley between the upper ranges, where we were to commence shooting; and at this point a commanding rock invited us to rest for a few moments and enjoy the beauty of the scene. What words can do justice to it? Nature in her most charming moods surrounded us on every side. Above us, heavy masses of grey mist rested calmly on the summits of the higher hills, now green and beautiful after the early rains. From below our feet thin wreaths of vapour curled slowly upwards from the dark ravines through which we had ascended, and vanished in air at our feet like ghosts at cock-crow. Every tree and grass-plateau wore its brightest tints; whilst the sound of rills awakening from the slumber of the hot months came mysteriously from the gloomy abysses around us, and added music to the other delights of the moment. The delicious freshness of the air reminded us of the Neilgherries, which could be seen stretching away to the south; but the hearts of both of us beat higher in the anticipation of hunting the mighty mountain-bull than they had lately done under the less exciting pleasure of deer-stalking, even in Ooty's heavenly clime, which now seemed a tame sport to that we were to engage in.

The best hours of the morning were, however, advancing apace, so we arranged for our men to follow the elephant's track in half an hour, and started with the elephant and the two trackers only for the swamp where we expected to find traces of the bison. Nor were we disappointed; the trackers soon pointed to the night's tracks of both bulls, and after going round the swamp found where they had moved off together up the valley. In following the trail we came upon two or three lots of sámbur which allowed the elephant to approach within twenty yards without showing any fear, as long as the men were concealed in the grass, but the instant they were seen the deer vanished. After going for about four miles through the most lovely bamboo-jungle and teak-forest, under huge trees whose giant trunks and limbs were covered with ferns—through gloomy marshes where the trees were plastered with black mud by the rubbings of herds of elephants—crossing and recrossing the picturesque stream that flowed and fell in occasional cascades down the valley,—we at length emerged into an open glade and beheld the mighty pair we were in search of, quietly browsing on the tender shoots of the bamboos on the opposite side, about a hundred yards away. We now left the trackers in the cover, and headed the elephant across the glade, as if to pass into the jungle to the left of the bulls, keeping the wind well in our favour. Our elephant was a young pad female (Soondargowry), only six and a half feet high (scarcely higher than the bulls), but steady under fire, and plucky; we had no mahout, managing her ourselves, and we used no concealment beyond having dark-coloured shooting-coats. Our guns deserve some mention: these were a couple of double-barrelled C.F. breech-loaders for spherical ball by W. W. Greener—one a No. 4, the other a No. 8 bore, weighing 19½ and 17 lb. respectively, and firing 12 drams each.

When within sixty yards the bison observed us, but evinced no alarm till we got nearer, when they seemed to notice something strange, and both came forward a few steps. We were now only thirty-five yards away, the bulls being on our right face, and as they were beginning to get fidgety, we turned the elephant partly round to bring them on to our near side for easier shooting. This movement was taken by one bull as the signal for decamping, and away he went, though P., to whom he had been assigned for slaughter, called a halt from him with the 8-bore; this, however, only hastened his retreat, the ball entering too high and far back, as the shot was a difficult one from P.'s position. Almost simultaneously with the crash of P.'s rifle the 4-bore opened upon the other bull, raking him from stem to stern, and dropping him on the spot.

The first bull had, after a desperate flounder, disappeared into the bamboos. Our stanch little elephant, who had never had such heavy firing off her back before, stood well through it all, and walked up to the fallen bull with perfect *nonchalance*. We jumped off, hobbled her, and leaving her to be brought on by our men, started with the trackers after the wounded bull. Blood was plentiful, and we had not gone more than half a mile when we sighted him entering some thick bamboo-cover ahead. We had to use some caution in following him into this, as it was just the place for him to pull up in; but he held on through it, and we lost a good deal of ground. In the forest on the far side we made the pace hot again: a short distance ahead was another bamboo-cover; and before we had got far into it, cautiously as before, the trackers pointed to the bull lying down. His head and shoulders were hidden by a bamboo-clump, but his huge dorsal ridge and heaving flanks could be seen pretty clearly. P. sent another 8-bore through him as far forward as he could, in acknowledgment of which the bull jumped up with unexpected agility and plunged off through the cover. We followed him fast now, as the noise he made insured us against stumbling upon him unexpectedly; but the two trackers outstripped us far, and in their eagerness not to lose sight of the bull, kept up with him into the open forest on the far side. When we emerged from the cover a fine piece of diversion was going on: the bull, unable to escape, and seeing his pursuers, had turned upon the trackers, and, snorting and plunging in a way which we thought would land him on his head at every bound, was lumbering after them through the forest about a hundred yards off. The men did not even take to trees, which they would have done if hard pressed, but the bull was much used up by his wounds, and had no chance of catching them. This only lasted for a minute or so, when the bull came to a stand under a tree about sixty yards from us, looking very bad. It would have been easy enough to drop him now, but as the place was a good one for a pitched battle, we advanced towards him, keeping several paces apart, so that only one of us could be charged, whilst the other would have a flanking-shot. Taken in front, and by a cross-fire between such weapons as we had, there was not much probability of the bull making good his charge.

The poor beast, sweating with the pain of his wounds and his run, snorted as we approached. We walked up to about thirty yards, when we thought it was the bull's turn to make a move; but just as we expected him to come on he turned to the left, and P. killed him with the neck-shot. Little blame to the poor beast for not courting battle; he was too badly wounded to think of anything after his unsuccessful chase of the trackers but to lie down and die peaceably; had he been less sick he would doubtless have given us some work.

The trackers were now despatched for the elephant and luncheon-basket, and whilst we smoked the pipe of peace, the men cut off both bulls' heads for stuffing, got out the marrow-bones, and with all hands laden with meat, we set off in the cool of the afternoon for the pass by which we had ascended in the morning, and commenced the descent just as the sun was setting. On the way down P. made a pretty shot with his express at a sámbur, about two hundred yards away across a ravine. Though the stag dashed into the nearest cover, the "phut" of the bullet came back clear and sharp—that "dull, soft thud" which the "Old Forest Ranger" so truly says is "as grateful to the sportsman's ear as the voice of her he loves." Bah! the sensations of a young lady on receiving her first proposal can be nothing to it! The place where the stag disappeared was difficult to get to, and we had no time to spare. As he had been fairly hit with the express, we felt sure he would not go far (this proved to be the case, as he was found dead by our people just inside the wood in the morning), so we pushed on down the pass, and reached camp soon after dark. The well-lighted tent and neatly-laid dinner-table, with glasses filled with pretty scarlet and white jungle-flowers, looked vastly comfortable after our day's tramp; and after a good dinner, assisted by the coolest and brightest of claret cup, the day's enjoyments ended with the post-prandial cheroots, and we turned in with feelings of charity for all men.

P. and I commenced the hunt of another old bull at the foot of the Billiga-runguns on the last day of his leave, but I had to finish the chase alone. We found his tracks in a gorge in the early morning, and after two hours' tracking we got near him, but he winded us and made off without giving us a chance. After waiting for an hour to let him settle, we tracked him for some miles further, when he again winded us. He was lying in a ravine, and we heard him crash away. This was bad, as it was likely he would now go far after being twice disturbed, as single bulls are often very cunning and go long distances before halting. However, there was nothing for it but perseverance, and though the day was warm we followed till late in the afternoon. Here P. mounted the elephant, whilst I thought I would just look through a small bamboo-cover near, where it was possible the bull might have stopped. Hurrah! he had lain down in it, and though he had gone on again, it was evident he was not suspicious, as he had loitered, so Gorrava and I pushed along in pursuit. At last Gorrava pointed in breathless haste to the bull walking leisurely through tree-jungle before us. What an exciting moment it was after our long hunt! I sank down for a moment to rest, as I was breathless and shaking with the haste we had made. The bull was eighty yards away, and his huge stern seemed to fill the space between the trees as he stalked along. We were meditating a closer advance when he winded us, and with a startled toss of his head he set off at a heavy trot, and though I ran my best after him for a long way, Gorrava carrying my rifle, he distanced us, and we had to stop.

However, I was not dissatisfied with the failure, and when I reflected on the joys which the possession of this redoubtable beast would bring, I felt equal to any exertion in compassing his downfall. We had done our utmost, and I had refrained from a risky shot, which was in itself a satisfaction. As he had not been fired at he probably would not go up the hills, and we determined to have him before long. Gorrava swore, touching the ground as his witness, that if I would persevere he would never let the bull escape, even if it "dug a hole and buried itself."

Next day I could not continue the chase as I had to accompany P. to Chámráj-Nugger. I was heartily sorry to part with so good a companion and sportsman. His last words to me were to "follow up the bull;" and the day after, I returned in the evening to my camp at Yerlsáriga. Gorrava had all the information about the bull's recent movements cut and dry: he had followed him the second day and had found him lying down, and on the third day had carried on his tracks from his lair of the second day till they were very fresh, when he left them for fear of disturbing the bull. As long as he did not go up the hills we were sure of him.

Next morning—the fourth day—we took up yesterday's track. Rain, that had since fallen, made it difficult at first, till we got on to the tracks made after the rain, when it was easy work. Since morning the bull had been making his way steadily, though grazing and loitering along, to a cover called Kul Bhávi Podaga, a place where we had finished many a good hunt of bear and bison before. When we reached it at mid-day, Gorrava, Jaffer, and I entered alone; the walking was quiet, there being no undergrowth amongst the bamboo-clumps, and we peered anxiously about as we stooped and crept along to catch sight of the bull if lying down. There was a fine wind in our favour, which was a godsend, as the breezes in valleys amongst hills are often very uncertain.

The bull was not to be seen, however. Gorrava followed his every step till we could see the open through the bamboo-clumps on the far side. We seemed to be doomed to disappointment; what could have become of him? Suddenly Gorrava pointed to him almost at our feet, drinking at a pool under the high overhanging bank of a ravine on which we stood, and which wound a tortuous course through the cover. The bull had first come to the point where we now were, but being unable to descend here he had got down elsewhere, and was now drinking below us! He had only been a few minutes before us; our advance was so silent that at ten feet distance he did not hear us. This was indeed poetical justice. What a tramp he had led us!—at least forty miles in all, though within a radius of ten.

A bamboo-clump hid his vitals and I had to fire at him too far back. Away he dashed at the shot, the bamboos obstructing my second barrel, out of the ravine and round through the cover. However, I knew that with that in him (an 8-bore ball and 12 drams), he was a dead bull, and we followed in great glee. The moments in which the result of the chase becomes no longer doubtful, amply reward the sportsman for his willing toil, and are the happiest of his life.

The bull was off for a well-known bamboo-cover, but not a thick or troublesome one; he was far from the foot of the glorious hills—his home for who knows how many years, and which he was never to see again! How little did he think when he left them, to escape the long grass and the myriads of flies, that he was never to return! It was an evil hour for him when the eye of Gorrava fell upon his tracks! The spare men having come up, we pushed along with only a small interval between us and them, and as soon as we got to the cover which the bull had headed for we found him lying down, and I gave him a shot with the 4-bore—which Gorrava always called the "*Mahá Táyee*" (the Great Mother)—through his ribs. This maternal whisper brought him to his feet very quickly, and he came blundering out just as the luncheon-basket party put in an appearance! He "went for" them instantly. Some got up the nearest trees, but the Shōlaga intrusted with the basket carefully deposited it before he made off! I gave the bull another shot and pursued him, when I suddenly met him almost face to face, coming back after he had lost the basket-carrier. I knew he had not seen me, and I stood quietly aside against a bamboo-clump, and as he passed I saluted him in the ribs. He now subsided into a walk, and I followed. He presently faced round and I gave him the 4-bore at thirty yards into the point of his shoulder. This even did not drop him, and he went on again, dead lame. When he faced round I walked up to within twenty yards, under shelter of a friendly tree, and as he stood shaking his head threateningly I brained him.

He was a gallant beast. He had given us a splendid run, the various incidents and excitement of which it is impossible to convey any just idea of. At the end he afforded a good example of what a bison can stand in the way of powder and lead: he had had five body-shots—two with the 4-bore and three with the 8—and then had to be brained. The body-shots were none of them very well placed. This difficulty in always getting at the right spots is the chief reason why heavy metal should be used on heavy game, otherwise the poor beasts may be caused much unnecessary suffering. This bull was a very old fellow, and much scored and battered by fighting.

CHAPTER XX.

THE TIGER (*FELIS TIGRIS*).

DIFFERENT SORTS OF TIGERS—THE CATTLE-LIFTER—USEFULNESS OF TIGERS—SMALL VALUE OF INDIAN CATTLE—THE GAME-KILLER—THE MAN-EATER—SIZE AND WEIGHT OF TIGERS —A TIGER KILLING AND EATING BEARS—CANNIBAL TIGERS—TIGERS AND WILD DOGS—TIGERS KILLING BISON—METHOD OF SEIZING THEIR PREY—FIGHT BETWEEN TIGER AND BUFFALO — HOURS OF FEEDING—TIGERS CLIMBING TREES — POWERS OF ENDURING HUNGER AND THIRST—HUNTING-RANGES OF TIGERS—BREEDING OF TIGERS—METHODS OF HUNTING TIGERS—BEATING WITH ELEPHANTS—DRIVING WITH BEATERS—SHOOTING OVER "KILLS" OR WATER—NETTING—EXCUSE FOR THIS METHOD—POISONING AND TRAPPING TIGERS.

THE late Capt. James Forsyth in his delightful book *The Highlands of Central India*, in which a most interesting account of tigers and tiger-shooting is given, has divided tigers into three classes, according to their habits — viz., those which habitually prey upon cattle; those which live upon game alone; and the few dreaded individuals of their race that frequently prey upon human beings.

This classification correctly defines the ways of life of different tigers. I have had extended opportunities of acquainting myself with their every-day habits, as, in addition to constantly following them for sport's sake, I was tiger-slayer to the Mysore Government for some time, and have had around me the most experienced natives, to hunt out and follow up tigers that were destructive to cattle or dangerous to human beings. The following descriptions of their habits are therefore founded upon somewhat intimate experience of them.

The cattle-killing tiger frequents jungles close to villages, and seizes a victim amongst the cattle when driven thither to graze, or picks up stray animals about the villages at night. In India cattle are carefully herded into the villages before nightfall, so the cattle-lifter usually has to secure his victim in broad daylight. The ranges of these tigers where not disturbed are generally confined to a few villages; but if they have been hunted and are shy, they extend their visiting circle considerably. The tigers in the vicinity of my camp at Morlay (the hunting of which will be described further on) had a range of about twenty miles in length by ten in breadth. To this tract there were eight tigers originally, all solitary except a tigress and her nearly full-grown cub.

The largest tigers are found amongst habitual cattle-killers. When a tiger becomes old and fat he usually settles down in some locality where beef and water are plentiful, and here he lives on amicable terms with the villagers, killing a cow or bullock about once in four or five days. Some tigers contract the habit, through being interfered with, of killing more than one animal in each attack. I have seen three, four, and five cattle on the ground together after attacks by single tigers, and on one occasion fourteen killed by one tiger, in a herd overtaken by a storm; many of the cattle were benumbed and unable to escape. Cow-herds in the habit of meeting tigers often behave very boldly when their charge is attacked. Where three or four men are together they seldom think of leaving a tiger in undisturbed possession of his prey.

Capt. Forsyth estimates the value of cattle killed by tigers in the Central Provinces at from £5 to £10 apiece; and that a tiger will kill from sixty to seventy such animals, or between £325 and £650 worth per annum. These figures seem excessively high. The value of nine-tenths of Indian village-cattle is certainly under £1 each. I never found difficulty in getting old cattle for baits for four shillings per head. I have the returns of domestic animals killed in Mysore for the past five years at hand, but they are of little assistance in estimating the total value of the animals destroyed, as goats, sheep, donkeys, &c. (mostly killed by panthers and leopards, and a few by wolves), are included with cattle.

The individual value of these animals may be set down at an average of Rs. 7 (fourteen shillings), as goats, sheep, and donkeys are worth only a few shillings. Allowing each tiger even seventy horned cattle per annum at £1 each, the loss would amount to £70 per tiger, which I imagine is nearer the mark than £650.

It may be thought that even this loss is sufficiently serious to warrant the advocating of a war of extermination against tigers, but the tiger might, in turn, justly present his little account for services rendered in keeping down wild animals which destroy crops. His agency in this respect goes far, in the opinion of many sportsmen of experience, towards counterbalancing the bill against him for beef. It is pig and deer—not the tiger and panther

—that attack the sources of subsistence; and these are only to be kept in check by the animals appointed to prey upon them. Were the tiger and panther gone they would soon gain the upper hand. Many cases have come under my notice where the tiger has proved himself the ryot's friend in a particular manner, in addition to his general services. I was once talking with an old ryot about some new cultivation he had pushed ahead of the other ryots' holdings into the jungle, and asking after its welfare. He said, "As soon as the crop was above ground some village-cattle that had broken from their pen strayed into it at night, but a tiger killed a bullock there belonging to the headman, worth at least Rs. 20 (£2), so the others took better care of their cattle. I could not have watched my field or gone to the expense of putting up a hedge the first year. The other ryots' holdings were all in a block, so a few hedges and watchmen sufficed for *them*, but I had to trust to the tigers. I put up scarecrows for deer and pig, but that did not keep them out long. However, the tiger and a panther killed two or three pigs, and they gave up visiting my field. I got a moderate crop, and am going to clear more ground this hot weather, and next year will be able to fence it." When it is considered that it is of such units that the vast total of Indian tillage is made up, the importance of the question of keeping destructive animals in check must be recognised. In many cases I have known of tigers pouncing upon a sow with young pigs and demolishing the whole family; and the sportsman will have occasional instances of their vigilance in finding his wounded game retrieved during the night by a tiger or panther.

It may be urged that were the tigers disposed of, the pig and deer could be left for the ryots; but this is mere theory, all practical sportsmen being agreed that deer and pig could never be kept within bounds except by the *Felidæ*. In thick, thorny, and continuous jungles they cannot be got at, and they would multiply unrestrictedly, and force upon the ryots the arduous work of watching their fields at night in unhealthy localities where the tiger and panther now keep the game in check. Cultivation would recede in many parts of the country were there no tigers. The balance of nature cannot be interfered with with impunity, and a general crusade against hawks, wild cats, *et hoc genus omne*, might be preached with as much reason on the ground of their abducting stray chickens, though keeping down destructive vermin at other times, as against the tiger for appropriating an occasional bullock. Of course all tigers are fair game to the sportsman; they can never be unduly reduced by shooting. The most destructive cattle-killers—the animals that it is desirable to get rid of—are those which, from being most easily met with, are sure to fall first; but for people who have only considered one side of the question to urge the pursuing of every tiger that can be heard of with poison, traps, and the incentive of high rewards to native shikáries, is advocating a measure which would lead to a deplorable state of things for the ryots.

As to the individual value of the cattle killed by the tiger, it is to be remembered that, it being against a Hindoo's tenets to take the life of the sacred cow, there is always about every village a large number of old, scraggy, and useless animals of no value to any one, in ridding the country of which the tiger does good to the community. When a ryot's bullock gets beyond ploughing, and his cow past milking, there is no sale for them, as they are as useless to every one else as to himself; so they are added to the other half-dozen or so of halt and blind in his fold, and sent with the two or three hundred of their kind owned by the village to the jungles to graze. A ryot is always careful of his really good cattle, taking them with him to his fields when working, and tying them there upon the divisions between the fields where there is good grass. The sight of the hordes of half-starved and mangy animals returning to Indian villages in the evening is a familiar one to residents in the country. These wretched beasts generate the cattle diseases from which few Indian villages are ever quite free, and their room is to be preferred to their company. Fortunately nature assists the tigers in effecting a clearance amongst these every year. At the time of the early rains the enfeebled animals eat ravenously of the young grass which then springs up, become distended, and die in a few hours.

The tiger is no unmitigated evil in the land. His pursuit affords excitement and recreation to many a hard-worked official whose life, except for an occasional day in the jungles, would be one of uninterrupted toil. Many officers see for themselves matters affecting the districts of which they have charge when visiting out-of-the-way localities for sport, which they would never learn otherwise. It is a pity to see the tiger proscribed and hunted to death by every unsportsmanlike method that can be devised, in response to popular outcries—chiefly in England—without foundation in fact, about his destructiveness. Trace out and slay every man-eater by all means possible, and at any expense; but ordinary tigers are exceedingly inoffensive, and have their uses. May the day be far distant when the tiger shall become practically extinct!

THE GAME-KILLER.

The game-killer confines himself entirely to thick forests, chiefly in hill-tracts, where he keeps to the feeding-grounds and hot-weather resorts of game; and though the sportsman has little cause to bless him, the would-be protectors of the ryots should rather give him their countenance than thirst for his blood, as he is most beneficial in keeping down the herds of deer and pig that would otherwise destroy much crop. The game-killer shuns the haunts of man, and wanders much in the cool forests at all hours. On one occasion in the Kákenkoté jungles I was following a deer-run one gloomy evening after a wet afternoon, when a slight movement behind attracted my attention, and I turned just in time to see some animal disappear silently into the jungle. I had not time for a shot. On examination we found a tiger's pugs in the moist earth where, crouched behind a bamboo-clump, he had been patiently watching for deer, and had cunningly allowed the tracker and myself to pass within a few yards of him before attempting a retreat.

Captain Forsyth states that the game-killer is usually a lighter and more active beast than the cattle-killer. This is, doubtless, the rule, as he has to travel farther for his food—but there are exceptions. One of the largest tigers I have killed was a pure game-killer. I shot him upon the carcass of a young elephant he had seized and partially eaten in the Chittagong hills, as described in Chapter XIII. I recently saw the carcass of a cow-bison killed and partly eaten by a tiger in the Billiga-rungun hills. This was the work of a powerful tiger, though a game-killer, as the bison was a full-grown animal, and a terrible struggle had ensued upon its seizure.

THE MAN-EATER.

This truly terrible scourge to the timid and unarmed inhabitants of an Indian village is now happily becoming very rare; man-eaters of a bad type are seldom heard of, or if heard of, rarely survive long. Before there were so many European sportsmen as there now are in the country a man-eater frequently caused the temporary abandonment of whole tracts; and the sites of small hamlets abandoned by the terrified inhabitants, and which have never been reoccupied, are not uncommonly met with by the sportsman in the jungles. The terror inspired by a man-eater throughout the district ranged by him is extreme. The helpless people are defenceless against his attacks. Their occupations of cattle-grazing or wood-cutting take them into the jungles, where they feel that they go with their lives in their hands. A rustling leaf, or a squirrel or bird moving in the undergrowth, sets their hearts beating with a dread sense of danger. The only security they feel is in numbers. Though the bloodthirsty monster is perhaps reposing with the remains of his last victim miles away, the terror he inspires is always present to every one throughout his domain. The rapidity and uncertainty of a man-eater's movements form the chief elements of the dread he causes. His name is in every one's mouth; his daring, ferocity, and appalling appearance are represented with true Eastern exaggeration; and until some European sportsman, perhaps after days or weeks of pursuit, lays him low, thousands live in fear day and night. Bold man-eaters have been known to enter a village and carry off a victim from the first open hut. Having lived in a tract so circumstanced until I shot the fiend that possessed it, and having myself felt something of the grim dread that had taken hold of the country-side, where ordinary rambling about the jungles, and even sitting outside the tent after dark except with a large fire, or moving from the encampment without an escort, were unsafe, I could realise the feelings of relief and thankfulness so earnestly expressed by the poor ryots when I shot the Jezebel that had held sway over them so long.

The man-eater is often an old tiger (more frequently a tigress), or an animal that, through having been wounded or otherwise hurt, has been unable to procure its usual food, and takes to this means of subsistence. It is invariably an ex-cattle-killer that, from constant intercourse with man, has become divested of its natural dread of our race, and interference with whose kills has caused collisions between itself and cow-herds which have finally led to its preying upon the hitherto dreaded man when other food fails. The man-eater is as cowardly as it is cunning, fleeing before an armed man, between whom and a possible victim it discriminates with wonderful sagacity. The slightest sound of any one in pursuit of it, even the whisper of a single sportsman with one or two trackers in its haunts, starts it at once; it will then probably travel for miles, though even whilst fleeing it may pounce upon some unwary victim, as I have seen an ordinary tiger seize a bullock when itself the object of hot pursuit. This combination of cowardice and audacity constitutes the difficulty there always is in bringing a man-eater to bag.

Though the belief that some tigers confine themselves entirely to human flesh is undoubtedly erroneous, a man is so much more easily overcome than any other animal that man-eaters frequently seize cow-herds in preference to the cattle they are in charge of. It is this which has led to the belief that, after having once tasted human flesh the tiger prefers it to any other. The reason why tigresses should be more frequent offenders than their lords is difficult to conjecture. Perhaps it is that when their cubs are young they are often put to great straits to obtain food for them, or urged to acts of boldness in their defence; or the fact that tigresses are as a rule more vicious, sly, and enterprising, as also more ferocious when pushed to extremities than tigers, may partly account for it. This may seem an ungallant representation by a sportsman, (and who is more tender-hearted, more ready to overlook the sex's failings than the true sportsman?) but it is the truth.

How the belief arose that man-eaters are usually mangy animals it is difficult to understand. I do not remember to have read of a single instance of any sportsman finding this to be the case. Were tigers apt to lose their hair, or to become lean in old age, a foundation for the belief might exist; though to say that this was the result of eating human flesh would be erroneous. But old animals merely become lighter in colour, the black stripes narrowing and becoming further apart, and very slightly mixed with grey hairs, whilst the yellow turns to a paler hue than in youth. As far as my own experience goes I have never seen a mangy or lean tiger.

Man-eaters are exceedingly rare in Mysore and the surrounding territories. In the past fifteen years there has only been one of great note—the Benkipoor tiger. This tiger flourished some twelve years ago, and caused great loss of life in the country about Benkipoor in the Nugger Division of Mysore. A large reward was offered by Government for his destruction, but in the number of tigers shot and brought forward as the man-eater there was a difficulty of identification. And though it is believed that he was at last shot by a native shikárie, as all killing ceased from the time that a male tiger with one fore-foot injured was brought in, it was not known at the time that the real Simon Pure had been slain, and the enhanced reward was never paid.

Regarding the size of tigers, once a much-disputed point, all careful observers are, I believe, agreed in accepting Dr Jerdon's view (*Mammals of India*) as thoroughly correct. He says: "The average size of a full-grown male tiger is from 9 to 9½ feet,* but I fancy that there is very little doubt that, *occasionally*, tigers are killed 10 feet in length, and perhaps a few inches over that; but the stories of tigers 11 feet and 12 feet in length, so often heard and repeated, certainly require confirmation, and I have not myself seen an authentic account of a tiger that measured more than 10 feet and 2 or 3 inches." I know two noted Bengal sportsmen who can each count the tigers slain by them by hundreds, whose opinions entirely corroborate

* From nose to tip of tail.

Jerdon. My own experience can only produce a tiger of 9 feet 6 inches, and a tigress of 8 feet 4 inches, as my largest.

It is not to be denied that tigers exceeding 10, 11, and even 12 feet in length are sometimes spoken of and have even been described. But it has invariably happened, in my experience, that whenever the narrator of such stories has been brought to book, he has been unable to appeal to any authority more satisfactory than his own memory, or the memory of his friends. Now, on such a point the memory is by no means an infallible guide. When a man has assured me that the length of a tiger—a length greatly in excess of the ordinary size—is indelibly impressed upon his memory, I have never failed to express my regret that it was not, at the time, indelibly impressed upon his note-book. A sportsman cannot be too careful in this particular. Perfect exactness in his description of the slaughtered animal is an aim he should always keep in view. For this purpose the memory is not a safe witness. It may be laid down as an axiom that the note-book carried by the sportsman is the only safe evidence; and that all other—whatever be its nature—must be disregarded.

I have only weighed one tiger, a very bulky, well-fed male. He weighed, by two different scales, 349½ lb., or 25 stone all but half a pound. I should have imagined this was about the extreme weight of any tiger, but I have seen heavier recorded.

It is difficult to ascertain the probable age to which tigers live. A large male that I shot, and which was said to have been perfectly well known about Morlay for twenty years, showed no signs of great age: his teeth were good, and he seemed in the prime of vigour and strength; his coat was, however, getting light-coloured. As cats not unfrequently live to upwards of twenty years, the tiger's span of life is probably longer than is usually supposed. A tiger has lived in the Regent's Park Zoological Society's gardens for ten years, but this is of course not a satisfactory test. The natives have an idea that the age of tigers and panthers can be told by the number of lobes of the liver, being one lobe for each year of age; but this theory is not, I believe, accepted by anatomists. It is true, however, and is a peculiar fact, that the number of lobes does vary considerably in different animals, and is greatest where other indications of age exist. I have shot tigers and panthers with from nine to fifteen lobes. If this has nothing to do with their age, it would at least be interesting if anatomists could give some reason to account for it.

A strange example of a tiger's departing from the usual food of the *Felidæ*, is that of a large male near Poonjoor some years ago, that is said to have killed and eaten several bears. The account of his doings in the Poonjoor jungles was given me by old Bommay Gouda, whom I have already mentioned as having lived all his life amongst tigers, bears, and elephants and as an authority whose interesting accounts of the habits and peculiarities of the occupants of the jungles could be relied on. It appears that this tiger killed several bears at different times whilst feeding, coming from behind and seizing them by the nape of the neck, and bearing them down (no pun intended), after a struggle, by his weight and strength. Towards corroborating this account some Shōlagas at the other end of the hills, twenty miles away, and who knew nothing of what Bommay Gouda had told me, gave me a similar account; adding that a bear had been thus killed and partially eaten in a clearing where they were watching their crops early one morning. This was doubtless the same tiger. My Morlay trackers also told me that some years ago they surrounded a bear and her three-parts grown cub with nets in a date-grove close to which my bungalow now stands at Morlay. The bears broke through the nets, the big she being severely speared in doing so, and both got clear away to a ravine a mile distant. Next morning they were found together, dead, and the large bear partially eaten by a tiger whose marks were all around. Whether she had died of her wounds or had been killed by the tiger the men had not taken sufficient notice at the time to be able to tell me, but the cub had been killed. This was also probably the work of the same tiger. The carcass of a bear which I once shot at Yerlsáriga, and which was dragged to some distance from the tents after being skinned, was partially eaten by a leopard that night, which shows that the *Felidæ* do not always confine themselves to cattle and game.

One of the strangest things I ever heard of in connection with tigers is an instance of three tigers devouring a fourth. This was also told me by Bommay Gouda and two Shōlagas who were with him at the time of the occurrence. For my own part I believe the story. It was that a male tiger killed a buffalo late one evening; the carcass was found partially eaten next day; and the following, or second morning, when some low-caste men, under Bommay Gouda's guidance, went to take whatever might be left, they found the head and shoulders of a large tiger, and some bones of the buffalo. The ground around bore traces of a savage fight, and it was found that a party of three tigers had disturbed the original slayer of the buffalo at supper, and the struggle which ensued for possession ended in his death. There was probably then only a little meat remaining, which the victorious party finished, and forthwith set to at their defunct relative (a beef-sausage !). These tigers' blood being up, and their appetites excited, not appeased, with the remains of the buffalo, and the dead tiger lying ready to hand, perhaps somewhat mangled, their eating him can be imagined as a not wholly improbable contingency, and is different from their having killed him with the intention of making a meal of him. I observe that Mr Walter Elliot, quoted by Dr Jerdon, says: "Another instance was related in a letter by a celebrated sportsman in Khandeish, who, having killed a tigress on his return to his tents, sent a pad-elephant to bring it home. The messenger returned, reporting that on his arrival he found her alive. They went out next morning to the spot, and discovered that she had been dragged into a ravine by another tiger and half the carcass devoured."

It is universally believed by natives that the tiger is occasionally killed by packs of wild dogs (*Cuon rutilans*). These animals are not numerous; their operations are of a character so destructive and harassing to game that no tract could support them in any considerable number. Their ranges extend over immense areas of country, whilst they seldom hunt in one neighbourhood for more than a few days, and that at considerable intervals, as the deer become so scared that they flee the locality. The wild dog is between a wolf and jackal in size, of a uniform deep rusty colour above, paler below, and with a blackish brush. They run both by sight and scent, and their perseverance and endurance are so great that they rarely fail ot kill any animal on whose track they start. From what I have seen of their style of hunting, and of their power of tearing and lacerating, I think there can be no doubt of their ability to kill a tiger. I can call to mind two examples of their powers. One morning two dogs chased a spotted hind past my tent. One of them halted at sight of the encampment; the other, which was within springing distance, made two snatches at the exhausted creature's abdomen, and then drew off. The bites were inflicted with lightning speed: the deer went but a few paces when she fell with her entrails protruding. On another occasion I heard the yapping of jungle-dogs, and a noble spotted stag came racing down an open glade, his branching antlers laid along his back, and three wild dogs at his flanks. They had only time to make a snap or two each when we interfered. The stag went but a few yards and fell, and was speared by one of my men. In the moment's biting it had been emasculated, and about four pounds of flesh torn from the inner part of its thighs.

Similar injury might easily be inflicted on a tiger. I have seen more than one flee from a pack of curs—a very mangy one gallantly holding on to the royal beast's tail on one occasion—and it is probable a tiger would turn from wild dogs. The latter's habit of hunting almost exclusively during the day would be in their favour in an encounter with a tiger. Their tactics are not to attack in front; they never expose themselves to the horns or hoofs of powerful deer. They would bite a tiger, should he run from them, in parts that might speedily cause his death. A Shōlaga told me that he once saw a tiger confronted by wild dogs, sitting on his haunches against a bamboo-clump. The dogs, ten or twelve in number, were making no active demonstrations, but walked close to him, in a most impertinent and unconcerned manner. The Shōlaga having no personal interest—a native's first consideration in all matters—in the result of the meeting, left the rivals. It is possible that in such a case, if the tiger maintained his position, the dogs would withdraw, as they could do nothing against him in a front attack. Causes of hostility may occasionally arise between the tiger and wild dogs through attempted interference with each other's prey. Otherwise it is not clear why the dogs should molest the tiger.

Bison are occasionally killed by tigers. A tiger's method of attacking a solitary bull-bison has been described to me by jungle-men as consisting in showing himself in the grass and leading the bison to charge, avoiding each rush of the bull, following him on the instant, and striking him behind with the intention of emasculating him. The largest and oldest-looking solitary bison I ever shot had a half-healed mark of a tiger's stroke on the outside of his thigh, a long raking wound of about eighteen inches, which could scarcely have been got in any other way.

I once saw the carcass of an old bullock which we had tied for a tiger, and which was killed by a small leopard somewhat in this way. The bullock had been beyond its strength, so it had seized it by the nose, and held on like a bull-dog till the bullock had fallen, when the leopard had bitten the inside of the hind-legs and torn the stomach, and thus killed the bullock without touching the throat. Wild dogs seize deer in this way, so it is possible that the tiger adopts the same plan with bison, whose strength is so much greater than his own. The largest tiger would, of course, have no chance in fair fight with a bull-bison. The latter's brawny throat, with its hide two inches thick, would afford him a difficult hold even could he attain it, and no wrench could dislocate the bison's powerful neck, whilst the tiger would be crushed out of all recognition if once caught between the ground and his antagonist's massive forehead or fore-legs. As I have already mentioned, however, a tiger occasionally succeeds in killing cow-bison. A case occurred near Morlay where a tigress and her two nearly full-grown cubs attacked a cow-bison that had become separated from the herd. One of the cubs was killed before the bison was overcome, and was found by my men next morning. A few years ago a tiger and a bull of the Amrut Mahál Government breed of cattle at the Commissariat depot at Hoonsoor, near Mysore, had a desperate struggle in the jungles.

The bull eventually beat off his antagonist, but was left in a woeful condition, and died in a few hours.

I have never witnessed a tiger actually seize its prey, but it has been described to me by men who have seen the occurrence scores of times within a few yards' distance whilst tending cattle. The general method is for the tiger to slink up under cover of bushes or long grass, ahead of the cattle in the direction they are feeding, and to make a rush at the first cow or bullock that comes within five or six yards. The tiger does not *spring* upon his prey in the manner usually represented. Clutching the bullock's fore-quarters with his paws, one being generally over the shoulder, he seizes the throat in his jaws from underneath, and turns it upwards and over, sometimes springing to the far side in doing so, to throw the bullock over, and give the wrench which dislocates its neck. This is frequently done so quickly that the tiger, if timid, is in retreat again almost before the herdsman can turn round. Bold animals often kill several head, unsophisticated cattle occasionally standing and staring at the tiger in stupid astonishment; but herds that are accustomed to these raids only enter the jungle with extreme unwillingness, and frequently stampede back to the village at even the rustle of a bird in a thicket.

Captain Forsyth says: "The tiger's usual way is to seize with the teeth by the *nape* of the neck, and at the same time use the paws to hold the victim and give a purchase for the wrench that dislocates the neck." Captain Baldwin, in his *Large and Small Game of Bengal*, says: "He launches himself upon his victim, and seizing it by the back of the neck (not the throat), brings it to the ground, and then gives that fatal wrench or twist which dislocates the neck. I have examined the carcasses of many scores of bullocks killed by tigers, and have, in the great majority of cases, found the neck broken, and the deep holes at the back of the neck caused by the tiger's fangs." Also: "A tiger, as I have before stated, almost invariably seizes his prey by the back of the neck; leopards and panthers not unfrequently by the throat."

Now, with due respect for Captains Forsyth and Baldwin's opinions on sporting matters, I beg to differ with them entirely on this point. The tiger does occasionally seize by the nape of the neck, in the case of having to deal with very powerful cattle, but I am convinced this is not his usual method. Out of some hundreds of kills that I have seen, there were only two animals seized in this way. One was a boar, which had eventually beaten off a tigress, though we found him dead several days after, with deep fang-wounds at the back of his head; and the other was a huge tame bull-buffalo, that might well have defied any tiger but such an one as he succumbed to. The bull was attacked when lying down, and had evidently been seized by the nape of the neck. His immense strength had enabled him to rise, the tiger probably at first maintaining his hold. The antagonists had then separated and closed several times. The ground was torn up, and the fallen leaves were red with blood from the buffalo; branches eight feet from the ground were splashed with blood blown from his nostrils, or thrown up in his efforts to rid himself of the tiger. He had at last, after a gallant fight, stumbled into a trench, used for conveying water to the gardens wherein the struggle took place, and had been there killed by his ferocious assailant.

It is evident that in the case of beasts with horns a tiger would find them considerably in his way in seizing by the back of the neck. Moreover, the beast would be borne to the ground, where killing it would be a longer affair than by dislocating its neck in the manner described. Dislocation could not be effected on the ground as well as by turning the throat upwards, when the inertia of the beast's carcass before it is overthrown presents a sufficient purchase to effect the dislocation. That the tiger does not seize by the nape of the neck is also apparent from the fact that the gape of the largest is insufficient to take in the neck of big cattle so as to bring the fangs to the lower part of the throat where the fatal marks are always found. I imagine Captain Baldwin must be alone in his experience of finding wounds at the back of the neck.

Cattle are seized by tigers when grazing in the jungles at any hour of the day, but more frequently after three o'clock in the afternoon. Should the tiger fail in his attempt to seize, he pursues the animal or others of the herd, striking savagely at their hind-legs to hamstring or upset them; or he gallops round through the bushes, and attacks again from the side or front. The tiger's powers of springing seem inconsiderable. I observed that tigers always forded, never jumped, an irrigation channel not more than eighteen feet wide, that flowed through the jungles near Morlay, and which they frequently crossed during their night's prowls. I have frequently measured the bounds of tigers that have pursued deer, and have found fifteen feet to be about the utmost they usually spring. I have seen it surmised, upon a consideration of the respective size and power of a tiger and of a cat, that the tiger can cover a hundred feet at a bound. Were a flea or grasshopper adopted as the basis of calculation, a much more startling result might be obtained. The popular belief that a tiger slinks away should he fail in his attack is erroneous, as also the belief that he can kill his prey by a stroke of the paw. I have never seen anything to support this belief, nor is it held by natives. Of none of the sportsmen or natives of whom we read as coming under tigers' hands has it ever, as far as I know, been recorded that limbs were broken or death caused by a stroke of the paw only. I have known several cattle escape from tigers, severely lacerated, where, had a heavy blow accompanied the strokes of the paws, bones must have been broken.

There appears to be no foundation for the venerable belief in tigers sucking the blood of their victims. The jugular vein is never, as far as I have observed, injured. It is by fracturing the vertebræ, not by blood-letting, that the tiger's prey is deprived of life. I have known several cases of cattle getting away from tigers after having been seized by them, but escaping the fatal wrench, from the interference of the cow-herds. All but one died of lock-jaw, or from inflammation of the wounds in the throat, but there was no bleeding. The tiger frequently retains its hold on its victim's throat for some time, but probably only till assured that life is extinct. The physical difficulty of producing a vacuum sufficient to cause a flow of blood, whilst the tiger's mouth is opened so widely as to grasp a bullock's throat, would be considerable. A little after sunset, or sooner if the jungles are quiet, the tiger returns and drags the carcass to some retired spot where he commences his meal. In eating the tiger invariably commences at the hind-quarters. The exact spot where the first mouthful will be taken can be told with certainty. The flesh of one or both thighs, and sometimes the flanks, or about 70 lb. of meat, is eaten the first night. Tigers seldom lie up far from their "*kill*," if the cover be thick and quiet; they eat whenever inclined either by day or night till the carcass is finished; this is usually on the third day, but it, of course, depends upon the size of the animal killed. After or during a meal the tiger drinks largely, often walking belly-deep into the water. One morning before it was quite light three of my trackers were going to see about some elephants near Morlay, when they heard a tiger on the opposite bank coming towards the river they were going to cross. They got up a tree and saw the tiger march into the water and immerse his head to the eyes, blowing and spluttering as if to wash his jaws. Having lapped as much water as he required, he crossed to underneath the tree up which the men had climbed, and sat down at the foot. They had only cudgels and their *cumblies* (black blankets) with them. These they threw down altogether upon the unsuspecting tiger, which, to their amusement, dashed off into the jungle with a "wough," in a great state of fright. This was the "Don," a tiger to be mentioned further on, and on which my men were always playing practical jokes.

After a pretty lengthy experience of tigers, and finding that all I had seen had dragged, not carried, their kills, I was disposed to doubt the truth of their ever lifting a full-grown bullock clear off the ground; but I subsequently saw where this feat had been performed on two occasions by two separate tigers. One of these, an immensely powerful beast, had taken up a bullock weighing probably 400 lb., and carried it through a very dense thicket for about three hundred yards. The other, a small tigress, carried an old bullock some distance through open jungle. These tigers' object in doing this was not apparent, except that their kills had been constantly meddled with, and they may possibly have had some idea of leaving no traces behind them, though it is doubtful if their intelligence were equal to such a flight as this. In both of the above cases the drag of one hind-leg of the bullock was observable here and there.

Tigers frequently astonish those most conversant with their ordinary habits by some erratic conduct, and it is unsafe to condemn as untrue almost anything that may be related of their doings (as long as it is nothing of which they are physically incapable) merely because it is unusual or unprecedented. An account given by two sportsmen a few years ago of a tigress climbing a tree in a wood on the Neilgherry hills was much criticised, and even laughed at, by many who had scarcely perhaps ever seen a tiger out of a menagerie, or at least had never happened to see one up a tree. Tigers are not physically incapable of climbing, and though their doing so is decidedly unusual, there is no reason why they should not occasionally use their powers. I have never seen a tiger in a tree myself, but their claw-marks are constantly to be found where they amuse themselves by springing and clutching the soft bark, sometimes at thirteen feet from the ground. The natives believe that this is done to sharpen their claws, or as a means of relieving irritation in the claws caused by putrid flesh; and the marks may sometimes be made by juvenile tigers at play. There is one kind of tree called in Canarese "muttaga" (the bastard teak, *Buttea frondosa*), the bark of which is very soft, and the sap, which it gives forth at the slightest wound, of a blood-red colour. The tiger is particularly fond of clawing this tree, and the imaginative natives ascribe this to his supposed delight at the sight of what he believes to be blood!

The tiger's powers of enduring hunger and thirst are very great. In January 1870, a tiger, tigress, and panther were surrounded with nets by some villagers in a valley near which a friend and myself were encamped. We shot the panther on the first day, but the enclosed thicket was so dense that we could not get the tigers to show, and we had no elephants. On the fifth day, however, we wounded them both. After this, as nothing would make them break cover, we were obliged to send to Mysore for elephants, and we killed them, still full of vigour, on the tenth day. The weather was hot, the circle in which they were enclosed was only seventy yards in diameter, and the heat of the fires kept up day and night all round was considerable. Still they existed without a drop of water for ten days, suffering from wounds half the time. A tiger can go much longer than this without food without serious inconvenience.

The hunting-ranges of tigers are extensive, and are traversed with great expedition. A tiger that I was after on one occasion travelled from Hássanoor to Morlay, about twenty-three miles, within ten hours; this was his own pace, as he did not know we were following him. Tigers are not often met with in the jungles when not the object of pursuit. During some years of wandering in tigerish localities I have only come upon them accidentally about half-a-dozen times.

Tigresses do not breed at any fixed season. I have taken cubs in March, May, and October. I have twice taken four cubs at a litter, but this is an unusual number—two, occasionally three, being more common; and male and female cubs appear to be in about equal proportions. How it is that amongst mature animals tigresses predominate so markedly, I am unable to say. The tigress probably does not breed oftener than once in two years. I have seen as many as three cubs about four months old with a tigress, but never more than two well-grown ones. The natives say that the tigress feeds her cubs when very young with gobbets of half-digested flesh, which she disgorges on her return from hunting. This is probable, as carrying meat to any distance would be an unnatural proceeding, and the half-digested flesh is probably better adapted to the requirements of young cubs. When even six weeks old the cubs move from place to place with their mother, but are left at home whilst she hunts. They are led to the feast, if near, when she kills. Even at this tender age they are very cunning, and immediately take a line of their own if intruded upon during their mother's absence. Two cubs, born near Morlay in November 1875, first began to hunt for themselves in the following June, when seven months old. They still, however, remained with the tigress. I returned from Bengal at this time, and took much interest in noting their progress. They had considerable difficulty at this age in killing even old cattle single-handed, and they scratched them greatly in their attempts. Nor did they attack loose cattle—only such as we picketed for them. On one occasion there were evident marks of the mother having sat by whilst the one cub that was then with her killed a bullock. I shot both these young tigers upon their return to feed on animals they had killed: one, the female, on July 29, when she measured 6 feet 3 inches, and weighed 118 lb.; the other, the male, on November 25; he measured 6 feet 11 inches, but I was unable to weigh him.

Tiger-cubs are very handsome little beasts, and exceedingly good-tempered; but it is essential that they should be taken very young, before they have any knowledge of jungle-life, or fear of man, or they cannot be tamed. A month is the outside age for taking them. They show much attachment to their master, following him everywhere, lying under his chair, and sniffing loudly with pleasure when noticed. As soon as meat is given, even to the youngest cubs, they turn up their noses at milk, and will take nothing but meat afterwards. The idea that uncooked flesh makes them savage is, I have satisfied myself, groundless. Cubs will only get on well on raw meat, and as long as they have enough of it, are the best-tempered little animals in the world. When four months old they become formidable in appearance and power, but they may safely be kept loose much longer. A pair which I gave to his Highness the young Mahárájah of Mysore were kept loose until eight months old, and used to play with each other or their keepers, and with a tame bear, very prettily. My experience of tame tigers is that they are neither treacherous nor likely to show any sudden savageness if well fed. I had one of considerable size that used to be loose in my room at night, and though I pillowed and thumped it when it would show its affection for me by jumping on to the bed as soon as I was asleep, it never showed any resentment. I sold a pair of cubs eight months old, as I was ordered to Bengal and could not keep them, for £100.

Having now given some notes on the nature and habits of the tiger, I shall endeavour to describe the usual methods of hunting him.

TIGER-HUNTING.

The pursuit of the tiger with a line of elephants is perhaps the most common method, the sportsman either shooting from the howdah, or from a post selected ahead, towards which the tiger is driven. This plan is chiefly adopted in Bengal in places where the grass is long, and where men on foot would be useless.

Beaters are employed instead of elephants in other parts of India, where the jungle admits of men getting through in line, and is perhaps too thorny or close at about the height of the howdah for shooting from an elephant.

In some parts of India, particularly in Mysore, tigers are surrounded with nets and shot from outside, or from the backs of elephants, or even on foot, inside.

Phototint. H. M. Wright & Co. London

A Night Watch

Watching for their return to a "*kill*," or at pools where they are known to drink, is the method chiefly practised by native shikáries.

Poison, spring-guns, pitfalls, and traps are also brought into play, generally where a man-eater is concerned.

I have had very little experience of beating in line with a large number of elephants; this method is hardly applicable to Southern India, where there are few savannahs of long grass as in Bengal, and where elephants are not so easily obtained.

In shooting either with elephants or beaters, it is essential that the sportsman or some of his men should know the ground well, and the tiger's usual paths to and from the cover to be driven, and the adjacent covers. A tiger scarcely ever moves through very thick cover, preferring paths and comparatively open passages amongst the bushes; and in driving along a ravine he almost invariably comes along the bank, very seldom down the bed. It is often of great assistance to have "dummies" of natives' clothes, hung here and there on conspicuous bushes, to guide the tiger, but these should be placed so that he may see them from some little distance and not come upon them suddenly, as in that case he may become alarmed and break away. In driving a ravine, a straight reach, and the point therein where the jungle is narrowest, should be selected by the sportsman for his post. In bends, or where the ravine is tortuous, the tiger is likely to cut across a corner. No beat should be begun too near a tiger for fear of alarming him, and causing him to pass the sportsman too quickly for a good shot. Some tigers show almost as soon as the first shout of the beaters is heard, others will not leave the cover till the last moment. It is a good rule never to be off guard until the last man has left the cover, as should the tiger whilst coming along have detected the sportsman, he may lie close, and let the beaters come very near before he breaks. Tigers and other animals display great intelligence in detecting the quarter from which real danger is to be apprehended, and will break back through a line of shouting beaters to avoid the silent sportsman they may have detected ahead.

I had particular facilities for enjoying the sport of tiger-shooting on foot, or from trees, at Morlay. My men were thoroughly up to the habits of the game, and we knew every inch of the covers. There is little danger in this sport if the tiger is not turned back by being fired at from in front. When alongside or past the sportsman he generally dashes ahead if wounded, but if fired at the instant he shows himself he may turn back. Beaters should be ordered to mass together as soon as a shot is fired, and to leave the cover in a body. I used an old bugle for signals, a blast from which meant danger. If it was not sounded when a shot was fired my men knew all was safe ahead, and came on with undiminished confidence. Beaters cannot be expected to drive out a piece of jungle boldly where there is a possibility of a wounded tiger being stumbled upon. I have been fortunate enough never to have had a single accident in tiger-shooting, though I am sure men would have been injured on some occasions had our arrangements not been good.

I generally managed to keep up communication with the men leading the beat by signals, and often found it of great advantage. I had a man posted at some distance from me in a tree, or open space, who could see the advancing beaters and myself. By a wave of a handkerchief, red or white, by the head of the beaters, which was telegraphed to me by the sentinel, I knew if the tiger had been found, had broken back, or was coming along; and when I have sometimes had to stop a beat I have been able to do so by a signal without losing time. It is very inconvenient to be unable to communicate with beaters without shouting, or sending some one down one's tree with a message.

All this training was excellent practice, moreover, for the Morlay people for the more important work of elephant-catching, in which signals with fires or flags upon hill-tops at a distance of some miles were sometimes used. Of course it is but few sportsmen who have opportunities for hunting tigers in this systematic way, but perhaps some of the above hints may be found applicable on most occasions.

There is perhaps no method of shooting tigers so seldom successful as watching for their return to feed on animals they have killed. Almost every sportsman has tried it again and again, and solemnly vowed upon each occasion that it should be his last, generally only to be found at his post on the next tempting opportunity. For my own part I confess to a great liking for the silent and solitary watch; and as this description of shooting requires the exercise of the sportsman's utmost vigilance and patience, I have never felt any qualms as to its legitimacy. In a shady green *mechán* * in some fine tree, watching at the cool of evening—that always bewitching hour in the Indian day,—when jungle-sounds alone break the stillness, and birds and animals, seldom seen at other times, steal forth, and can be watched at leisure—whilst intense excitement is kept alive by the possibility of the tiger's appearance at any moment,—I have often wondered how any one can consider being perched upon a tree under a blazing sun whilst a tiger is being driven towards him sport, and use the term poaching in reference to this. How many men have killed their forty or fifty tigers who have never succeeded in bagging one by watching,—

* A screened platform.

the fair outwitting of the subtle beast on his own ground! Give him who prefers the horn-and-tomtom system his diabolical appliances, his calorific post; but the solitary watch in the hushed evening hours for the lover of nature, for him who can feel the true romance and poetry of solitude in the jungles.

It was not until I had made many unsuccessful attempts to shoot tigers by watching—never even seeing one—and had cheerfully put down my want of success on each occasion to sheer bad luck, that I began to consider in the ample hours I had aloft for reflection, whether there might not be some mistakes in the arrangements we made for their reception to account for tigers never putting in an appearance, especially as any carcass that was not watched was always revisited. I then saw some of the errors we made, and since rectifying them have been fairly successful. I will therefore venture upon some hints which may perhaps be of service to others.

The reasons why tigers fail to show again at their kills are, either that they have been disturbed in their mid-day retreat whilst the platform was being put up, or have winded or heard the sportsman upon returning to feed. As the tiger kills his prey with the intention of eating it, so he will surely return unless disturbed. To avoid alarming him, the best plan is to tie up a bullock (a natural kill will seldom do as well) in some quiet locality two or three hundred yards from any place where he can remain during the day, and where the line he will take in returning to the place is well defined. This is necessary, as the sportsman can thus have his platform prepared without fear of the tiger's being within hearing, and post himself so that his scent (it should be remembered that the prevailing breezes often change at sunset) may not be blown towards the tiger on his return. These essential points being seen to, it only remains to have the *mechán* comfortably prepared, and for the sportsman to keep absolutely quiet, and take up his post sufficiently early. The *mechán* should be about six feet long and three broad, with its length towards the kill, a hole about six inches square being left amongst the leafy branches with which it is to be screened, to see and shoot from. A mattress, pillows, rug, and water-bottle should not be forgotten, as without comfort much of the pleasure of the sport is lost. A book should be taken to read till dusk. I never hesitated to smoke whilst upon the watch; it can do no harm, as if the tiger is in a position to wind the smoke he will most certainly smell the smoker, and tobacco will then add no extra terrors to his flight. I need hardly say that the sportsman must make no audible movement, and can only remain perfectly still if lying down; in sitting up the feet go asleep, and it then becomes impossible to avoid moving. The leaves for screening the platform should be of a kind that will not dry soon, nor rustle if touched. Some kinds shrivel up in a couple of hours, and crackle with the slightest movement. No one should be allowed on the platform with the sportsman; a native is absolutely certain to cough at the critical moment. The platform should be placed about fifteen or twenty feet high, when possible, to lessen the chances of the tiger's scenting the sportsman. A tiger rarely looks up unless his attention is attracted by some sound; but there is great danger of his winding the sportsman. There is no objection on the score of safety in having it lower, as tigers never attempt an escalade when suddenly startled. The cases in which they have injured sportsmen in trees have occurred when their ire has been roused by being driven about by beaters.

As soon as the jungles are quiet the tiger may be expected, and the sportsman should seldom watch for him beyond half-past eight in the evening, as if he intend to come he will have put in an appearance before that time. Nor should he take up his post later than four o'clock, as a tiger often comes long before sundown. A tigress for which I was watching on one occasion returned to her kill at three in the afternoon of a very hot day. I expected her early and had taken up my post at two o'clock. On this occasion the position was a difficult one, as there was no choice between a bush too close to the "kill" and a tree too far away. I was obliged to take the former, and laying some poles across the bush I had an elephant's pad placed on them, and green boughs arranged round as a screen. I was only seven feet from the ground, and on a very unstable arrangement. I had been watching about an hour, when suddenly, without other notice of her approach, there was the cautious but firm tread—that sound which there is no mistaking, and which once heard cannot be forgotten—of the tigress in the dead leaves under me! She had, unfortunately, approached from behind, and taking advantage of my bush as a last point of observation, had entered it! I was within three feet of her! I need not say she detected me in an instant, but drew back so stealthily that I did not hear her leave, and I remained in the pleasant position of imagining her within arm's-length for a quarter of an hour. At last the excitement overpowered my physical control, and I could not help moving, and looking I found she was gone. I left, so as not to risk frightening her further, and she returned after dark and dragged the bullock away.

Mosquitoes never give much trouble in fine weather up till half-past eight at night. Three or four days before full moon, and about two days after, is the best time for watching. Nothing can be done in dark nights. The kill may be dragged a few yards to afford a better shot if necessary.

Phototint. H. M. Wright & Co. London.

Tiger-Netting.

Tigers do not mind this at all; but it should be left within easy sight of the place where it was left, so that when the tiger returns he can see it immediately as it lies. The idea that touching or interfering with a kill will prevent the tiger's devouring more of it is quite unfounded. Carcasses are constantly pulled about by vultures and jackals during the tiger's absence. Let any one move a carcass a few yards—one that is not watched; it will be seen that the tiger returns to it without hesitation.

In tying a live bullock for a tiger, the rope should be put round the base of his horns or one fore-leg. I have had to secure some bullocks with a chain when I wanted the carcass left on the spot, to prevent tigers that had acquired the habit from biting the rope, which they will do if they want to drag their prey to cover, and cannot break the tie.

TIGER-NETTING.

In some parts of Mysore the villagers are accustomed to surround tigers with nets, and then to shoot or spear them. This is the only method (except watching) by which they can be brought to bag where the cover is too continuous to be easily driven. It may seem unsportsmanlike to shoot a tiger through a net, but as far as danger goes there is perhaps as much as in shooting him from a tree.

The method of enclosing the tiger within the nets is as follows: The nets used are made of ½-inch rope with a 9-inch mesh, and are 40 feet long by 12 deep. When a tiger is known to be in any particular cover, perhaps a densely-wooded ravine, a path is cleared across some distance from where he lies, and a line of nets is set up 8 or 10 feet high, the extra depth lying on the ground; the nets are extended into the open on both sides. A hundred or a hundred and fifty Torreas or Oopligas, the only castes who take part in this sport, are usually engaged.

Men armed with spears conceal themselves behind the row of nets at different points, and a flanking line is posted on each side of the cover to prevent the tiger breaking out sideways. A few climb commanding trees to give notice of his movements, whilst the main body of beaters commence at the head of the ravine and drive him towards the nets. Under these circumstances tigers and panthers act very differently. Panthers frequently rush ahead and precipitate themselves into the nets, when they are speared on the spot, or effect their escape. But a tiger, however much he may be alarmed at the noise behind, keeps a careful look-out ahead. His passage onwards is signalled by the men in the trees, and when he appears near the nets the spearmen show themselves; he then generally draws back, and as care is always taken to enclose a particularly thick piece of jungle within the nets, he conceals himself. The beaters close in from behind in a compact line, carrying spare nets. Should the tiger try to break back he is received with shouts, which generally drive him back. Having reduced the area to about a hundred yards in diameter, the nets are quickly run up all round. The main ropes (which pass through the bottom and top meshes all along the nets) are fastened to convenient trees; the nets are supported at the height of ten feet by forked poles inside and out, inclining towards each other, and secured together at the top; logs of trees and heavy stones are laid upon the foot all round, and pegs are driven in to prevent the logs being moved. The extra depth of two feet or so of nets is brought up round the logs, and wattled above with cross sticks, thus making the net double for about two feet from the ground. In this way a barrier of great strength is formed; it cannot be easily pulled down by the tiger, and is too pliable to afford him an effective blow. It is a strange fact that tigers never attempt to jump over the nets, as they might easily do; panthers occasionally do so. At night fires are lit all round, and spearmen drive the tiger back if he shows himself. A whole day is often taken up in rendering the enclosure secure.

Preparations for killing him are now commenced. Fifteen or twenty picked spearmen enter the enclosure with a few men provided with long-handled choppers; the duty of the latter is to clear a path fifteen feet in width across the enclosure, thus dividing it into two parts, the spearmen acting as a guard the while. The object of the path is that the tiger may be shot when driven across it. This going inside an enclosure with a tiger that has been excited perhaps for two or three days, and has failed in all his attempts to escape, would appear, to those who do not know the true nature of the animal, to be inviting certain death; but the men keep well together, and a tiger has never been known to charge home amongst them. His position seems to have the effect of cowing him. After he has been wounded the men seldom venture within the nets.

If, after being fired at, the tiger keeps in the thick cover, and every means fail to stir him, and elephants are not at hand, the looking him up is a service of sufficient danger. The tiger may be dead, but he is perhaps only badly wounded; in such cases the only thing is for the sportsman to go in with a strong body of men with spears (these would, of course, be of little use in meeting a charge, but the having some weapon in hand gives confidence), when the tiger can be shot as he lies, or in charging, or retreating. I have on several occasions hunted up tigers in this way, and I must say

I never yet saw one really charge home into a body of men. Fifteen or twenty men used to such work, and who will stand and not be intimidated, as many of the Oopligas and Torreas of Mysore will do, are, I am sure, quite safe. I do not believe that any tiger—man-eater, wounded, or tigress with cubs,—dares to charge home into a determined and close party of men.

Tiger-netting is generally carried out for the amusement of European officers by the headmen of villages, but the natives will occasionally, if a tiger becomes troublesome, hunt him in this way themselves. In such cases, as they seldom have firearms to shoot him, nets are set up in the cleared path across the enclosure, and arranged so as to collapse to his charge, and envelop the tiger when he is driven across. A dozen bold fellows station themselves behind a screen of bushes, and the rest go inside and drive the tiger towards them, when he is generally speared as he struggles in the nets. The spears used have blades a foot long and three inches broad, with bamboo handles six feet in length, and can be driven through a tiger. A few seconds thus suffice to make an end of him. Should he get free at the moment the men rush upon him one or two are often knocked over, but the nets generally hold him.

Strychnine is occasionally used for destroying tigers. As I have before said, I was for some time employed by orders of Government in killing the tigers in parts of Mysore; and though I only poisoned three—the others that I killed being by legitimate methods—I turned my attention at the time to experiments with poisons.

There is no difficulty in making a tiger take a dose. I tried strychnine on several occasions until I found out the best way to apply it. The first time I gave four grains to a large tiger. He ate about half the quantity of meat he would otherwise have done, the poison affecting him before he completed his meal, and he then vomited and drank at a pool near, rolling at every few yards, evidently in great agony. This tiger was severely affected for some days, and my men brought me news of him, groaning and roaring in different parts of the jungle. I was too busy with elephant-catching at the time to look after him, and he recovered. In the second case I used nine grains; a tiger, tigress, and large cub fed off the carcass, but the tigress alone took the poisoned portion. She threw up a good deal of flesh (and covered it over with dry leaves), and rolled about a good deal. Further on she threw up the strychnine upon some fine clean sand in the bed of a ravine, and the saliva sinking into the sand the grains of strychnine were left almost intact upon the surface. This tigress then went for miles without showing any further symptoms of being affected. In the third case I put nine grains into a bullock, after looking for the tiger that had killed it during the day. We had disturbed him, so he did not return that night. Next morning the bullock had swelled to an enormous size and the wound was dripping a gelatinous matter. I put a couple of men to watch during the day to keep off the vultures, and by evening fully a quart of fluid had dripped and coagulated below. The tiger returned at night and ate half the bullock, and finished it the next night, so he could not have felt the poison; and I believe, from this and similar experiments, that strychnine is worked off from dead flesh in a few hours.

I subsequently hit upon a fatal method of applying poison. I do not intend to divulge the secret, as district officers with strongly-developed utilitarian views would be enabled to poison off all the tigers in their ranges by this means, which, judging from the operations in a single district in Madras, some who do not pause to consider the useful features of the tiger's presence might not hesitate to do. The success I attained in my first, and I hope last, experiment, as far as tigers are concerned, was painfully complete. Two old bullocks that were yoked together were killed by a tiger close to my camp. The original slayer was joined at dinner by two tigresses, and the three ate the whole of one bullock, leaving the other untouched. In the morning I had the remaining carcass guarded from the vultures, and late in the afternoon I applied the poison in the way I had devised. Next morning we found the three tigers had dragged the bullock into some rocks and bushes about a hundred and fifty yards distant, with bare country all round, and no water in the rocks. Not knowing that they were dead, I sent to Captain C. of the Revenue Survey, who was in camp at a village four miles distant, and with another friend, who was staying with me, set out with five elephants about 11 A.M. We posted ourselves in trees across the line we expected the tigers to take, and sent the elephants with the trackers on them to beat them out of the rocks.

From my tree I could see the elephants clambering about the rocks, and the men keeping a sharp look-out; presently I heard a shout that one tiger was dead, and soon afterwards another. The mahout of an elephant that was in advance now found the third. Shrieks of laughter and much merriment followed an inspection of the "bodies," and a tracker came running for us. I confess I had never expected such slaughter. I was not certain, having only seen tigers affected before, that my new plan would succeed, and I felt like a murderer when I viewed the unfortunate victims. My men took a very different and exceedingly cheerful view of the case, exclaiming delightedly, "Oh, this is good! here have our master and we been risking our throats" (clutching their necks with appropriate gesture, and giving the dislocating twist that they considered we had been placing ourselves in peril of) "in poking about after tigers for months, when one dose of this capital 'medicine' would have done. This is the thing for the future." And when the tigers were padded they preceded the elephants, singing anything but a dirge. My own feelings as we followed the *cortège* may be imagined, nor did my companions spare me.

I should say that the male tiger had commenced to eat first, and the poison must have been almost instantly fatal, as he lay within four yards of the carcass. He had not struggled at all; he must have felt the poison, turned away, and dropped dead. One tigress was on her back thirty yards distant, the other near her; the latter had struggled slightly. As a proof of the almost instantaneous effect of the poison in this instance not more than half-a-dozen pounds of flesh had been eaten. Upon being moved, a quantity of blood ran from the nostrils of all three tigers.

Traps are not now often used for tigers: a few used to be caught alive in ordinary mouse-trap-shaped cages in the time of the late Mahárájah of Mysore; and there was, when I was last there, one of these cages, mounted upon wheels, decaying in the Hoonsoor jungles. The bait used was a goat, partitioned off by iron bars at the far end of the cage, as a native is loath to give even a sprat to a whale if he can catch him without. How tigers can ever have been such simpletons as to enter these structures is incomprehensible. I once saw a novel kind of trap in a hill where a tiger had been recently caught by propping up a flat slab, as in an ordinary brick-trap for birds, over a recess between two rocks, and baiting with a goat. Tigers are occasionally caught in pitfalls. One fell into a sámbur-pit that some Shōlagas on the Billiga-rungun hills had dug near their cultivation whilst I was there shooting on one occasion, but though severely staked it got out: the pit was only four feet deep, but narrow at the bottom, and the tiger had had a long task to free himself. Old Bommay Gouda used to kill a good many tigers in his younger days by dead-fall traps, made of bamboos and loaded with stones; the natives construct these very ingeniously. I once had a huge iron spring-trap like the ordinary scissors rat-trap. It was originally made by a sporting district officer for catching panthers, which did a good deal of damage amongst the game in his domain, but was found to be too slow for them, as they sprang away in time to avoid the jaws. It was twelve feet long, with two springs that required a man of ten stone weight standing on each to put down. The bait-plate was eighteen inches square, the jaws about three feet long, and closing at a foot and a half above the plate. I am convinced no tiger would ever have got out of it if he could only have been got in, unless he had left his leg behind; but though it was sprung by a famous tiger—the "Don," to be mentioned further on—we never got hold of him. I used to set it by cutting a recess in a thorny bush, and tying a goat inside, with the trap, covered with a few twigs or grass, at the entrance; the ends were thrust into adjoining bushes. How the Don found the snare out the first time we could never tell, but he forced his way through the bush from behind and took away our goat. He did this again at a second place. The third time we fenced the goat in, except on the side of the trap, with such horrible thorns that even the Don could not get through them. This time he sprang the trap, and must have jumped back at the same instant: he then secured the goat. We tried the trap at different places; but he took the goats away, springing the trap each time, and then carrying them off at his leisure, so frequently, that we had to bring back our inglorious trap after the loss of a small flock of goats, and I never tried it again. This showed astonishing intelligence in this tiger—a point in which the animal is entitled to rank high in the brute creation. The shrewdness displayed by them on occasions—shrewdness removed from mere instinct—is very marked. The most unsophisticated tigers, after being hunted unsuccessfully once or twice, become so alive to danger from any source that it is most difficult to circumvent them.

CHAPTER XXI.

TIGER-SHOOTING IN SOUTHERN INDIA.

REMARKS ON TIGER-SHOOTING ON FOOT—NOT NECESSARILY FOOLHARDY SPORT—EFFECT OF THE TIGER'S ROAR — THE IYENPOOR MAN-EATER — HER RAVAGES — KILLS A MAN AT NÁGWULLY—ANOTHER VICTIM—AN UNSUCCESSFUL CHRISTMAS DAY'S HUNT—A HERDSMAN'S FATE—A PRIEST CARRIED OFF—THE MAN-EATER'S CUB—HORRIBLE DEATH OF A VILLAGER—AN UNSUCCESSFUL PURSUIT—HER LAST VICTIM—AN AFFECTIONATE SON-IN-LAW—NEWS OF THE MAN-EATER—AN EVENING WATCH—HER APPEARANCE—KILL HER—THE VILLAGERS OF HEBSOOR—TERRIFIED AGRICULTURISTS—THE "DON" TIGER —HIS HABITS AND PECULIARITIES—EFFIGY OF THE DON—AN INLAND CYCLONE—THE DON'S GLUTTONY—WE HUNT HIM—AN AFTER-DINNER RUN—WOUND HIM—HE ESCAPES FOR THE TIME—CONTINUE THE CHASE NEXT DAY—HIS DEATH—REGRETS—BOILING DOWN THE DON'S FAT.

TIGER-SHOOTING on foot is very generally condemned, but as in most matters of choice there is something to be said for, as well as against, it. It is never followed systematically by any man, but circumstances occasionally arise when it must be resorted to, or sport be sacrificed. At this point some men abandon their quarry, some stick to it. Those without experience of their game do well to pause; but one who knows the beast he has to deal with, may kill many dangerous animals on foot without accident or even serious adventure. Almost every accident that occurs is directly traceable to ignorance or carelessness. The sportsman is a tyro, and over-venturesome; or due precautions are not observed when a wounded beast is on foot, and some one, moving about where he does not think the animal can possibly be, is seized.

Tiger-shooting on foot can never, of course, be safe sport; but a sportsman is not supposed to look for absolute safety on all occasions, any more than does a soldier. Risks must be run, but if properly conducted dangerous game-shooting on foot is not the mad amusement usually supposed. Speaking for myself, I have been fortunate enough to kill several tigers and panthers, and a large number of bears and other formidable beasts, on foot, so I will venture to state what I think are the chief precautions to be observed.

It makes all the difference in the world whether the animal to be attacked is wounded or not. The sportsman occasionally comes upon a tiger when after other game, or one is driven from a cover without being much bullied. There is no danger to speak of in firing first shots at a hundred such beasts. But if a tiger has been much harassed and irritated, and imagines himself unable to escape—or wounded, and is followed up whilst pain and exhaustion have forced him to stop—he proves a very different beast to the retiring animal he ordinarily is, though he is always an abject coward if firmly faced. It is true that in shooting with elephants tigers frequently get on board some of them; but a tiger fears man more than any other being, and though he will charge pluckily enough to all appearances, he always shirks the last ten feet if boldly received. In netting tigers I have seen this so constantly that I am quite sure a few determined men, keeping together, are quite safe from any tiger in open ground.

Whether a tiger should be attacked on foot or left alone depends greatly on the nature of the jungle in which he is found. In the grass plains and thick undergrowth of such parts of Bengal as I have seen, tigers can only be shot from the elevation of elephants' backs; but in many parts of Southern India the jungle is clear inside, and the ground is broken, so that rocks and ravines may afford advantageous positions. The tiger can also be shot even without such aids when he can be seen at some distance.

None but the utterly ignorant would think of following a wounded tiger into long grass or close cover, where it has every advantage, and the sportsman may be seized before he has time to use his rifle. As well might one follow it on a dark night. In such cover the tiger rarely makes any demonstration from a distance, seeking to avoid observation, but when almost stumbled upon he attacks like lightning. In doing this he is seldom seeking to make a reprisal, and only acts in self-defence when he thinks himself discovered.

One of the most powerful elements in the tiger's attack is his voice if the attack be commenced very near. The startling, coughing roar is almost paralysing to the coolest in such cases. But if the tiger has to come on from any distance he rarely does more than grunt, and the sportsman's attention is concentrated on the beast himself, and his demonstrations pass unnoticed. The power of the tiger's voice at close quarters may be understood by any one who has an opportunity of seeing a newly-caged tiger. It is almost impossible to watch a charge against the bars, if standing within a yard or so of them, without flinching; but if seen at twenty yards' distance it is nothing.

If a moment's time be given for preparation, a tiger's charge loses much of its power. In following any dangerous game the excitement felt when the beast is known to be near, but not visible, amounts to positive nervousness. A quail rising at his feet startles the man who the next moment faces an elephant or tiger with *sang froid.* As soon as the game is seen, nervousness gives place to the most perfect coolness, and if a tiger's charge can be anticipated it loses most of its danger.

I never myself hesitate to follow wounded animals on foot if the ground be favourable. In such cases the chief precautions to be observed are: to trust no place as not holding the tiger till it has been ascertained not to do so; never carelessly to approach thick cover from which a beast may make a sudden attack; and, if possible, to have men who will all stand firm. Under no temptation should the sportsman's last shot be fired at a retreating beast.

I will now recall, with the aid of my hunting-journal, some scenes in tiger-shooting, and will endeavour to select occurrences illustrative of the nature and peculiarities of the animal. Amongst them I will relate one or two incidents in tiger-shooting on foot, to show how I consider the sport may be managed when occasion demands.

When I pitched camp at Morlay in September 1873, to commence the elephant kheddahs, the country-side was in a state of considerable alarm from the attacks of a man-eating tigress. This tigress's fits of man-eating seemed to be intermittent, as after killing three or four persons some months before, she had not been heard of till about the time of my arrival at Morlay, when she killed two boys attending goats. I anticipated some trouble from her in our kheddah work, as it would be unsafe for one or two men to go alone through the jungles; but whether it was from the disturbance caused by seven or eight hundred work-people, or other reasons, we heard nothing of her for some time.

On November 30th, when the work-people had dispersed, news was brought in that a man, returning to the village of Nágwully (about six miles from Morlay) with cattle, had been carried off the evening before. From an account of the place where the mishap had occurred I knew it was useless to look for the tigress after the lapse of eighteen hours, as she would have retired to impracticable jungle. I urged the people to bring news of further losses at the earliest possible moment.

On December 19th another man was carried off close to the village of

Iyenpoor, five miles from Morlay, but I did not hear of this till two days afterwards.

On Christmas-day I thought I would look up the jungles in the Iyenpoor direction, so took an elephant and some trackers in hopes of learning something of the tigress's habits. The unfortunate man's wife, with her three small children, were brought to me as I entered the village. The woman, with the strange apathy of a Hindoo, related what she knew of her husband's death without a tear. I gave her some money, as she would have to expend a small sum in accordance with caste usage to rid her of the devil by which she was supposed to be attended on account of her husband's having been killed by a tiger, before she would be admitted into her caste's villages; and then, accompanied by the headman and others, went to the scene of the last disaster. A solitary tamarind-tree grew on some rocks close to the village; there was no jungle within three hundred yards, only a few bushes in the crevices of the rocks; close by was the broad cattle-track into the village. The unfortunate man had been following the cattle home in the evening, and must have stopped to knock down some tamarinds with his stick, which, with his black blanket and a skin skull-cap, still lay where he was seized. The tigress had been hidden in the rocks, and in one bound seized him, dragged him to the edge of a small plateau of rock, from which she jumped down into a field below, and there killed him. The place was still marked by a pool of dried blood. She had then dragged her victim half a mile, to a spot where we still found his leg-bones.

After walking about for two hours with the trackers, in the hopes of seeing recent marks of the tigress, but without success, the village cattle were sent for and herded into the jungles in the hope of attracting her if near. The poor beasts were, however, so frightened by the constant attacks of tigers, that we could scarcely get them to face the jungle, and a partridge rising suddenly was too much for their nerves, and sent them, tails up, to the village before they had been out half an hour. After some time they were got back. About 1 P.M., as they were feeding near a cover in a hollow encircled on three sides by low hills covered with bamboo, and a very pretty spot for a tiger, a wild scurry took place as a large tiger rushed amongst the foremost of them. Strange to say they all escaped, two only being slightly wounded; a few plucky buffaloes were in advance, and interfered considerably with the tiger's attack, as these animals never hesitate to do.

Up to this time I had been walking, rifle in hand, amongst the cattle, but the heat was considerable, and at this unlucky moment I was some little distance behind getting a drink, or I might have had a shot. As the herdsmen were not certain that the tiger had not secured something in his rush, we went in force to look through the cover. We only found footprints, however, and knew they were not those of the man-eater, but of a large male who was a well-known cattle-killer about the place. We shortly heard a spotted-deer bark over the saddle of the hill to our left; the tiger had moved off in that direction upon his discomfiture. We saw nothing more of him that day, or of the man-eater, and I returned to camp by moonlight. It was so cold that I was glad of an overcoat. A good camp Christmas dinner was awaiting me; and had I only been lucky enough to bag the man-eater, I should have been able to enter this amongst my red-letter days.

After this nothing was heard of the tigress for a week, when the trackers and I were going to look after some wild elephants, and at the ford in the river below the Koombappan temple found a tiger's pugs that were immediately pronounced to be hers. I sent back two men on my riding-elephant to warn the people of Morlay that the tigress was in our jungles, as her usual hunting-grounds were to the east of the river, and the people on our side were liable to be off their guard. We tried to follow her, but she had crossed open dry country, in which tracking was impossible, and we had to give her up. During the day I made arrangements for hunting her systematically next day should she still be in our jungles.

Whilst at dinner that evening, I heard voices and saw torches hurriedly approaching my tent, and could distinguish the words "*naie*" and "*nurri*" ("dog" and "jackal") pronounced excitedly. The Canarese people frequently speak of a tiger by these names, partly in assumed contempt, partly from superstitious fear. The word "*hooli*" (tiger) is not often used amongst jungle-men, in the same way that, from dread, natives usually refer to cholera by the general terms of *rōga* or *járdya* (sickness). The people were from Hurdenhully, a village a mile and a half away, and had come to tell me that their cattle had galloped back in confusion into the village at dusk, without their herdsman. Only one man had been with them that day, as there was some festival in the village. We suspected he had fallen a victim to the tigress, but it was useless to attempt a search that night. The cattle had been two or three miles into the jungles, and we had no indications where to look for the unfortunate herdsman, who was, moreover, probably now half devoured. So ordering some rice for the men, I sent them to Morlay to tell the trackers, and to sleep there and return with them in the morning.

At dawn we started on the back-trail of the cattle from Hurdenhully till we found the point where they had begun to gallop, just below the embankment of a small channel drawn from the river near Atticulpoor, and supplying the Hurdenhully tank with water. The ground was hard and much trodden by cattle, and we looked for some time for the tigress's tracks in vain, till the distant caw of a crow attracted us to the place where we found the man's remains; only the soles of his feet, the palms of his hands, his head, and a few bones were left. We lost no time in taking up the tigress's track, and used every endeavour to run her down, as we had over a hundred men ready at camp to beat her out could we but mark her into some practicable cover; but though she had eaten so much she had recrossed the river as usual, and had gone into the jungles towards the hills, where there was no chance of finding her.

About a week after this the priest of a small temple ten miles due west from Morlay, and in comparatively open country where a tiger had not been heard of for years, was jogging along on his riding-bullock one morning, to sweep out and garnish the small jungle-temple in which he officiated, and to present to "Yennay Hollay Koombappah" the offerings of the simple villagers whose faith was placed in that deity. Suddenly a tigress with her cub stepped into the path. The terrified bullock kicked off his rider and galloped back to the village, whilst the tigress—for it was the dreaded Iyenpoor man-eater, far out of her ordinary haunts—seized the hapless *poojáree* (priest), and carried him off to the bed of a deep ravine near.

Upon hearing next day of this, my men and I thought it must be some other tiger, as this fiend had managed with such cunning that we did not then know that she had a cub; and it was not till we found this out subsequently that we traced this death to her also. Up to this time she must have left her cub in the thick jungles along the hills, making her rapid hunting forays alone, as the cub had never been with her before; and this accounted for her invariably crossing the river and making for the hills after a raid. The absence of the tigress from the vicinity of Morlay during September and October was probably caused partly by her keeping out of the way when this cub was very young.

The next death was of a horrible description. Several villagers of Rámasamoodrum were grazing their cattle in a swampy hollow in the jungle near the temple, when the tigress pounced upon one man who was separated from the others. She in some way missed her aim at his throat, seized the shoulder, and then, either in jerking him, or by a blow, threw him up on to a thicket several feet from the ground. Here the wounded and bleeding wretch was caught by thorny creepers; whilst the tigress, as generally happens when any *contretemps* takes place, relinquished the attack and made off. The other men and the cattle had fled at the first alarm. The village was some distance away, and there was not time before nightfall for a party to search for the man, whose being still alive was not known.

Next morning the lacerated wretch was found. In his mangled state he had been unable to release himself; he was moaning and hanging almost head downwards amongst the creepers; and he died soon after he was taken down.

Before long the tigress visited my camp, but fortunately without doing any mischief. Close to my tent (my bungalow was not built then) was a large banian-tree: every night a fire was kindled near it, and here I sat and discussed plans for work or sport with my men. One morning when the trackers came to wake me early, they found the man-eater's tracks leading down a path close to the banian-tree in question. As we thought she might still be on our side of the river, I accompanied the men to examine its vicinity, and to ascertain if she had recrossed it towards the hills; if not, we intended to hunt the different covers on its banks during the day.

Upon reaching the river we walked down the sandy bed overshadowed by drooping *hongay* (the Indian beech, *Pongamia glabra*) trees. The scene at early morning was very pleasant. Gaudy kingfishers fluttered and poised over the pools and shallow runs of clear water into which the river —a considerable stream in the rains—had now shrunk. At a bend we came upon a troop of lungoor monkeys (*Presbytis priamus*) feeding upon some fallen fruit; these ran nimbly across the sand to the sanctuary of the large trees when we appeared. In one stretch a spotted stag and several graceful hinds were drinking at the cool stream, perchance admiring their shapely forms in nature's mirror; but for the nonce they passed unheeded. The soothing cooing of doves, the scream of the toucan, the cheery and game cry of the jungle-cock (*Gallus sonneratii*) perched aloft, whilst his ladies ruffled themselves in the sand below, combined to make one of those tranquil phases of beauty in nature which are such a contrast to the wildness and grandeur of other scenes.

The trackers moved quickly and silently along. We passed two or three pugs, but these elicited no notice, except one into which Dod Sidda drove the butt-end of his spear without a word; this was the night's track of the tigress to our side of the river. We had nearly got to the temple, below which it was not likely she would have crossed, and were in hopes of not finding her out-going trail, when a single track across an unblemished stretch of sand caused an exclamation of disappointment, and one glance showed it to be the unmistakable small oval pug of the man-eater. We felt our chances of finding her that day were very small, but there was nothing like trying; so sending for an elephant to come to the temple and there await my return, we cast ahead towards the hills, and again hit off the trail. After several hours' work, finding tracks now and then in the sandy beds of ravines, but all leading to a country where the cover was continuous, we were obliged to give it up as useless, as we could neither keep the trail nor have done anything towards driving such extensive cover had we even found where the tigress lay hidden. We were forced reluctantly to return, consoling ourselves with the hope of finding her in more favourable country soon, and vowing to leave no stone unturned till we bagged her. It had become quite a point of honour with the trackers; we had never been played such successful tricks before by any animal, and they said the tigress was "throwing dirt into their mouths."

We got back to the temple late in the afternoon; here I found the elephant and several of my people, and a man with a note from Captain C., of the Revenue Survey, who was in camp a few miles from Morlay. I started the messenger back with a reply, and though we were pretty certain the man-eater was miles away, it was a nervous job for him to get through the jungle till he reached open country on the far side. He left us, already casting furtive glances around him, to the great amusement of my men (who had not the job to do themselves!). Before he had got far, one of them, who was a bit of a humorist, called him back. The man came, when the wag, assuming a concerned air, said: "You know, *keep a good look-out ahead of you*—never mind the *rear;* if a tiger seizes a man from behind, what could any of us do? but, you know, *you can see her if she is coming for you from in front,* and you might try a run for it. Good-bye! Koombappah be with you! *Don't* delay; it's rather late as it is!" The poor villager grinned painfully at the joke, which the rest enjoyed immensely; but I saw he was in such a fright—and reflected that, with the uncertainty of her class, the tigress might as likely be near as far away—that I sent half-a-dozen men (the joker amongst them) to see him safely into the cultivated country on the other side.

Shortly after this, work took me to Goondulpet, twenty-five miles from Morlay, on the Neilgherry road, and I returned on the 14th January 1874. As I rode into camp about mid-day the trackers were waiting for me, and informed me that they had heard the "death-cry" raised at a small village called Bussavanpoor below the Rámasamoodrum lake, and some two miles from Morlay, that morning; and that on inquiry they found a woman had been carried off by the man-eater out of the village during the night, but that they had not followed the tracks, as I was not with them. Bussavanpoor was a small hamlet situated in the middle of open rice-fields, then bare as the crop had been cut. There was no jungle to cover the man-

Phototint.

H. M. Wright & Co. London

The Man-eater's Victim

eater's advance, and a tiger had never hitherto been heard of near the village. This attack was therefore the more unlooked for and terrifying to the villagers.

Immediately breakfast was over and an elephant ready I started and soon reached Bussavanpoor. The attack had been most daring. At one end of the single street of the village stood a shady tree, round the base of which a raised terrace of stones and earth had been built as a public seat; within ten yards of this tree the houses began. From the marks we saw that the tigress had crouched upon this raised terrace, from which she commanded a view of the street. The nearest house on one side was occupied by an old woman, the one opposite by her married daughter. The old woman, it appeared, sometimes slept in her own house, sometimes at her daughter's. The night before she had been going to her daughter's, and as she crossed the street, only a few feet wide, the tigress with one silent bound seized and carried her off. No one heard any noise, and the poor old creature was not missed till morning.

When I arrived the son-in-law came forward, and with the other villagers gave an account of the mishap. The son-in-law's grief was really painful to witness; and when he told me how all his efforts to find any trace of his mother-in-law had been unsuccessful, he gave way to the most poignant outbursts. Now, knowing pretty well how little store is placed upon an old woman in India, I could not but regard this display of feeling by the fat young son-in-law as rather strange. A mother-in-law is not usually so highly esteemed (amongst natives) that her loss is deemed an irreparable calamity; and when I further noted that the afflicted youth could only give a shaky account of his exertions in looking for the body, I thought something was wrong, and had him taken along with us.

The tigress had gone towards the river; and though cattle and people had been over the fields, and it was now afternoon, the sun hot, and a strong wind blowing clouds of dust about, the trackers carried on the trail very cleverly, and pointed out that several footmarks had followed it before us, for which the prostrated son-in-law found some difficulty in accounting. After passing through a field of standing rice in which the broad trail was very distinct, and where in the soft mud we got a fair impression of the tigress's pugs, and through some bushes where strips of the woman's blue cotton cloth were hanging, we came to a cocoa-nut garden near the river, and here, amongst some aloe-bushes, we missed the drag. There was a place which looked as if the tigress had lain down, probably to eat, as there were marks of blood; but there were no remains, and her trail continued across the river, whither we followed.

The trackers soon thought something was amiss, as no trace of the body's being dragged could be found. One of them remarked that the tigress would hardly eat the whole at once; whilst, had she carried off the remainder in her jaws, she must have laid it down at the pool in the sandy bed where she had drunk. There was no trace of her having done this. We returned to the aloe-bushes. After examining these for some time, one of the men looked inside a thicket, and with an exclamation turned upon the son-in-law, and giving him a sound box on the ear asked him "what he meant by it." "It" was that the villagers had followed the track with horns and tomtoms (as we subsequently learned) in the morning, and had burnt the remains to avoid police inquiry, the dejected son-in-law acting chief mourner. The ashes of a fire which the tracker now pointed to inside the thicket sufficiently explained the affair.

The woman was of good caste. Had her death been reported, the remains would have been handled by out-castes, and have formed the subject of a sort of inquest by the police at Chámráj-Nuggar; to avoid this, the relatives had burnt the remainder of the body as soon as found. What could be done when the foolish villagers either brought us news too late, or acted in this way? We sent the now truly smitten son-in-law back to the village, bewailing his mother-in-law more sincerely probably than before; and finding that the tigress had gone east we returned to Morlay, it being useless to follow her in that direction.

This death caused great consternation. The villagers concluded that they would now not be safe in their houses at night, and some of the outlying hamlets would have been temporarily abandoned had the tigress lived much longer. But this was to be her last victim; though our chances of killing her seemed still as remote as ever, a few more hours were to end her bloody career.

Next day, the 15th January, I determined upon a more organised plan of hunting her. I arranged that Bommay Gouda and three trackers should go to Iyenpoor, at one end of her usual range, whilst I remained at Morlay. In case of any one being killed near Iyenpoor the men were to let me know immediately; and I supplied them with strychnine, and a gun charged with powder, as a safeguard in their jungle wanderings. The four men started early in the afternoon. About an hour afterwards one of them came running back, pouring with perspiration and covered with dust. I feared some accident had happened until he found breath to say that the party had met the tigress, and that she was then in Kárraypoor Guddah, a small hill two miles from camp. This hill rose to a height of about two hundred feet out of a level cultivated plain. On three sides it was almost bare granite, a few bushes and boulders being the only cover, and the country was open all round it. On the east face there was a little more cover, and the main jungle was distant five hundred yards, but between it and the hill was open ground, so that the tigress was in an isolated position.

I ordered a pad-elephant at once, whilst I thought over the best plan for hunting her. Such a chance as getting her into a detached hill could hardly be hoped for again, and the present situation offered a fine opportunity of extinguishing her. The only plans were to drive her out, or to watch for her return to the carcass. The first I saw would not do, as all the Morlay men,—the only ones amongst the villagers who would have been useful for this service—the others were too terrified,—were at their fields, and time would be lost in collecting them; and though this might possibly have been effected, and the tigress have been driven out, as there was no doubt she would flee readily from a hunting-party, it would be impossible for one rifle to command the entire east side of the hill, at any point of which she might break. I therefore decided to watch for her return to the carcass, and hastily securing a bottle of water and some bread, and an overcoat in case of night-watching, I started.

On the way the tracker told me how the party had met the tigress. They were going across open fields and saw an object moving over the bare ground which they could not at first make out, but presently discovered to be a tiger on the far side of, and partly hidden by, a bullock, which it was half dragging, half carrying towards the hill. They immediately divined it to be the man-eater, and ran shouting towards her, obliging her to drop the bullock at the foot of the hill, up which she sullenly trotted. One tracker then hastened to camp; the others remained to prevent her returning to the bullock before I arrived.

I need here hardly say, except for the information of those who have had no experience of man-eating tigers, that they never refuse a bullock or other prey, if such offers, and that when opposed by man they give way at once. Their tactics in attacking man may be described in one word—surprise; and if discovered in their attempt they generally abandon it. The most confirmed man-eaters never lose the innate fear with which all inferior animals regard human beings, and unless they can stalk and catch an unwary cow-herd or wood-cutter in their own fashion they are not to be dreaded. When the tables are turned on them they flee as readily as other tigers.

When we got near the hill we left the elephant and joined the trackers. The only cover near the carcass was a large rock, but the wind was wrong for watching from that quarter. About seventy yards away in the plain was one solitary bush, not sufficiently large to hide a man; there was neither tree nor other cover within a couple of hundred yards. The situation certainly presented difficulties, and it was not easy to decide what to do. At last I hit upon a plan, and sent the men to bring leafy branches and creepers; when these came we walked past the bush in a body, and the branches were thrown on to make it larger; at the same time Bommay Gouda and I hid behind it, the others going on in full view from the hill. By this manœuvre, should the tigress be watching, she would not perceive that we had concealed ourselves.

We sat till evening. The sinking sun threw a strong light from behind us upon the granite hill, whilst in the distance the Billiga-runguns were bathed in purple light, deepening to blue in the gorges. The smoke of evening fires began to ascend from the small hamlet of Hebsoor away to our left, and a thick white cloud of dust moving slowly along the river-bank towards the village marked the return homewards of the village herds. There would only be sufficient light to shoot at so long a range as seventy yards for half an hour or more, and I was beginning to fear the tigress might not return during daylight. The afternoon had been hot, and I had drunk all the water in the bottle, whilst patient Bommay Gouda, who being of good caste could not drink from my bottle, had sat with his bare back exposed to the grilling sun, watching without a movement. At this time of the year—January—the change in temperature in Mysore, and, in fact, the whole of India, between day and night, is very considerable, sometimes upwards of thirty degrees, and as the sun neared the horizon the evening quickly became chilly; but this disturbed Bommay Gouda no more than the heat in his imperturbable watch. A couple of hares appeared from somewhere and gambolled in the space between us and the hill; and a peacock perched himself upon a rock, and with his spreading fan of purple and gold opened to the full, turned slowly round and round, courting the admiration of a group of hens who pecked about, more intent upon their evening meal than the admiration of their vain swain. Satisfaction with himself, however, rendered him oblivious to the want of homage in his harem.

We had been whispering quietly, as we were out of earshot of the cover, and Bommay Gouda had just said, after a glance at the sinking sun, that it was the time, *par excellence*, for a tiger's return to its prey, when a peahen which had been hidden amongst boulders on the hillside to our right, rose with a startling clamour. This signal, as well known as unmistakable, made us glance through the leafy screen, and there we saw the man-eater, a handsome but small tigress, her colour doubly rich in the light of the sinking sun, walk from behind a rock across the side of the hill, here a bare sheet of blue granite, and come downwards towards the carcass. She halted now and again to look far out into the plain behind us. Was the beast dreaded by thousands, hunted by us so long, and which we had never even seen before, the guilty midnight murderess, really before us? Could nothing but some untoward failure now avert her fate?

I followed her with my rifle so eagerly that Bommay Gouda whispered to me to let her get to the carcass before I fired. When she reached the bullock she stooped, and at the same instant I fired at her shoulder, broadside on, with my express. Bommay Gouda could contain himself no longer, and jumped up before I could stop him; I did so also, but could see no tigress! It was extraordinary, certainly; we looked up the hillside, but she was not there. Was she really a devil as all believed, and had she vanished in air? Just then up went a tail on the far side of the bullock in a convulsive quiver; she had fallen exactly behind the carcass. I ran along the hill-side to intercept her should she gain her feet; but it was all right; she was only opening her mouth in spasmodic gasps, and I settled her. The trackers came up in great glee; they had seen the tigress come over the summit of the hill and enter the rocks on our side half an hour before we saw her: they were in a large tamarind-tree away in the plain. On examining her we found that she was in milk, which was the first intimation we had that she had a cub; she was in the prime of life and condition, and had no lameness or apparent injury to account for her having taken to man-killing.

I may here say that we never killed her cub. It was heard calling to its mother for several nights around Iyenpoor, but we could not find it in the daytime, and it must have died of starvation, as had it lived we should certainly have encountered it.

We soon had the tigress padded (after the trackers had beaten her with their slippers and abused her in dreadful terms); and as our way to Morlay lay through Hebsoor, a messenger started off in advance with the news; and before we had gone far we were met by almost the whole community of Hebsoor, with torches and tomtoms, and begged to parade the tigress through the village. The women and children were delighted, though half terrified, at the sight of her. They had never seen a tiger before, there being no Zoological Gardens handy in India except those of Nature, and the creature was only known as a fearful beast which had eaten papa or mamma or sons or daughters. Soondargowry, the elephant, was fed with cakes, balls of sugar and rice, and plantains by the pleased housewives, and seemed to enjoy herself, though at first the torches and shouts made her rather nervous, especially as this was the first tiger she had carried; she had been a wild animal herself not long before.

On the way to Morlay beyond Hebsoor we entered an extensive stretch of rice-fields, then dry and the crops cut, but yet on the ground, below the Rámasamoodrum lake. Ordinarily fires were kept up at the threshing-floors, and much merriment went on all night; but the dread of the tigress latterly had been so great that all was quiet and apparently deserted. Not a fire was to be seen nor a voice heard. Dotted about the plain were large trees which we knew sheltered the anxious watchers of the threshing-floors below. We had brought torches and men from Hebsoor, and after much calling that the tigress had been shot, voices were at last heard from different trees, lights began to appear, and watchers came from all directions, some shouting to us from the distance to let them come up and see the "dog." We humoured them and they were delighted, all remarking what a huge tiger it was! (was there ever a small tiger to the native mind?)

I was struck at the quick return of everything to its old groove after this. Instead of small bodies of people hurrying fearfully homewards early in the afternoon, and not a villager visible after five o'clock, as had lately been the case, odd villagers now used the path past camp after dusk, and the rice-fields were again the scene of work and harvest merry-making. There was little doubt from the place where the tigress was found that she was the man-eater, though we could not be positive of this, as there were several tigers about. I was relieved, therefore, as time progressed, by finding that all killing ceased. It will be years, however, before the recollection of the Iyenpoor tigress is lost in that part of the country; and her name will be preserved in legend, with exaggerated accounts of her doings and the manner of her death, long after all fact regarding her has been lost.

Contemporary with this tigress there lived in our jungles, amongst others of his race, a male tiger of the largest size. He had been locally known as the "Donnay" tiger for many (it was said upwards of twenty) years. Donnay in Canarese means a cudgel, and is applied to persons rough or rude; this tiger had gained the *sobriquet* from his immense size and imposing appearance. But as far as human beings were concerned he was the most harmless and good-natured beast imaginable; he never hurt the smallest cow-boy, and was really rather liked than otherwise by the villagers. He was, however, a glutton at beef; he required his steaks both regularly and of good quality, and from long experience had become a most accomplished hunter of cattle. There was no avoiding him; he understood the habits and ways of the animal man perfectly, and probably knew all the cow-boys personally. If the cattle were not seized out at graze, it was only because the Don was waiting for them near the village, and would seize one on their return in the evening; but as he had a large circle of villages where he was upon visiting terms, he never degenerated into an oppressor to any community in particular. The only mishap to his friends the Morlayites that ever happened through him was once when he knocked over one of them whilst netting hares in a small ravine within a few hundred yards of the village; in this place the Don had ensconced himself with some designs in connection with his main object in life, beef, and the villagers unwittingly surrounded him with their nets and went inside to beat. In escaping he had to "over" one man to clear the way, but it was universally agreed that it was a pure accident; and though the man died soon afterwards, the Don lost nothing in public esteem by the mischance.

From a long course of immunity from misadventure to himself the Don had come to be regarded as enjoying the especial protection of Koombappa of the temple, the great jungle-spirit; and it was universally believed that when that deity went the rounds of his jungles the Don was chosen by him as his steed. The villagers had even made an effigy of the Don, respectably got up in wood and paint, and looking truly formidable, with a seat on the back, and on wheels, which they dragged round the temple and down to the river in solemn procession on feast-days. Though the Morlayites always entered with delight upon any hunts I organised, hardly any of them believed the Don would ever be shot, and it thus became a point of importance with me to slay this notable rival. Accordingly, as soon as I got through the work of putting everything in train for elephant-catching, I turned my attention during the hot months of 1874 to circumventing him.

It would fill pages to relate our unsuccessful days, the number of times he escaped us in almost miraculous ways, and the devices which I planned against him. He ate quite a small herd of cattle picketed for him, but no return for the outlay was to be had but bootless drives and unsuccessful night-watchings. Never had a tiger so many lives, never did one retain his skin more cleverly. The Don bore no malice withal, and after a day's hunting we would find his huge square pugs next morning close to camp! He was not going to quarrel about trifles, and had probably taken a bullock during the night to relieve us of apprehension on that score.

On one occasion he did a most extraordinary thing, which was, however, quite on a par with his general uncertainty and originality. A cow was in the habit of straying into the fields at night, so her owner secured her by a yoke to an old bullock when sent to graze. Instead, however, of the cow's becoming reformed, the ancient bullock was corrupted through his close association with so loose a character; and one evening, instead of returning to his peaceful pen, allowed himself to be led into a field of *avaray*, a kind of bean (*Dolichos lablab*), of the sweet-smelling flower of which cattle are very fond, close to my bungalow. Whilst feeding here the Don chanced upon the pair, killed the cow, and ate more than half of her, whilst the wretched bullock remained secured by the yoke, a terrified spectator of the scene. The bullock and half-eaten cow were found in this position in the morning. Why the Don left the bullock untouched it is impossible to conjecture, except that he was very lean; he generally slew and spared not. As it happened he supped off this bullock not very long afterwards, when he had not the option of anything more choice.

At last the Don's day came. In May 1874 we had a severe storm; the rain came down in sheets with a biting wind, the cold was extreme, and there was no break for twenty-four hours. The effects of this storm, occurring as it did in the height of the hot weather, were most disastrous over the whole of the south-eastern portion of Mysore and the adjoining Madras district of Coimbatoor. Thousands of cattle died from exposure. Out of a drove containing some hundreds sent from the plains up the Billiga-runguns for the hot-weather grazing I was informed that the sole survivors were three cows. The whole country round Morlay stank for a fortnight with the rotting carcasses—the *Hòlayas*,* vultures, pariah-dogs, and jackals, being unable to dispose of so many animals. I was told that pea-fowl and other birds were picked up dead in some places in the jungle.

However, it is an ill wind that blows no one good. At Atticulpoor, five miles from Morlay, some *Brinjárries* † had an encampment and a large number of cattle. The latter were caught in the jungle in the storm, and in a few hours were so benumbed that they could scarcely move. Whilst returning in this plight to the encampment the Don appeared on the scene. This put a little life into them and they made the best of their way homewards, the Don bowling over all that he could catch. He hunted the main body into the village after killing fourteen; many were dispersed in the jungle and perished from cold during the night. I saw the carcasses of those killed next day, and believe others were overtaken in the bed of a stream, and carried away by the water.

The Don was now set up with beef for some days; he was not likely to leave the neighbourhood soon, and as the ground was saturated and tracking would be easy for some time, I decided with my Morlay men to give him a grand dusting, even though we should fail to bag him. On this point even I had latterly become quite sceptical.

* Outcasts who eat carcasses of animals that have died or been killed by wild beasts.

† Nomadic cattle-graziers, and carriers of grain and salt into remote localities.

Phototint. F. M. Wright & Co London.

The Tiger's Siesta.

The slaughter of the cattle had taken place on the 6th May; the weather was not settled till the 8th; and on the 9th, having made careful arrangements in the interval, I commenced with the only five elephants I happened to have and a hundred picked men.

The trackers soon ascertained that the Don was lying in a cool green cover on the river, just above an old stone dam which raised the water to a sufficient level to be drawn off by the channel that fed the Rámasamoodrum lake. Into this cover the tiger had dragged three carcasses, and had been there since the 7th. The only place I could find to command his line of escape was a point on the opposite side of the river, where the bank was some four or five feet high. His retreat would be across the river to that side, and I commanded the bed for a hundred yards up and down; the stream was about thirty yards wide, and the water some two feet deep. I did not mount a tree, as I could see better on foot.

After the lapse of a quarter of an hour the beat commenced. It was a slow and quiet one, most of the men merely acting as stops outside, whilst the trackers crept in till they found the half-eaten carcasses; the Don was lying near them, but retired from the men's intrusion, which information they shouted to me. The cover was a narrow strip and the men worked him along, following his pugs nearly to the end of it. I now saw him slip noiselessly into the water under the shelter of an overhanging bush about one hundred and twenty yards from me down stream. He stood for a moment, his back almost level with the water, pricking his rounded ears and looking wistfully at the opposite bank. I thought I might not see him again, and fearing to lose even this opportunity I fired. We found afterwards that this shot just grazed his back. He sprang up the bank with a growl, but came face to face with an elephant, upon which he turned and sprang with a short roar far out into the river, and in two or three bounds was up the bank on my side.

The cover which he had gained was a corresponding slip to the one he had left, and ended at the stone dam some four hundred yards further down. I now lost no time in running to the dam to try and head him, as his line would be still down stream. I hoped I had succeeded in this; but when the beaters and elephants had crossed, and beat out the cover, we found he had passed before I got there. We now feared he would travel far. The next cover of importance was a mile away inland, in a ravine between which and ourselves lay a difficult stretch of hard country covered with scrub-jungle, where tracking would be no easy work. The day was hot, however, and we knew the tiger was gorged, so we determined to keep to his track. Leaving the elephants and beaters at the dam, the trackers and I started.

After following the trail across burnt open country for some little way, it turned suddenly sharp down towards the river again, some distance below the dam. The tiger had supped the night before without calculating on being called upon to run for a mile on a hot day across open country, and with a trifle of a hundred pounds or so of beef inside him he apparently did not feel equal to the exertion. That intemperate dinner, the fatal determination to try the small covers along the river, cost the Don his life. Each step that we followed towards the cool river assured us that he was putting himself into our power, and our hopes rose high. The river below the dam flowed rapidly over gravel and rocks; crossing here the Don had entered a thick patch of cover on the opposite bank, about two acres in extent, between the river and the Honglewaddy channel.

I at once took up my post in a small tree on the upper side of the channel with one tracker, as the men said that he would not keep between the channel and river to the next small cover, but would cross the channel, travel under cover of a thin strip of bushes on its upper bank, and recross it into cover further down. Almost at the first shout of the beaters the tiger trotted out and crossed the channel exactly as the trackers had predicted; but as soon as he came to the open ground near my tree he broke into a fast gallop, coming straight under me. He was an immensely heavy tiger, short on the legs, but long in the body and thick set, and as he ran his fore-arms looked bowed out to deformity by the great development of muscle. He breathed heavily as he galloped—a husky chuckle, I fancied, at the way in which he thought he was outdoing us. Had he but looked up and seen the eager eyes and grim rifle following him! As he came under me I gave him the express down into his neck (this shot hit to the right of the vertebræ), and the left took him in the right thigh, downwards; but neither we afterwards found got well into him, though both were severe wounds. He rolled over and over with horrible growls, going heels over head with the sudden check to his impetus; but picking himself up, he got into cover before I could turn in my awkward position. We felt, however, that his fate was sealed, and great was our jubilation.

The trackers and beaters having now collected we made a grand redistribution of forces. Men were immediately started off in couples to all the important points far and near, with instructions to climb commanding trees and to mark the tiger down when we moved him. Having given them time to reach their posts, the trackers and I, on elephants, followed the tiger's blood-trail to the end of the bushes, about two hundred yards, where there was a dense and thorny thicket twenty yards in diameter. Having ascertained that the tiger had not crossed the channel, we knew he must be in this.

The only stanch elephant was old Bheemruttee, which I was riding. I had no howdah, but was mounted on her pad. I had my heavy 8-bore and express, and tucking my legs under the ropes, her mahout and I pushed her into the thick thorns. This was certainly a very unsafe way of looking up a wounded tiger, but there was no help for it. None of the other elephants could be got in; they were Commissariat animals, and were more accustomed to carrying tents and baggage than to this kind of thing. They were now engaged in skirmishing with Tinker, a white terrier I had, a very good dog at finding game; but whenever he appeared on the scene, anxious to do something, he was received with such rapping of trunks, grumblings, trumpetings, and short charges, that he was driven almost wild. The elephants evidently connected the whole disturbance and sense of danger with his presence, and kept a sharp look-out on him in consequence. After being subjected to small showers of earth and pebbles kicked at him with unerring aim, and other demonstrations, the unhappy dog was reduced to such a state that he went and sat in the same bush with the tiger!

When we were within about ten yards of the wounded brute he charged from the front with a loud coughing roar. Bheemruttee did not budge an inch. In another step he would have been visible, and would have had both barrels, but his heart failed and he drew back, growling threateningly. The cover was so matted at four or five feet from the ground that he could not have sprung upon the elephant, but might have seized her legs, though Bheemruttee would doubtless have given him a warm reception. I could not see him as he charged, though he came within five yards.

We pushed on step by step. When a tiger once gives way he seldom makes a home charge afterwards, and in this instance he did not face us again, but jumped into the channel and got into a small cover between it and the river.

Crossing the channel with the elephants, I took up my post in a tree nearly at the end of the cover. There was only one thicket behind me, and then open jungle; the jungle he was in was about two acres in extent. The elephants beat up to me, but the tiger could not be found. I fancied I had heard a slight movement in the solitary thicket behind me during the beat, and a low whistle from one of the stops in a tree in the open beyond now attracted my attention. I called up Bheemruttee and was just getting on to her, when with the usual short roars out the tiger came, and back through amongst the elephants. One of the trackers, who was on foot alongside an elephant, threw his cudgel at the tiger as he passed and got some blood on it, at which he was much pleased. I was in an awkward position, but wounded him slightly with one barrel. I had climbed the tree from the elephant's back; had I gone to it on foot I should have had to do so within a few feet of the tiger, which shows the danger of moving about when a wounded animal is near.

We hunted him about for a couple of hours more, but though I posted myself ahead whilst Bheemruttee drove towards me, and went in on her once or twice, I had not the luck to get another shot at him. Strange to say he would not fight despite all this badgering, but kept moving about with only Bheemruttee following him. It grew late, and we had to leave the sulky monster at nightfall, growling in a thicket into which we durst not put an elephant as there was a high bank in the centre on which he was lying, and from which he might have jumped upon us.

Next morning I was joined by a first-rate sportsman, who had unfortunately missed the fun of this day, and we went to the cover together. We found the tiger had left it, and it was not till the trackers had been engaged for three hours on the trail, across hard stony ground, that we reached a ravine which he had entered. It was not known whether he had remained here or passed out, so we got up trees and the elephants and trackers on them went in. A low growl was soon heard, but the men were divided in opinion as to whether it was one of the elephants or the tiger that had uttered it. They, however, at last ascertained that the tiger was lying in a very dense patch of grass and thorny shrubs, and Bheemruttee was sent for me. When I pushed in, the wounded monster, too sick to move, growled again, and I settled him with the 8-bore. I was obliged to lie in an awkward position on the pad to get this shot, and forgetting to hold the heavy rifle as tightly as I should have done, it recoiled and drove the hammer deep into my nose, so that I was soon almost as bloody as the tiger. I had 12 drams of powder in the cartridge, which had been loaded for bison-shooting. One elephant standing near with several spare men on the pad moved a step forward at the shot, and the rearmost man went a back summersault, clutching at the ropes, and landing upon his feet, rather astonished, at the elephant's tail. She, thinking this was the tiger at last, made off with her cargo at her best pace for some distance, to the general amusement.

Thus ended this famous tiger. We really regarded the fallen hero with pity. One tracker said emphatically, as he leant on his long spear and looked reproachfully at his fellows, "*He never hurt any of us.*" He had died as he lived, managing cleverly to the last, and he perished with clean hands; not the life of one of his old friends could be laid to his charge. We had lived on such intimate terms with him that I, for one, now that the chase in which we had followed him with such ferocious persistency was over, would not have been sorry had he been alive and unhurt again. What would our jungles be without the Don ?

On the way to Atticulpoor, where we were going to meet Captains S. and D., Dowlutpeary, the elephant who had the honour of carrying the fallen hero, behaved very badly. My friend and I were on the pad with the tiger, when a gust of wind carried away his sun-hat; this alarmed her in her already excited state, and away she stampeded despite the mahout's efforts to stop her. We hung on to the tiger, but all nearly came off together. We arrived at Atticulpoor in a very lop-sided condition through her vagaries, the pad and the tiger having slipped to one side, whilst we sat perched on the other to maintain some sort of equilibrium.

We cut off the Don's head, leaving a good neck, and next day managed to stuff it pretty fairly, using arsenical soap and filling it with coir, and paying it constant attention until set and dry. We were astonished at his fatness, and we set to work to boil him down. We got two large pots, and extemporised a fireplace under a banian-tree; here we grilled the pieces of fat in one pot, running off the pure grease into the other, in which it got a final boiling. If boiled until so hot that a drop of water flies from the surface as from molten lead any fat will keep good for months.

Two rolls of fat like those from the inside of a hog were the *pièces de résistance;* the rest was cut from his inside and flanks, and the out-turn of the boil was *twenty-four* ordinary quart beer-bottles, or *four imperial gallons* of pure grease: the natives believe it possesses wonderful medicinal virtues in rheumatism and cattle diseases. From six to nine bottles is a fair yield for a tiger; but, as my men said, the Don's fat was "the fat of a thousand kine." Huge tiger though he was, he only measured 9 feet from tip of nose to tip of tail; but his muscular development was enormous.

CHAPTER XXII.

TIGER-SHOOTING IN SOUTHERN INDIA—(*continued*).

A GRIFFIN'S EXPLOIT—A NETTED TIGRESS—OUR NARROW ESCAPE—A SMALL BOY'S ADVENTURE WITH A TIGER—A VISITOR WELCOME AT ANY HOUR—NEWS FROM POONJOOR—A TIGRESS RESISTS BOMMAY GOUDA'S RESEARCHES—I ASSIST IN PURSUING INVESTIGATIONS—THE CAUSE OF HER CONTUMACY—SHOOT HER ON FOOT—A COURAGEOUS CUB—BOMMAY GOUDA'S WORTHLESS SON—A TIMID TIGRESS—WOUND HER—A MARKER TREE'D—LOOK FOR THE TIGRESS ON FOOT—A CLOSE INTERVIEW—WE RETIRE GRACEFULLY—A DEAD TIGER COMES TO LIFE AND ESCAPES—A NIGHT-WATCH—KILL THE TIGRESS—A CAUTIOUS TIGRESS—MOONLIGHT SCENE—SHOOT THE WOULD-BE DESTROYER—JACKALS AT A CARCASS—THE TIGER'S ARRIVAL—A WARM RECEPTION—SEARCH FOR THE WOUNDED TIGER ON FOOT BY MOONLIGHT—RECOVER HIM.

AMONGST many incidents connected with tiger-shooting which I remember, one happened to a friend and myself in the days of our griffinage, when we had a very narrow escape from a wounded tigress. This tigress had been netted in the method already described, and we had fired at her as she bounded across the line cleared through the enclosure; and as after this neither fireworks nor showers of sticks and stones moved her, we determined to go inside and look her up. We had no elephants, so went in on foot. We, however, designed some method in our madness, and arranged to have a net carried on uprights by men with us, and a good display of spear-points through it, whilst the jungle was to be cleared for our advance by long-handled choppers used under and through the net. If the tigress charged, the spears were to do what they could towards keeping her off, whilst we were to receive her with our rifles, and doubted not our ability to extinguish her!

The service of going inside was, however, quite at a discount amongst the men; they were now giving way and asking each other reproachingly "why they didn't go in," whilst only three headmen expressed themselves ready to accompany us; these were actively engaged in abusing their followers. We should have taken warning from the reluctance to enter exhibited by men who had, before the tigress was fired at, gone in without hesitation; but thinking they only wanted an example, we selected a point of entry where there was a clear space between the nets and the jungle inside of about six feet in width, and entered, followed by three gun-bearers and our volunteers.

In front of us was a thick hedge of bushes, four and a half feet high; this had been thrown up by the spearmen the evening before as a defence whilst waiting for nets to complete the circle; beyond the hedge was dense jungle. I believe other Torreas would have followed, as they were by no means wanting in pluck, but at this moment one of the three spearmen thrust his spear into the hedge to make a gap. The tigress was lying behind it and sprang up with a short roar, rearing on her hind-legs. The upper half of her body only was visible; she held her paws high, and I felt she towered over me, as I was in advance. In another instant we should probably have been struck down, when we both fired into her chest. She glared at us for a brief instant, in which she might certainly have seized either of us, as I was pulling wildly at the trigger of the already discharged barrel, this being my first experience of a tiger at very close quarters, and M. for some reason had not followed up his shot. She at last sank slowly out of sight, much to our relief I have no doubt. She must have been within a few feet of us when we entered, and was probably regarding our calves with much interest through the hedge.

After she disappeared we effected an orderly retreat. She was now seen from outside lying dead, so having fired two more shots into her to make sure, we again went in and brought her out. She had only moved ten feet from where we shot her. One bullet had entered the centre of her chest and had come out alongside her spine; the other had gone through her right shoulder. She was not more than two feet from the muzzles of our guns when we fired, and her chest was singed. We can only account for her not springing upon us by supposing either that the shot near the spine crippled her, or that her astonishment overcame all other feelings when, instead of encountering the "mild Hindoo" of the country, she received such a warm reception from two "Sahibs." Truly a good angel watches over griffins.

A small boy near Morlay had a narrow escape from a cattle-killing tiger on one occasion. He was a youngster, eight years of age, the son of one of my men, and whilst tending sheep had formed his little black blanket into a bag, and swung it, filled with reeds, on his back. Whilst stooping amongst the bushes collecting more reed, a tiger, taking him for a sheep (when hard pressed a tiger does not despise mutton), seized him from behind, or rather seized the bag. The boy fell over; and the astonished tiger, not knowing what to make of the bag of grass in its embrace, bolted forthwith. The boy is now in my employ: his father died of jungle-fever in one of our excursions after elephants. Little "Koombappah" still bears a long scar where the tiger clawed him. This incident illustrates what I have already said about tigers being easily disconcerted when seizing their prey by any unlooked-for *contretemps*.

One night I was awakened by talking outside my bungalow at Morlay, and rousing myself to listen I found it was Bommay Gouda from Poonjoor, who was telling my men in excited whispers something about a tiger. I jumped up and welcomed the old boy, whose information was always to be relied on, and learned that a tiger had killed two cows near Poonjoor that afternoon; that he went to see the carcasses with two Shōlagas, but the tiger would not let them come near the place; that he then took several other men, but the tiger charged out determinedly, and entirely refused them admittance. So he had come to tell me, as such a bold animal could not, he thought, but give good sport.

Bommay Gouda had been unable to get any one to come with him to Morlay, thirteen miles along a jungle-road, so he had set out by himself, and arrived at midnight. Next to his anxiety that the tiger should be proceeded against, the old fellow was particular in requesting that some fitting chastisement should be inflicted on his eldest son for refusing to come with him. I knew the youth in question as an unworthy descendant of so sporting an old sire. How often had he tried to extract rupees from me by making himself very busy when anything was shot and all the danger over! I promised to have him accommodated with a little wholesome discipline.

The moon was bright; the trackers were sent for from the village, and, though it was midnight, were soon in camp, and started at once with Bommay Gouda. I followed at daylight.

The place where the cattle had been killed was a piece of high ground dotted with small thickets and overlooking a bamboo-cover on lower ground, some two hundred yards distant, through which a ravine ran. I saw that if the tiger was in the cover below it would not be likely to leave it after the sun got high, as the country was bare for some distance all round; so we decided to wait till the day got hot before making a commencement.

Bommay Gouda and the trackers were of opinion that we had only to follow the trail and the tiger would dispute an advance and could be shot.

I thought it was probably a tigress with cubs, as it had been so bold in facing man; though Bommay Gouda, on whom its determined resistance to intrusion had made a considerable impression, declared it was a huge male, and showed by holding his arms to represent capacity that its head must be about the size of a schoolroom globe!

We spent the interval till noon in a cool old temple overgrown by a peepul-tree (*Ficus religiosa*), whose roots had displaced, but firmly embraced and upheld, many of the huge old slabs of which it was constructed. It had long been abandoned, and Bommay Gouda said bears used it as a retreat in continued rains.

At twelve o'clock we went to the thicket on the high ground where the tiger had been last seen. We found it quite untenanted. One cow had been eaten, the contents of its stomach and its leg-bones being all that remained; and the other had been dragged down the gentle slope covered with short grass, towards the bamboo-cover. We followed the track in a body, and soon got to the ravine in which we were pretty sure the tiger was lying. The bamboos were in clumps, and there was plenty of room to walk together amongst them; we could see well on all sides, and entered with due caution. We had no apprehension of a tiger's attacking so many men (there were nine of us), who all had confidence in each other, and would stand firm.

When we got to the small sandy ravine, in which a little water was flowing, Koon Sidda whispered "Cubs," and I saw a fine young cub running up the opposite bank from the carcass of the cow, which lay partially eaten in the water. The little glutton was feeding at noonday! At the same moment his mother, who we subsequently found had been lying under a bamboo-clump, came growling threateningly towards us from the direction the cub had taken. She stopped in the bamboo-cover where we could only see her indistinctly.

Had I only succeeded in wounding her now by firing an indecisive shot we might have lost her altogether, and as I knew she would not leave the cover with her cub at that hour unless much frightened, we moved along the bank of the ravine, down stream, to find a better place to cross.

The tigress, however, kept parallel with us, but hidden, just hinting now and then that we were to leave the place. We soon found a crossing and advanced towards the ravine bank, at which she growled more loudly. I looked at my men; their faces beamed with pleasurable excitement, whilst they whispered objurgations and disparaging remarks concerning the "jackal." I felt proud of them.

When we reached the bank the tigress came forward almost to the edge of the opposite cover, about twenty-five yards away. I could see her chest pretty fairly, so I gave her a barrel of my 8-bore. This shot struck to one side of the centre, smashed her shoulder, and came out behind it, as she was not standing so much end on as I thought when I fired. It did not get well into the cavity of the chest.

As I stepped back to be clear of the smoke the tigress made a blind purposeless rush into the ravine. She was hidden by the bank we were on, and took off down the bed under overhanging bushes, and then came up our bank, about one hundred yards away, and lay down under a small tree, where there was a slight depression in the ground, the grass in which was three feet high. We heard her groan and went cautiously towards the spot; but when about thirty yards away I noticed that all was still, and that her heavy breathing ceased. I suspected she was still quite able to do damage, so we agreed to wait for an hour, and moved to a shady tree ten yards further back. At this moment Dod Sidda saw her peering at us through the grass. She had crept to the edge, and was watching us intently with her head between her paws. I knelt, and with a steady shot with the express brained her.

We then went up and found the first shot had smashed her right shoulder, entering at the chest, and raking her down the ribs. She would have died in a few hours. As it was, had she charged on three legs I think I could have settled her; but we did the correct thing in retiring to wait and watch her.

The cub had cleared out at the commencement of the action and we could not find him anywhere. We saw by the marks that there was only one, and we arranged to catch him on the morrow. We sent to Morlay for men and several hare-nets, with which we surrounded the thicket near the remains of the cow next day, where we knew he must be. We went in after him with sticks, when the little beast came straight at me, roaring and striking with his paws in a most determined way. His powers of offence were not very great, but he had all the will. I whacked him soundly about the head with a thick rattan, but he followed up his charge manfully; he was clumsy, however, and fell over, and I got him down, and he was soon secured. He was about the size of a clumber-spaniel, and weighed 40 lb. A stretcher was made, on which on a soft bed of leaves he was conveyed to Morlay. He was too old (about two and a half months) ever to become tame, and I sold him at six months for Rs. 500 (£50). Out of this sum I maintained an alms institution for the old men and women and very young children of Morlay for some months, as grain was very dear at that time, giving them a little rice, curry-stuffs, and tobacco daily.

When we shot the tigress I gave old Bommay Gouda the Government reward, Rs. 50; and whilst paying the men I presented his son, who had, as usual, made himself conspicuous after the tigress was shot, with *one* rupee —a great disappointment and disgrace to him, as he was of good caste, and even his own servants, the Shōlagas, got more.

On another occasion the Morlay people were beating a tigress up to me, and had got her to the edge of a thick cover. She then had to cross open ground for seventy yards to the next patch. I was posted in an old tree between the two covers, somewhat nearer the latter. The tigress was a terribly timid creature, and I heard much fun going on with her inside as she skulked about. The men, in threes and fours, were creeping through the cover, which was pretty open underneath, with spears, cudgels, or fire-brands in their hands, and had hemmed her in by forming a semicircle, with its extremities resting on the open ground at the edge of the cover. A cat pursued by a pack of dogs could not have exhibited more fear than the tigress.

At one time I heard Dod Sidda call to his mates that he could see something red, but did not know whether it was the tigress or an ant-hill. Three or four of them crept nearer to investigate, when the object got up and slunk away. "Who's to the east there? look out! stop her!" they shouted. "Just let us have her by the whiskers in this corner, and we'll hold her till 'Doray' (our master) comes and shoots her," replied Mada and other choice spirits guarding in that direction. The men understood this particular tigress's disposition so well, and the security numbers and coolness give, that they were doing what even I thought rather rash, though I had every confidence in their astuteness in jungle matters.

At last the tigress slyly showed her head in my direction, and looked at the open space before her. For some time I only saw the tips of her ears; she then came forward a few yards, but instead of advancing she crept along the edge of the jungle to outflank the men, and to escape back into the cover from which she had been driven. There was no one to stop her and turn her in my direction, so waiting till she was clear of the men I fired. I confess to having nearly missed her, as the ball, instead of taking her in the shoulder, hit her under the left eye, crossed through the nasal bones, and blew out her right eye, also smashing the articulation of the jaws in her right cheek, making a mummy of her face without killing her. She would have been unable to bite any of us, as we subsequently found, had she got hold of anybody. I missed her with my left as she rushed back into cover.

All had massed together and now came to me, except a few who climbed trees inside the cover to keep watch. These men said the tigress had not gone far back, and was near the place where she entered.

We retired to talk the matter over, and to give her time. After the lapse of half an hour one of the men shouted from a tree inside that the tigress was about fifteen yards from him, but he could not see her for the denseness of the thicket; that she had breathed hard for some time, sobbing occasionally, and at last, after three gasps, had become perfectly still, and he thought she was dead, as she had made no sound for a quarter of an hour. Upon this we approached in a body, and I sent Tinker in, but he returned without showing any excitement, as we thought he would have done had the tigress moved. This was very extraordinary, as she was really alive at the time.

One maniac—a new hand from Hurdenhully, who wanted to distinguish himself—now said he would go in if permitted. My men ironically begged him to do so, offering him the choice of their cudgels, and asking him to leave his address and any messages he had for his relatives. Also to say who would pay them for burying decently what was left of him. One offered to perform the offices of cremation for him, as firewood would cost nothing, if he would give him a legacy of his blanket, and hand it over now. After much bantering he was shoved away from the council circle.

We knew the cover well inside. It was a capital place to look up a tiger. There was no thick undergrowth, and we could see for several yards on all sides, whilst the stems of young saplings and thick leafless creepers would make it impossible for any large animal to make a sudden or straight rush. We had often been through it in search of spotted-deer and pig.

The five best trackers and I decided to go in. We knew where the tigress was lying, from our informant in the tree, and of course made all our arrangements on the expectation of finding her alive, though it appeared probable she was dead. I carried my 8-bore myself, and Jaffer my express. If she were still alive and charged, I felt sure of being able to almost literally blow her from the muzzle, as I need not fire in such cover till she was within a yard, if she ventured so near. If a man can keep cool, a less difficult matter when he knows what to expect than if surprised, it is of course almost impossible to miss a large animal at such close quarters.

We approached the tigress's position with every care, but when we got to about ten yards from where we knew she lay we found that an inequality in the ground hid her from us. We could not go nearer than we then were without risk of being attacked suddenly; so I told one of the men to throw a stone into the depression.

As soon as it fell we heard the crackling of a stick, and the tigress rose slowly, and looked at us over the low bank. Her sound eye was conspicuously bright from the absence of the other, which left a hideous blank, and both sides of her face were covered with blood. We did not know till now that my shot had taken her in that quarter. No one moved or spoke, and without doing anything more the tigress sank down in a few seconds as before. She had not even grinned at us; she only regarded us steadfastly. She could not have been quite dazed by her wound or she would not have paid any attention to the fall of the stone; but though conscious, she apparently did not know exactly what she was about.

I kept her covered with my rifle as she looked at us, in expectation of a charge. I did not fire, as there were sufficient twigs and creepers in the way to render the glancing of the bullet possible; whilst to have enveloped ourselves in the smoke of one barrel with the tigress so close might have been dangerous. Had I let her get to close quarters I could then have given her both almost against her chest.

Upon her disappearance we backed quietly out, the object of our reconnaissance having been attained. A hearty laugh was raised when we were safely outside at the ridiculousness of the whole position—the tigress's lugubrious appearance, her not coming at us as we had expected every instant, and at the tracker "tree'd" close to her. Mada pantomimed the expression of her face for the amusement of the rest of the men, screwing up one eye in hideous contortions. Some inquired of the marker in the tree what he would like for supper!

It was improbable that the tigress would leave the cover, or die, at least for some time, of her wounds. Had she been shot in the body, only time would have been required; but in most cases with head-shots, if an animal is not killed on the spot it improves rather than grows worse with time. I may instance the case of a friend, a noted Madras sportsman, who floored a large tiger some months subsequently from the very tree in which I had wounded this tigress. The tiger dropped as if brained, and did not move a muscle for some time. I was in the tree with my friend, and we remained in our places for a little, the beaters also keeping their distance by order, as we neither wished to spoil the tiger's skin by an unnecessary shot, nor risk approaching him until there could be no doubt that he was dead. Suddenly, without the slightest warning, and after he had lain stunned for at least four minutes, the brute raised his head, regained his legs for a brief moment, and fell forward into the thicket before we could raise our rifles. Leaving my friend (who had a wife and several small children!) in the tree, I got down, and with my men surrounded the cover with nets, and then sent in some small dogs to rouse the tiger. Out the brute came as if nothing was the matter with him, dashed through the nets, was missed by both of us owing to intervening bushes, and made good his escape. So much for head-shots, which should generally be avoided, except at close quarters.

In the present instance we might have gone in again from the other side, and perhaps have shot our tigress as she lay; but there was a safer, though less expeditious, way of bringing her to bag, and as we never courted danger unnecessarily we changed our plans. I sent to Morlay for all the tiger-nets, and by evening the cover was securely surrounded by men and fires; the circle was about a hundred yards in diameter. Our first care on the completion of the circle had been to go in force and cut a path up to the tree where the tracker was, from an opposite direction to our former advance, and we released him without seeing the tigress.

We spent a night of merriment at the surround. I ordered four sheep from camp, which the hunters decapitated at the spot where it was decided to enter the enclosed space on the morrow, and after sprinkling the nets and ground with blood, they mounted the heads on spears and carried them three times round the circle with torches, horns, and tomtoms. Some particular plant also had to be hunted up in the dark, to be worshipped in accordance with the observances on such occasions, at the proposed point of entrance. The sheep were then divided, and between feasting and story-telling the time passed agreeably. One man did a feat which amused everybody. It constituted a good example of the cleverness of natives at this class of performance, of which sword-swallowing, splitting cocoa-nuts on their bare pates, &c., are instances. He took a piece of stout twine about four feet long, and introducing one end, by the aid of a stick, into one of his nostrils, he brought it into his mouth through the hole of communication near the palate, and then drew the end out of his mouth. There was no deception. I tested the genuineness of the feat by observing a mark on the string outside the mouth, and by merely pulling the end brought it down the nostril, and *vice versâ*. To this string the performer tied a weighty stone, and carried it about!

The tigress only showed herself once, about five in the morning, but upon a blazing firebrand alighting on her already damaged head she withdrew promptly. I had got old Bheemruttee from Chámráj-Nuggar overnight, and under her protection I now entered the surround and climbed a tree, past which Bheemruttee soon drove the tigress, still perfectly active, and I killed her.

On this occasion it will be seen that we went into a favourable cover only, and kept well out of the immediate reach of the tigress; and though there seemed every chance of her being dead, we formed our plans on the supposition of finding her still in the flesh, and allowed no one to go in but experienced hands.

I remember an impressive scene by moonlight when watching for a tigress, and I might have seen a bullock seized on this occasion had I not hurried matters at the critical moment. A tigress had killed a cow towards daybreak not far from Morlay, and having no time to eat it had dragged the carcass into a thicket, going herself two miles away to lie up for the day. As there was no chance of getting a shot at her when eating in the thicket, I had a live bullock tied to a stump in a perfectly open space a few yards from the carcass, and a comfortable *mechán* prepared in a tree near. This was one of the favourable occasions which should be chosen for watching. We had tracked the tigress to a distance, so that our preparations could not alarm her; whilst, not having eaten any of the carcass, she was certain to return early in the night.

I commenced to watch at 5 P.M. Daylight had given way about seven o'clock to a brilliant moon that rendered everything almost as distinct as in the day, when I heard the distant, low, grating voice of the tigress as she came up from the cool river-covers where she had spent the hours of a hot Indian day.

The first intimation I had of her close approach was an uneasy movement of the bullock, which had been quietly eating some grass with which we had provided him to make his last moments as happy as possible. I had expected his immediate seizure on the tigress's arrival, and with a view to keeping as still as possible till the noise of the scuffle commenced, I was lying at full length on the elephant-pad, where I had made myself comfortable with a pillow. A hole six inches square had been left in the leafy screen, just above my head, through which to fire.

On hearing the bullock start I raised myself slowly and saw the tigress sitting on her haunches within six feet of the bullock, eyeing him. He was secured to a low stump with only three feet of rope, the remainder being wound round his horns; the tigress was facing me about three feet beyond the stump, the unhappy bullock being at the length of his short tether with the stump between him and the tigress. There was a quiet bloodthirstiness in the scene which was very impressive, and made me remember, even in the excitement of the moment, the many evidences I had seen of similar scenes of unwitnessed midnight bloodshed.

The tigress knew that the bullock could not escape her, but her air was not one of gloating over her victim, but of some suspicion regarding the rope round his horns. I was only ten feet from the ground, and thirty from the tigress. So intense was the stillness that the slightest movement on my part would have been heard.

Neither the tigress nor bullock moved for full three minutes, when the former stood up, satisfied with her investigation, and stepped towards the bullock. Her jaws were within a foot of his throat; there was going to be no spring or rush, and in another moment he would have been seized; when a wish to save the poor helpless beast that had been my only companion during the still watch impelled me, and I drew myself quickly up and put the express to my shoulder, pushing the barrels through the screen, which I had not done hitherto for fear of the moonlight's glinting on them.

At the slight sound I made the tigress drew herself up instantly, standing close to the bullock, and looked straight at my *mechán;* in a moment she would have been off, when I fired at her shoulder and rolled her over. I stood up and gave her another shot over the screen as she was gasping convulsively; this settled her.

Till now the bullock had remained perfectly quiet, but at the shots he commenced to dash madly round and round the stump, roaring with fright, and jumping over the tigress as he passed. My trackers were anxiously waiting at some distance, and on my giving the well-known signal, three barks in imitation of the spotted-deer, they came running up. By this time I had got down the tree and was examining the tigress, and as my bungalow was only half a mile away some more of my people soon hastened up with Soondargowry, the pad-elephant. This young lady was very amusing in all her ways: she walked up to the tigress and sniffed it, and then with a growl, as much as to say, "A tigress to-night, eh! is that all?" knelt down to receive her burden, and marched off sturdily with it to camp.

On another occasion when watching for a tiger by moonlight I was entertained until his arrival by the proceedings of three jackals. Two arrived before sunset, and their elaborate care in approaching the carcass of the bullock the tiger had killed, though it lay in open ground, and they might have known the tiger could not be secreted in very close proximity, was highly amusing. When close to it they would suddenly scamper off, apparently with the object of drawing some movement from the tiger if it were anywhere near. Having at last plucked up courage to begin, one fell to voraciously, tugging away at the skin and making a great noise, whilst the other watched assiduously, never essaying to taste the tempting flesh. Presently the sentry raised every hair on its body and tail, lowered its head into the attitude of a dog in vomiting, tucked in its tail, and made a quick shuffling movement forward, ludicrously like an aggressive turkey. Here comes the tiger, thought I; but presently I descried the cause in the shape of a third jackal. The jealous sentry—the first-comers were evidently a pair—would not permit its approach, and the new-comer at last lay down with an assumed air of unconcern to await its turn.

The jackal had been tugging away at the dead bullock for about half an hour, the sentry not having had its turn yet, when both started away from the carcass and looked fixedly in a direction almost under my tree. They then commenced to make a peculiar sniffing noise, and changed places restlessly, running first a few paces to one side, then to the other, but never taking their eyes off the object that had attracted them. I knew they had viewed the tiger. I had never seen a tiger's reception by jackals before; but their demeanour was so marked that I felt certain to what to attribute it. It was a moment of intense excitement, as I could not turn to look in the direction from which I felt sure the tiger was approaching. Presently the jackals, after changing their note to a sort of sharp twittering, evidently intended to conciliate their lord and master, retired to some little distance, and I shortly heard the quiet, measured footfall of the tiger almost below me. I had the wind in my favour. Presently the striped head and shoulders came into sight, and after one or two pauses their owner marched to the tail of the bullock, and stood looking in the direction of the jackals. He exposed his full broadside towards me, and looked very large in the moonlight. I knew if he lay down he would offer a more difficult mark, so I lost no time in firing. With a loud "wough, wough," the stricken brute galloped heavily away, but I felt sure I heard him fall when about sixty yards distant. I listened—there was a low groan. Again the sound was repeated—the peculiar sobbing groan of a dying animal.

I waited for twenty minutes and then signalled to the trackers, who were in a tree at some distance, in a direction in which we previously knew their presence would not interfere with the tiger's approach. I had been amused by their answering some spotted-deer which began to bark soon after my shot, and not far from me, and which they mistook for my signal. The five naked and odoriferous, but simple and attached fellows, were soon safe with me in the tree. We agreed to wait for half an hour and then to look the tiger up. We considered that there was no necessity to wait till morning, as the moonlight was very bright, and there were only a few trees dotted about in the otherwise open ground, and we were sure of one point—namely, that if the tiger had any strength remaining he would have used it ere this to put as great a distance as possible between himself and us. We decided only to look as far as the spot where I was of opinion he had fallen. If he were not there we would defer further search till morning.

On getting down the tree we found the trail was very distinct. The grass was about eighteen inches high, quite dry, and almost white, as it had seeded and withered. The bent blades, upon which the moonlight glinted brightly, showed a glistening path where the tiger had passed. When we had got to about the spot where I supposed the tiger to be, one tracker pointed silently to a dark object lying where the silvery path ended abruptly, and beyond which the grass stood undisturbed. "It looks like a log," whispered one. "A log with stripes and a tail, then," said the quicker-sighted Murga. It was the tiger, quite dead.

CHAPTER XXIII.

THE PANTHER, LEOPARD, AND CHEETA OR HUNTING-LEOPARD.

THE DIFFERENCE BETWEEN THE PANTHER, LEOPARD, AND CHEETA OR HUNTING-LEOPARD —DISTINGUISHING MARKS—THE BLACK LEOPARD—HABITS AND DISPOSITION OF THE PANTHER AND LEOPARD—THE CHEETA OR HUNTING-LEOPARD—DR JERDON AND GENERAL SHAKSPEAR'S DESCRIPTIONS—ANTELOPE-COURSING WITH THE CHEETA.

THERE are three animals of the genus *Felis* which in India usually pass incorrectly as to two of them, under the common denomination of cheeta. These are the panther (*Felis pardus*), the leopard (*Felis leopardus*), and the cheeta or hunting-leopard (*Felis jubata*). Of the handsome spotted skins that grace many Indian bungalows, and which are generally referred to as cheeta-skins, at least ninety-nine out of every hundred are those of the panther or of the leopard.

The accompanying illustration shows the characteristics of the first and the third named animals, the panther and cheeta. The distinction between the panther and the second, or leopard, is practically small, and lies chiefly in the inferior size of the leopard. The markings, habits, and general appearance (except size) of the two animals are almost identical. But neither can be confounded with the cheeta, even by the most casual observer. It will be seen that, irrespective of the difference of the physical conformation of the panther and cheeta, the spots of the panther (and also of the leopard) are grouped in rosettes, enclosing a portion of the ground colour; whereas those of the cheeta are solid, and are separate from each other.

Between the panther and leopard the distinction is, as above stated, less marked, and is chiefly interesting to zoologists and critical sportsmen. The general observer may be pardoned for confounding the two. All interested in the question in India are aware of the prolonged controversy that has been carried on upon the subject, but most are now, I think agreed in accepting Dr Jerdon's view, based upon the most reliable evidence —namely, that the panther and leopard are mere varieties of the same species. Though they differ greatly in size, the former attaining, in exceptional cases, almost to the dimensions of a small tigress, whilst the latter is frequently, when full-grown, under fifty pounds in weight—in fact, not larger than our large bull-dogs—there is not more radical difference between the two animals than exists between horses and ponies, or large dogs and little ones. Their habits and haunts are almost identical, such divergences as occur being due mainly to the relative powers of the two animals. Thus, whilst the panther seizes cattle as well as the smaller domestic animals, and large deer, the leopard is content with goats, dogs, and even fowls; and in the forest it preys upon pea-fowl, hares, and such small game. Much of the confusion that has arisen regarding panthers and leopards has undoubtedly been caused by the fact that adult animals are found, varying in size as much as do the dray-horse and the child's pony, or the mastiff and toy-terrier. As there are also various shades of colour amongst them, the question has puzzled many who have not had opportunities of examining numerous specimens of both animals. The following distinctions, compiled chiefly from Dr Jerdon's *Mammals*, will, I trust, assist the inexperienced sportsman to a correct classification of such animals of the two varieties as he may shoot.

The panther (*Felis pardus*) varies in size from six to eight feet from nose to tip of tail. Ground colour generally pale fulvous yellow, or rufous fawn, with dark spots grouped in rosettes, except on the spine and towards the extremities, where they are distinct black marks. Fur short and close. The ground colour is lighter in old than in young animals.

The leopard (*Felis leopardus*) varies greatly in size, but probably never exceeds six feet in length from nose to tip of tail. Some individuals are little larger than a large tiger-cat. The leopard is stouter in proportion to its size than the panther, and the skull is rounder. The spots are more crowded, and the fur is longer and looser than in the panther.

A variety of the leopard perfectly black all over, in which the spots show but indistinctly as still darker marks, is not altogether uncommon in Mysore and other parts of India, and is less rare in certain localities in the Malay peninsula and Java. In Mysore it is never found out of forest-tracts. In its habit of confining itself entirely to heavy forests it differs somewhat from the common leopard. I have never seen the animal in its wild state, but I have seen two nearly full-grown ones in captivity, and more than one skin. The two I saw are now alive in England, and are apparently cubs of one litter. This circumstance would seem to militate against the view

Phototint

H. M. Wright & Co London

(1). Panther, (Felis Pardus).
(2). Cheeta, or Hunting Leopard, (Felis Jubata).

held by some naturalists and sportsmen that black leopards are only *lusi naturæ;* and the fact that they never occur amongst ordinary leopards in the open-country localities of Mysore also seems to point to the conclusion that the black leopard is quite distinct. On the other hand, there is said to be no anatomical distinction between the two animals, and testimony exists to show that amongst ordinary leopards, from heavy forest tracts at least, melanoid individuals do occur. The following information on this point has been obligingly given me by the director of the Zoological Society's Menagerie at Amsterdam: "In regard to the black leopards from Java my experience leads me to suppose them to be merely a variety of the *Felis leopardus* from Java. We have had two young ones from a black female; one was black, the other of the ordinary colour. This female took the male in liberty, so there is no proof as to what the father was. The black leopards from Java have all sorts of shades, from jet-black to light brown." It would appear from this, and other evidence, that whilst the black leopard is entirely confined, at least in India, to heavy forest tracts, it does not there refuse to inter-breed with the ordinary leopard.

Both panthers and leopards are exceedingly common in Mysore. I will proceed to describe their habits as I have observed them.

The panther takes rank after the tiger among the beasts of prey of India. Though his powers of offence are inferior to those of his larger relative, he frequently proves himself a more dangerous animal for the sportsman to encounter, as less provocation suffices to rouse him, and he is exceedingly courageous in his retaliation. The panther does not systematically frequent heavy forests. His favourite resorts are the light belt of jungle on the borders of, or intersecting, cultivated lands, and, even more frequently, the rocky hills, or *droogs,* formed of large masses of rock piled in wild confusion upon each other, and forming endless caverns from which he cannot be dislodged. The leopard is also found in these places, though his more favourite habitat is forest country. The isolated hills mentioned are a peculiar feature of Southern and portions of Central India, and rise abruptly from the level plains, being often entirely free of brushwood and trees. From their strongholds in these panthers and leopards watch the surrounding country towards sunset, and descend with astonishing celerity and stealth, under cover of the rocks, to cut off any straggling animal among the herds or flocks on their return to the village at nightfall.

From their habit of lurking in the vicinity of the habitations of man, to prey upon cattle, ponies, donkeys, sheep, goats, and dogs, the panther and leopard are frequently brought into collision with Indian villagers; and a panther or leopard being mobbed in a garden, or field of sugar-cane or standing corn, from which he will charge several times and bite and claw half-a-dozen people before he is despatched or makes his escape, is no uncommon occurrence in India. At night panthers and leopards frequently find their way into goat-folds or calf-pens, climbing over walls or the roofs of native huts in their burglarious inroads, and carrying off their prey with great boldness and agility. They appear to have a peculiar *penchant* for dogs; and I have known many villages in parts of Mysore where panthers and leopards were numerous, in which not a dog was to be found, or perchance but one or two, which would be pointed out by their owners as "very lucky" ones, they having escaped, sometimes from the very clutches of their unceasing foe, whilst their companions had successively fallen victims to his stealthy attacks.

I have never known a case of a panther or leopard taking to man-eating in Mysore, though many such instances are recorded from other parts of India. Further information regarding the habits and disposition of these animals will be gleaned from a perusal of the next chapter, which I propose to devote to recitals of adventures in hunting panthers and leopards.

The cheeta or hunting-leopard is, as I have already shown in the game-list of Mysore (Chapter III.), almost unknown in the province. During thirteen years I have only seen two skins, both shot by native shikáries. I have never seen the animal in its wild state myself. I shall therefore only give a short description of it, which I transcribe from Dr Jerdon's *Mammals*, and from an article that appeared in *The Field* of September 7, 1867, on the *Felidæ* of India, from the competent pen of Major-General H. Shakspear.

Dr Jerdon's description is: "Bright rufous fawn with numerous black spots, not in rosettes; a black streak from the corner of each eye down the face; tail with black spots and the tip black; ears short and round; tail long, much compressed towards the end; hair of belly long and shaggy, and with a considerable mane; pupils circular; points of the claws always visible; the figure slender, small in the loins like a greyhound; limbs long. Length, head and body, about 4½ feet; tail, 2½; height, 2½ to 2¾ feet.

"The hunting-leopard is found throughout Central and part of Southern India, and in the north-west from Khandesh, through Sind and Rájputána to the Punjaub."

Major-General Shakspear says: "The cheeta or hunting-leopard has the foot and toe-nail of the dog, without any more retractile power, and is therefore canine. Though his height is equal to the panther's, he does not weigh much more than half as much as that animal. He is as truly made for speed as the greyhound—indeed he must be for a short distance much faster, since he can give the antelope a start of a hundred yards and catch him in another two hundred; and the antelope is the fastest known animal in the world, the greyhound having no chance of running him down on the hard soil which he usually roams over. The great depth of chest, long forearm, hocks nearly down to the ground, light sinewy limbs, prominent elbow-joints, and very light waist, all denote his vast speed.

"The cheeta is tamed and taught to hunt antelope. For this sport he is never caught until he has come to his full strength, for if caught young he never acquires the speed and power necessary to course and kill the antelope. Hunting-leopards used to be kept a good deal by wealthy natives for the sport they show, and sometimes by European gentlemen. They become very tractable and tame, though, being kept for coursing only, and not as pets, they are not allowed to run loose. They are not more formidable than a large dog, and I never heard of their attacking man."

Jerdon says: "I had a young one brought to me at Saugor, only a very few days old. I brought it up with some greyhound pups, and they soon became excellent friends. Even when nearly full grown it would play with the dogs (who did not over-relish its bounding at them), and was always sportive and frolicsome. It got much attached to me, at once recognising its name (Billy), and it would follow me on horseback like a dog, every now and then sitting down for a few seconds, and then racing on after me. It was very fond of being noticed, and used to purr just like a cat. It used to climb on any high object—the stump of a tree, a stack of hay—and from this elevated perch watch all round for some moving object. As it grew up it took first to attacking some sheep I had in the compound, but I cured it of this by a few sound horse-whippings; then it would attack donkeys, and get well kicked by them; and when not half-grown it flew one day at a tame full-grown nil-ghai, and mauled its legs very severely before it could be called off. I had some chikáras (*Gazella Bennetii*) caught, and let loose before it to train it. The young cheeta almost always caught them easily, but it wanted address to pull them down, and did not hold them. Occasionally, if the antelope got too far away, it would give up the chase; but if I then slipped a greyhound, it would at once follow the dog and join the chase."

Regarding the mode of coursing antelope with the cheeta, Dr Jerdon quotes as follows from Buchanan Hamilton: "On a hunting-party the cheeta is carried on a cart, hooded, and when the game is raised the hood is taken off. The cheeta leaps down, sometimes on the opposite side to its prey, and pursues the antelope. If the latter are near the cart the cheeta springs forward with a surpassing velocity, perhaps exceeding that which any other quadruped possesses. This great velocity is often continued for three or four hundred yards. If within this distance the cheeta does not seize his prey he stops, but apparently more from anger than from fatigue, for his attitude is fierce; and he has been known immediately afterwards to pursue with equal rapidity another antelope that happened to be passing. Sometimes, but rarely, the cheeta endeavours to approach the game by stealth, and goes round a rock or hill until he can come upon it by surprise."

Mr Vigne (quoted by Jerdon) says: "It requires strong epithets to give an idea of the creature's speed. When slipped from the cart he first walks towards the antelope with his tail straightened and slightly raised, the hackle on his shoulder erect, his head depressed, and his eyes intently fixed upon the poor animal, who does not yet perceive him. As the antelope moves he does the same, first trotting, then cantering after him; and when the prey starts off, the cheeta makes a rush, to which (at least I thought so) the speed of a race-horse was for the moment much inferior. When we consider that no English greyhound ever yet, I believe, fairly ran into a doe antelope, which is faster than the buck, some idea may be formed of the strides and velocity of an animal who usually closes with her immediately.

Jerdon adds: "I have often seen the cheeta, when unhooded at some distance from the antelope, crouch along the ground and choose any inequality of surface to enable it to get within proper distance of the antelope. The cheeta, after felling the antelope, seizes it by the throat, and when the keeper comes up he cuts its throat, and collects some of the blood in the wooden ladle from which it is always fed. This is offered to the cheeta, who drops his hold, and laps it up eagerly, during which the hood is cleverly slipped on again. Shikáries always assert that if taken as cubs they are useless for training, till they have been taught by their parents to pull down their prey. This opinion is corroborated, in part at least, by my experiences with the tame one mentioned above."

CHAPTER XXIV.

SPORT WITH PANTHERS AND LEOPARDS.

MY FIRST INTRODUCTION TO THE PANTHER—THE SHRÁVANA BALAGŌLA IMAGE—A NOCTURNAL VISITOR—A LARGE PANTHER AT MUDDOOR—UNSUCCESSFUL HUNTS AFTER HIM—BAG HIM AT LAST—TWO PANTHERS NEAR RÁMANHULLY—THEIR STRONGHOLD—DRIVE THEM—IN A BUSH WITH THE PANTHERS—SHOOT ONE—HINTS ABOUT POSTING MARKERS—THE TORREAS OF MYSORE—NEWS OF A LARGE PANTHER—HIS HAUNTS—JAFFER'S DIPLOMACY—HUNT THE PANTHER—AN OBTRUSIVE BOAR—THE PANTHER TURNS RUSTY—WOUNDS A BEATER—ESCAPES TO ANOTHER STRONGHOLD—WE ATTACK HIM THEREIN—THREE MORE MEN CLAWED—THE PANTHER ESCAPES—SHOOT A FEMALE PANTHER AND CAPTURE HER CUBS—INTRACTABILITY OF PANTHER-CUBS—A PIG-HUNT—A NIGHT-RAID INTO CAMP BY A PANTHER—SHE CARRIES OFF OLD ROSIE—PROMPT PURSUIT—ROSIE'S ESCAPE—SHOOT THE PANTHER.

THE panther was the first wild animal of the dangerous order that I met with after my arrival in India. I had been but a few months in the country when I accompanied a friend to a place called Shrávana Balagōla, forty miles N.N.W. from Seringapatam, where he was desirous of photographing some ancient monuments of the almost extinct (as to Mysore) sect of *Jains*. Shrávana Balagōla is a small town of about one hundred and fifty houses, and is situated, together with a very fine tank or reservoir about four hundred feet square and forty deep, between two remarkable hills, each formed of a mass of granite covered more or less with enormous boulders that have been riven and piled up in the most singular positions by some violent convulsion, and which form large caves and dens that shelter panthers and leopards, to the damage of the neighbouring flocks. These hills are characteristic specimens of the piles of rock that abound in the Mysore territory. Upon one of the hills there is a huge image of a naked human figure in granite. It is upwards of sixty feet high, and about twenty-five feet across the shoulders. From the thighs upwards it is in full relief; downwards it is attached to the rock behind. It is evident that a lofty, towering rock has been cut away, leaving the figure; and it appears that the whole summit of the hill has been levelled, by incalculable labour, to form the plateau on which the image and its surrounding wall and sacred buildings stand. The face of the rock at the feet of the figure is cut away, so that the image appears to stand upon a lotus-flower. On both sides, near the feet, the rock is hewn to resemble white-ant hills, with sacred serpents emerging from their galleries. Though the image is certainly one, probably two, thousand years old (the ancient inscriptions on the rock at its feet cannot be deciphered with certainty at the present day), its surface has undergone no change, and it appears as if just fresh from the hands of the sculptor. The face has the serene expression generally seen in Buddhist statues; the hair is curled in short spiral ringlets all over the head; while the thick lips and long ears give the impression of an Egyptian pattern for the statue. Could a model of this stupendous testimony to the state of art and culture of long-forgotten ages be erected in England it would dwarf Cleopatra's Needle into insignificance, and would truly astonish the natives around the Thames Embankment.

We arrived at Shrávana Balagōla about midnight, having been piloted across many miles of wild open country by successive village *talliáries,* or watchmen. The village was wrapt in slumber as we rode through its silent main street. We dismounted and left our ponies here, in charge of their grooms, and proceeded with the coolies and guides, who carried our bedding and provisions, to the building in the centre of the north side of the tank, and which is seen in the illustration (from a photograph taken by my friend) facing the beholder. This building, it will be observed, is open on the side facing the tank; it is composed of hewn granite, and the roof is supported by massive granite pillars. Here we intended to sleep till morning.

The whole scene was bathed in a flood of soft light from a full moon, and the contrast between the bold and frowning masses of granite, and the quiet slumbering sheet of water between them, was effective and engaging. As I walked along behind our party, lingering to enjoy the scene alone, I was startled by a low jarring sound in the rocks just above me. It was repeated five or six times in succession, beginning low and swelling into a harsh grating noise, somewhat like that caused by a pump that will not draw, but much louder. It reverberated across the silent tank, and was re-echoed from the opposite hill. I knew it must be caused by some wild animal of the dangerous order, and on joining my friend he told me that the guides said there were several panthers frequenting the caves in the hill. This was exciting news to me, and gave a double interest to the locality. How I longed to be able to converse in Canarese that I might

Phototint H. M. Wright & Co. London.

Granite Rocks at Shrávana Balagōla.

question the guides about the animals! During the time we were preparing a cup of tea the panthers frequently grunted out their peculiar harsh cry, which half delighted, half frightened me; and I remember that before I followed my friend's example of falling asleep on a mattress on the floor, I frequently glanced at the small open doorway which led through the side of the building, and which appeared to me to be peculiarly adapted to admitting the panthers to the reservoir, to slake their thirst thereat in case they felt so inclined. I hardly thought, however, that they really used this means of reaching the water, or I certainly should not have fallen asleep.

I had not been unconscious long when I was awakened by a low growl from my dog "Spot," which slept at my feet on the mattress. I raised myself instantly. Horrors! there was a panther within a few feet of my toes, its head and shoulders clearly outlined against the sheet of silvery water outside the open building! I should say that the floor of the building was divided into two levels, one half being raised some three feet above the other, like a stage. The door through which the panther had found ingress opened on to the lower level, and coming through this with the intention of drinking, ignorant of the presence of two sleepers on the raised portion, the animal had smelt us, or the dog, and when I started up was standing on its hind-legs and peering at us! Had I not awoke it would doubtless have carried off the dog. But this was not to be Spot's fate at that time, though he fell a victim to a leopard two or three years later, having been carried off from the verandah of a house in Hoonsoor.

The panther withdrew almost before I had time to shout. My friend took all this very coolly when I aroused him, and beyond anathematising the panther and turning over, paid no heed to the occurrence. I naturally conjured up visions of being pounced upon when asleep, exaggerating, like all novices, the danger connected with unwounded wild animals, and my further slumbers were not of the most tranquil description. Next morning, whilst my friend busied himself about his photography, I took my gun, and with several natives clambered over the rocks, expecting, I do believe, to fall in with the panthers! I was informed that they not unfrequently basked upon the rocks for an hour or two in the early morning sunshine, but of course it was not likely such wary animals would be surprised by a party such as I headed. I have since shot panthers and leopards by marking them from below when basking, and then stalking them alone; but it requires intimate knowledge of the locality, and of the animal, to make a successful advance upon such watchful creatures.

In the evening I watched with two natives over the entrance of one of the panther's caves, hoping they might show themselves; but though we heard them growling and snarling at each other within, night fell without their emerging, and we made the best of our way down.

I made many subsequent fruitless attempts to bring panthers and leopards to bag in rocky hills of this description, but it was not till I had killed even more than one tiger that I succeeded in outwitting my first panther. This animal cost me much labour and perseverance, but was a splendid specimen, and an ample reward for my past ill-luck. He was a male of the largest size I have ever myself seen (seven feet two inches from nose to tip of tail), and had lived for many years in an isolated *droog*, or hill, about three miles to the south-east of the travellers' bungalow at Muddoor, on the road from Bangalore to Mysore. The country thereabouts is quite open and free from jungle. Whilst staying at Muddoor I had at different times made attempts upon his life, but he was exceedingly cunning, whilst I was very ignorant, which combination did not result in affording me the close interview I sighed for. However, I speedily gained some knowledge from my failures, and the day of course came round when perseverance was crowned by success. Two days before this, on a blazing hot afternoon, I had climbed the hill with a native shikárie of the locality, and having secured a kid, which will always bleat in a manner most seductive to panthers and leopards, in the path down which the panther generally came, as reported by the villagers, we watched from the shelter of a rock near. About sunset I heard a slight noise behind us. I turned, expecting to find myself face to face with the panther, but there was only a large monkey with his family, sitting on a rock watching us. We knew at once that the panther must be on the other side of the hill, and that the monkeys had come here to avoid him, as panthers and leopards prey upon them. We therefore descended, and returned to Muddoor. In Southern India it is always dark by 6.45 P.M., so that there is not much time for watching after sunset, unless there is a brilliant moon.

The next afternoon we again went after the panther, ascending the hill as before in the blazing sun, to gain our posts before he should be stirring, and tied another kid in a likely spot. Its bleating must have been heard all over the hill; but unfortunately a heavy thunderstorm succeeded the sultry day, and we were driven to Muddoor amidst the pelting rain. I have observed that few wild animals venture forth during the terrific crashes of thunder and the lurid lightnings of Indian storms, so we deemed it useless to watch during the strife of the elements.

The Fates seemed in favour of the panther. Next day, however, I returned to the hill. It was still early in the afternoon, so I determined to take a stroll round its base. Several villagers were with me, when one suddenly pointed upwards to the panther lying under an overhanging rock, on the shady side of a cluster of rocks, and surveying us, and the country below, from his comfortable and secure position. He looked very fierce and beautiful through my field-glasses; but thinking I should have more leisure to admire him after I had shot him, if peradventure such good fortune was to attend my efforts, I walked on with the men as if we had not observed him—a point on which many animals are very sagacious—and when out of sight we held a consultation as to what we should do. It was decided that two of the men should drive some donkeys, which happened to be proceeding along the village path laden with salt, past the panther's position in full view, whilst I and the native shikárie stalked him from above.

Would that I had gone by myself, as the fellow spoilt the first act of the sport. I had nearly reached the point from which I expected to get a shot at the coveted animal when the shikárie clinked my spare gun against a rock he was climbing. I ran hastily forward, but only caught a glimpse of the panther as he jumped down amongst the boulders below. Presently I heard the spare men beneath hallooing amongst the lower rocks. I ran forward as best I could over the uneven ground till I came near them, when I found that, seeing the panther get off the rock, they had run forward to the cave for which they knew he would make, and they had now got on to a large rock and were hallooing and waving their cloths to keep him out of his retreat. The panther had come up, but fearing to enter the cave, was sitting behind a rock at some distance. I could not see him from where I stood, though the men were able to do so. I had been told that he had another cave on the top of the hill, to get to which I knew he must come directly past where I was standing, so I took up my position above a wide, smooth, sloping surface of rock, across which he must pass; and I knew that being thus above him I should at least keep him back, as if I failed to kill him with my first shots, when wounded he would be more likely to roll down the rock than to come at me.

I now called to the men to frighten him away, if possible towards me; but not an inch would he move. He evidently considered me the dangerous person, partly perhaps from my not making a noise like the others, as also from deliberately standing in his path. Getting tired at last of waiting, but still against my better judgment, I agreed to the request of the men on the rock to join them and shoot the panther from their position. No sooner had I left the way clear and commenced to descend, than up the panther got, and made towards where I had been. The men screamed, "He's going! he's going!" I heard he was, though he was partly hidden by a few bushes that grew near the spot. I turned and endeavoured to regain my position, but I was no match for the panther at climbing. As I scrambled forward I saw the yellow-and-black-spotted hide of the brute through the fringe of bushes as he glided easily upwards, about eight gun-lengths distant. I could not see him distinctly enough to make sure of a vital part, and I was fully imbued with the popular idea—which I have since, however, come to regard as resting upon rather doubtful foundation, as I have seen as many beasts charge up hill as down—of the danger of firing at a formidable beast on higher ground than one's self. However, there are cases where cautious calculations weigh little; and after my various disappointments with this animal, I had no intention of letting him escape me if possible. I therefore promptly fired both barrels of the rather inadequate weapon I was armed with—a 14-smooth-bore—into his ribs. There was a deep growl, a momentary silence, and then the panther rolled down the smooth rock on the far side of the bushes, whilst I seized my spare gun from my attendant, and we endeavoured to reach a more safe position. The wounded beast was, however, beyond doing mischief, and after a few struggles he died at the foot of the shelving rock where he lay. Both bullets had passed completely through him close behind the shoulders.

Need I dilate upon the delight of a young sportsman at such an issue to his hunt? The men shared my pleasure, and plumed themselves with just cause upon their action in intercepting the panther's retreat into his cave. Had they not done this I should probably never have had a shot at him. It was doubtless well for us that this beast was killed outright, as he was an old male, and would not have been likely to stand on ceremony after being maltreated. Amongst such boulders and chasms as those around us, an attack might have been fatal from falls from the rocks without the assistance of teeth or claws. Some of the men ran to their village for a couple of bullock-yokes for carrying the panther, and quickly returned accompanied by almost the whole community, male and female, young and old. The panther was quickly raised aloft by half-a-dozen willing fellows, and carried to Muddoor. We were rather long on the way through having to parade the beast through several villages on the line of march. The panther had been, with others of his race, on rather more intimate calling terms at these places than the owners of stock had hitherto relished; but they welcomed him heartily under the circumstances of his present visit, and the bearers collected a few pence for the obligation of carrying him to the chief inhabitants' doors.

The next panther I killed was one of two which some villagers informed me had been long settled in a strip of bush-jungle and thickets bordering the Tippoor channel, one of the irrigation works drawn from the Cauvery river, and of which I then had charge. These panthers were represented to have killed most of the dogs in the villages for some distance round, and to be very destructive among the ryots' sheep, goats, and light cattle. It was the height of the hot weather, and I had not had any shooting to speak of for some time, so I was delighted at this chance of breaking the monotony of everyday work. I sent two trusty shikáries with the villagers to bring more certain news of the panthers' retreats, and their account being favourable I asked the ryots to collect a hundred men next day, and promised to ride over to their village, Rámanhully, that evening after dinner, so as to be ready to commence early next morning.

At 8 P.M. I started for my tent near the village. In front four coolies carried my cot and bedding on their heads. After them came my cook and "boy"—a youth of about fifty—and a couple of coolies carrying the cooking utensils. In front of me two shikáries bore my rifle and smooth-bore, their polished barrels glancing brightly in the moonlight. Then myself on pony-back. Behind, a horse-keeper and two dog-boys leading my dogs. Another man with my shot-gun brought up the rear. We travelled by the footpaths across fields till we came in sight of my tent, pitched under a fine banian-tree, and here I found the hundred men ordered duly collected. When I rode up they blew a loud blast on a horn, and whilst the cook was getting coffee ready I sat outside and talked with their headmen about tomorrow's arrangements. Most of the beaters had rusty spears—heirlooms of a time when this part of the country was better wooded, and their forefathers used them in killing wild pigs—and these, long unused, they now busied themselves in cleaning. They had also got together a good number of nets, which they were overhauling and patching by the firelight.

By 6 A.M. next morning the beaters had eaten their morsels of rági-bread, and we were on our way to the cover. We found the night's tracks of the panthers near it, and the fresh skulls and remains of two dogs which, despite the scarcity of those animals in the villages near, they had managed to surprise during their nocturnal prowlings. The cover was a strip of bush-jungle about half a mile long, and nowhere more than a quarter wide. It was bordered on one side by the Tippoor channel and open rice-fields, then bare and dry; and on the other three the country was open. The cover was not very dense, as most of the bushes had lost their leaves under the influence of the hot winds and scorching sun of March, and the panthers' only strongholds were a few evergreen thickets which afforded cool lying during the hot hours of the day. At one place, about the middle, the cover narrowed very much. As we were not certain in which half the panthers then were, we set up a line of nets across the narrow part, whilst, in the absence of trees or other vantage-ground, I sat in a thick bush some little distance behind the nets. I was fenced in on three sides so as to be invisible, whilst the fourth was only screened breast-high as I knelt, to permit of my shooting. The bushes in front of me were cleared so that I might see the panthers as they crossed the open space. The line of nets was intended to check them if going fast, and thus afford me a better shot.

Having sent the beaters to commence with the less likely half of the cover, I took up my position with my three guns and a trustworthy man who knew the locality well. We scarcely expected to find the panthers in this beat, as their chief strongholds were in the other portion; but it is often necessary to beat out the thinnest parts of a cover first, as if the animals sought happen to be in them they may be scared away by the noise required for beating the thicker portions before the thinner, whereas if in the dense cover they will not leave it for the slight disturbance necessary to drive the more open parts. Our conjectures were correct; the first drive proved blank. We were now certain of the panthers being in the other half of the cover, and the men began the drive with a will. The excitement of waiting for such brutes as panthers, seated on the ground, must be experienced to be understood. They usually come so quietly as scarcely to be heard, whilst there is a certain amount of danger in the sportsman's position that makes it interesting. He is kept almost painfully on the alert from the beginning to the end of the beat.

On this occasion the beaters had not been at work very long when I heard them calling, "There they go! there they go! look out, sir, they're coming towards you!" The panthers had been thoroughly frightened, and as the cover was thin, they had given up their usual sneaking dodges, and now came galloping along like two large dogs. I could not see them, but presently we heard them as they made their way rapidly through the bushes towards the narrow waist of the cover where we were ensconced. It unfortunately happened, however, that the beaters were some distance behind, so the panthers decided to take breath, and instead of crossing the open space in front of me, they bounded from behind our position into the very thicket in which we sat hidden! I was somewhat of a novice at this time, and I must say I was startled by the suddenness of the occurrence. The two beasts panted and growled from the combined effects of their run and their ire at being thus rudely roused, and sat themselves down in the middle of the thicket within a couple of yards of us, behind! I of course thought they would attack us, and the fact of having my back to them added a great deal to the unpleasantness of the position. It was fortunate we were screened in, as had the panthers come thus suddenly to close quarters they would assuredly have made an attack, from their own fears. As it was, winding us, but being merely aware of the close proximity of danger without seeing the cause, they sprang away towards the nets, which they could not see from the bush. With the retreat of the enemy I was myself again, and seeing that my chance of a shot from our stronghold was gone, I scrambled out and ran after them. I had not gone a dozen yards when I saw one panther hesitating at the nets. I instantly gave it right and left, and seized my second gun from my companion, who had fortunately followed in my steps. The panther had its head towards the nets, which it instantly charged and knocked down; and the other panther went over the gap like a flash of lightning, not giving me time for a shot. I then brained the first panther, and the beaters coming up it was taken under shade, and we proceeded to redispose ourselves for beating up the escaped animal, which was the male, and much the larger of the two.

I had unfortunately, however, neglected to post men at a distance to observe if he left the cover. This should never be neglected, and the young sportsman will find a little time spent in posting markers before a beat is commenced is rarely time lost. When an animal gets past the guns, or is temporarily lost sight of, immediate information as to the line he has taken, and a prompt chase, often lead to his being found; whereas if there be no markers to direct the hunt, insurmountable difficulties, in loss of time or perplexities of tracking, may be met with. In this instance we had made too sure of our game. We had not expected them to leave the cover. After beating twice through it without finding the escaped panther we therefore had nothing to guide us in our further search for him. The ground was dry and hard, and tracking impossible; and it was equally likely that he might have betaken himself to some jungle-covered islands in the Cauvery, about a mile away, or to some light jungle and broken ravines beyond, or even to some dense patches of sugar-cane nearer at hand. We did what we could. We searched the nearest likely places; but the day was hot, and I was soon tired, and we had to give up the chase. The panther must have crossed a wide expanse of open ground in leaving the cover whichever direction he took, and had two or three men been posted on the chance of such a contingency, there is no doubt we should have killed him in a very short time after his companion. However, wisdom can only be gained by experience.

This panther never returned, as far as we knew, to the cover. He must have finally retired to some rocky *droogs* on the other side of the Cauvery, from which, indeed, the pair was known to have come originally. The ryots were on the look-out for some days, but nothing more was seen of him; and the last time I visited this locality the jungle had been almost destroyed by woodcutters, and it will probably never again harbour a panther. Such changes may be very satisfactory from a utilitarian point of view, but the sportsman cannot look upon the transformation of spots where he once followed his favourite pursuits without a feeling of regret. The supplanting of natural and animal attractions by corn-fields and cattle-pens robs localities of all their romance.

The men who had assisted me in hunting these panthers were of the *Torrea* caste, the professional hunters of Mysore. The gradual decrease of game attendant upon the spread — or it may be more correct to say resumption—of cultivation in tracts that were laid waste in the time of Hyder and Tippoo, has of late years debarred the Torreas in great measure from following their former pursuits. Pig and deer have decreased or disappeared in many places where they were formerly numerous, and nothing larger than hares or pea-fowl now remain to the Torreas. These remarks apply to the outlying coverts in the province only, as the great belt of forest that almost encompasses Mysore is probably, owing to forest regulations and other causes, now as full of game as it ever was. Much of the old spirit and traditions survives among the Torreas, even among those almost cut off from opportunities of the chase; and in such hunts as the one with the panther, they are proud of being called upon to show that their craft is not entirely lost. I always took pleasure in encouraging this feeling among those of the tribe with whom I became acquainted.

The praise I had bestowed upon the villagers of Rámanhully was wafted to a community of Torreas at Chuttra, a village three miles on the other side of my camp near Rámanhully: and one morning four *naiks*, or tribal chiefs, came to say that a large male panther was in the habit of staying in some covers near their village during the hot-weather months each year; that he was there then, and might be easily made to "eat the bullets" of so redoubtable a sportsman as myself!

I determined to survey the surrounding country well, and take my measures with deliberation, before commencing upon this panther; so I appointed an early hour next morning to meet my new friends at their village. I found them awaiting me, and we made a tour of examination through the neighbourhood. It was a much less feasible place for hunting a panther than the scene of our late hunt. Several square miles were covered with low jungle, with heavier patches here and there in numerous small ravines; these drained into one main ravine, capable of carrying off their accumulated discharge in the rainy season. At one point of this main ravine there was a dense cover of some ten acres in extent, composed of matted thickets of creepers and a peculiar evergreen bush, the foliage of which bent to, and touched, the ground on all sides, making a thick screen that prevented a view into the interior without parting it with the hand. These bushes are favourite retreats of panthers, pig, &c. The Torreas said the panther in question almost invariably lived in this cover, but that if disturbed he would betake himself to a place called Kul Bhávi, or the stone well, where there were a few similar thickets. This was a cover in one of the tributary ravines, about three-quarters of a mile from the large cover. Should he be dislodged from this, he would either, they said, make back to the big cover, or endeavour to reach a small rocky hill a mile further on, where he had a cave. He ordinarily only used the latter as a den on occasions during the wet months, when mosquitoes are very troublesome in close green thickets. We found his tracks, those of a very large male, almost like a small tigress, in the sandy bed of the main ravine which ran through the cover. Down it we crept silently in Indian file, that I might gain an idea of the nature and extent of the panther's haunts.

We decided to try and drive him out of the main thicket towards the Kul Bhávi, or smaller one. I was to be stationed at the point where he would most likely emerge from the large cover; and such nets as we had were to be stretched across his line of escape, some distance out in the open ground beyond where I stood. We hoped that if he got past me this obstacle would delay him, and afford me the chance of a second shot. The prominent points for a mile round were to be occupied by markers, to avoid the chance of our losing a second panther by the want of foresight that had cost us our last. I saw, however, that to drive so large a cover effectively, a greater number of men was required than the Torreas of Chuttra, so I proposed to them to invite the villagers of Rámanhully to join them. There is much jealousy among the various Torrea communities, who have the country apportioned into hunting-tracts for each village, and I had some difficulty in getting them to fall into my views with cordiality. But the eloquence of Jaffer—who explained to them that the Rámanhully Torreas, being strangers to the ground, would only be required as stops, and for duties of quite a secondary nature, and would have little of the honour and few of the rupees to be obtained in the event of the death of the panther—at last prevailed, and two of the headmen proceeded to Rámanhully to give their kinsmen an invitation for the hunt. Jaffer declared himself ready to go with them; and I have no doubt he represented to the private ear of the Rámanhully people that they were the men to show his "Sahib" sport, as they had already done, and that the assistance of the Chuttra Torreas was merely called in as a matter of etiquette, the cover lying in their boundaries. Jaffer plumed himself greatly, and not without cause, on his skill in getting opposing factions among the sporting villagers with whom we became acquainted to coalesce in his master's interests; and he was at the same time a great favourite amongst them for his never-failing vivacity and pleasant company.

An early day for the hunt having been appointed, the combined forces of Rámanhully and Chuttra collected the evening before near the latter village, but they encamped outside it. It is a great point to get beaters, if intended to work early, away from their houses, to obviate the difficulty always experienced in collecting them early. As there was a fair road from my camp to Chuttra I drove over in my across-country pony-trap at sunrise. The various markers were at once despatched in couples to take up their allotted stations, whilst the beaters waited until the sun was well up, to allow the panther time to return to his stronghold in case he had been to a distance for his night's prowl. Before commencing, the nets were set up some distance from the cover in the open, and I took post on the edge of the thicket where a path entered it, and by which we expected the panther to appear. The hunters ascertained that he had entered the cover before daybreak, and some one said a large boar, of which there were a few about, had also retired to it for the day; but I paid little heed to this latter piece of news at the time, in the all-absorbing attention regarding the particular beast we were after. I was, however, speedily to be reminded of the boar's presence.

The beat commenced, and I soon heard a heavy animal making its way stealthily but rapidly towards me. I thought of nothing but the panther, when I was suddenly confronted by the boar, a huge grey old fellow, who pulled up almost at the muzzle of my rifle as I levelled it at him. I had no time for hesitation. I was directly in his path, and only a few yards distant. I should probably have been cut down in another instant in the style in which a boar can do this to any one opposing him, so I fired at his long narrow forehead and dropped him dead. Some men who were stationed not far off ran up and dragged the boar out of the way, and one of them was sent to inform the beaters, who had ceased driving at the firing. This occurrence was unfortunate, as the disturbance ahead must have alarmed the panther, for a beater shortly came to say he was in a thicket but would not move. The messenger assured me that I could shoot him as he lay without more ado, and that the headmen were anxious for me to come at once. The chance was a tempting one, but still it was decidedly against my better judgment that I left my post and went to the place, where the headman of Rámanhully, with only a spear in his hand, volunteered to show me the brute. He parted the screen of green leaves of a thicket a little way in advance and peered in. I could see nothing, anxiously though I strained my eyes. My companion begged me to accompany him nearer, and we crept into the thicket in a stooping posture, till I caught sight of the panther lying among some roots and dry briers. I delayed for a moment to enable me to see exactly how he lay, as it was desirable to put him *hors de combat* at the first shot; but the checkered sunlight and quivering shadows of the boughs matched so closely with his spotted hide that this was no easy matter. Just as I was going to fire he sprang up with a loud " wough, wough," and after a short rush in our direction, to intimidate us, suddenly changed his course, and was out of sight before I could pull trigger.

I now more than ever regretted having left my original post, and made the best of my way back to it. Here I found the nets lying in disorder on the ground, but the panther had, a marker informed me, retreated to the cover after struggling a few minutes in the toils. We now decided that I should take post a short distance to the right, considering it unlikely that the brute would again break cover at the same place; and the drive began again. In a very few minutes I was startled by screams and shouts, and then all was still. I feared some accident had occurred, and one of the men was brought to me rather severely bitten in the upper part of his left arm. It appeared that he had been separated from his companions, and that the panther had sprung upon him as he was entering a thicket and had inflicted the injury. Other men being near, the brute left him. I handed him over to the care of one of my peons, who had had some instruction as a dresser in the Mysore hospital; and having instructed the men, who were really plucky fellows and nothing daunted by this mishap, but rather inspired with a determination to have the panther killed, to keep in compact parties and to carry lighted bundles of dry date-fronds in their hands, the beat recommenced.

A shout behind me now caused me to run towards the line of nets, which I saw falling in all directions, and I found that the panther, with the peculiar crassness often exhibited by wild beasts, had made his way out of the cover at the same place as before, had knocked down the nets in his rush, and was now well on his way towards the Kul Bhávi ravine!

We were soon all together, and after seeing the wounded man's arm washed and bound up, and having despatched him in my trap to Mysore, twelve miles distant, we proceeded to the ravine where the markers informed us the panther had taken shelter. They were able to tell to within a few yards where he lay, so surrounding the place with the nets in a circle of about a hundred yards diameter, we threw stones and lighted sticks in, but could not get him to move. Something desperate was evidently required. We were all much excited, and when I proposed to go at him there was no hesitation on the part of the plucky Torreas. A large number accompanied me, all armed with boar-spears, which were, however, too long and top-heavy to be used effectively, except for a deliberate thrust. We formed up inside the circle in a wedge-shaped mass, I taking the apex or most advanced point with my rifle, and the spearmen guarding both flanks. We advanced slowly, throwing stones and firebrands to the place where we knew the brute was hiding. He was lying, as we subsequently found, in a shallow fissure covered with briers, where none of these missiles reached him, and he probably could not see us distinctly or he would not, I am convinced, have attacked so formidable a party. When we were close upon him, all of us wound up to the highest pitch of excitement, out he came with the usual grunting roars of an attacking member of the *Felidæ*, passed me like a flash of lightning, and struck down the man the third to my left. Almost before he fell the panther had sprung from him on to a second and a third of the line, growling and cuffing right and left, and then away he went behind us, into the jungle-overhung ravine. His movements were so rapid, and I was so hampered by the people grouped about, that I had not a chance of firing. The men had failed, from the length of their spears, and the short hold which they were obliged to take of them, to make them of any service in keeping him off.

This was vastly well. Four men *hors de combat*, and not a shot fired on our side. It was fortunate that the panther had been so flurried that he had no time to do more mischief. None of the men were even bitten. One was clawed on his chest, one on his abdomen, and the other over his shoulder. I do not look upon this undertaking as one we ought to have failed in had the men had better spears. There is no reason why a few determined men should not make short work of an animal not much bigger than a mastiff, even though it possess the cat's agility. I know of one case of a panther having been killed by a few natives with bill-hooks. He was lying in a garden and attacked one of them who approached him unawares. The others rushed in and finished him at once. In November 1873 a ryot near Morlay killed a tiger, upwards of two-thirds grown, that attacked him when similarly stumbled upon. The brute held him by the left arm until the man killed him with his *cutty*, or heavy chopper. I saw both the dead tiger and the wounded man immediately after the occurrence, and the plucky fellow had the good fortune to recover from his wounds, severe though they were.

We could now do nothing but wait till the markers observed where the panther stopped; but he had been so thoroughly alarmed that he forsook both the covers and the rocks, passed our most distant markers, and made his way towards an extensive tract of scrub-jungle, where pursuit was useless. The day was hot and we were all half dead with thirst, whilst there was no water nearer than Chuttra, so we were obliged to content ourselves with the thought that we had done all that we could to make an end of him, and to return to the village. The slain boar proved a source of some consolation to the men. I should have liked to have kept his skin for a saddle, but one of the old Torreas represented in such touching terms that the crackling was the *bonne bouche*, that, rather than lessen their enjoyment, I let them take him away entire. I fancy, however, that they must have found the integument of this old stager offer something more than a "coy resistance."

This, happily, was the only occasion but one on which I have had men injured whilst shooting. The other was a similar case, two Morlayites having been bitten and clawed, though not very severely, by a large male panther which we were badgering in his stronghold, and which I shot whilst coming at myself. The Torrea whom I sent into Mysore was sufficiently recovered to return to his village in ten days, and I think he did not regret the occurrence on the whole, as I always gave him the much-valued rupee when we met afterwards. The scratches of the other three men were trifling. I never bagged this panther. He appeared to take offence at our usage of him, and though he returned now and again he never stayed long enough to admit of our organising a second hunt for him. I killed a female panther, however, and captured her two cubs, very probably his wife and offspring, eight days after our adventure with the old gentleman himself. I had returned from a morning inspection of a channel when news came that a panther, smaller than the last, and accompanied by cubs, was in the cover; also that the Chuttra headmen were collecting such of their followers as they could, in view to my returning with the messengers. I swallowed a hasty breakfast and drove to the place. Only about twenty men had been collected. I had very little faith in the efforts of so small a party in so extensive a thicket, though, as very often happens, this hastily-improvised drive was more successful than our more elaborate arrangements had been.

By the advice of the men, and accompanied by one of them, I took up my post inside the large cover on the edge of a narrow glade or path that ran through it, and at a particular spot at which they assured me the panther would cross. Hunters with thorough local knowledge can frequently tell to within a yard where beasts will pass, even in what appears to a stranger to be an ill-defined jungle, where it might be supposed there could be little preference of route. But wild animals generally keep to certain lines very closely, to tracks well chosen in the first place, as being in the most direct line to other strongholds, or to particular points where they must cross ravines.

My attendant and I stole to our post with the utmost caution, moving slowly and heeding every step lest a crackling twig or rustling leaf should betray us. We knew the panther must be lying very close to where we were, that being the most secure part of the cover. We stood on the ground near a wild-date tree, and in a few moments the beaters began to make noises at some distance. I had cautioned them not to begin too close, as a suddenly-awakened animal often dashes away too fast to give the sportsman a good chance.

The patch of jungle was small in extent, but dark as night, and though the beaters made every conceivable noise as they approached, the panther did not show itself, and I was beginning to fear it had slipped away in some other direction, when a slight movement, but without any sound, caught my eye to the right. Turning my head quietly I saw the panther's head and shoulders just past a bush. I felt instantly I had her! She was only five yards off, and her quickest movement could scarcely save her one shot at least. She had not caught sight of me as she was looking to see if the coast were clear, so I brought up my rifle quickly. She caught the movement and turned full on me, crouching with lightning speed. At the same instant a bullet through her lungs knocked her out of time altogether. With a convulsive spring backwards and sideways she disappeared in the thicket. There was dead silence among the beaters at the shot and growl that followed, and I heard the panther gasping and choking with blood a few yards inside the thicket. The gasps became fainter and slower, and then all was still. I made my companion climb a tree to mark, whilst I retired and joined the beaters.

We decided, after a little consideration, to go, after the lapse of half an hour, in a strong body to the place where she had disappeared. When we did so we caught sight of her dark-spotted skin, and we speedily dragged its defunct wearer forth. She was a large panther for a female (6 feet 8 inches), and the men were delighted to think that so few of them had effected more than five times their numbers did before.

We sent the panther to camp, and with my two bull-terriers, Boxer and Rosie, proceeded to hunt up her two cubs. These little spit-fires were speedily seized by the dogs, and we succeeded in capturing them before they were much hurt. They were somewhat larger than cats, but proved themselves such graceless and intractable little beasts that I sent them, after keeping them for a few weeks, to the public gardens in Bangalore, where they are, I believe, to this day. I have never been able to make pets of panther or leopard cubs. They seem almost untamable, and are certainly never to be trusted as young tigers may be. The latter become as faithful and reliable as dogs, and I have never found any difficulty in keeping them till they attained formidable dimensions. They appear to have more of the dog than of the cat in their disposition.

The beaters now said there were some wild pigs in a ravine two miles away, and if I would wait for a few minutes they would run to the village for their nets, and would hunt them under my auspices. Arrived at the ravine, I sat on the side of a hill under a tree whence I had a good view of the sport. Presently three pigs tore along the opposite side of the valley before the pursuing beaters, but coming to the nets, which they winded, they turned down-hill, crossed the ravine, and came rattling up close on my left. Then such a shout arose among the beaters! Their expectations of pork, as far as these rested on the netting process, were gone. I was their last hope of meat for supper. They called out, "Sir, sir!" (in Canarese, of course,) in every tone of voice, from the exhorting and imploring to the despairing. This quite put me off my shooting. Had they kept quiet I think I was good for one, if not two, of the pigs at the distance at which they passed me, but their desperate, still hopeful shouts, tickled me so that I missed with both barrels. What delight had been theirs had a pig rolled over! I comforted them, however, by telling them not to mind the pigs, as they had behaved like men in the panther beat, and should have three sheep in lieu of the escaped pigs.

I have already spoken of the boldness panthers and leopards display in entering villages at night in quest of dogs, goats, &c. They not unfrequently venture into the sportsman's encampment on similar enterprises, and their inroads are generally so well-timed that the chances are in favour of their carrying off the object that has attracted them. I once, however, frustrated a panther in the following manner: Captain R. and I were doing a little shooting together in the Hoonsoor jungles, and were encamped near the village of Hullada Copple, which we were told was infested by a panther that had carried off all the dogs, and was troubling the ryots greatly by its boldness. The jungles were too extensive to attempt beating for it with any prospect of success, and, in fact, we gave it little consideration, being more intent on a search for a tiger. On the night of our arrival we suggested to our servants to be doubly cautious in keeping the camp-fires burning, and after our post-prandial cheroots, were soon sound asleep.

Before turning in I took care that my only dogs, Boxer and Rosie, should be chained close by in a small tent in which two servants slept, near to our own.

I happened to be partly awake about midnight when I heard a sudden rush past my bed-head outside the canvas wall of the tent, a momentary scuffle in the small tent, and then the despairing yells of one of the dogs as it was being carried off towards the jungle. I sprang out of bed and dashed out, wholly unarmed, just in time to see the white form of old Rosie in the jaws of some marauder. With a shout I gave chase, hoping to force the animal—I did not know at the moment what it was—to drop its prey. R., startled by my cries, and missing me, feared I had been carried off by a tiger, and being an old campaigner, proceeded to pull on his trousers preparatory to heading a relieving force!

The panther gained the jungle, closely followed by me. The worrying sound here gave place to choking sobs from the bitch. I thought she had been dropped, and ran in to pick her up; her white form was just visible among the bushes by the dim starlight. Just as I stooped I became aware that the panther was lying on its back hugging the bitch, which was uppermost, in its paws. Feeling my position to be an awkward one, I hurried back to camp, which was by this time in an uproar. To seize the rifle that Jaffer held ready, and call for a torch, was, as our novelists say, the work of a moment; but to find a torch under the circumstances was another matter, and the only light forthcoming was an inch of tallow candle. Jaffer, shading this with his cloth, accompanied me back to the scene of action; but the Fates were against us, for before I could get a shot we found ourselves in the position popularly ascribed to an ancient patriarch—the candle having gone out! The panther growled in unpleasant proximity, when R., with a blazing bush, lit by some one in camp, advanced to our assistance, and the panther, seeing the approaching numbers, made its exodus. With rifles on full-cock we hunted about—I being all this time in my night-shirt—but could find neither bitch nor panther. Returning to camp we saw, to our great surprise and joy, the old bitch sitting under the table, licking her wounds. I picked her up in my arms where she shivered and growled by turns at the recollection of what she had gone through. Her collar had saved her from serious injury.

The panther, possibly feeling sheepish after its night's disappointment, turned its attention next day to mutton. As we were sitting at breakfast a villager ran in to say that one of his flock had been seized and dragged into a piece of jungle by the panther. The cover being too extensive to be driven with beaters, we tossed up for places for watching. R. won, and took

up a convenient position over the last victim, in expectation of the panther's return to his mutton. I procured a kid, whose bleating panthers always find difficulty in resisting, and tied it up in another part of the jungle. I watched from behind a bush near, seated on the ground, and had hardly settled myself comfortably when the sharp chirruping of a squirrel in the cover warned me that the panther was moving. In another moment the kid's cries were stifled in its grasp, but a right and left from me sent it off, badly wounded, before it had time to do the kid any injury. No elephants being available, we waited for half an hour before following it up on foot. After creeping along its bloody tracks for about two hundred yards, I observed it raise its head from a patch of rushes ahead, glance at us, and crouch again. We had picked up a piece of bone two inches long on its trail, and knew by this that one of its legs was broken. We now slipped the dogs who quickly brought the crippled enemy to bay, and I shot it.

No wonder Rosie had escaped. The panther was an old female; her fangs were worn down to mere stumps, and were almost useless; and she was emaciated and weak from hunger. She measured 6 feet 3½ inches in length, and 2 feet 2 inches high at the shoulder. Fleshy protuberances, the size of pigeons' eggs, had grown under her tongue and on the insides of her mouth, and must have interfered with her feeding. Surely the last days of the large carnivora must be some expiation of all their past evil deeds, when, unable to catch deer, pig, &c., they die by inches, or are prompted to deeds of daring with regard to domestic animals which sooner or later bring them to grief.

CHAPTER XXV.

SPORT WITH PANTHERS AND LEOPARDS—(*continued*).

NEWS OF A PANTHER AND TWO LEOPARDS — SHIKÁRIE SUBBA — A FRIEND'S ILL LUCK — THE MÁDERHULLY GARDEN — ARRANGE PLANS FOR DRIVING THE PANTHER AND LEOPARDS — THE HOLOYA CASTE — THE NATIVE BEER OF MYSORE — INVEST IN A DONKEY — THE BEAT — SHOOT THE LEOPARDS — THE PANTHER'S CUNNING RUSE — A SUDDEN EVICTION — SHOOT THE PANTHER — A GOOD BAG BEFORE BREAKFAST — GOVERNMENT REWARD FOR SHOOTING PANTHERS AND LEOPARDS — CIRCUMVENTING CUNNING PANTHERS—OUR EARS DECEIVE US—MY LAST MEETING WITH A PANTHER —HIS STRANGE BEHAVIOUR—THE INTERVIEW TERMINATES UNSATISFACTORILY.

ONE of my most fortunate days with panthers and leopards occurred in May 1872, when I had the luck to bag three before breakfast. I happened to be stationed at the time at a place called Nursipoor, in a part of Mysore where, as there were no jungles near, there was very little game, so I had no better amusement for my spare hours than shooting the few antelope that were to be found, and crocodiles in the Hemávati river. I was therefore gratified at the intelligence brought to me one morning by a man named Subba, a local shikárie, that he had heard that some panthers had been long established near a village called Máderhully, thirty miles from Nursipoor, and he proposed that we should take an early opportunity of looking them up. Native report is not always reliable however, so I sent Jaffer with Subba to make more careful inquiries. They returned in a few days with a satisfactory report; but as my duties did not admit of my beating up the panthers' quarters just at that time, I sent Subba to live at Máderhully till I could take a holiday, and to learn all he could the while about the panthers' goings and comings. Subba was one of the few natives one meets with who have the English love of roving, and unconcern for home ties. To the ordinary Hindoo, house and family are all in all. Even when pressed by such exigency as starvation he prefers to die in his own village rather than go to a distance to obtain relief. I have met some natives, however, of sporting tastes, who would roll up their blanket, tie up their simple cooking utensils, and start upon any service, perhaps to be absent for a month or more, at a moment's notice, merely asking that something should be sent to their wives, a point which the Hindoo never forgets. Subba was one of these rovers, and in consequence was looked upon as somewhat of a vagabond by his stay-at-home neighbours. As a tracker he had the great recommendation of being a taciturn man, never speaking till he was sure, and never substituting imagination for facts.

It so happened that before I went to Máderhully I made a more distant excursion after certain bears with a friend, and whilst four fell to my rifle he shot none. I was moved with compassion at his disappointment, and sent him to Máderhully after my preserved panthers, which Subba had been reporting for some time were to him as "the dogs of his own house"—*i.e.*, that he was as certain of being able to lay hands on them. I ordered him to show my friend every attention, as some consolation for his ill luck with the bears; but the same cause which had led to want of success in the one case—viz., lack of knowledge of his game—again operated in his panther-hunt; and though Subba and the beaters did their best, my friend rendered their efforts futile by leaving the place where he had been posted for one he himself deemed better, and by committing other blunders, and he finally crowned the whole by missing the panthers when he did get a chance at them! He tried again the following day; but Subba made no apology when relating the circumstances to me afterwards for having, with the villagers, purposely misled the "Doray" (gentleman), as, though they knew well where the panthers were on the second day, they feared they might only be frightened away, not secured; and it is not unnatural that men, whose hopes of reward rest on the death of the animals they may have spent much time in watching and marking, should not like to see them lost, and with them their hoped-for guerdon, by an unskilful sportsman.

The panthers—or two leopards and one panther, as they turned out to be—lived in a large, partly abandoned, and jungle-overgrown garden beneath the embankment of a lake or tank, the water of which had formerly been used for irrigating it. The proximity of this stronghold to Máderhully and other villages, in the environs of which dogs, goats, and stray cattle might frequently be pounced upon, rendered it a suitable retreat for the panther and leopards, and here they had lived unmolested for a long time, as none of the villagers had firearms. Having allowed them a few days to recover from any alarm they might feel at the late hunt, I appointed the 25th of May as an auspicious day for further operations against them; and as it is always desirable for the sportsman to learn all he possibly can of the locality where he intends to shoot, I sent my tents to Máderhully and arrived there myself on the morning of the 24th. After a cup of coffee I proceeded with Subba and his chief auxiliaries amongst the villagers to inspect the ground.

The garden was about a mile long and a quarter of a mile broad. The middle part, throughout its entire length, was thinly planted with cocoa-nut and plantain trees; whilst, from the state of decay into which it had fallen, the hedges had become overgrown patches of aloe-bushes, creepers, and thorny thickets. The length of the garden lay north and south. The best covers for the panthers and leopards were respectively the northern half of the east boundary hedge, and the southern half of the west one. Subba said that the leopards were generally to be found in the former, and the panther in the latter place; and we therefore decided that on the morrow the men should begin to beat the east hedge from the north corner, and that I should be stationed at a point about half-way down it, where a thin fringe of bushes ran across the garden and formed a line of communication between the thickets on each side. Of this connecting fringe we knew any animal retiring before the beaters would take advantage, to cross the otherwise open ground to the thickets in the south-west corner. There were no covers outside, and disconnected with, the garden itself, except one small patch of dense aloe-bushes, about a hundred yards away from the south boundary hedge. Having noted the places where markers should be stationed, and having pointed out their posts to the men with us, to be occupied by them next day, I returned to camp to breakfast. In the afternoon sixty stout fellows—all Holoyas, or low-caste Hindoos—were enrolled as beaters, and each had a gun-wad given him as a voucher, as after a beat many who only help latterly, or not at all, will appear at the time of paying, and either the sportsman is put to double expense, or the amount is divided amongst so many as to make no one much the better. With tickets, the black sheep have no opportunity of obtaining money under false pretences.

The Holoya caste is one of the few amongst Hindoos to which the use of intoxicants is permitted; and every afternoon those Holoyas who have leisure, and who are lucky enough to have the necessary coppers, betake themselves to the nearest beer-shop. This is a cleanly-swept spot under a shady tree, and is screened from the gaze of passers-by with plaited cocoa-nut leaves. It is always situated at a little distance from the village, in deference to the prejudices of the more numerous abstaining inhabitants. The liquor supplied in the booth is the fermented sap of the wild date-tree (*Phœnix sylvestris*), largely diluted with water. It stands in large froth-covered earthen jars, each containing several gallons, and is served out into the customers' own drinking-vessels, usually gourds or lengths of the giant-bamboo, at about a farthing a quart. *Henda,* as this liquor is called, is to the low-caste Hindoo what beer is to us; and it appears to be a wholesome beverage if not abused. It is not highly intoxicating when used fresh, as is customarily done; whilst it contains a large amount of nutritious saccharine matter. The contract for the sale of this product throughout Mysore is leased out by Government, and brings in a large revenue. The consumption of spirits (arrack) is comparatively trifling, and is chiefly confined to large towns. Many of the drinkers of *henda* never taste spirits, which are more difficult to procure, and almost prohibitory in price. The supply of *henda* to the people is effected by petty contractors who rent one or more of the numerous groves of the wild date that are scattered throughout the country. The trees require no attention or culture. The sap is drawn from them by an incision made just below the leafy crown of their otherwise bare stems, and the earthen vessels into which it drains are emptied daily into skin-bags borne by donkeys or ponies (the sacred bovine tribe is never used for this somewhat discreditable work), and is despatched direct to the places where it is consumed.

I had just made arrangements with my Holoya beaters when I saw a string of donkeys and ponies laden with the wobbling bullock-skins of fermented liquor dear to their hearts, and I immediately despatched Subba to purchase a load as a present for them. He returned shortly, accompanied by the contractor, and driving a donkey whose hocks rubbed painfully against each other, and whose hind-legs had the appearance of almost crossing each other as it walked, from its being systematically overloaded, and having been used when too young. Such is the condition of most of the *henda* contractors' cattle. Subba had arranged for the transfer of the load for a small sum, and he represented that he had further negotiated the purchase of the donkey for one rupee and three-quarters (three and sixpence) if approved, and advised its being taken as a bait for the panthers. I agreed to this, as it was advisable to give the animals a feed overnight to make them less inclined for exertion on the morrow. It may seem cruel to tie up a living animal as a lure for the carnivora, but this is often a necessary measure towards compassing their destruction, and by the sacrifice of one the salvation of many scores may be effected. So the donkey and its load were driven off by the delighted Holoyas to a shady tree at a distance, and when relieved of its burden, the wretched creature was led away to the garden to be tied up as a last repast for the leopards and panther. As I sat outside my tent after dinner that evening, I could not help pitying the poor donkey left to its fate. The night was starlit and quiet. Fireflies glancing near the border of the lake, and in and out amongst the dark foliage of the garden, were the only signs of life in that direction, but I knew that a dark deed was being done, or would be done there before morning.

As soon as it was light the men collected at the tent. I sent Subba and two others to see what had become of the donkey, and as we were starting we saw them running excitedly towards us. They had seen the two leopards enter the thicket in the north-east corner where the donkey had been tied. They had killed and dragged it some distance, and had eaten more than half of it. The beaters formed line near this spot, whilst I took the markers with me and saw each one safely up his tree in different parts of the boundary-hedges, and in the middle of the garden. They were cautioned on no account to come down, nor shout to us whatever they saw, but merely to keep their eyes open, and be able to let us know when we wanted information. Knowing how cunning panthers often are, I thought it possible that, if hotly pressed in the garden, one or other of them might betake itself to the detached clump of aloe-bushes which I have already mentioned as being situated a hundred yards beyond the south boundary-hedge. There was a large tree growing in the centre of the clump, so I ordered an old fellow to climb into it on the remote chance of his being useful there. The men were so disposed in the trees along each boundary hedge that it was impossible for any animal once afoot to hide itself where it would not be under the silent observation of one or other of them.

I mounted my tree in the narrow belt of jungle that, as aforesaid, crossed the garden and linked the two chief thickets together, whilst a man was posted in the open ground outside the garden who could see me and also the advancing beaters. I arranged a code of signals with him for guiding the beaters. Accidents or failure frequently ensue in driving dangerous game from want of communication with the beaters. Either a wounded animal turns back and meets the advancing men, who imagine it has been killed or has gone forward, and continue the beat; or if they take the precautionary measure of leaving the cover upon hearing shots, when the beast may in reality have been missed, or have gone forward, his mate or others of his kind in the drive may take the opportunity of slipping back and escaping.

I sat alone. I have too often found that an attendant moves or coughs at the critical moment to desire company. I occupied myself until the beat began by settling myself comfortably. My seat was a blanket rolled round a thick bough. With my knife and a saw-blade I lopped off such surrounding twigs as obstructed the view. I fastened my spare gun to a branch with my handkerchief, ready to hand, and planted my large pewter tankard, full of cold clear water, in a fork above me. It was refreshing even to look up through its glass bottom and the limpid fluid, the sportsman's safest tipple. One is sometimes kept a long time in a tree if the beaters experience difficulty with the game, and this in a hot Indian May day is unpleasant without water. The tree I was in was shady and comfortable, but the heat in the air makes the sportsman thirsty. Underneath me was a dry sandy water-course, with a narrow border of bushes on each side. The crisp leaves of deciduous trees lay thickly in its bed, and I knew that even the stealthy tread of a leopard upon them would not be unheard by me, even before it came in sight. My view extended for about fifty yards up the bed of the water-course.

The distant yells of the beaters soon warned me that the sport had commenced. Some little time passed when I saw my signalman raise both arms, a sign from the beaters that the two leopards were afoot. I was expecting their speedy appearance when an extra storm of yells, and an interchange of abuse amongst the men, followed by a sudden silence, told me that the leopards had broken back, I only hoped without accident. The men ran back to head them, and they recommenced at the original place and beat up merrily. Presently I heard a rustling in the dry leaves, and saw one leopard sneaking down the sandy ravine. It came on very cautiously and hesitatingly, and I amused myself by watching it. Though full grown it was a small animal (few if any leopards exceed five and a half feet in length), and I felt rather ashamed of being in a tree to shoot such a creature. I would have met it on foot with pleasure. It looked as if half inclined to turn back, but each yell of the men appeared to call to its mind some act of spoilation for which it feared retribution, and to make it dread a return more than an advance. On it came, and when directly under me I dropped it dead with a bullet through the neck. It never moved, but lay prone as it fell, with one paw before it in the attitude of advancing. I telegraphed "dead," and the beaters came on with redoubled cries.

Soon the male leopard approached with slow and stealthy step down the bed of the ravine. He looked very pretty to a sportsman's eye, grinning with mingled fear and anger at being disturbed in his early sleep. His belly almost touched the ground as he crept along. Fortunately the wind was from him to me, so he did not scent his dead spouse, nor did he even observe her as she lay. He seemed to have thoughts of leaving the bed of the ravine before he reached me, and drawing his head level with the bank he peered cautiously through the garden to see if the coast were clear in the line of his meditated departure. He gave me a rather difficult shot, but I rolled him over. He got up and rushed up the bank, but I tumbled him over again into the ravine. He now cantered back, but I caught my empty rifle between my knees and seized the spare one, and just as he was getting out of sight I killed him with a lucky shot in the ear.

Having laid out our game in the shade, I sent Subba to inquire of the markers along the other boundary-hedge of the garden if they had seen anything. After some time he came back to say that every man along the line reported that one panther, some said two, had passed him, and that the old fellow in the tree in the aloe-clump signalled that there was something hiding near its foot. I plumed myself greatly on my foresight in having stationed this marker in his present post. The panther (for such it was) had, with the cunning common to its class, left the garden at the disturbance we made over the leopards, and had secreted itself in this unpretentious spot, hoping, no doubt, that we should confine our search to its regular haunts. The idea was a good one, but unfortunately for it, not quite novel; I had been played the trick before, successfully on that occasion, and had not forgotten the circumstance. The day was getting hot, but Subba's information was as refreshing as ice! I sent the men to the tank to get a drink of water, and we then set out without a word, as the place where the panther lay hidden was so small that the slightest alarm might have made it leave it. The old fellow in the tree had taken the precaution of climbing to the topmost branch (panthers have been known to pull sportsmen out of trees; a friend of mine shot one when in a tree which it had ascended to a height of thirty feet from the ground on being mobbed in a garden by some villagers), and he now directed us by silently pointing to the exact spot in the thicket where the hiding beast lay. The men formed up on the far side of the thicket without a sound, whilst I took post on foot close to the south hedge of the garden. I placed my spare rifle on full-cock against a tree ready to hand. Between the aloe-thicket and my post was a stretch of the greenest turf, as, though it was then the end of the hot weather in Mysore, the ground here was damp and marshy. The panther would have to cross this open space, close past me and in full view, in returning to the garden.

The men awaited my signal with upraised clubs, and a fiendish howl ready, no doubt, on each tongue. A little in advance of them stood Subba, with a lighted stick in one hand and a rocket in the other, waiting for orders to eject the animal. I raised my hand. The lighted stick was applied to the rocket, which fizzed slowly; when properly agoing it was thrown into the very spot where the beast lay, and its terrors supplemented by the said pent-up yells of the beaters. The panther came out like a jack-in-the-box! It had the air of having been blown out by the explosion of the rocket, so sudden was its appearance. The startling character of the demonstration against it was certainly sufficient to terrify any wild animal out of its ordinary demeanour; and with a series of springs and continued roars, the beast made straight for the garden. I stood almost in its path. I had set out in the morning with the usual resolves to be cautious, but it is more easy to make such vows at home than to keep them in the field. Prudent resolutions often vanish under excitement. Whilst awaiting the turning out of the panther I was anxious enough, and pondered within myself whether I should not be safer in a tree; but when it came bounding towards me I only thought of bagging it by a neat shot. It never saw me, its attention being centred on diving into the garden to escape the awful racket it had just listened to. Its rich, tawny, spotted skin glanced like a race-horse's coat, and contrasted beautifully with the green turf as it flew towards me. The instant it started the beaters stopped their yells, and looked on at the impending event with breathless interest. The panther's roars were the only sound which now broke the stillness. It would, in the course it was taking, pass about fifteen yards to my right. I kept it covered with my rifle from the moment it started; and when it was just passing me, and about twelve yards distant, I fired. My shot was rather too far forward, however, and merely grazed its chest; but the left barrel smashed both its shoulder-blades, and the beast alighted heavily on its chest, rolling over with the impetus of its spring. The beaters ran up, and we stood round the beautiful but fierce creature as it lay, biting at the turf and even its own paws in its impotent rage at being unable to rise. We watched it for a few seconds, when I put an end to its sufferings.

We now went to look for the reported fourth panther, and having found the point in the thicket where it had been last seen, I once more took up my position on foot, in the absence of a suitable tree, and the beat began. No panther, no trace of one, was to be found, however, but a very large wild cat made its appearance. This was evidently what the markers, seeing it indistinctly in the thicket, had mistaken for a panther. I killed it with a bullet.

I now returned to breakfast with a complacent mind. We had had a capital morning's sport. The arrangements had been perfect; the shooting had been—ahem! I will leave my readers to judge; nothing, even to the cat, had escaped us; and all this before ten o'clock!

People came from adjacent villages to see the three animals, which lay in a row under a tree near my tent. The sight afforded them evident satisfaction, as there was scarcely one of them whose flocks or dogs had not suffered from their depredations. The first two were a pair, and were the true leopards or *kerkals* of Mysore, having all the characteristics given by Elliot, and quoted by Dr Jerdon in his *Mammals.* The measurements of the animals from nose to tip of tail were: Panther (female), 6 feet 10 inches. Leopards—male, 5 feet 4 inches—female, 5 feet 2 inches; both full grown.

The Government reward in Mysore for killing a panther or leopard is 25 rupees. I gave 40 rupees of the amount due for the three to Subba, who had taken great trouble in their pursuit. As a native can live well on 5 rupees a-month, this would suffice to make him happy for some time, especially in the matter of drink, to which he was much devoted. The remaining 35 rupees gave the beaters great satisfaction.

I have before mentioned the panther and leopard's habit of living in rocky hills near villages, and of preying upon domestic animals. Such depredators keep chiefly to deep and intricate caves, from which they cannot be dislodged even with fireworks; and almost the only plan of getting a shot at them is to watch, either before or after nightfall, over a live goat tied as a bait. Some cunning panthers, however, will not approach such a lure, as their suspicions are at once aroused by the sight of a solitary goat stationed near their retreats. With such sly animals I have found the most effective plan to be, to hide early in the afternoon amongst the rocks at the foot of the hill on the side where the panther will most probably be on the look-out about sunset, and, having an accomplice in the goat-herd, to have a goat quickly tethered and left behind as the flocks are driven villagewards in the evening. The sight of this apparent straggler, which bleats loudly for its fellows, will often deceive the most wary panther or leopard. It descends from its elevated post of observation with marvellous rapidity, and if the sportsman has chosen his post well, so that he may neither be seen nor winded by the animal, he will have a fair chance at it when it is seizing the goat.

I remember an absurd occurrence in connection with these hill-panthers. A pair was said to frequent an isolated pile of rocks in open country, so I proceeded one morning with some villagers of the neighbourhood to inspect their retreat with a view to devising plans against them. We separated amongst the rocks to look for recent marks. One villager accompanied me. Seeing an entrance to a likely-looking cave under a shelving sheet of rock, I stooped down and peered in, when I immediately heard a low, tremulous sound in the deep recesses which I took to be the growl of the objects of our search. I drew back, and the sound ceased. I was under no apprehension, as my experience of panthers and leopards is that they never charge out of the darkness to attack a person outside their retreats. I have even known a leopard in a cave to be poked with bamboos for a length of time. It could not be shot, and it refused to come out, though the titillation amongst its ribs must have been, one would think, not less hurting to its dignity than distressing to its bodily feelings.

On the present occasion, to make sure I peered in again. There could be no mistake; it was evidently a suppressed growl. The villager with me said it could not be the panthers, as the cave was not so extensive as others in the hill, and was never frequented by them. He walked up to the entrance and looked boldly in. His mien changed, however, in a moment. He evidently heard what I had heard, and he drew back with a gesture of astonishment and apprehension. I laughed at his change of countenance, and sent him to call the others, and when they came we proceeded to examine the vicinity of the cave, but could find no footprints. We approached the entrance, when the same sound was again audible. One of the men, after listening intently, laughed, and saying, "I'll show you the panthers that made that noise," crept into the cave, from which large numbers of bats began to issue. It was the tremulous sound produced by the movements of these creatures within, which, resounding in the hollow cavern, closely resembled a low growl. When the entrance had been darkened by our looking in the bats were disturbed, and fluttered their wings as they hung from the roof, and some of them flew about.

I have related at the commencement of the last chapter how the panther was the first wild animal of the audacious class that I made the acquaintance of in India. It strangely enough happened that it was also the last I encountered before leaving India. I am obliged to say I did not acquit myself in the leave-taking interview with as much address as I ought to have displayed. To have failed with my first panther through inexperience was natural enough; but the same excuse cannot be made for the loss of the last by a combination of indifferent shooting, and what was worse, want of strategy. The occurrence happened as follows:—

I was to leave Morlay, so long my jungle-home, for Madras next day, *en route* to England, so, wishful for a last evening stroll I took a rifle and drove in my pony-trap along the jungle-road which I had had cleared so as to be feasible for driving from Morlay Hall to the Koombappan Goody temple. Shooting was not my object so much as a quiet saunter through the scenes to which I had become so much attached, so leaving my trap at the temple, Murga (a tracker) and I wandered silently along the river-bank. The jungle was unusually thin and leafless even for the season of the year (the hot weather), owing to the lack of proper rain for many months, which had affected vegetation in the wilds as well as crops and pasturage. The ordinary water supplies of the country having dried up, spotted-deer, monkeys, jungle-fowl, and smaller creatures, were collected in unusual numbers in the neighbourhood of the Honhollay river. Such was the drought that no water had flowed in its bed for months, and the supply was now confined to a few pools.

It would have been inexcusable butchery to have shot many of the deer thus forced to the locality by the most pressing of creature wants, thirst; so contenting myself with one fat stag, to afford my men a parting feast, I wandered on, watching the different animals and scenes till sunset, and then mounted my trap and drove homewards. I was allowing the pony to jog along at his own pace, and thinking of the months that must elapse before I should again set foot in these free and beautiful wilds, when Murga, who was sitting behind me, touched my shoulder and said "Panther." I looked, and at a bend in the narrow track, about forty yards ahead, I caught sight of a large panther just disappearing into the jungle. We knew him instantly as an old brute that had defied all the arts of the trackers and myself to bring to book since I settled at Morlay. There were only two panthers in our jungles; the second was a female, and smaller than the male. This cunning old fellow would never kill our "ties," nor lie up in thickets where we could find him during the day. He procured his prey (dogs and stray cattle) in villages far in the open country, and was thus independent of the picketed animals with which we strove to tempt him, in the hope of tracing him, when gorged, to his lair. He was never to be found in any of the larger thickets, but resorted to straggling, undefined country, where it was impossible to arrange any sure plans for driving him. He had become so cunning, through being subjected to several unsuccessful hunts, that we latterly gave up making special search for him, and trusted to some accident to throw him into our hands at last. Here was such a chance.

Oh that I had only seen him a moment sooner! thought I. My rifle was at hand, and I could hardly have failed to bag him. Murga was of opinion that he might show himself again. He said, "You know, sir, he invariably keeps along paths. If you run quietly to the bend you may see him." Seizing my double express I reached the place where the panther had disappeared, leaving Murga with the trap. I noticed that his footprints led along this part of the road, and he must therefore have been visible from the trap, had we but been looking ahead, some time before we saw him. I peered into the jungle. All was quiet. I went a few paces forward and looked round the bend. There was the brute, walking along in the silent manner peculiar to panthers, neither looking to right nor left, and appearing as if he had never been disturbed in his life! He was seventy yards away, and end on, presenting a difficult shot; but I knelt, and taking a steady aim, fired. The brute only gave a start, and without looking behind him galloped heavily forward for a few yards, and then subsided into the same unconcerned pace! I was determined to make a better shot now, so waiting until the panther turned a bend in the path I ran quickly and silently after him, as I knew another bend, which the path almost immediately made, would give me a broadside view further on. Peeping eagerly ahead I saw the panther going round the second bend with an air of the most perfect abstraction. Here goes an awakener—to his doom—thought I, as I pressed the trigger. He was then only fifty yards away, but the light was failing, and though I certainly ought to have bagged him, I made one of those distressing misses which every sportsman does now and again. The panther sprang forward with a gruff growl, and as my rifle was empty, and the spare cartridges were in the trap, I ran back for them.

I found there were only two. It was fast growing dark, so we left the pony standing, and Murga ran back with me to where I had last fired, to where—as we did not then know I had missed—we expected to find the panther dead, or at least wounded. To our astonishment there was no blood, whilst his tracks kept on in the path, and at his former deliberate gait. "He's a devil," said my superstitious companion as we ran on round the next two bends. Still the track led forward. At the third turn we came suddenly on the brute, looking inquiringly over his shoulder in the direction in which he heard our footsteps. Almost before I could bring up my rifle he bounded into the cover, and I missed him again, though there was some excuse this time in his rapid movements. The chief strategic mistake we made occurred at this point. Instead of going back to the pony as we did, imagining that as the panther had now seen his enemies clearly, and had been deliberately fired at from the distance of a few yards, he would not show himself again, I ought to have hidden myself in the thicket bordering the path, and I should certainly have obtained a shot at him, at a few yards' distance, almost immediately.

We met the pony coming slowly along with the trap, cocking his ears and stepping like a startled deer, as he well knew from a lengthy jungle experience that the shots and smell of the panther meant something serious. Jumping in I gave him his head, and as he was anxious to get home—all domestic animals in India evince the greatest disinclination to remain in the jungles after sunset, their instinct warning them of the danger they incur in so doing—we rattled rapidly forward, when, as we rounded the corner where I had last fired, we nearly drove over the brute of a panther, seated coolly on his haunches in the middle of the road! He bounded quietly into the jungle again. I had the presence of mind not to pull up, as we should probably have alarmed him by so doing—if anything would have done so! —so continuing less quickly I handed Murga the reins, and jumping out of the trap hid myself by the side of the path about forty yards further on, whilst he drove away. This ruse succeeded, and the panther, thinking the coast clear, stalked out and sat down again, looking after the receding trap. I tried to sight him, but it was now so dusk that though he could be seen plainly enough when my head was raised, with one eye closed and the other directed along a rifle-barrel, with a dark background, he was invisible. I tried repeatedly but could not get a sight, when he rose and came a few yards down the path, and then turned into one at right angles to it, and which led past me, but through bushes on my right. I had only one barrel loaded, but was determined to have the panther unless it were positively predestined that such was not to be my luck. I therefore slipped quietly through the bushes to cut him off in the small path he had now taken. I however made the mistake of stepping into it instead of waiting until he came level with me. I met him face to face at about five yards' distance, but a bush which overhung the narrow path obscured him; and whilst I delayed an instant to make certain of him—as in the dangerous position in which I stood it would not have done merely to wound him—he drew back with great quickness and vanished in the failing light.

This was the last I saw of him. I can only account for his extreme contumacy throughout by supposing he never saw clearly what we were, being confused by the presence of the trap, and also from the fact that many wild animals, even the most timid, are often very bold at night, as they are not accustomed to meet man abroad at that time. Deer may be approached much more easily late at night, or just as it grows light in the morning, than at other times, as they are not accustomed to being disturbed by people moving about at those hours.

CHAPTER XXVI.

THE INDIAN BLACK BEAR (*URSUS LABIĀTUS*).

DESCRIPTION OF — HABITS AND DISPOSITION — SHE-BEARS CARRYING THEIR CUBS — WOUNDED BEARS ATTACKING EACH OTHER — FOOD — BEARS DRINKING HENDA — EATING FLESH — DANGER OF MEETING BEARS — MODES OF HUNTING BEARS — A HARD BUT SUCCESSFUL DAY — BAG FOUR BEARS — JUNGLE-SURGERY — BEARS AT SAKRAPATAM — THE IYENKERRY LAKE — FELONIOUS BEARS — EXECUTE TWO OUT OF FIVE — MAKE A FURTHER EXAMPLE OF TWO MORE — BOXER AND ROSIE — SHOOT A BEAR BEFORE A LARGE ASSEMBLY — NATIVE BELIEF REGARDING BEARS CARRYING OFF WOMEN — KILLING BEARS WITH DOGS AND A KNIFE.

THIS is the common bear of India and Ceylon: it is sometimes called the sloth bear. It is found from the extreme south of India to the Ganges. Two other species occur in the Himalayas, but *Ursus labiātus* is the only one inhabiting the plains. It does not hibernate, and though covered with so thick a coat seems quite at home in the hottest localities. The hair is black, coarse, and shaggy; the muzzle and tip of feet whitey-brown; and a crescent-shaped mark on the breast—in sportsman's parlance the horse-shoe—is white or yellowish in different individuals.

The largest bear I ever killed weighed exactly 20 st., stood three feet high at the shoulder, and approached six feet in length.

Bears have formidable claws, four inches in length, with which they dig for insects. The sole of the foot is very like that of a man's in shape, but shorter and broader; and the print left by it is sufficiently like a man's to admit of a mistake being made regarding it by any one unaccustomed to tracking.

The male and female bear frequently live together, except when the female has cubs. Three bears are not unfrequently found in company, in which case it is usually a mother and two large cubs. The female has two, sometimes, I believe, three, young at a birth, and often carries them on her back during her travels. It is an amusing sight to see the youngsters dismount at the feeding-grounds and scramble up again if anything alarms them. The young are thus carried on occasions until they are several months old, and so large that only one can be accommodated. I once shot a she-bear carrying one young one whilst the other followed, through a thicket where it was a wonder the young bear, which was as large as a sheep-dog, could keep its seat.

Bears are exceedingly affectionate animals amongst themselves, and are capable of being most thoroughly tamed when taken young. Either wild or tame they are very amusing in their ways, being exceedingly demonstrative and ridiculous. Though hard to kill they are very soft as to their feelings, and make the most hideous outcries when shot at, not only the wounded animal but also its companions. It has frequently been stated by sportsmen that if a bear be wounded he immediately attacks his companions, thinking that they have caused his injuries. But I think this is not quite correct, at least in the majority of cases. I have observed that a wounded bear's companions generally rush to him to ascertain the cause of his grief, joining the while in his cries, when he, not being in the best of humours, lays hold of them, and a fight ensues, really brought about by the affectionate but ill-timed solicitude of his friends.

Bears are numerous in some parts of Mysore, especially in the jungles at the foot of hill-ranges, where they find shelter in small detached hills. Those in Mysore are frequently formed of granite boulders, amongst which are numerous caverns and cool recesses. Bears will, however, lie out in the forest, at the foot of a bamboo-clump or shady tree, or in a thicket. They retire to caves chiefly in the rains, when mosquitoes and gnats are troublesome in the thickets. In localities where they are not liable to be disturbed, bears sometimes sleep during the day in very exposed situations, and do not mind an amount of sun that would be thought disagreeable to creatures with so warm a coat. They are usually in their retreats by eight o'clock in the morning, and are again on the move an hour before sunset. In showery, cloudy weather, especially at the commencement of the rains, when they have been put to straits to obtain a livelihood during the hot months, owing to the hardness of the ground preventing their digging for insects, they may be found feeding throughout the day in quiet places.

Their sight is poor, nor is their hearing particularly good, and when engaged in searching for food they may be approached to within a few paces. But their sense of smell is wonderfully acute; by it they discover insects deep under ground, honey in trees overhead, and are able to detect a man to windward at an immense distance.

The food of the bear consists chiefly of black and white ants, whose underground colonies he is ever attacking; the larvæ of large beetles; and fruit. He is particularly fond of the pods of the *Cassia fistula* (a very common shrub in the Mysore jungles), which contain a sweet black gum between the seeds, of a highly laxative character. Bears are fond of sugar-cane, jak fruit, and melons. In some places they are troublesome in the groves of wild date-trees (*Phœnix sylvestris*), from which *henda*—the fermented sap of the tree—is obtained. The date-trees are seldom more than twenty feet high; the bears climb them, and by tipping up the pot in which the juice is collected with their paws they manage to drink its contents. The *henda*-drawers would not begrudge them a few quarts, but they break a large number of pots by their clumsiness before they get what they require. The natives are unanimous in asserting that the bears drop down backwards instead of taking the trouble to climb down, and that they constantly get drunk with their potations. This seems not unlikely from the manner in which monkeys and other animals are affected by strong drinks. Bears are also very fond of the fruit of the date-palm, which they find on the ground under the trees, and of honey when they can obtain it.

Ursus labiātus is usually believed to be non-carnivorous, but I have known of one case of a bear devouring a jungle-sheep (muntjac-deer), which one of my men had shot and left in the jungle overnight, being unable to carry it home. It rained heavily before morning, so there was no mistaking the footmarks of the marauder, which might otherwise have been supposed to have been a panther or hyæna. I have seen where bears have gnawed the dry bones of cattle that have died in the jungles. They do not, however, attempt to kill any animals for food, and their eating flesh at all is decidedly exceptional.

Bears are dangerous to an unarmed man. Woodcutters and others, whose avocations take them into the jungles, are frequently roughly handled by them. They are most dangerous, like all wild animals, if suddenly stumbled upon, when their natural timidity leads to their becoming the aggressors. Perhaps fewer accidents occur under such circumstances of sudden meetings from tigers and panthers than any other animals; they are naturally quick-witted, and not so much embarrassed by an unexpected encounter as some other creatures. The blundering fear of a suddenly aroused bear is distinct from any fierceness of disposition. Bears are very peaceable if left alone, and even when wounded and sorely provoked frequently behave in a pusillanimous manner. Injuries inflicted by them are less commonly fatal than from the *Felidæ*.

The usual methods of hunting the bear are, driving him with beaters if in jungle, or sitting over his cave at daybreak and shooting him on his return from his night's wanderings if his quarters are amongst rocks. In the forests about Morlay I always shot bears by following them with trackers. As they seldom ceased feeding in wet weather before 9 A.M., if we hit off a trail early in the morning we could generally catch the animal up before it retired for the day. There were no caves of any magnitude, and the bears were generally found lying under the shelter of a rock or bamboo-clump, if not overtaken whilst yet afoot. Tracking is most easy in September and October, when the grass is about two feet high and the dews heavy. A bear leaves a very plain trail through this.

PART II.—INCIDENTS IN BEAR-SHOOTING.

Bear-shooting is one of the most entertaining of sports. Some sportsmen have spoken disparagingly of it, and I daresay sitting up half the night watching for a bear's return to his cave, and killing him without adventure, may be poor fun. I have never myself tried it. But bear-shooting conducted on proper principles, with two or three bears afoot together, lacks neither excitement nor amusement. It is not very dangerous sport, as the animal can be so easily seen, whilst he is not so active as a tiger or panther. Still he is very tough, and to any one who would value him for his demonstrations he would appear sufficiently formidable. If a bear charges he can generally be killed without more ado by a shot in the head when within two paces. The belief that a bear rises on his hind-legs when near his adversary, and thus offers a shot at the horse-shoe mark on his chest, is groundless. I have shot several bears within a few feet, and they were still coming on on all-fours. No doubt when a bear reaches his man he rises to claw and bite him, but not before. Nor do they hug an adversary with intent to crush him. I have had satisfactory demonstration of this in hunting them with dogs.

One of the best days I ever had with bears was on the 5th May 1874. Perhaps I should rather say one of the most productive days, as the sport itself was tame in comparison with other adventures I have had with them. I had been encamped in the Poonjoor jungles since the 1st; three days had been unsuccessful ones, and on the fourth I had only killed one bear out of a family of three encountered. I had lost the other two entirely through the villanous conduct of some untrained gun-bearers. One of these, who bore a prominent part in the misconduct, excused himself afterwards by saying he really hardly knew in his perturbation which was

I and which were the bears, as we had mixed ourselves up so, and all seemed to be holding out our paws for the gun he carried, until he didn't know rightly who was who, and so bolted! Two of the three bears had rushed towards us at my shot, and had got rather close, which he made an excuse for flight.

I generally considered that in the bear-ground about the foot of the Billiga-rungun hills I ought to keep up my average when bear-shooting to one a-day for a week or so, so I started on the fifth morning four bears in arrears. It was about four o'clock in the afternoon that Jaffer and I were seated on the top of a hill, which rose some five hundred feet above the general level of the jungles round Poonjoor. Fortune seemed to be against us. It was a lovely day—not in the English acceptation of the term, but from the Indian sportsman's point of view—showery and overcast. As we sat facing the west, from which quarter the wind was blowing freshly, bringing up clouds from the Malabar coast that for the next two days poured down a monsoon deluge on the Mysore plateau, destroying by its violence an immense number of cattle, and even birds in the jungle, we scanned the open glades in the forest below us in hopes of seeing a bear. We had been singularly unsuccessful all day. Since early morning Bommay Gouda, some Shōlaga trackers, Jaffer, and I, had done all we could to find bears, but we had not even seen a single recent track. Our wish was to find marks of the night before, when the Shōlagas could follow the bear to its retreat. There had been a heavy fall of rain—the one thing needful in bear-shooting—during the night, and the delightful coolness of the day had enabled us to keep on without intermission, except for breakfast on the banks of the Poonjoor river. Still we had seen nothing till afternoon, when we found some scratchings, made early that morning, at the foot of the hill Jaffer and I were now seated on. The soil was stony, and the occasional showers during the morning had dimmed such traces as there were, so the following the trail was not an easy task. Nevertheless Bommay Gouda & Co. had girt up their loins and buckled to, and were now engaged on the footprints in the forest below us.

It was slow work, however, and as the day was so overcast I had thought it likely that bears might be abroad feeding, so Jaffer and I had ascended the hill to look round. The cool breath from the gathering clouds was very invigorating after the three months of hot weather we had passed through, and the prospect over the wide expanse of forest, now in young leaf, a refreshing one. Whilst admiring it I did not, however, forget the main object of our ascent; but seeing nothing from where we were, we crossed the narrow piece of level ground on the top of the hill to take a look on the east side. Just as I seated myself the mark of a bear's paw—one scratch at a place where some insect dainty had been concealed—attracted my attention. It was fresher than any sign at the foot of the hill, and I immediately divined that the bear or bears—we could not tell how many there were—must be somewhere on the top of the hill. It was evident they had ascended it as it was quiet, and neither woodcutters nor wandering Shōlagas would disturb them; and they could not in that case be far away, as the level on the top of the hill was only about six hundred yards in length. It was throughout about fifty yards wide, and there were a few rocks here and there on it, but no caves.

We deliberated for some minutes as to the advisability of Jaffer's returning for the trackers, but fearful lest, if we made any delay, the bears might be off feeding again, we proceeded at once to look for them. I had only brought my express rifle, loaded, and Jaffer had two spare cartridges; this gave me four shots. We might have thought twice before attacking three bears with these had we known the number of the enemy, but we thought there was probably but one, or a pair, so started to find them.

The wind was blowing strongly from the west, and so we kept along the eastern edge of the plateau, Jaffer going occasionally to the west face to look amongst the few rocks there. We traversed the plateau nearly to the end in this manner without seeing anything of the bears, though there were places below boulders where they had lain on previous days. It was highly exciting work, as we expected to be face to face with them each time we peeped round a boulder; still every likely place proved a blank. At last—lying on a level rock about ten feet square, under the lee of a perpendicular one some eight feet high which stood upon it—I saw a black and shaggy mass, some thirty paces distant. I caught Jaffer's shoulder and pointed it out to him. We had the wind all right, and the bears were fast asleep, so we approached nearer to see how they might be disposed of most effectively. When within even ten yards we could not see a head in the indistinct mass. I was thinking of firing into them when Jaffer very sensibly pointed to the top of the overhanging rock, and to a stepping-stone behind it, by which we might get above the bears. Of course that was the thing to do. I gave him a pat of approbation, and sat down to unlace my heavy shooting-boots. In another moment we were looking down upon the sleeping beauties, only two gun-lengths below us! We now saw that there were three of them. Their deep snoring was pleasant music after our long day's hunt, and we gazed on their placid, upturned countenances with rapture. Some might have thought their expression piggish: to us it was perfect!

Phototint. H. M. Wright & C° London.

The Sleeping Beauties Awakened.

Had I had a second rifle, or more cartridges, I would have given the bears a better chance for their lives by startling them before firing, but I could make no such allowance, situated as we were, and I commenced with right and left behind the shoulders of two of them. The uproar that ensued on this sudden alarm may be imagined. The unwounded one and one of the others fell to at each other with horrible yells of fear, the third going a few feet, where it fell dead. Before the fight had lasted half a minute the unwounded one found it had a corpse in its arms. Having anything but a clear idea of the awful misfortune that had robbed it in one fell moment of its two companions, and had occasioned a most sulphurous smell all round, it made off with lamentations, whilst one of the exploded cases had got jammed in the express and I could not extract it. However, I at last got a fresh cartridge in, and over the bear went down the hill in a number of summersaults, till it was brought up by a young tree, where it died in a few moments.

A low whistle informed the trackers at the foot of the hill, who could not see what had occurred for the forest, that they might advance, and they soon came panting to the top, delighted at the turn our unlucky day had taken. But this was not to be the last of our good fortune. We had just got the trio on to the pad-elephant that had accompanied us, and the trackers were laughing over the fusilading and cries of the wounded by which they had been so suddenly and pleasantly startled, when we heard the simulated barking of a spotted-deer; and on our replying, Kára, a Shō-laga, joined us with news of a large male bear marked down two miles away. I have forgotten to mention that Gorrava and Kára had been despatched in the morning to try and find this bear, an old fellow that had given us a great deal of trouble for two or three days, and had successfully eluded us owing to want of rain and consequent difficulty of tracking. They had now found him, and Kára had been running about the jungle all alone since mid-day, searching for us. The firing had reached his ears, and he was now soon heading our party to the place where the bear was asleep. We sent the elephant home with the three bears.

Gorrava met us when close to the spot, much relieved by our arrival, after his long and anxious watch over the sleeping beast, which, he said, was still asleep and undisturbed by the firing. Gorrava, Jaffer, and I now went to where he was lying on a flat rock overshadowed by a single tree. He was a magnificent bear, both in size and perfection of coat. I asked Gorrava to step up and shout into his ear, promising to knock him over as he got up to reply, but he did not fancy the commission; so we roused him with a stone, and I shot him as he came open-mouthed in our direction, and when within six feet of us. Soondargowry (the elephant) was brought back from camp after she had deposited the three bears, and we soon had this one padded. The first herd of elephants that had come down the hills after the hot season were close at hand, encouraged by the rain and cool weather in the low country, and they were very noisy, feeding and disporting themselves, as we passed. We accompanied Soondargowry in a body in case we met any of the wild ones, who might have frightened her. I took care after dinner to provide the men with all the requisites for making a merry night after our successful day. It rained in torrents, but they were under snug shelter; and from the sounds of merriment that went on, I think they enjoyed themselves none the less for the weather without.

The Shōloga Kára whom I have mentioned was an excellent and patient tracker, but he frequently fell lame from a deeply-seated ulcer on the inner side of his right foot, just where the sole of a boot is joined by the "uppers." I imagined a thorn to be the cause of the mischief, as all natives of the lower classes in India go barefooted, and wounds from thorns and stones are not uncommon. It did not yield to common treatment, however. The wound, though two inches deep, had an orifice that would barely admit a straw. One day, during a halt at noon in the jungles, I saw Kára and two of his brother Shōlagas doing something to the wound, and found they had introduced a leech—the small Indian jungle-leech—into it, in the belief that it would eat away the gangrenous flesh! This I found Kára had been doing at intervals for months, keeping the leeches plugged in for some hours! Kára was only a lad of nineteen; he had suffered from the ulcer for two years; and as it appeared likely to cause him incessant trouble, I determined to send him to Nunjengode, twenty-eight miles from Morlay, where a Government dispensary had recently been opened. Of course it would not have done to let him know of my benevolent intentions. He would have been as little likely as a bison to appreciate any plan involving a journey into open country, amongst the dwellers in towns, and would speedily have been *non est.* So I sent a tracker for him to come to Morlay, and when he arrived Jaffer marched him off to Nunjengode with a letter to the dresser. I sent a quantity of rági to his wife, and an explanation of what had become of Kára; but I believe, before he returned after an absence of twelve days, his disconsolate spouse had fully settled in her own mind that we had sacrificed him to evoke success in hunting! The use of the knife upon Kára had, however, been confined to his foot, and the wound healed rapidly. He has lived to be thankful that his views were not consulted in the matter.

I shot several bears in 1872-73 at a place called Sakrapatam in the

Kuddoor district of Mysore. There is a high conical hill at this place, rising about 1500 feet above the plain, furrowed with deep water-courses and sparsely covered with stunted trees. Near its summit are several detached rocks, and occasional caves, in which, and in the dry water-courses, bears had their homes. At the foot of the hill is a large lake called Iyenkerry, formed by an embankment thrown across a narrow gorge between the large hill and a smaller one. This *bund* obstructs the waters of the valley, and forms a splendid lake about five miles in circumference, ornamented with two or three well-wooded islands. From the far shore rise the Bábábooden hills, clothed with forest.

This artificial lake is a work of great antiquity. Its waters are drawn off by a sluice through the embankment for irrigating the land (many square miles in extent) below it, which is cultivated with rice-fields, and betel, areca, and cocoa-nut gardens. A good deal of land which was tilled in former days has relapsed into jungle from the decrease or desertion of population, probably owing to Mahratta invasions and other troubles upwards of a hundred years ago. Much of it is now covered with date-trees, from which *henda* is drawn. This liquor and the fruit of the trees, together with the patches of sugar-cane, jak fruit, and other products of the gardens, formed a combination of attractions too great for the virtue of the bears in the adjacent hill, and they had abandoned themselves to the habit of making almost nightly predatory excursions in search of these dainties.

Having ascertained this failing of theirs, and procured two good trackers, I proceeded one morning before daybreak with a friend, Captain M., to waylay the robbers on their return from their nefarious enjoyments. M. took up his position on a commanding spur of the hill near the bottom, I on another half a mile distant, and as daylight advanced we scanned the plain below us for the returning depredators. I had not been at my post long before a native who was with me saw a bear engaged in turning over stones (for insects) about half a mile above us on the hillside. We had a steep ascent to make, and did it at pace, when I found myself within fifty yards of the still unconscious bear. After resting for a few minutes I fired, but I was not very steady, and only broke his forearm, bringing him down the hillside with lugubrious howls. At this another bear—his mate, which had been hidden till now—came shuffling after him, yelling in concert. Poor creatures, they certainly stand by each other in all their trials! I stepped forward to meet the she, when she charged without hesitation. I brained her in the attitude in which she was advancing, and then ran after my wounded bird. I soon caught him up, when he made a show of charging. I reserved my fire so as to kill him neatly at the muzzle, but he turned round unexpectedly and made off with redoubled cries. On being pressed he again turned on me, but at the sight of the barrels covering his head away he went the faster. The next time I killed him the moment he turned; I could not afford to be sold three times by one bear.

I now sat down after my run, when my gun-bearer Birram saw three more bears going at a quick pace along the hillside high above us. I was too unsteady to risk a shot; they had been alarmed by the firing, and were shambling off in a great hurry. The climb was very stiff, but at last we got on to their track, and followed along the breast of the hill till we found they had entered a deep cave from which it was impossible to dislodge them. M. had no luck.

We had two blank days after this, not even seeing a bear. On the fourth the luck again fell to my share. The day previous we had beaten up all the covers below the lake, in order to frighten the bears back to the hill if they were taking shelter in the low country; and believing that going to our places early in the morning was likely to disturb them on their way homeward, we took our blankets, coffee, &c., with all our men, up the hill in the afternoon, and camped during the night on the summit, in a place sheltered from the wind, and where our small fires would not be seen. There was no dew, and the night was warm and fine, so we slept in the open air for the nonce, though it is a thing to be avoided.

Having taken a cup of coffee we were at our posts at the earliest dawn, each watching a different side of the hill. No bears appeared before 7 A.M., so I took a long shot (two hundred yards or more) at a sámbur standing under a tree. It dropped, but recovered itself and went off. We now started down the hill to beat some ravines at the bottom for sámbur, when a fine stag got up, an easy shot to M., but he missed him with both barrels. He was a hundred and fifty yards off before I got a chance, owing to his taking off up the bed of a ravine; I missed both shots. M. then had two more as the stag was topping a rise two hundred yards away, and more by accident than good shooting broke one of his fore-legs. A great hunt then began. Boxer and Rosie, two bull-terriers I had with me, followed the stag, and we found them hanging on to him, and covered with blood, in a ravine two miles away. We killed the stag, and having nothing better to do, set to work in the cool and shady ravine to skin him. We had nearly finished when one of a party of markers whom we had left on the top of the hill on the off-chance of bears returning after 7 A.M., came to say two had entered a rocky ravine on the far side of the hill from where we then were, and were safely settled there for the day. We looked at the steep and hot hillside, enough to daunt anybody but sportsmen. However, game is not to be obtained, any more than other good things, without labour, and we commenced the climb, leaving some men to finish skinning the sámbur. We had no water, and would have given five pounds for a mugful before our task was completed. However, after many halts to breathe and to wipe the streaming perspiration from our faces and necks, we reached the summit.

The ravine the bears had been marked into was half-way down the other side of the hill. At its head grew two or three magnificent trees, the only shade-giving ones on the hill at that season—the height of the hot weather. Beneath them was a dripping, moss-grown well of excellent water. How we posted down towards it, over large boulders and through long grass! In our hurry M. fell and damaged himself considerably, and I narrowly escaped denting my rifle-barrels, which would have been nearly as bad as breaking my legs. At last we got to the haven, where we drank and rested for half an hour, and considered ways and means with the local shikárie.

The ravine was about half a mile in length, and debouched into the plain below. The adjacent ground sloped steeply into it on both sides, whilst its dry bed was strewn with large boulders. M. elected to keep along parallel with the ravine and about fifty yards up the slope on the left side. I knew the bears must be amongst the boulders at the bottom, so I went down the bed with the men to put them up.

We searched for some distance, occasionally turning our eyes to the men whom we had left on the top of the hill to signal if the bears left the ravine, and to mark them down again if we failed in our attack upon them, till Birram's quick eye spied the pair lying on a ledge of rock above us, under the shade of another rock, and fast asleep. I fired into them as they lay. Out they came, and I hit them both again as they bundled down the ravine. They were desperately wounded, but both kept on, whilst I stayed to reload. M. fired, but was too far off, and missed. I now ran after the bears. Boxer and Rosie had got one into a small side ravine, and great fun was going on; I knew they could keep him, so I ran on after the other and larger bear—one of the largest females I have killed. I found her lying as if dead, but I gave her another shot to make sure, when up she got and bolted; my left barrel stopped her for ever. When I got back the other bear had died from his wounds, and the dogs were lying near him, panting with heat and thirst, and nearly choked with hair and blood.

Just as I was firing at the bear at the beginning of the brush I heard M. call out something about a panther. It now appeared that, just before I first fired, a large panther had been disturbed in the ravine, and had raced up towards us, but without seeing us owing to a sharp turning. We should have met face to face in another instant round the corner had I not happened to fire at the bears at that moment. I never saw the panther; it escaped in the confusion. M. persisted in a wild-goose chase after it, whilst I set to work, well contented, to skin my bears. They had no fat on them.

In the cool of the evening my men and I walked down the ravine to the lake, where I had a refreshing wash, and thence returned to Sakrapatam, three miles. I never neglect to take a towel, dry flannel-shirt, and a piece of soap with me on all shooting-days. Personal comfort, and the benefit to health in being able to exchange a wringing wet shirt for a dry one, are thus easily secured. I was only out for four days this trip, and kept my score up to a bear a-day, with which I was quite satisfied.

I once shot a bear which I should have been sorry to have lost, though I came near doing so, for there were a number of spectators of the scene. It happened near the temple on the summit of the Billiga-rungun hills. I was encamped there in December 1874, when one afternoon two men came from the temple, which is perched on the edge of a precipice of some two hundred feet of sheer rock, in company with a cluster of houses of the employees attached to it, from the Bráhmin priest to the humble sweepers of its courtyard, to say that a bear was feeding in an open space below the rock. The patch in question had been cleared for cultivation, and in it were some manure-heaps in which Bruin was now grubbing for the larvæ of beetles.

We had half a mile to descend from my camp to get at him. All the people living in the temple, and some low-country folk who had come up to worship, had assembled on the rock on hearing that the Sahib had gone forth to slay a bear; and as my gun-bearers and I rapidly descended a path round the foot of the precipice, I saw the goodly body of spectators, comprehending a number of nut-brown beauties, to fail before whom would be ruination. The grass was very high and dry in the forest round the clearing. I did not know the ground well, and the man who was leading us was not much of a shikárie. It thus came to pass that I was introduced to the bear with much less ceremony than I could have wished. "There he is! see him!" said our guide as he ushered me suddenly into the open space. I did see him, and what was less satisfactory, he saw me. The noise of our approach in the long grass had attracted his attention before we appeared. I made a too hurried shot, especially as there were some twigs between us, and away the bear went into the undergrowth. Madness! and all those ladies looking on! I raced after him, and nearly fell over the brute in the long grass at the edge of the clearing. He had not seen us well, and not knowing what the disturbance was about, had foolishly stopped to listen. Right and left through his ribs must have enlightened him as he rolled over. He had severe wounds on his head from fighting, which quite marred his beauty.

The people on the rock shouted with delight, and some of low caste ran down to help us. Soondargowry (the elephant) had been got ready and sent after me, and she now came and carried up the bear among rocks and difficulties which would have been very troublesome without her. I ordered the animal to be laid in an open space near the temple, as a mark of respect to Billiga-runga Swámi, the presiding deity of those parts, and that all the people might have a chance of seeing it. My men, who were very jealous of their master's reputation, explained to the people that the first shot had not missed—none fired by their Sahib ever did—but had gone down the bear's throat as it stood facing us, which accounted for the bullet-hole not being visible! In support of this they pointed to the blood issuing from the mouth from internal bleeding.

There is a common, but I need hardly say groundless, notion amongst the natives of the jungle-tracts in Mysore, that solitary male bears will carry off women should they meet them alone, and keep them alive. I asked some of the damsels who were standing near, peeping shyly at the bear and his slayers round the corners of their cloths, what they would have thought of such a fate had this one waylaid and abducted them when coming up to the temple. Jaffer, who was always ready with some sally, said he wouldn't mind being the bear in such case,—upon which they all ran off laughing.

I have shot a large number of bears in the Mysore jungles. With good trackers they have little chance of escaping, though some cunning ones occasionally baffled my men and myself on many successive occasions. I have, however, latterly hunted them entirely with dogs and a knife, which is much the most interesting method of taking their lives. I propose to give an account of this sport in the next chapter.

CHAPTER XXVII.

DOGS FOR INDIAN HUNTING.

JACKAL-HUNTING WITH FOX-HOUNDS—GREYHOUNDS—FOX AND HARE COURSING—A FOOT-PACK IN DACCA—DOGS FOR HUNTING FORMIDABLE GAME—SIR SAMUEL BAKER'S SPORT IN CEYLON—BULL-DOGS FOR HUNTING BEARS, BISON, BUFFALOES, ETC.—CONSTITUTION OF A PACK—INCIDENTS IN LARGE-GAME HUNTING WITH DOGS—MY FIRST ATTEMPT—THE PACK SEIZE A BEAR—ANOTHER BEAR-HUNT—OBLIGED TO SHOOT THE BEAR—DAMAGE SUSTAINED BY THE PACK—A BISON-HUNT—BILL SYKES—MOTTO FOR SEIZERS—THE DOGS ARE ALMOST CHOKED—THE PACK SEIZE A YOUNG ELEPHANT—A COMMEMORATION DINNER—BILL SYKES DISTINGUISHES HIMSELF SINGLE-HANDED—FIGHT WITH A PANTHER—OBJECTION TO SPIKED COLLARS FOR HUNTING DOGS.

IN a few Indian stations the European residents keep packs of imported fox-hounds for hunting jackals. The sport is not of a high order, but it affords a morning gallop before the sun gets high. A few greyhounds are kept where the country is feasible for coursing foxes and hares. The Indian fox (*Vulpes bengalensis*) is a very different little animal to its English congener, being more grey in colour, weighing only seven or eight pounds, and living almost exclusively in open plains, where it has numerous burrows. Owing to the latter circumstance, little sport can be had with it with fox-hounds, but when surprised at a distance from its retreat a good course can be had with Arab or English greyhounds. It doubles with astonishing quickness and dexterity, and trusts more to eluding its pursuers by this means than by straight running. In Dacca (Eastern Bengal) we used to have excellent fun with the *bágdos*, or large civet-cat (*Vivera zibetha*), an animal weighing about twenty-five pounds. Two friends and myself kept a small pack of nondescript dogs, mostly half-bred terriers and spaniels, for hunting it. The *bágdos* is much like a badger in general appearance. It is not fast, and therefore does not often trust itself to open ground, but dodges from one patch of tangled grass and briers to another. It also climbs low trees, goes to ground, and takes to water freely, as means of escape from its yapping pursuers. It thus affords a good run on foot, and always winds up with a fierce resistance. We found a powerful bull-terrier was generally required to finish a chase. The *bágdos* is generally found in thickets in close proximity to villages, where it preys upon fowls. One of the largest I have killed was slain in a drain in the town of Chittagong, after a prolonged subterranean conflict with a redoubtable bull-terrier I possessed at that time. The same dog killed another *bágdos*, single-handed, in the culvert under the steps of the dâk bungalow in Chittagong.

A few English sportsmen keep spaniels, but it is seldom that dogs used only with the gun can be turned to account in India. Scent is generally bad, and there are neither facilities for training young dogs, nor sufficient practice for old ones. In snipe or quail shooting native attendants are handier than dogs, and consequently a spaniel or terrier that will bring a duck out of a weedy tank is generally the Indian sportsman's only canine auxiliary in the field.

Previous to the time when my duties led to my living entirely in the jungles, I always kept one or two good bull-terriers for encounters with jackals, wild cats, &c. On the few occasions when I had the chance of using these dogs at formidable beasts they so distinguished themselves as to impress me with a high opinion of their prowess, and of their ability to overcome larger animals than might be thought possible; and I conceived the idea of setting up half-a-dozen couples of really stanch dogs, with which and a knife only, to kill bears, panthers, leopards, &c. It has not been until lately, however, that I have been in a position to carry out my idea; but since I have lived almost wholly in the jungles, I have had opportunities of gaining some knowledge of what can be done in dangerous-game hunting with the aid of dogs. It is only to a few sportsmen, chiefly those who happen to be forest-officers or planters, to whom my experiences are likely to be of service. But in the hope that those in a position to try the sport for themselves may find them of some little use, I propose to record what I have myself learnt. I also believe that the general reader who has a taste for such subjects as form the theme of my book will feel an interest in reading of instances of courage shown by that infinitely more courageous animal than all the wild beasts of Asia and Africa together, the only creature in the world that fears no animate or inanimate object—the British bull-dog.

The hunting of large and dangerous game with dogs may be managed in two ways: either with a pack merely to find and bay the animal wherever it goes, sufficiently discreet to keep out of its reach until the sportsman comes up with his rifle; or with dogs that will seize any beast at once and hold it until it can be speared, or killed with a knife. The latter sport is naturally much more exciting than merely shooting an animal found by dogs; and whilst the former method is useful for tigers, especially wounded ones, almost all other smaller animals may be killed with dogs and the knife alone. It is of this latter class of sport that I propose to treat.

I first took the idea of hunting large animals with nothing but dogs and a knife from Sir Samuel Baker's *Rifle and Hound in Ceylon.* Every one interested in the subject should read that book. In Ceylon the game hunted is the sámbur deer (*Rusa Aristotelis*), and occasionally the wild hog. But there not being a sufficient number of sámbur in accessible localities in Mysore to make them an object of pursuit, I determined to make a trial with bears, bison, panthers, and wild hogs. Since commencing I have killed several bears, panthers, and bison, and also captured a young wild elephant which the pack seized without hesitation.

In recommending a pack of dogs for seizing big game, I would do so only to men who are able to find bears, bison, or buffaloes. These animals will not give much of a run, which is a necessary condition, as the heavy dogs for seizing are not good at chasing. A bull-dog that is invaluable if the game can be fought with but little running, is useless in a chase of any duration; therefore he can only be employed where animals can be brought to bay at once. The excitement of the sport consists in seeing the valour of the dogs, and in killing the animal with nothing but a knife. Nothing can be finer than to see the headlong attack of dogs that know not what fear is. Some persons may take exception to the sport on the ground of cruelty to the dogs, but I do not think sportsmen will—not that they are less tender-hearted than other people, but because they understand better what the dogs' feelings are. Many people speak of cruelty and pain in the abstract, without reference to the circumstances of the cases to which they apply the terms. Some would think nothing of keeping a bull-dog chained up for months, but would decry exposing it to the chance of being knocked about by a wild animal. Any one who understands the nature of such dogs knows that in excitement they do not feel pain, whilst depriving them of liberty and exercise is a real infliction to them. Their natural instincts find the greatest pleasure in fighting and bloodshed. Can any one doubt which of the two the dogs themselves would choose,—to be loosed at a beast, or be tied up in a kennel? If so, he knows nothing about the disposition of bull-dogs.

It is remarkable how little injury the dogs sustain in this rough style of hunting. The simultaneousness of their attack overpowers a bear or panther, and prevents its paying attention to any dog in particular. The

bull-dog's habit of fixing on to the nose or cheek of a foe renders the animal it seizes unable to do much injury by biting when once it has been seized. Then, though bears and panthers can inflict a severe blow when the object struck is at arm's-length, when it is very close their paws and claws are comparatively powerless. A bear's claws are so blunt that when a dog is holding him he cannot tear his skin, or make any wound, though at arm's-length he might cuff him soundly; and a panther, though his claws are so sharp, can do little more harm. A bear never hugs the dogs; his nose makes a splendid hold; and from what I have seen, I consider two really good bull-dogs a complete match for any bear, if they get a fair chance of flying at him together. Once seized by the snout a bear is a helpless creature, and does little but roll over and howl.

A pack for dangerous-game hunting should comprise about three couples of seizers, and three or four couples of good terriers and crossbreds for finding game and bringing it to bay for the operations of the seizers. These finding dogs should not be too small, otherwise they may not give tongue sufficiently loudly; and one or two should be fast. They should be plucky enough to keep in attendance on a beast whatever demonstrations he makes against them, but not so courageous as to go at him.

The seizers should be bull-dogs or bull-mastiffs. In using the word bull-dog, I mean the dogs—usually bull and terrier—commonly termed bull-dogs. I need hardly say pure bull-dogs are very rarely seen, nor, if procurable, would they answer so well as the cross between bull and terrier. The pure breed is seldom large enough, and the true bull is a particularly unintelligent and peaceable animal. It is necessary to hit a happy medium. The bull-dog's determined courage and forward attack must be joined with the terrier's vivacity and intelligence. With too much of the bull in his composition a dog will be stupid; whilst if the terrier element preponderates too strongly his courage may be doubtful, and, what is fatal in a seizer, he may go at some other part of the animal than the head.

The duty of the seizers in hunting is to fix on to any animal at which they are loosed. It must be remembered that imported dogs are generally useless until they have had a little teaching, as their instincts are seldom developed or encouraged in England, where a dog that would attack other animals would be a nuisance. But dogs of the right stamp all have it in them, and a little training upon stray cattle, or one of the gaunt village pigs which can be bought for a few rupees in India, will be sufficient to teach them. One of the best dogs I ever had for seizing large animals knew absolutely nothing when I received him from England.

The seizers should not weigh less than from 35 to 40 lb. Excellent dogs of this class can be got in England for a few sovereigns. Show-dogs are not required. Sometimes suitable dogs may be bought from European soldiers in India, but the general run of their bull-terriers are not heavy enough, nor are they always reliable as to courage. Perhaps the best plan in starting a pack is to get a couple of heavy, well-bred country bitches (bull-terriers), and to import a dog for them. The progeny live better in India than imported dogs. They can be used when nine months old, and should be trained to worry raw skins, jackals, &c., as soon as they get their permanent teeth. I have amused myself in an evening by having a rope thrown over a branch of a tree under which I happened to be encamped, with a skin fastened to one end, whilst a whole litter of bull-puppies would fix on to the skin, and might be hauled up thirty feet and kept there some time without danger of their letting go. One of these surprised some friends with whom I left him on one occasion, when full grown, by springing up and hanging to the punkah as it waved over the dinner-table. He had not been accustomed to see such things in his master's jungle-bungalow, and it reminded him of the skin exercise of his puppyhood!

It is worse than useless to have a pack of dogs in which there are but one or two good ones. The others urge these on, and they will be sacrificed through not being supported. It is cruel to set an insufficient number of dogs to attack an animal. Six will be as many as are required for any bear, bison, or panther, and indeed four will generally suffice, or even two with most bears. Anything like a running hunt is to be avoided, as the dogs may be disposed of in detail as they come up. They should be slipped well together, and not before they all see clearly what they have to do. Unless they understand that there is a common enemy, such excitable and pugnacious dogs are liable to fall upon each other. It is necessary to keep them all on as friendly terms as possible, but this can sometimes only be managed by keeping them apart, as rivals will fight whenever they get a chance.

I shall best convey an idea of how the sport of tackling large game is to be conducted by describing a few hunts in which the efforts of myself and pack have met with success.

The first animals I introduced my pack to were a couple of bears. I had the following six seizers then:—

MARQUIS.	An imported bull-mastiff, weighing 40 lb.
LADY.	A country-bred bull-terrier bitch, 35 lb.
BISMARCK. VIPER. FURY.	Pups of the above, weighing about 30 lb. each, nine months old.
TURK.	A country-bred bull-terrier, weighing 40 lb.

Phototint.
H. M. Wright & Co. London

Bear-hunting with Dogs.

The above was not a strong pack; Marquis was old, and three were only pups. However, there was nothing for it but to make a trial.

One morning my men succeeded in marking two bears into a favourable locality among some rocks on a hillside near Morlay. The hill sloped gently to the plain below, and was clear of bushes. We approached the rocks from one side. There was no cave, but the bears were sitting on a table-rock, overhung by a larger one, enjoying the early warmth of the sun preparatory to turning in. Upon our appearance within thirty yards they made off. I killed the female on the spot with my express. She tumbled off the rock and rolled a few yards; the male jumped after her, and with howls made off down the hill. The dogs were with us in leash, and as soon as the bear was well started they were slipped. Unfortunately Turk tackled the dead bear; the other five pursued the fugitive one. Marquis was up first, and sprang at the bear's head, and over the two rolled amidst fearful shrieks from the bear. I thought no dog could have held on under such summersaults as they turned; but when they stopped, Marquis was fast to the bear's cheek. The bear now reared up, and might have punished the dog, but Bismarck at this moment seized one ear, Lady the other, and Viper and Fury his snout. From that time the bear was unable to rear, the dogs pulling him over sideways, or keeping his head to the ground, at each attempt. He tried hard, but in vain, to clear his head with his paws. I had expected he would cut the dogs up a good deal, but they kept his head down so much that he could not strike out, and at close quarters he could not tear them. In about ten minutes the bear was quite done, and two thrusts with my knife behind the shoulder settled him. I might have killed him the moment I came up, but there was no necessity for it, as the dogs were masters of him after he was seized. None of them sustained any injury on this occasion.

Two days after this, one of the largest male bears I have ever seen was marked into a small detached jungle. Captain P. had joined me in the interim, and with the dogs and a few men we started after the bear. A couple of trackers, P., and I, took the dogs inside, whilst other men were posted round the jungle, and directed to keep up sufficient noise to deter the bear from breaking out. Their occasional shouts unfortunately distracted the dogs when slipped, and they ran wherever there was most noise. I had Marquis by the collar myself, so when Viper and Bismarck found the bear I slipped him, and he went straight in. The bear made off, fighting and growling fiercely. We had considerable difficulty in following fast enough, but at last we got up. The three dogs and bear had then been at it about two minutes. When I appeared on the scene the dogs were holding on to the brute's stern, the only part they could attack during his retreat through the thick undergrowth, whilst he struck at them with his fore-paws. As soon as he saw me within ten feet of him he came straight at me, and I was obliged to brain him with a shot. This was a pity, as we had hoped to knife him. The other dogs came up at this moment, and but for the *contretemps* there would have been a fair fight. Bismarck was severely injured. A bite in the throat narrowly missed his windpipe, and he was so roughly handled that he could not stand up for a day or two. He, however, did many doughty deeds before his death, a year later, from a kick by a stag sámbur. Marquis and Viper were more or less clawed, but not seriously. This bear weighed exactly 280 lb., or 20 st. Our discomfiture was entirely owing to the dogs not having been able to get at the bear's head, and to their being separated.

I have not had many fair chances at bison with my dogs. The solitary bulls that lie out by themselves are the best animals to attack. Buffalo might also be hunted in this way in many parts of Bengal and other places where they are found. When it is considered with what ease one good dog can pull down the largest tame buffalo or bullock, it may easily be imagined that a bison or wild buffalo has no chance against three or four. His enormous power is of no avail to him against such pigmy antagonists. A less powerful but more active animal would stand an infinitely better chance of escape by shaking them off, and betaking itself to flight, than does a bison.

In approaching bison or buffalo, and in fact all animals, with dogs, it is necessary that the men keep out of sight if possible, as many animals will stand to fight dogs which make off at once if they suspect the presence of man. When the dogs have got to work their master may put in an appearance. From what I have seen on occasions such as the following, I have no hesitation in stating my opinion that four good dogs should hold any bison or buffalo so that it may be hamstrung.

It was on the 30th August 1876 that I started from Poonjoor with a strong pack in search of bison. There were seven couples in all, of which Bill Sykes, Bismarck, Turk, Tiger, and Lady were the seizers, and the rest were finders. Some of the latter were quite plucky enough to join the attack when an animal was seized by the big dogs. The seizers were in single leashes, the others in couples, so that I had some ten men with me leading them, in addition to the trackers. As we could not find a solitary bull's track we followed a herd.

We came on the bison in bamboo-cover after two hours' tracking. The finders were all slipped at them, but the seizers were kept in leash till one of them should be brought to bay. A bull made off up a hill by himself, with the finders after him, and they badgered him so much that he soon stopped to fight, whereupon the seizers were taken forward and slipped. I came in view just in time to see Bill Sykes fix on to the bull's nose, when he turned and thundered down the hillside past myself and men, at a pace which was astonishing in so heavy a beast. Bill Sykes of course hung on, though he was carried through two or three thick places where any but a most determined dog would have been swept off. He was a model seizer; he always went in straight, and never waited for a more favourable opportunity, nor the assistance of the other dogs. Dogs may be sacrificed by this reckless courage on occasions, but the general safety is best insured by all going in without hesitation, and holding on under any punishment. How often curs with just enough pluck to make them take a snap or two are killed by going within reach of a dangerous animal, whereas dogs that fix and hold render the beast comparatively harmless. Seizers should act by nature on the tactics recommended by Nelson to his young officers in their dealings with the enemy: "Never mind manœuvres; always go at them."

The other dogs did not get a chance till the bull was at the bottom of the hill, when they sprang at his head one after another as they came up, and pulled him down. They kept his nose to the ground whilst he bellowed with fright and pain, and made but poor attempts to gore them with his horns. Thus a few dogs prove more troublesome assailants to a bison than a tiger does, as the latter, from his size, can be more easily tossed or trampled on.

It is difficult to keep seizers in good working condition as to their wind; they soon become blown, as they cannot have sufficient practice. On this occasion (I finished the bull with a shot through the neck), they were so exhausted by their worry when we got them off, that they lay around, casting longing glances at the dead bull as they gasped almost to choking from the heat and exertion, but unable to get up, though anxious to attack him again. I was really frightened at Bismarck's condition; his tongue was purple, and swelled to an enormous size, and he gasped in a manner which made me think he would choke. Fortunately we were not far from a stream, whither we hurried with him and the other seizers in our arms, and soon restored them by sousing their heads with the cool water. They were kept in the shade till the cool of evening, whilst we skinned and cut up the bison, and packed part of it on the elephant. The dogs were fed with roasted collops off the bull, and none of them were seriously the worse for such bruises as they had received.

On the following day we made one of the most extraordinary captures that I suppose was ever made with dogs—namely, a young elephant. This animal, a male five feet high, had in some way become separated from its herd, and had been about in the Poonjoor jungles, living a solitary life for some months. I had taken out the dogs and men to try and find a bear, and we were filing along through tolerably open jungle when we saw the elephant coming towards us over a rising knoll fifty yards away, throwing dust over its back. I instantly decided to have a try at it, so the dogs were slipped.

The elephant had seen us and was already making off. He had not gone two hundred yards, however, before Lady was up, and single-handed sprang at his cheek, and hung there; in another moment Bill Sykes and Turk had him by the trunk; he stumbled, when Bismarck seized the top of the ear furthest away from him, across the head, so that when the elephant rose and raced off, Bismarck was riding on his head, holding on to the ear on the off side, and having his hind-legs hanging down on the near. Such a scene now ensued as beggars description. The elephant roared lustily, and dragged Bill Sykes and Turk along, often on their backs, and apparently in imminent risk of being trampled to death. The jungle was full of dry bamboos, amongst which pursued and pursuers made a great crashing. All the smaller dogs, maddened by the excitement, were yelling and snapping at the elephant's hind-legs as if it had been a sheep, regardless of the kicks they received. It seemed certain that some dogs must be killed—Bill Sykes and Turk had the most dangerous places—but unless they were killed on the spot, none of the seizers were dogs that would let go.

The encounter had been so unexpected that we had no ropes with us, but there were some with the pad-elephant nearly a mile behind. It took time to get these, and meanwhile the elephant rushed about, kicking and dragging the dogs through bamboos and in and out of ravines. It followed us when we got in front to head and delay it till the ropes came, but was too much hampered to catch any one. When the ropes arrived, Bismarck, Lady, and Bill Sykes were still at their holds, but Turk was so thoroughly exhausted that he had been shaken off: though the flesh was weak, however, the spirit was willing, and he still tottered after the elephant, which had now subsided into a walk. Had the ropes not come when they did the seizers would have been wearied out, and the elephant might have escaped.

I had two Chittagong elephant-catchers with me, whom I had brought from Bengal, and as soon as the ropes arrived they caught the elephant's hind-legs in running nooses, and got a turn round a tree. When both legs were secured we got the dogs off, which was dangerous work, as they had to be caught hold off and half choked within reach of the elephant. They had to be carried from the spot and bathed in a stream near: there were no bones broken, but they were much bruised. However, what did that matter to dogs of their stamp? Plenty of milk and good soft beds of straw soon put them all right.

Soondargowry (the elephant) was now brought up, and the captured youngster was secured to her and led to the river, and then to camp. It was about two years old, and weighed probably 900 lb., a good feat in seizing for dogs under 40 lb. Its wounds were not serious, and in ten days were quite healed. I brought it on to the strength of the elephant department, but when the Chief Commissioner learnt how it had been caught he made me a present of it. I had a soft saddle made and rode it for some months—it was quite tame in fifteen days after we caught it—and I finally sold it for £50. I gave the dogs a sumptuous dinner of two courses—roast-mutton and rice-pudding, both unlimited in quantity and first-rate in quality—on the occasion.

As an instance of the dauntless courage of the above-mentioned Bill Sykes (an imported dog, for which I paid £20 in England), I may mention that before I had had him long he one day, when let loose, seized Soondargowry by her trunk, and hung on until we succeeded in catching her after she had run through the jungles until she could scarcely put one foot before the other! He could never have seen an elephant before, but a bull-dog is not dismayed by any object, however strange. In this respect he differs from every other created being.

I have never killed a panther in the jungles with dogs only, but I once let a full-grown leopard out of a cage in an open plain with Bill Sykes, Turk, Bismarck, and Tiger. They speedily rendered him *hors de combat*, though I had to put a knife into him at last, as it is impossible for dogs to kill a panther or bear outright, though they can make them unable to leave the spot. Turk was the only dog bitten, and he was not severely hurt. Panthers or leopards in caves might be easily overcome with such dogs. For use against panthers or bears a leather collar, almost as thick as a trace, and three and a half inches wide, is ample protection for the dogs' throats. There should be no spikes or plates on the collar, as whilst a panther will seize the throat (which he cannot harm through the leather) if there be no spikes, their presence is likely to make him lay hold elsewhere, where he may do more damage.

Published by

Facsimile Publisher
Ashok Vihar, Delhi-110052 (India)
Website: www.facsimilepublishers.com

Distributed by

Gyan Books Pvt. Ltd.
5, Ansari Road, Daryaganj, New Delhi-110002 (India)
E-mail: books@gyanbooks.com, Website: www.gyanbooks.com

8 888000 823223